STAYING WELL AFTER PSYCHOSIS

STAYING WELL AFTER PSYCHOSIS

A Cognitive Interpersonal Approach to
Recovery and Relapse Prevention

Andrew Gumley

University of Glasgow

and

Matthias Schwannauer

University of Edinburgh

John Wiley & Sons, Ltd

Email (for orders and customer service enquiries): cs-books@wiley.co.uk
Visit our Home Page on www.wiley.com

Reprinted February 2006

Other Wiley Editorial Offices

John Wiley & Sons Inc., 111 River Street, Hoboken, NJ 07030, USA

Jossey-Bass, 989 Market Street, San Francisco, CA 94103-1741, USA

Wiley-VCH Verlag GmbH, Boschstr. 12, D-69469 Weinheim, Germany

John Wiley & Sons Australia Ltd, 42 McDougall Street, Milton, Queensland 4064, Australia

John Wiley & Sons (Asia) Pte Ltd, 2 Clementi Loop #02-01, Jin Xing Distripark, Singapore 129809

John Wiley & Sons Canada Ltd, 22 Worcester Road, Etobicoke, Ontario, Canada M9W 1L1

Wiley also publishes its books in a variety of electronic formats. Some content that appears in print may
not be available in electronic books.

Library of Congress Cataloging-in-Publication Data

Gumley, Andrew.
    Staying well after psychosis : a cognitive interpersonal approach to recovery and relapse prevention /
Andrew Gumley, Matthias Schwannauer.
        p.   cm.
    Includes bibliographical references and index.
    ISBN-13: 978-0-470-02184-2 (hbk) – 978-0-470-02185-9 (pbk)
    ISBN-10: 0-470-02184-5 (hbk) – 0-470-02185-3 (pbk)
    1. Schizophrenia – Treatment.   2. Schizophrenia – Relapse.   3. Psychotherapy.   4. Cognitive therapy.
I. Schwannauer, Matthias.   II. Title.
    [DNLM: 1. Psychotic Disorders – therapy.   2. Psychotic Disorders – prevention & control.
3. Recurrence – prevention & control.   4. Cognitive Therapy – methods.   WM 600 G974s 2006]
    RC514.G786 2006
    362.2'6–dc22

                                                                                    2005024833

British Library Cataloguing in Publication Data

A catalogue record for this book is available from the British Library

ISBN-13 978-0-470-02184-2 (hbk) 978-0-470-02185-9 (pbk)
ISBN-10 0-470-02184-5 (hbk) 0-470-02185-3 (pbk)

Typeset in 10/12pt Palatino by SNP Best-set Typesetter Ltd., Hong Kong
Printed and bound in Great Britain by TJ International Ltd, Padstow, Cornwall
This book is printed on acid-free paper responsibly manufactured from sustainable forestry
in which at least two trees are planted for each one used for paper production.

CONTENTS

ABOUT THE AUTHORS

Andrew Gumley is Senior Lecturer in Clinical Psychology on the University of Glasgow Doctorate in Clinical Psychology training programme, a practising clinician as Honorary Consultant Clinical Psychologist in ESTEEM, North Glasgow Early Intervention Service, a trainer in cognitive behavioural psychotherapy at the Glasgow Institute for Psychosocial Interventions (GIPSI) and external consultant to the State Hospital at Carstairs Psychosocial Interventions Programme. His research interests include the evaluation of cognitive behavioural therapies for individuals who are considered to have severe and enduring mental health problems. In recent years, he has contributed to a number of randomised controlled trials of cognitive therapy involving individuals who have had or are recovering from distressing psychotic experiences, and individuals who have been diagnosed with borderline and antisocial personality disorders. His primary clinical and research interests focus on developing a psychological understanding of individual vulnerability and transition to the recurrence of psychosis. In this context Andrew is particularly interested in how the interplay between the experiences of psychosis and cognitive and interpersonal factors may prevent detection of at-risk mental states for relapse, contribute to affect dysregulation during relapse, or result in persistent and distressing emotional states such as fear of recurrence. These clinical and research interests are directed towards the development, refinement and evaluation of psychological therapies for recovery and staying well after psychosis.

Matthias Schwannauer is Lecturer and Research Supervisor in Child and Adolescent Clinical Psychology on the University of Edinburgh Clinical Psychology Training Course, Research Co-ordinator in the Young People's Unit in Edinburgh and practising clinician as consultant clinical psychologist in an adolescent onset psychosis service in Lothian. His current clinical and research interests include the relationship between interpersonal and cognitive factors in developmental models of severe and enduring disorder groups. He is particularly interested in the developmental onset of severe mental health problems with regard to psychological factors of vulnerability and resilience to psychiatric disorders. In the past few years Matthias has investigated developmental models of interpersonal and cognitive aspects of emotion regulation in a number of populations, such as depression in a highly vulnerable group of single, young homeless adolescents with an early onset psychosis and individuals suffering from bipolar disorder. He is interested in the advancement of a developmental psychopathology model of affect regulation in a range of populations with severe and recurring psychological difficulties.

PREFACE

When writing this book we made a number of decisions about the language used to refer to individuals who have had distressing psychotic experiences. We do not refer to diagnostic entities such as schizophrenia. We consider psychosis as an integrative and collective term used to describe a range of human experiences, such as hearing voices or suffering from persecutory paranoid beliefs. In addition, we wanted to use small case vignettes and patient–therapist narratives to illustrate therapeutic processes. In doing so, we have had to consider a range of our own clinical and supervision experiences when creating characterisations of therapy issues. We have given our characterisations of typical and recurring therapeutic issues names so that readers can follow the progress of therapeutic scenarios. These named characterisations do not portray individual clients.

In the past 15 years there has been a revolution in our understanding of psychotic experiences. This revolution is linked to the emerging acceptance of psychological models of psychosis, the growing importance and centrality of user involvement, and the evolution of an empirical evidence base, which attests to the effectiveness of cognitive behavioural therapies for psychosis. However, so far the evidence that individual psychological interventions such as CBT are effective in preventing recurrence of further distressing psychotic episodes is lacking. This is in contrast to family-based interventions, which have demonstrated significant and important effects on reducing the likelihood of recurrence of psychosis and readmission to hospital. However, the uptake and provision of family interventions in the UK and elsewhere have been limited and many families do not find these very accessible. In addition, many people who have experienced psychosis do not necessarily live with their families, and may be living alone and be socially isolated but also their perceived key problems may not be situated within a family context or relationships. This is a group who are also at an elevated risk of recurrence. Furthermore, the impact of recurrence of psychosis can be devastating for individuals themselves, their loved ones and their family. Psychosis can also have long-term effects on individuals' lifespan development, particularly in terms of the individual's social and vocational development, which is often significantly compromised by the sequelae of the onset of a first episode in late adolescence. For example, individuals often experience personal trauma associated with the psychosis itself or the experience of hospitalisation; there is often a loss of expectations and hopes for the future, impaired secondary individuation and personal independence, increased disengagement of friends and family, and significant levels of stigma and socio-economic discrimination. Repeated recurrence of psychosis brings about additional losses, re-traumatisation, more pervasive and distressing psychotic experiences, and greater social disabilities. Therefore, we feel that there is an urgent need to develop an individually based psychological therapy aimed at the prevention of relapse. In attempting to do so, we describe an integrative cognitive interpersonal approach to support individuals who are recovering from psychosis. A framework of psychological treatment is presented here that incorporates various treatment strategies, which are designed to facilitate emotional recovery from psychosis, the prevention of psychosis recurrence and to optimise interpersonal and social development. This book is based on the premise that psychosis is fundamentally a normal human experience, the form and content of which reflect core cognitive, interpersonal and developmental life tasks and experiences.

This book has been structured in such a way that those interested in the wide-ranging theoretical and empirical evidence that we have drawn upon for our therapeutic approach should read Chapters 1, 2 and 3. Part II provides an overview of the structure, style and organisation of therapy. Specifically, Chapter 4 deals with issues of therapeutic structure and style, while Chapter 5 provides a closer view of our approach to the process of engagement and formulation.

Throughout the first five chapters we make frequent reference to attachment theory. This is a major theme of this book and our approach to staying well after psychosis. There are numerous theoretical and empirical reasons for this and we would direct readers' attention to Chapters 2 and 3 for a detailed exposition. However, we see the rationale for this as rather straightforward. Asking people with psychosis to seek help in the context of emotional distress and during a period of heightened risk of relapse is a highly complex and demanding task. For many people, being asked to monitor their early signs and activate a prearranged action plan is challenging. Consider how difficult it is for an anxious patient to maintain the belief that his palpitations are normal in the midst of a panic attack! Attachment theory provides a developmental understanding of clients' experiences of seeking help or proximity seeking in the context of distress and suffering. Attachment theory also helps us reflect on our own responses, either individually or as a service to clients' attempts to seek support. Hence we can understand staying well in the context of this reciprocal interpersonal process. This theoretical stance has helped us operationalise what we try to achieve as caregivers in providing a sympathetic, accepting, empathic, non-judgemental, caring and sensitive approach to providing psychological therapy in response to recovery and relapse prevention after psychosis.

In writing this book, we have attempted to avoid being prescriptive. It does not necessarily follow that the flow of treatment should reflect the flow of chapters in Part III of the book. Part III details the specific cognitive and interpersonal strategies that we have found useful and which have their basis in our clinical experiences and our research experience (see Gumley et al., 2003). We have organised Part III to reflect commonly recurring issues in recovery and relapse prevention. This includes interventions to support emotional and self-reorganisation following psychosis (Chapter 6), strategies aimed at addressing interpersonal distrust and suspicion (Chapter 7), strategies aimed at alleviating the traumatic effects of psychosis (Chapter 8), interpersonal interventions aimed at supporting individuals negotiating the multiple demands of their social and interpersonal context (Chapter 9), schema-focused strategies (Chapter 10) and working with fear of recurrence of psychosis (Chapter 11). We hope that readers will access specific chapters based on their clients' specific problem lists and goals, and use chapters to cross-refer to recurring themes developed within the book. We hope that Chapter 12 will support readers in this task.

In discussing the recurring themes developed in this book, we have relied heavily on the work of attachment theorists, including Mary Main, Peter Fonagy and Mary Dozier. We have also taken the view that psychosis is a severe life event, which leads to the development of associated emotional distress. Understanding emotional distress following psychosis requires an understanding of the process of emotional adaptation to psychosis. For this we have relied heavily on the work of Max Birchwood, Tirril Harris and George Brown. We hope that this treatment manual will be useful to therapists who conduct family interventions for carers and loved ones of those suffering from psychosis. In writing this manual we have been greatly influenced by the work of Christine Barrowclough. Finally, in the process of attuning cognitive and interpersonal therapeutic strategies in an attachment context, we would like to acknowledge the work of Paul Gilbert, who has influenced and will continue to profoundly influence our thinking as therapists, clinical psychologists and researchers.

The approaches and techniques described in this book are governed by two further principles. These are that interventions must be developmentally tailored and that the expression of psychotic experiences is understood as an adaptive and meaningful response to personal life experiences. Psychosis disrupts important developmental processes, thus skewing or stalling personal life trajectories. At the same time, psychosis appears to arise in a particular developmental context leading us to suggest that specific developmentally sensitive interventions need to integrate developmental tasks and transitions. Finally, we propose that psychotic experiences are an expression of individuals' developmental adaptation and response to critical life events and transitions. Those who develop psychosis have frequently experienced early adverse experiences, which impact upon cognitive, emotional, and interpersonal development.

Andrew Gumley and Matthias Schwannauer
Glasgow and Edinburgh
26 June 2005

FOREWORD

Tom McGlashan, following many years of psychotherapy research and practice at the Chestnut Lodge Institute in the USA, lamented, 'What has become of the psychotherapy of schizophrenia?' (McGlashan, 1994). It seemed doomed due to the power of neuroscience. At the same time, there was a renaissance of psychotherapy for psychosis in the UK, under the aegis of cognitive therapy. We rediscovered the 'person' in psychosis: people with psychosis were no longer passive sponges of psychotic experience, but were active agents searching for meaning and control of their changed mental life. Recently there has also been a re-marriage of emotion and psychosis (still at the courtship stage, I suspect), following Jaspers' view that we should separate 'emotion from madness proper'. This has allowed us to explore the interaction of emotion and psychosis (Freeman & Garety, 2003) and the various pathways to emotional dysfunction in psychosis (Birchwood, 2003).

These paradigmatic changes have been embedded in the application of cognitive therapy to psychosis (CBTp). The first generation of such studies was successful and was evaluated using traditional psychosis outcomes used in drug trials (psychosis symptoms, relapse). Thus CBTp won approval in National Schizophrenia Treatment Guidelines in the UK and USA; however, there has been a growing discomfort that we have done so at the expense of the true origins and real purpose of CBT and therefore we adopted the neuroleptic metaphor for CBTp to regain respectability for the psychotherapy of schizophrenia.

We are entering a new phase of CBTp in the way emotional and interpersonal processing in psychosis is at the core of our thinking. We have come out! We understand, for example, how secondary appraisal of psychosis can lead to depression and suicidal thinking or traumatic reactions; and we are beginning to understand how the social context can interact with developmental vulnerability to influence distress in psychosis and help-seeking behaviour. Distress and emotional dysfunction are now becoming the primary outcomes of CBTp, not hallucinations and delusions alone.

Andrew Gumley and Matthias Schwannauer have been among the vanguard of these new developments in CBTp: they have undertaken breakthrough work in relapse prevention by focusing not on the re-emergence of psychosis symptoms *per se*, but on the subtle changes in mental life and individuals' catastrophic appraisal of them.

This is a magnificent book. It defines what I'm sure will characterise the 'new wave' of CBTp for psychosis, based on powerful evidence for the inter-relationship of developmental vulnerability, cognition and emotion in psychosis, informing interventions with a distinctive emphasis, not simply to be wheeled out when neuroleptics fail. The title of the book and its emphasis on recovery and staying well are apt. It combines a scholarly approach to theory, bringing together the tenets of attachment theory and social cognition which evolves seamlessly into their cognitive interpersonal intervention protocol, illustrated with colourful and lucid clinical material. Above all, this is a very practical volume that deserves to be widely read and implemented by frontline clinicians.

REFERENCES

Birchwood M (2003). Pathways to emotional dysfunction in first-episode psychosis. *British Journal of Psychiatry*, **182**, 373–375.

Freeman D & Garety PA (2003). Connecting neurosis and psychosis: the direct influence of emotion on delusions and hallucinations. *Behavioural Research and Therapy*, **41**, 923–947.

McGlashan TH (1994). What has become of the psychotherapy of schizophrenia? *Acta Psychiatrica Scandinavica*, **384**(suppl.), 147–152.

Max Birchwood
*Professor of Mental Health, University of
Birmingham and Director of the
Birmingham Early Intervention Service*

ACKNOWLEDGEMENTS

We are obliged to many people for their support and inspiration for this project. First of all, we want to acknowledge and thank our clients and their families who have shaped and made sense of our clinical experiences. Our clinical experiences have inspired us to pursue an understanding of adaptation to psychotic experiences and to develop and operationalise the therapy approach outlined in this book. We also want to acknowledge the patience and support of our colleagues and friends in our clinical and academic work. In particular, we want to aknowledge the support of our clinical colleagues in ESTEEM, North Glasgow Early Intervention Service, and EPSS, the Early Psychosis Support Service at the Young people's Unit in Edinburgh.

We also want to thank the following people for their inspiration to us: Aaron T. Beck, Tony Morrison, Max Birchwood, Nick Tarrier, David Fowler, Philippa Garety, Douglas Turkington, Gillian Haddock, Mick Power, Kevin Power and Kate Davidson. We would also like to pay special tribute to Angus Macbeth, Nicola Clark and Emma Seel for their assistance in preparing this manuscript. Finally, it takes many hours to prepare a book, time that is taken from many weekends and evenings. Therefore, we would like to thank our families, friends, and our partners, Lee-Anne and Claire for their consistent and patient support.

PART I

THEORETICAL OVERVIEW

CHAPTER 1

CURRENT PERSPECTIVES ON RELAPSE, RELAPSE DETECTION AND PREVENTION

INTRODUCTION

In this chapter, we will briefly review the evidence for psychological therapies in the prevention of relapse. Following this brief review, we describe a psychological approach to conceptualising the early signs of relapse in psychosis. We will argue that relapse needs to be understood from (1) the context of the person, their beliefs and appraisals of relapse and psychosis; (2) the individual's interpersonal context; and (3) the manner in which service systems respond to the challenge of relapse prevention for individuals who are prone to recurrent psychotic experiences. Our general definition of relapse is as a medical term that is used to describe the recurrence of an episode of illness or the exacerbation of illness symptoms, which had been partially remitted. Importantly, however, in relation to psychosis, relapse refers predominantly to the return or exacerbation of positive psychotic experiences that are likely to be associated with high levels of emotional distress and impaired social, vocational and interpersonal functioning. The combination of psychotic experiences, emotional distress and impaired functioning may lead to the person being voluntarily or involuntarily admitted to hospital. It is important to recognise that there is the breakdown of educational, vocation and social resources that accompanies relapse. Furthermore, relapse brings with it greater threats to the family structure and functioning.

Relapse has been associated with the evolution of greater residual and pervasive psychotic experiences (Wiersma et al., 1998), greater social disability (Hogarty et al., 1991), increased risk of depression and suicidal thinking (Iqbal et al., 2000) and heightened, more intense levels of family distress (Barrowclough et al., 2001). In psychological terms, relapse is a potentially devastating and critical life event with profound consequences for the emotional and psychological well-being of the person and their family or loved ones. In addition, the effects of an individual's relapse on care staff and health professionals connected with their well-being should not be under-

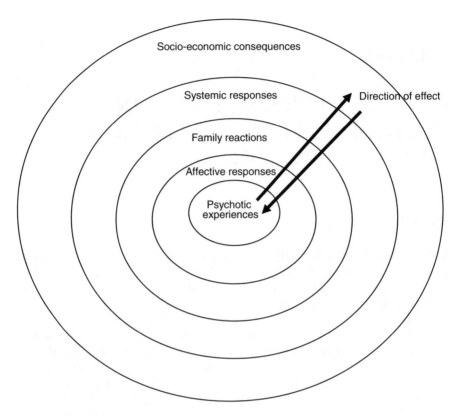

Figure 1.1   Personal, interpersonal and systemic context of relapse

estimated. Many staff may experience feelings of disappointment and self-criticism, or, in contrast, feelings of frustration and anger. Therefore, any attempt to develop a comprehensive formulation of relapse needs to fully integrate factors at the individual level (for example, personal meanings and appraisals, affective reactions and behavioural responses), the interpersonal level (for example, family attributions and their associated emotional and behavioural reactions), and the systemic level (that is, the responses of services, health professionals and care staff). The bidirectional relationship between the personal, interpersonal and systemic factors is graphically illustrated in Figure 1.1.

PSYCHOLOGICAL THERAPIES AND RELAPSE PREVENTION

Before describing our psychological approach to conceptualising the early signs of relapse, we will briefly review the current evidence for psychological treatments being effective in the prevention of relapse among individuals diagnosed with schizophrenia. In particular, we focus on family therapy and cognitive behavioural therapy (CBT). We will argue that while there is robust evidence for family interventions being an effective approach to supporting families and individuals in staying well after psychosis, there is a need to develop individually based therapies that can support and enhance family-based work, or indeed stand alone as a psychological approach to the prevention of relapse.

Family Interventions

Pitschel-Walz and colleagues (2001) described a meta-analysis of 25 studies, which evaluated the effectiveness of family interventions for relapse among individuals diagnosed with schizophrenia. Previous meta-analyses (Mari & Streiner, 1994, 1996; Pharoah et al., 1999), containing up to 13 studies, had suggested that family interventions for schizophrenia were moderately effective in decreasing the frequency of relapse and re-hospitalisation. Pitschel-Walz and colleagues were able to include more studies unpublished at the time of these earlier reviews. In total, they identified 39 studies; four were excluded because of lack of control group, nine studies were not randomised studies, and in one study group comparisons were missing. Twelve studies compared family intervention with usual care (Goldstein et al., 1978; Leff et al., 1985; Spiegel & Wissler, 1987; Spencer et al., 1988; Tarrier et al., 1989; Kelly & Scott, 1990; Hogarty et al., 1991; Posner et al., 1992; Vaughan et al., 1992; Randolph et al., 1994; Xiong et al., 1994; Zhang et al., 1994). Pitschel-Walz and colleagues found that family interventions were better than routine care at 6, 9, 12, 18, and 24 months after therapy. Longer-term therapies (those lasting between 9 to 24 months) were more effective than shorter-term interventions (those lasting less than 3 months). Furthermore, in five studies that combined family intervention with individual intervention (Cranach, 1981; Kelly & Scott, 1990; Hogarty et al., 1991; Buchkremer et al., 1997; Pitschel-Walz et al., 1998) this combination of therapies performed better than routine care. However, adding individual therapy to family intervention did not result in significant improvements in relapse rates compared to family intervention alone. A further six studies compared family intervention with individual therapy (Ro-Trock et al., 1977; Falloon et al., 1982, 1985; Kelly & Scott, 1990; Hogarty et al., 1991; Telles et al., 1995; Hogarty et al., 1997a, 1997b). There were no significant differences in efficacy between the two interventions during the first year after study entry. However, two years after participants entered the studies, the family intervention performed better than individual therapy in the prevention of relapse. In addition, five studies (Clarkin et al., 1998; Colom et al., 2003; Miklowitz et al., 2000, 2003; Rae et al., 2003) have also shown that family-focused interventions in bipolar disorders are also effective in preventing relapse.

Cognitive Behavioural Therapy

The basic design, participants, outcomes and follow-up periods are summarised in Table 1.1. A total of 35 papers describing 23 randomised controlled trials involving the comparison of CBT with at least one other treatment condition, involving a total of 2,206 participants with a diagnosis of schizophrenia or similar was identified.

The studies identified for this review were heterogeneous in terms of the participant populations and outcome measures used. One study (Barrowclough et al., 2001; Haddock et al., 2003) focused on participants with co-morbid substance use problems. Four studies (Drury et al., 1996; Haddock et al., 1999; Lewis et al., 2002; Startup et al., 2004) delivered cognitive therapy during the acute/recovery phase. Eight studies (Lecompte, 1996; Garety et al., 1998; Pinto et al., 1999; Tarrier et al., 1999; Sensky et al., 2000; Turkington & Kingdon, 2000; Durham et al., 2003; Trower et al., 2004) focused on those with drug-resistant symptoms. Two studies (Daniels, 1998; Bechdolf et al., 2004) studied group cognitive therapy. Two studies (McGorry et al., 2002; Morrison et al., 2004) delivered CBT to individuals who were at ultra-high risk of developing psychosis. Two studies (Kemp & David, 1996; Turkington et al., 2002) focused on the development of insight as the primary outcome. Only four studies (Buchkremer et al., 1997; Hogarty et al., 1997; Bach & Hayes, 2002; Gumley et al., 2003) had relapse or readmission as their primary outcome.

Although a wide variety of outcome measures was used, there were three main primary outcome measures employed including the Brief Psychiatric Rating Scale (BPRS: Overall & Gorham, 1962), the Comprehensive Psychiatric Rating Scale (CPRS: Montgomery et al., 1978), and the Positive and Negative Syndrome Scale (PANSS: Kay et al., 1987). The BPRS was employed in Buchkremer et al. (1997), Daniels (1998), Garety et al. (1998), Haddock et al. (1999), McGorry et al. (2002), Pinto et al. (1999), Startup et al. (2004) and Tarrier et al. (1999). The CPRS was used in Sensky et al. (2000), Turkington and Kingdon (2000) and Turkington et al. (2002). The PANSS was used in Barrowclough et al. (2001), Bechdolf et al. (2004), Durham et al. (2003), Gumley et al. (2003), Lewis et al. (2002) and Morrison et al. (2004). Other studies used the Psychiatric Assessment Scale (PAS: Drury et al., 1996), the David Insight Scale (Kemp & David, 1996; Turkington et al., 2002), the Voice Compliance Scale and the Beliefs About Voices Questionnaire (Trower et al., 2004) as primary outcome measures. Over this time period, CBT studies seem to have been concerned with symptomatic improvement and therefore have been orientated to psychiatric ratings of outcome. CBT studies have been less concerned with emotional recovery, quality of life, social functioning and staying well. In this respect the Trower et al. (2004) study marks a shift towards more CBT-specific outcomes.

Table 1.1 Randomised controlled clinical trials of CBT for schizophrenia or similar[1]

Study	Country	Design	Diagnostic criteria	Treatment conditions	Main outcomes	End of study results	Length of follow-up	Follow-up outcomes	Follow-up results	Comments
Bach & Hayes, 2002	United States	RCT		ACT (1: n =) TAU (2: n =)	Relapse	1 > 2	NA	NA	NA	This was the first trial of Acceptance and Commitment Therapy (ACT) with individuals with psychosis
Barrowclough et al., 2001	United Kingdom	RCT	ICD-10 DSM-IV	CBT + MI + FI (1: n = 18) TAU (2: n = 18)	GAF[9] PANSS Relapse	1 > 2 1 = 2 1 > 2	18 months	Patients: GAF PANSS Carers: BDI[10] GHQ[11]	1 > 2 1 = 2 1 = 2 1 = 2	Main outcomes reported for 9 and 12 months following randomisation MI = Motivational Interviewing FI = Family Intervention

Table 1.1 Continued

Study	Country	Design	Diagnostic criteria	Treatment conditions	Main outcomes	End of study results	Length of follow-up	Follow-up outcomes	Follow-up results	Comments
Bechdolf et al., 2004	Germany	RCT	ICD-10	GCBT (1: n = 40) GPE (2: n = 48)	PANSS[5] Compliance	1 > 2 1 = 2	6 months	Relapse PANSS[5] Compliance	1 > 2 1 > 2 1 = 2	Therapies were delivered with a 6-week treatment envelope with follow-up reported at 6-months post-treatment GCBT = Group CBT GPE = Group Psychoeducation
Buchkremer et al., 1997	Germany	RCT	DSM-III-R	PMT + L (1: n = 32) PMT + L + KC (2: n = 35) PMT + CP (3: n = 34) PMT + CP + C (4: n = 33) L (5: n = 57)	Readmission BPRS[2] SANS[3] GAS[4]	1,2,3,4 = 5 4 > 5 1,2,3,4 = 5 1,2,3,4, > 5	5 years	Readmission BPRS SANS GAS	1,2,3,4- = 5 4 > 5 1,2,3,4 = 5 1,2,3,4 = 5 1,2,3,4 = 5	Main outcomes for this study are reported at 2-years post-randomisation PMT = Psychoeducation L = Leisure group KC = Key-person Counselling CP = Cognitive Psychotherapy

Study	Country	Design	Diagnosis	Groups	Measures	Group differences	Follow-up	Follow-up outcome	Follow-up result	Comments
Daniels, 1998	United States	RCT	DSM-IV	IBT (1: n = 10) WL (2: n = 10)	GAF CGI[20] QLS[21] BPRS	Group differences not reported.				CBT participants significantly improved on GAF, but not CGI, QLS, BPRS Group treatment was conducted over 16, twice-weekly sessions. Outcomes are at post-treatment. IBT = Integrative Behaviour Therapy WL = Waiting List
Drury et al., 1996, 2000	United Kingdom	RCT	WHO	CBT (1: n = 20) ATY (2: n = 20)	12 weeks: PAS[17] Positive PAS Disorganisation PAS Negative 9 months: PAS Positive PAS Disorganisation PAS Negative	1 > 2 1 = 2 1 = 2 1 > 2 1 = 2 1 = 2	5 years	Readmission PAS	1 = 2 1 = 2	ATY = Activity/recreation

Table 1.1 Continued

Study	Country	Design	Diagnostic criteria	Treatment conditions	Main outcomes	End of study results	Length of follow-up	Follow-up outcomes	Follow-up results	Comments
Durham et al., 2003	United Kingdom	RCT	DSM-IV ICD-10	CBT (1: n = 22) SP (2: n = 23) TAU (3: n = 21)	PANSS PSYRATS[6] GAS	1 = 2 = 3 1 = 2 = 3 1 = 2 = 3	12 months	PANSS PSYRATS GAS	1 > 2,3 1,2 > 3 1 = 2 = 3	End of treatment results were taken at 9 months with 3-month follow-up. SP = Supportive Psychotherapy
Garety et al., 1998	United Kingdom	RCT	DSM-III-R	CBT (1: n = 28) TAU (2: n = 32)	BPRS	1 > 2	18 months	BPRS Delusional[7] distress Hallucinations[7] frequency	1 > 2 1 > 2 1 > 2	
Gumley et al., 2003	United Kingdom	RCT	DSM-IV	CBT (1: n = 72) TAU (2: n = 72)	Relapse Readmission PANSS SFS[8]	1 > 2 1 = 2 1 > 2 1 > 2				PANSS positive, negative and global psychopathology scales analysed separately
Haddock et al., 1999	United Kingdom	RCT	DSM-IV	CBT (1: n = 10) TAU (2: n = 11)	Days to discharge BPRS PSYRATS	1 = 2 1 = 2 1 = 2	24 months	Readmission	1 = 2	

Study	Country	Design	Diagnostic criteria	Intervention groups	Outcome measures	Results	Follow-up	Results	Notes
Hogarty et al., 1997	United States	RCT	RDC	PT (1: n = 74) FT (2: n = 50) ST (3: n = 53)	Relapse (psychotic and affective)	Trial 1 1 > 2,3 Trial 2 1 < 3			Outcomes for patients living with (Trial 1: n = 97) and outwith family (Trial 2: n = 54) were analysed separately. Results are presented at 3 years following randomisation: PT = Personal Therapy FT = Family Therapy ST = Supportive Therapy
Kemp, 1998	United Kingdom	RCT	DSM-III-R	ComT (1: n = 39) TAU (2: n = 35)	Compliance Attitudes to treatment[12] Insight[13] GAF	1 > 2 1 > 2 1 > 2 1 > 2	18 months	Compliance 1 = 2 Attitudes to treatment 1 > 2 Insight 1 > 2 GAF 1 > 2	ComT = Compliance Therapy
Lecompte, 1996	United States	RCT		CBT (1: n = 32) Con (2: n = 32)					Con = Non-directive Conversation

Table 1.1 Continued

Study	Country	Design	Diagnostic criteria	Treatment conditions	Main outcomes	End of study results	Length of follow-up	Follow-up outcomes	Follow-up results	Comments
Lewis et al., 2002	United Kingdom	RCT	DSM-IV	CBT (1: n = 101) SC (2: n = 106) RC (3: n = 102)	PANSS PSYRATS	1 > 2,3 1 = 2 = 3	18 months	PANSS PSYRATS Readmission	1,2 > 3 1,2 > 3 1 = 2 = 3	CBT was associated with faster improvement compared to SC and RC SC = Supportive Counselling RC = Routine Care
McGorry et al., 2002	Australia	RCT	N/A	CBT + Risp (1: n = 31) CM (2: n = 28)	Transition BPRS SANS	1 > 2 1 = 2 1 = 2	12 months	Transition BPRS SANS GAF	1 = 2 1 = 2 1 = 2 1 = 2	End of treatment outcomes reported at 6 months. Trial conducted with people at ultra-high risk of developing schizophrenia. CBT + Risp = CBT in combination with low-dose risperidone. CM = Case Management

Study	Country	Design	Diagnostic criteria	Intervention	Outcome measures	Results	Follow-up	Outcome measures	Results	Notes
Morrison et al., 2004	United Kingdom	RCT	N/A	CBT (1: n = 37) Monitoring (2: n = 23)	Transition PANSS	1 > 2 1 > 2				Outcomes reported at 12-months post randomisation Trial conducted with people at ultra-high risk of developing schizophrenia
Pinto et al., 1999	Italy	RCT	DSM-IV	CBT (1: n = 20) SP (1: n = 21)	BPRS SAPS[14] SANS	1 > 2 1 > 2 1 = 2				All participants in receipt of Clozapine. Outcomes reported at post-treatment, 6 months following randomisation
Sensky et al., 2000	United Kingdom	RCT	ICD-10	CBT (1: n = 46) BF (2: n = 44)	CPRS[15] MADRS[16] SANS	1 = 2 1 = 2 1 = 2	18 months	CPRS[15] MADRS[16] SANS	1 > 2 1 > 2 1 > 2	Post-treatment outcomes taken at 9 months BF = Befriending
Startup et al., 2004	United Kingdom	RCT	DSM-IV	CBT (1: n = 47) TAU (2: n = 43)	SAPS SANS BPRS SFS	1 > 2 1 = 2 1 > 2 1 > 2	12 months	SAPS SANS BPRS SFS	1 > 2 1 > 2 1 > 2 1 > 2	Post-treatment outcomes taken at 6 months

Table 1.1 Continued

Study	Country	Design	Diagnostic criteria	Treatment conditions	Main outcomes	End of study results	Length of follow-up	Follow-up outcomes	Follow-up results	Comments
Tarrier et al., 1999	United Kingdom	RCT	DSM-III-R	CBT (1: n = 33) SC (2: n = 26) RC (3: n = 28)	BPRS Readmission	1 > 2,3 1,2 < 3	12 months 24 months	BPRS Readmission BPRS Readmission	1 > 3 1 = 2 = 3 1,2 > 3 1 = 2 = 3	Follow-ups took place 12 and 24 months post-treatment. Treatment duration was 3 months.
Trower et al., 2004	United Kingdom	RCT	ICD-10	CBT (1: n = 18) TAU (2: N = 20)	Compliance[18] Malevolence[19] Omniscience[19] PSYRATS Control	1 > 2 1 = 2 1 > 2 1 > 2	12 months	Compliance Malevolence Omniscience Control	1 > 2 1 = 2 1 > 2 1 > 2	
Turkington & Kingdon, 2000	United Kingdom	RCT	ICD-10 DSM-IV	CBT (1: n = 13) BF (2: n = 6)	CPRS MADRS	1 > 2 1 = 2				Outcomes reported at 6 months
Turkington et al., 2002	United Kingdom	RCT	ICD-10	CBT (1: n = 257) TAU (2: n = 165)	CPRS Insight[13] MADRAS	1 > 2 1 > 2 1 > 2				Outcomes presented at 20 weeks

Notes:

1 Based on the search strategy conducted by Cochrane Schizophrenia group (2004) supplemented by further search strategy combining SCHIZOPHRENIA with COGNITIV* and/or BEHAVIO* and/or THERAP* in CINAHL, EMBASE, PsychINFO, MEDLINE databases.

2 Overall JE & Gorham DR (1962). The Brief Psychiatric Rating Scale. *Psychological Reports*, **10**, 799–812.

3 Andreasen NC (1989) Scale for the Assessment of Negative Symptoms (SANS). *British Journal of Psychiatry*, **155**, 53–58.

4 Endicott J, Spitzer RL, Fleiss JL & Cohen J (1970). The Global Assessment Scale. A procedure for measuring overall severity of psychiatric disturbance. *Archives of General Psychiatry*, **33**, 766–771.

5 Kay S, Fizbein A & Opler L (1987). The Positive and Negative Syndrome Scale (PANSS) for Schizophrenia. *Schizophrenia Bulletin*, **13**, 261–275.

6 Haddock G, McCarron J, Tarrier N & Faragher EB (1999). Scales to measure dimensions of hallucinations and delusions: the psychotic symptom rating scales (PSYRATS). *Psychological Medicine*.

7 Brett-Jones J, Garety PA, Hemsley D (1967). Measuring delusional experiences: a method and its application. *British Journal of Clinical Psychiatry*, **163**, 257–265.

8 Birchwood M, Smith J, Cochrane R, Wetton C & Copestake S (1990). The Social Functioning Scale: The development and validation of a new scale of social adjustment for use in family intervention programmes with schizophrenic patients. *British Journal of Psychiatry*, **157**, 853–859.

9 American Psychiatric Association (1994). *The Diagnostic and Statistical Manual of Mental Disorders*, 4th edn. Washington, DC, American Psychiatric Association.

10 Beck AT, Ward T & Mendelsson S et al. (1961). An inventory for measuring depression. *Archives of General Psychiatry*, **4**, 561–571.

11 Goldberg D & Williams PA (1988). *Users guide to the General Health Questionnaire*. Windsor, NFER Nelson.

12 Hogan TP, Awad AG & Eastwood R (1983). A self report scale predictive of drug compliance in schizophrenics: reliability and discriminative validity. *Psychological Medicine*, **13**, 177–183.

13 David AS (1990). Insight and psychosis. *British Journal of Psychiatry*, **156**, 798–808.

14 Andraesen NC (1984). *The scale for the assessment of positive symptoms (SAPS)*. Iowa City, University of Iowa.

15 Montgomery SA, Taylor P & Montgomery D (1978). Development of a schizophrenia scale sensitive to change. *Neuropharmacology*, **17**, 1053–1071.

16 Montgomery SA & Asberg M (1979). A new depression scale designed to be sensitive to change. *British Journal of Psychiatry*, **13**, 382–389.

17 Krawiecka M, Goldberg D & Vaughn M (1977). Standardised psychiatric assessment scale for chronic psychiatric patients. *Acta Psychiatrica Scandinavica*, **36**, 25–31.

18 Beck-Sander, Birchwood M & Chadwick P (1997). Acting on command hallucinations: a cognitive approach. *British Journal of Clinical Psychology*, **36**, 139–148.

19 Chadwick P & Birchwood M (1995). The omnipotence of voices: II The beliefs about voices questionnaire (BAVQ). *British Journal of Psychology*, **166**, 773–776.

20 Guy W (ed.) (1976). *ECDEU Assessment manual for psychopharmacology (ADM 76-338)*. Washington, DC, US Department of Health Education and Welfare.

21 Heinricks DW, Hanlon TE & Carpenter WT Jr, (1984). The quality of life scale: an instrument for measuring the schizophrenic deficit syndrome. *Schizophrenia Bulletin*, **10**, 388–398.

CBT was compared with Treatment as Usual (TAU) in 11 trials (Garety et al., 1998; Kemp et al., 1998; Haddock et al., 1999; Tarrier et al., 1999; Barrowclough et al., 2001; Lewis et al., 2002; Durham et al., 2003; Gumley et al., 2003; Morrison et al., 2004; Startup et al., 2004; Trower et al., 2004). A total of 12 trials incorporated a comparison psychological intervention into the study design (Drury et al., 1996; Lecompte, 1996; Buchkremer et al., 1997; Hogarty et al., 1997; Pinto et al., 1999; Tarrier et al., 1999; Sensky et al., 2000; Turkington et al., 2000; Lewis et al., 2002; McGorry et al., 2002; Durham et al., 2003; Bechdolf et al., 2004). One trial (Daniels, 1998) compared CBT to a waiting list control.

In terms of overall psychiatric symptomatology, CBT shows encouraging evidence of being more effective in comparison to TAU (Garety et al., 1998; Tarrier et al., 1999; Barrowclough et al., 2001; Turkington et al., 2002; Gumley et al., 2003; Bechdolf et al., 2004; Morrison et al., 2004; Startup et al., 2004; Trower et al., 2004) or another psychological intervention (Drury et al., 1996; Pinto et al., 1999; Tarrier et al., 1999; Turkington & Kingdon, 2000) post-treatment. However, the results comparing CBT to other psychological interventions are less clear. CBT was also associated with a reduction in relapse in comparison to treatment as usual in one study (Gumley et al., 2003), in comparison to group psychoeducation (Bechdolf et al., 2004) and in comparison to the family therapy (Hogarty et al., 1997). On the other hand, Tarrier et al. (1999) did not find a reduction in relapse, and indeed for patients who are living alone, Hogarty et al. (1997) found an increase in relapse rate in comparison to Supportive Therapy. Two studies (Drury et al., 1996; Lewis et al., 2002) found that CBT was associated with a faster time to remission, or a more complete remission (Drury et al., 1996). However, Lewis et al. (2002) found that the advantage for CBT (compared to TAU) at four weeks was lost at six weeks; in other words, patients who receive CBT during their acute phase achieve remission two weeks before patients treated in routine care or with supportive therapy. Kemp and David (1998) and Turkington et al. (2002) found that CBT improved attitudes to drug treatment and increased acceptance of illness. McGorry et al. (2002) and Morrison et al. (2004) found that CBT was associated with a lower rate of transition to psychotic disorder, including schizophrenia.

Of the 22 trials, 11 have reported follow-ups beyond 12-months post-randomisation (Drury et al., 1996; Buchkremer et al., 1997; Hogarty et al., 1997; Garety et al., 1998; Kemp & David, 1998; Haddock et al., 1999; Tarrier et al., 1999; Sensky et al., 2000; Barrowclough et al., 2001; Lewis et al., 2002; Startup et al., 2004). These follow-ups were conducted at 18 months (Garety et al., 1998; Kemp et al., 1998; Sensky et al., 2000; Barrowclough et al., 2001; Lewis et al., 2002; Startup et al., 2004), 24 months (Haddock et al., 1999; Tarrier et al., 1999), three years (Hogarty et al., 1997) and five years (Drury et al., 1996; Buchkremer et al., 1997). Therefore, in terms of quantity of studies completed, the best evidence for the maintenance of treatment gains post-treatment comes from the six studies that have conducted 18-month post-randomisation assessments. In the Barrowclough et al. (2001), Garety et al. (1998), Kemp & David (1998) and Startup et al. (2004) studies, immediate treatment gains were largely maintained at follow-up. All these studies compared CBT to TAU. The Sensky et al. (2000) study did not find a difference between CBT and befriending (BF) at post-treatment. However, at 18 months those who received CBT had continued to improve, whereas those who received BF had lost much of their gains. The Lewis et al. (2002) study (reported as Tarrier et al., 2004) did not find a specific effect for CBT at 18 months, rather, receipt of psychological intervention appeared to improve outcome although this positive finding did not translate to relapse or read-mission outcomes. To date, there is no evidence for a specific effect for CBT at two years (Tarrier et al., 1999). The Hogarty et al. (1997) study did find an effect for Personal Therapy for those patients who lived with families at three years; however, treatment had been continuous over that period. Finally, there was little evidence for the efficacy of CBT at five-year follow-up (Buchkremer et al., 1997; Drury et al., 2000). However, the Drury et al. (2000) study found that those who relapsed more than once during the interven-ing period had a very poor outcome, raising the importance of relapse pre-vention for this group. There was a little evidence from the Buchkremer et al., (1997) study that receipt of CBT in combination with psychoeducation plus counselling protected participants against relapse compared to leisure activity control over the intervening five years.

In their Cochrane review, Jones et al., (2004) concluded:

> the use of cognitive behavioural therapy has been associated with some reduc-
> tion in symptoms, especially the positive symptoms of schizophrenia.
> However, there is considerable variability in the findings of the various studies
> and, at present, it is not possible to assert any substantial benefit for cognitive
> behavioural therapy over standard care or supportive therapies.

We would argue that some of this variability in findings is due in part to a number of factors including the variety of measures employed by the research teams and the different populations (in terms of symptoms and diagnoses) investigated in trials. It does not seem reasonable to compare CBT for stable yet drug-refractory positive symptoms with CBT delivered during the acute phase. In addition, it has recently been argued by Birchwood (2003) that the outcomes for CBT should not be the same as the outcomes for antipsychotic medication. In an example of this, Trower et al. (2004) have reported positive outcomes for their trial of cognitive therapy for command hallucinations. There are also limited data pertaining to the maintenance of therapy gains following treatment; further research is needed in this regard.

In addition, there is insufficient evidence at this juncture to support the use of CBT as a relapse prevention strategy. This may in part be due to the fact that many trials recruit participants who have chronic drug-resistant psychotic symptoms, but who are otherwise stable. In addition, few studies have had relapse as their primary outcome. However, examination of the treatment manuals adopted by trial investigators reveals that relapse prevention strategies are included within these protocols (Kingdon & Turkington, 1994; Fowler et al., 1995). These strategies focus on helping individuals recognise and respond to early signs of relapse by seeking help but do not specify particular cognitions or behaviours associated with the development of relapse acceleration, nor do these manuals specify psychological strategies to address cognition or behaviour during relapse. It would not seem unreasonable to suggest that the current lack of results with regard to relapse could, perhaps, be due in part to the inadequacy of existing CBT treatment protocols for relapse in psychosis. Indeed, those studies that specifically target the prevention of relapse (Bach & Hayes, 2002; Gumley et al., 2003) as a primary outcome show that cognitive behavioural intervention can be effective in the maintenance of recovery and staying well after psychosis. Therefore, there is a need for a specific manualised psychological intervention aimed at facilitating emotional recovery and relapse prevention. This book aims to achieve this goal.

AFFECT, MEANING AND RELAPSE

A key aspect of relapse is the experience of high levels of emotional distress and affective dysregulation in the period before, during and following the acute phase of psychosis. This has long been recognised by researchers and clinicians alike. For example, Docherty and colleagues (1978) proposed that prior to the development of a full-blown relapse there were identifiable and sequential phases, which they saw as an unfolding of a series of psychological states. These phases were conceptualised as being characterised by feelings of over-extension, restricted consciousness, behavioural and affective disinhibition, psychotic disorganisation and resolution. During the first phase of over-extension, the person experiences a sense of being overwhelmed by stressful demands or internal/external conflicts and is accompanied by feelings of fear, threat, anxiety and nervousness. This phase is followed by the appearance of a variety of intrusive mental phenomena, which limit the person's ability to concentrate and think. The person experiences feelings of helplessness, hopelessness, dissatisfaction and loneliness. During the disinhibition phase, the ability of the individual to modulate or regulate their internal impulses becomes impaired. The signs and symptoms of this phase are thought to be rage, panic and hypomania.

This precedes increasing perceptual and cognitive disorganisation, loss of self-identity and fragmentation of control during the active phase of psychosis. Docherty and colleagues' formulation emphasises a sequential view of the nature of relapse, where relapse is characterised by the progression of increasing non-psychotic symptoms, through increased emotional distress, affective dysregulation, psychological fragmentation, and feelings of loss of control, culminating in the evolution of psychosis.

The importance of the role of affect in psychotic relapse has been consistently demonstrated in a number of retrospective and prospective studies examining the prediction of relapse itself. Retrospective studies of individuals and their families (Herz & Melville, 1980; McCandless-Glimcher et al., 1986; Birchwood et al., 1989) show that the most commonly reported early signs of relapse are fearfulness, anxiety, poor sleep, irritability, tension, depression and social withdrawal. In their seminal study, Herz and Melville (1980) made the first attempt to systematically identify and characterise the early signs of relapse. A total of 145 people who had been diagnosed with schizophrenia and 80 of their relatives in the study were asked for their responses to the following question: 'Could you tell if there were any changes in your thoughts, feelings, and behaviours that might have led you to believe that you were becoming sick and might have to go to the hospital?' Approximately 70 per cent of participants reported noticing changes. Families were marginally more likely than the patients themselves to identify changes and, in about 66 per cent of cases, both families and individuals were in agreement. For most individuals and their families the time interval before relapse was more than one week. Between 50 and 60 per cent of individuals and families sought professional help; however, less than 4 per cent had been advised by a health professional to do so. In addition, Creer and Wing (1974) also reported in a survey of 80 relatives that virtually none had been given advice about the nature of early signs of relapse. The experiences described by relatives were ranked in terms of their frequency of being reported. The most commonly reported experiences were fearfulness/anxiety, tension and nervousness, sleeplessness, trouble concentrating, and loss of appetite and pleasure. These data are consistent with Docherty and colleagues' (1978) proposal that the earliest stages of relapse appear to be characterised by increased anxiety, fearfulness and tension. Herz and Melville's findings have been confirmed by three further retrospective studies (Thurm & Haefner, 1987; Kumar et al., 1989; Hamera et al., 1992).

The consistency with which early signs have been reported has led to the development of prospective investigations of early signs. In essence, these studies have sought to identify the sensitivity and specificity of these early signs as an indicator of emerging relapse. Clearly if these early signs are sensitive and specific to relapse, the monitoring of such signs, and associated emotional distress, would help facilitate earlier interventions – potentially leading to the prevention and/or amelioration of relapse. In the investigation of the predictive power of early signs monitoring, *sensitivity* refers to the ability of the monitoring system to correctly identify a forthcoming relapse. It is essentially the proportion of individuals who experience early signs prior to a relapse. *Specificity* refers to the power of these early signs to correctly identify those individuals or times when a relapse will not occur (see Table 1.2).

Table 1.3 provides a summary of prospective studies of early signs and relapse. Three of these studies (Jolley et al., 1990; Gaebel et al., 1993; Marder et al., 1994) were conducted in the context of a concurrent intervention trial which makes the relationship between early signs and relapse more difficult to ascertain due to the impact of interventions on this relationship. Four studies investigated observer-rated early signs alone (Subotnik & Neuchterlein, 1988; Tarrier et al., 1991; Gaebel et al., 1993; Marder et al., 1994), three studies investigated both observer- and self-rated early signs (Birchwood et al., 1989; Malla & Norman, 1994; Jorgensen, 1998) and one study investigated self-rated early signs alone (Hirsch & Jolley, 1989). Subotnik and Neuchterlein (1988) reported a prospective study of early signs in relation to relapse among 50 individuals. Participants were monitored fortnightly and relapse was defined by a rating of severe or extremely severe on the BPRS Unusual Thought Content, Conceptual Disorganization, and/or Hallucinations items. Greater suspiciousness and thought disturbance symptoms correctly identified 10 out of the 17 relapses. This gave a sensitivity to relapse of 59 per cent. Birchwood and colleagues (1989) recruited 17 individual participants who were monitored fortnightly using the self-rated or observer-rated Early Signs Scale over a nine-month period. Relapse was defined as any hospital admission or a clinician's judgement of imminent relapse or probable admission. Some 82 per cent of those who experienced a relapse had an increase in early signs prior to relapse; 62 per cent of those who did show an increase in early signs went on to have a relapse, meaning that 38 per cent had an increase in early signs but did not go on to relapse. Tarrier et al. (1991) monitored 56 participants on a monthly basis. Relapse was defined as a reappearance of positive psychotic symptoms or the worsening of persistent or residual positive symptoms, which lasted for at least one week. Depressed mood alone was associated with a sensitivity of 50 per

Table 1.2   Sensitivity and specificity

	High	*Low*
Sensitivity	Low false positives	High false positives
Specificity	Low false negatives	High false negatives

Table 1.3 Studies of the sensitivity and specificity of early signs to relapse in schizophrenia

Study	Assessment of early signs	Number of relapses	Sensitivity (%)	Specificity (%)
Subotnik & Neuchterlein (1988)	Observer-rated	17	59	NR
Birchwood et al. (1989)	Self-rated Observer-rated	8	62	82
Hirsch & Jolley (1989)	Self-rated	10	73	NR
Tarrier et al. (1991)	Observer-rated	16	50	81
Gaebel et al. (1993)	Observer-rated	162	8	90
			14	70
			10	93
Marder et al. (1994)	Observer-rated	42	37	NR
			48	
Malla & Norman (1994)	Self-rated Observer-rated	24	50	90
Jorgensen (1998)	Self-rated Observer-rated	27	78	45
			30	58

cent and specificity value of 81 per cent. When depression was combined with hallucinations, the sensitivity value increased to 62.5 per cent and the specificity value was 87.5 per cent. Malla and Norman (1994) monitored 55 participants on a monthly basis over a period of at least 12 months (range: 12–29 months). In this study many increases in psychotic experiences were not preceded by increases in emotional distress, unless accompanied by increases in psychotic symptoms. Jorgensen (1998) monitored 60 individuals, 30 of whom had residual positive psychotic symptoms ('symptomatic'), and 30 who were fully remitted ('asymptomatic'). Participants were interviewed every fortnight over six months or to relapse. A priori, different cut-off points were selected to identify early signs. These cut-off points were defined as changes in early signs scores ≥5, ≥10 or ≥15. Sensitivity and specificity values in Table 1.3 are given for ≥5. In total, 45 per cent participants relapsed, 27 per cent of whom were readmitted to hospital. For symptomatic participants sensitivity of early signs to relapse was 88 per cent and specificity 64 per cent, and for asymptomatic participants the sensitivity value was 73 per cent and the specificity value was 89 per cent. Across the eight studies reporting sensitivity and specificity for early signs to relapse, the findings on sensitivity values range from 8 to 88 per cent, and for specificity values from 45 to 93 per cent. Strict comparison across these studies is problematic given the nature of differences in methodology and design. However, a number of conclusions are possible on the basis of these data.

Observer versus Self-rated Detection

While it is not easy to group together studies examining observer-related and studies examining self-rated early signs due to important methodological differences, it is noteworthy that the median sensitivity of observer-rated early signs (Subotnik & Neuchterlein, 1988; Tarrier et al., 1991; Gaebel et al., 1993; Marder et al., 1994) was 37 per cent, while for those studies incorporating self-rated early signs monitoring (Birchwood et al., 1989; Malla & Norman, 1994; Jorgensen, 1998; Hirsch & Jolley, 1989) the median sensitivity results were 68 per cent. As the reader will recall, sensitivity refers to the ability of early signs to correctly identify a forthcoming relapse. Therefore, in this case self-rated early signs seem much more powerful in predicting relapse, suggesting that individuals' unique knowledge of their own experiences gives them a better ability to predict relapse than the health professionals who provide support and treatment for them. This also means that it is likely that individuals are detecting their own idiosyncratic signs of relapse at an early stage. Depending on their experiences of previous episodes of relapse/psychosis, this is likely to generate a high degree of emotional distress.

Emotional Distress as a Psychological Reaction

It is also apparent that when studies include positive psychotic experiences or incipient psychosis in their definitions of early signs (Subotnik & Nuechterlein, 1988; Birchwood et al., 1989; Tarrier et al., 1991; Jorgensen, 1998), this increases the sensitivity of early signs detection to relapse. The inclusion of low-level positive psychotic symptoms, such as ideas of reference or thought control, suggests that the development of emotional distress signals the person's emotional reaction to the re-emergence of psychotic experiences. The consistency of the findings on specificity of early signs to relapse, which is reported across these studies (64 to 93 per cent), is supportive of this proposal. That is, when there is a relapse, there is almost always an increase in emotional distress beforehand.

Underlying Experiences

It is likely that individuals may well be responding to quite subtle changes in their cognition, perception and attention that are psychologically significant or reminiscent of psychotic experiences. Early studies (e.g. McGhie & Chapman, 1961; Chapman & McGhie, 1963; Freedman & Chapman, 1973;

Docherty et al., 1978; Henrichs et al., 1985) found in clinical interviews that idiosyncratic changes in the perception of cognition, emotion and interpersonal experience appeared to be associated with psychosis, and that these experiences are different to those whose psychosis has remitted or those suffering from depression (Cutting, 1985). Chapman and McGhie (1963) suggested that individuals with psychosis become aware of unusual experiences, and that their reactions to these experiences may play an important role in the development and maintenance of psychosis. They recommended that a psychotherapeutic understanding of the individual's perceptual and experiential difficulties would aid improved communication. In addition, they suggested that psychotherapy should aim: (1) to discover individuals' subjective experiences and cognitive difficulties; and (2) to reduce unhelpful or ineffective reactions to these experiences. Bowers (1968) argued that self-experienced changes in perception and awareness were critical to the transformation of normal experience into psychosis. In an experiential account drawn from interviews with 15 people with psychosis, Bowers described changes in heightened awareness of internal and external stimuli. Associated with these perceptual changes, he described individuals as having an increasing sense of urgency, reduced need for sleep, exaggerated affect, and a heightened sense of self. Alongside this heightened experience, internal and external events and stimuli normally outside awareness became meaningful and self-relevant. Individuals described becoming engaged, fascinated, perplexed or indeed scared by their own experience. This state of heightened awareness of self gave way to what Bowers referred to as 'a dissolution of self' or 'loss of mental self-representation'. This loss of meaning combined with a heightened awareness of internal and external stimuli, gave way to the development and evolution of delusional beliefs constructed to make sense of 'heightened and altered sensory influx and self experience, widened categories of relevance and a push for closure or meaning' (1968, p. 352).

A COGNITIVE BEHAVIOURAL MODEL OF EARLY SIGNS AND RELAPSE

There have been a number of psychological conceptualisations of relapse (Thurm & Haefner, 1987; Birchwood, 1995; Gumley et al., 1999). All these models have emphasised how individuals interpret subtle signs (e.g. cognitive perceptual changes) and/or isolated symptoms (e.g. interpersonal sensitivity) as evidence of a forthcoming relapse of their psychosis. In this context individuals' interpretations of their experiences will be informed by their specific autobiographical memories (of psychosis). For some individuals who do not accept the construct of psychosis or illness, these signs may signal elevated interpersonal danger (e.g. 'if my doctor sees that I'm suspicious, he'll put me in hospital again'). These memories and appraisals drive the development of heightened emotional distress and trigger affective dys-regulation. Coping strategies adopted by individuals may enable them to reduce their levels of emotional distress or support affective stabilisation. For example, being able to talk with a trusted friend or family member, being able to self-soothe, having a kindly, accepting and compassionate attitude to oneself, being able to decatastrophise relapse, or being able to access appropriate support and assistance available may all positively impact on coping. Three studies (Brier & Strauss, 1983; McCandless-Glimcher et al., 1986; Hultman et al., 1997) show that patients monitor and regulate their symptoms in order to prevent relapse. Among individuals with bipolar disorder, Lam (1997, 2001) reported on the use of spontaneous cognitive and behavioural coping strategies during prodromal stages, and also the impact that these had on functioning. They reported that the use of behavioural coping strategies had an effect on reducing the likelihood of manic relapse. On the other hand, having few interpersonal resources, living in a highly stressful environment or being socially isolated may well limit the availability and flexibility of coping strategies or the opportunities for help-seeking. The use of coping strategies such as substance use or medication discontinuation (to reduce side effects) may provide short-term relief but enhance relapse risk in the medium and long term. Social avoidance and withdrawal may enhance interpersonal sensitivity, rumination and emotional distress leading to feelings of helplessness, hopelessness and suicidal thinking. Hultman et al. (1997) found that individuals with a withdrawal-orientated coping style were more likely to relapse than individuals who had a socially orientated coping style. In addition, problematic thought control strategies or avoidance strategies may prevent disconfirmation of excessively negative beliefs about relapse, thus (1) maintaining an elevated sense of threat of relapse; and (2) increasing the likelihood of greater relapse acceleration at the manifestations of early signs. Safety behaviours are a kind of coping strategy specifically targeted at attempting to avoid a feared outcome. Not only do these behaviours attempt to avert a feared outcome, they also prevent the individual from disconfirming unhelpful beliefs, and thus play a role in the maintenance of anxiety and psychological distress. This clinical account of relapse is summarised in Figure 1.2.

Freeman et al. (2001) examined safety behaviours associated with persecutory delusions among individuals with psychosis. In this study all participants reported the use of safety behaviours to reduce the perceived threat arising from their persecutory beliefs, and the authors hypothesised that these safety behaviours were involved in the maintenance of delusions by preventing disconfirmation of threat beliefs. In a modification of the Freeman et al. (2001) interview, Gumley and colleagues (in preparation) found that when participants with psychosis (n = 24) were asked if they had done anything to prevent or minimise relapse or readmission to hospital in the month

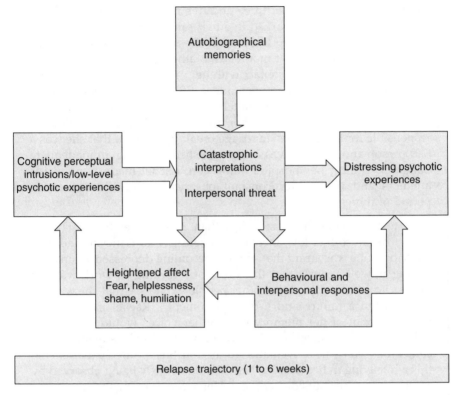

Figure 1.2   A cognitive behavioural model of early signs and relapse

prior to interview, 20 (83.3 per cent) reported using some strategy to prevent recurrence. These strategies included avoidance of people or places (n = 14, 58.3 per cent), help seeking from friends, family or mental health staff (n = 10, 41.7 per cent) or avoidance of thinking about relapse or memories of relapse (n = 12, 50 per cent). These studies emphasise a particular pathway of avoidant coping strategies which may well be influenced by further emotional and interpersonal processes.

Rachel

Rachel lives alone in a block of flats. She has had two periods of being in hospital after experiencing frightening voices telling her that she was evil, that she should kill herself, and that other people were plotting to kill her and her family. On both occasions Rachel was admitted to her local psychiatric hospital under section. Both admissions were prolonged, lasting for three and five months respectively. Prior to her first episode she worked in a hair salon and was in the second year of her apprenticeship to be a hairdresser. In the twelve months before her first episode her mother and father split up. She had made strong efforts to keep up contact with her mum and dad but frequent arguments between her parents made it difficult for Rachel not to feel that her loyalty was being stretched. Rachel became increasingly depressed and paranoid before her first episode of psychosis. She felt responsible for her parents' marriage break-up, she felt that she was a bad person and that she was being punished for being an inadequate daughter. During her hospital admission, Rachel made two suicide attempts and was under constant observation for a considerable period of time.

Prior to her second admission less than a year after her discharge, Rachel began to feel low, increasingly sensitive to criticism and self-conscious. She was afraid that she was becoming depressed again ('I'm getting unwell again'), that the stress of returning to work was too much ('I can't cope') and that other people would see that she was not coping ('I'm a failure and a disappointment'). Rachel gave a vivid visual account of her memory of how her voices would talk to her, telling her to kill herself for the sake of her family. This memory was contextualised by her psychiatric admission. She recalled experiencing this while lying in her hospital bed, simultaneously being observed by a nurse sitting just outside her room. Her accompanying thoughts were that ('I am defective, obsolete'). Rachel began to experience increased feelings of demoralisation, shame and helplessness. Her self-critical thoughts became amplified and when she began to hear a voice telling her that she was useless, Rachel experienced high levels of panic. She felt that she couldn't tell anyone, that she would have let down her parents, her doctor, her colleagues at work and her community nurse. In addition, the intensity of distress was overwhelming, undermining her ability to reflect upon her own thoughts and memories and find a way of communicating these to others. In addition, it is noteworthy that it was Rachel's perception of others' opinions of her that triggered negative self-appraisals. She withdrew further, fearful that she would be punished if people found out that she was unwell again.

Rachel's relapse formulation was collaboratively developed with her during her recovery following her second hospital admission. As you will see, this formulation emphasises the dynamic nature of relapse and aims to give form and structure to her experience rather than relying on a simple checklist of signs and symptoms. Previously we have argued:

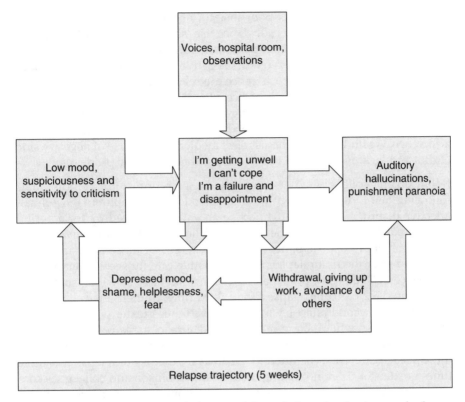

Figure 1.3   Rachel: A cognitive behavioural formulation of early signs and relapse

definitions that are used to capture the sensitivity of early signs could well benefit from definitions more closely allied to those negative beliefs about self and illness, which are hypothesised to dictate relapse speed and acceleration – rather than relying on a more closely delineated set of individual signs and symptoms alone.

(Gumley et al., 1999)

Figure 1.3 shows Rachel's formulation of her relapse.

ANTIPSYCHOTIC MEDICATION AND RELAPSE

The routine care received by individuals with psychosis emphasises the prescription of and adherence to antipsychotic medication. For many individuals, adherence to antipsychotic medication is difficult. In a systematic review of the literature, Lacro and colleagues (2002) found an average rate of non-adherence to antipsychotic medication between 41.2 and 49.5 per cent. In the 39 articles included in the review, the factors most consistently associated with non-adherence included poor insight, negative beliefs about medication, previous non-adherence, substance use, shorter duration of psychosis, poor discharge planning after inpatient treatment, and poorer therapeutic alliance. It seems interesting to us that negative attitudes to medication, lack of insight and previous non-adherence are related to non-adherence. These factors seem to suggest a lack of acceptance of psychiatric constructs of illness which are then used by investigators to define insight or describe attitudes to medication. This seems to lead to circularity in conceptualising non-adherence. We find that our clients reject medication because of negative side effects and lack of successful experiences of help for their problems.

Robinson and colleagues (1999) conducted a long-term study of individuals following being diagnosed with a first episode of schizophrenia or schizo-affective disorder. A total of 104 participants were followed up for a period of five years. At the end of the five-year follow-up, the cumulative rate of relapse for the 104 participants was 81.9 per cent. Of those participants, 63 recovered after the first relapse. The cumulative rate for second relapse was 78.0 per cent. Of this group, 20 made a recovery after a second relapse. Among this group, 86.2 per cent relapsed for a third time. In their analysis, the risk for a first and second relapse was almost five times greater when not taking medication than when taking medication. Thirteen stable participants who were not taking antipsychotic medication dropped out of the study. When these participants were included in the analysis, the risk of relapse was three times greater for those not taking medication. Robinson and colleagues considered that the relationship between discontinuation of medication and relapse may have been an artefact of discontinuation as a result of the relapse process itself (for example, loss of insight). This was examined in subsequent analyses by looking at the length of time between stopping medication and relapse. The effect for this relationship remained significant using 14-, 28- and 56-day time differences, thus indicating that medication discontinuation was unlikely to be a manifestation of relapse itself. Those who discontinued their medication also showed poorer pre-morbid adjustment in terms of social isolation and poor adaptation to school. In conclusion, this study shows that sudden discontinuation of antipsychotic medication is a risk factor for early relapse.

Another important study of antipsychotic medication is the Northwick Park First Episode Study (Johnstone et al., 1986) that followed up 120 individuals with a diagnosis of first episode of schizophrenia. For the first month following discharge from hospital, all participants remained on their antipsychotic medication. Participants who completed this one-month phase without readmission were then randomly assigned to receive either placebo or active medication. Relapse was defined as (1) readmission to psychiatric care for any reason; (2) readmission considered necessary but not possible; and (3) the prescription of antipsychotic medication considered essential by the person's psychiatrist due to features of imminent relapse (i.e. early signs).

Table 1.4   Northwick Park Study of first episodes of schizophrenia. Relapse outcome at 6, 12, 18, and 24 months

Group	Entered N	Relapsed N (%)	Relapse-free (months) (N, %)			
			6	12	18	24
DUP < 1 year						
Active	31	10 (32)	25 (80)	25 (80)	22 (71)	18 (59)
Placebo	51	26 (51)	39 (66)	23 (45)	21 (42)	21 (42)
Total	82	36 (44)	64 (72)	48 (59)	43 (54)	39 (48)
DUP > 1 year						
Active	22	15 (75)	17 (76)	7 (33)	6 (26)	4 (18)
Placebo	13	13 (100)	3 (23)	1 (8)	–	–
Total	25	28 (80)	20 (55)	8 (23)	6 (14)	4 (10)
Whole group						
Active	54	25 (46)	43 (79)	33 (62)	29 (54)	23 (42)
Placebo	66	41 (62)	38 (57)	24 (37)	22 (33)	20 (30)
Total	120	66 (55)	81 (67)	57 (48)	51 (42)	43 (35)

Johnstone and her colleagues found that of those on maintenance anti-psychotic medication, 46 per cent relapsed, and of those on placebo, 62 per cent relapsed by 24 months. These results are illustrated in Table 1.4. It is of interest that Table 1.4 shows that for those with a duration of untreated psychosis (DUP) greater than one year the relapse rate for those on maintenance medication is 75 per cent and those on placebo is 100 per cent. In contrast, those with a DUP less than one year, the relapse rates are 32 per cent and 52 per cent respectively. This shows how adjustment to early psychosis (as measured by DUP) mediates the impact of antipsychotic medication on relapse rate. Indeed, for those with a shorter duration of untreated psychosis, 50 per cent remain relapse-free on placebo.

Low-dosage or Discontinued Antipsychotic Medication

Although research shows that adhering to antipsychotic medication is an effective way of preventing relapse (for example, Crow et al., 1986; Robinson et al., 1999), antipsychotic medication exerts a social cost, and a number of serious complications can occur after prolonged use. Indeed, the occurrence of extra pyramidal Parkinsonian side effects is a major problem, which compromises both the long-term use and acceptability of antipsychotic medication. Even new so-called atypical medications exert major metabolic side effects including clinical obesity cardiovascular difficulties and height-ened risk of Type II diabetes. Robinson et al. (2002) found that the major predictor of discontinuation in their 1999 study (described earlier) was the occurrence of Parkinsonian side effects. Low-dose strategies have been developed, with the aim of establishing the minimum dosage needed to prevent relapse. Such an approach to treatment is based on the proposal that antipsychotic dosages can be prescribed at dosages less than those required in the acute phase (Marder, 1999), and that the dosage can then be increased if necessary to prevent relapse. Barbui and colleagues (1996) conducted a meta-analysis of randomised controlled studies, which had compared low-dosage antipsychotic medication with conventional dosage (Kane et al., 1983; Marder et al., 1984 1987; Johnson et al., 1987; Hogarty et al., 1988; Inderbitzin et al., 1994). A total of 415 individuals (214 in low dosage, and 201 in the conventional dosage group) participated in these studies. In all the studies selected, relapse was defined as either an increase in two or more points on the BPRS (Overall & Gorham, 1962) or a worsening of psychotic experiences requiring hospital admission. Low dosage was defined in three of the trials as 20 per cent of the conventional dosage (Marder et al., 1984, 1987; Hogarty et al., 1988); 10 per cent in one trial (Kane et al., 1983) and 50 per cent in two trials (Johnson et al., 1987; Inderbitzin et al., 1994). All studies employed a 12-month follow-up, except two, which followed participants to 24 months (Marder et al., 1987; Hogarty et al., 1988).

Table 1.5 illustrates the results of this review. In Table 1.5, relative risk refers to the risk of relapse in the low-dosage group compared to the risk of relapse in the conventional group. A relative risk ratio of 2.00 means that the risk of an event occurring in an experimental group is two times greater than the risk of that event occurring in a control group. Relative risk reduction (RRR) is the complement of relative risk, expressed as a percentage. The results showed that there was a significant increase in relapse rate associated with low-dosage antipsychotic medication over 12 months. However, over 24 months, relapse rates did not significantly differ. There are two implications of these findings. First, over 12 months at least, it was not possible to make substantial reductions in antipsychotic dosage without increasing the risk of relapse. There is a fine balance between maximising the protection against risk of relapse, and minimising the social costs exerted by antipsychotics. Second, it is notable that no significant differences were found between low and conventional dosages for relapse rate over 24 months. Therefore, those who do not relapse within the first year following a reduction in their medication dosage tend not to relapse in the second year.

Gilbert and colleagues (1995) conducted an extensive systematic review of studies investigating relapse rate following the withdrawal of antipsychotic medication. In this review 66 studies including a total of 4,365 participants conducted between 1958 and 1993 were reported. Twenty-nine of these studies involved paired comparisons with groups who continued to receive their antipsychotic medication. Overall, the risk of relapse among those who

Table 1.5 Low-dosage studies of antipsychotic medication and relapse. Intention to treat analysis at 12 and 24 months

Study	Relapse		Relative risk (95% CI** RR)	RRR* (%) (95% CI RRR)	p
	Conventional	Low dosage			
Kane et al. (1983)	48	77	1.60 (1.20–2.13)		<0.001
Marder et al. (1984)	36	29	0.79 (0.35–1.76)		NS
Johnson et al. (1987)	10	34	3.56 (1.09–11.07)		<0.05
Hogarty et al. (1988)	24	35	1.45 (0.69–3.05)		NS
Inderbitzin et al. (1994)	35	35	0.99 (0.44–2.25)		NS
12 months overall				−47 (−15 to −88)	<0.005
Hogarty et al. (1988)	42	43	1.02 (0.59–1.75)		NS
Marder et al. (1987)	45	49	1.08 (0.64–1.80)		NS
24 months overall				−5 (28 to −52)	NS

Notes: *RRR: relative risk reduction. **CI: Confidence Interval.
Source: Barbui et al. (1996). Low-dose neuroleptic therapy and relapse in schizophrenia: meta-analysis of randomized controlled trials, *European Psychiatry*, **11**(6), 306–313.

discontinued their antipsychotic medication was greater (53 per cent versus 16 per cent) over an average follow-up period of almost 10 months. Risk of relapse was greatest in the first three months after discontinuing medication (50 per cent versus 4 per cent) demonstrating that relapses occur early following discontinuation and that those who remain free of relapse after three months tend to remain relapse-free for the longer term. Of the studies included in the review, 33 involved abrupt discontinuation of medication (less than 14 days and usually one day). These studies found that the risk of relapse was three times greater following abrupt withdrawal compared to gradual withdrawal, and those receiving a higher antipsychotic dosage were at even higher risk of relapse.

The above findings support the proposition that antipsychotic medication reduction strategies are feasible, advantageous and effective for many individuals, but do not necessarily require complete drug withdrawal (Carpenter & Tamminga, 1995). Low-dosage strategies are associated with an increased risk of relapse over 12 months, but at 24 months, 50 per cent of those on lower dosage remain well. Similarly, in drug discontinuation studies the risk of relapse is heightened considerably, particularly in the first three months after medication is withdrawn. However, over the longer term, almost 50 per cent remain relapse-free without medication. Indeed, the Johnson study suggests that those who remain well at 12 months continue to remain well at 24 months. Those with a longer duration of untreated psychosis (Crow et al., 1986), those who have an unplanned (Robinson et al., 1999, 2002) or abrupt discontinuation (Gilbert et al., 1995) are at very high risk of relapse and relapse itself is likely to occur within three months of discontinuation. It is important to consider the very high rate of relapse (81.9 per cent over five years) in the Robinson study, as this study strongly indicates that adherence to antipsychotic medication is a necessity to prevent relapse. However, in this study, discontinuation from medication was defined as an *unplanned* period of non-adherence from medication lasting at least one week or longer. These discontinuations were therefore likely to be abrupt and not in consultation with those involved in the individuals' care.

More recent evidence from Gaebel and colleagues (2002) showed that 58 per cent of individuals who have a *planned* discontinuation of their medication following a first episode of psychosis and who are offered systematic regular early signs monitoring (with reinstatement of medication if a possible relapse is indicated) remain relapse-free, compared to 62 per cent of individuals with a first episode of psychosis who continue on maintenance antipsychotic medication. Furthermore, Gitlin and colleagues (2001) followed up 53 individuals who had a planned discontinuation of their medication for an average of 18 months. During that period 78 per cent and 96 per cent experienced an exacerbation or relapse within one year and two years respectively. That notwithstanding, when hospitalisation was used as the principal relapse criterion, only six out of the 50 experienced an exacerbation or relapse that required readmission. This study shows the importance of continued support, follow-up and early signs monitoring (with prompt intervention if indicated) for those individuals who have the opportunity to discontinue or reduce their overall antipsychotic medication. It is striking that few, if any, studies describe provision of concurrent and robust psychological therapies for individuals who are participating in lower dosage or medication discontinuation studies. Furthermore, many of the aforementioned studies were conducted in an era that predates the (relatively recent) development of cognitive behavioural therapies specifically designed for individuals with psychosis.

IMPLICATIONS FOR STAYING WELL AFTER PSYCHOSIS

We have argued that the early signs of relapse are best conceptualised within a psychological framework, where affective experiences including fear, helplessness, shame, embarrassment and humiliation arise from the person's appraisal of subtle cognitive perceptual or low-level psychotic experiences. Individuals' appraisals have their origins in the specific and often distressing autobiographical memories of previous episodes of psychosis and their personal, interpersonal, social and vocational consequences. Individuals' emotional and behavioural responses to the emergence of early signs of relapse have the potential to accelerate, decelerate or prevent the onset of a full-blown return of psychotic experiences and re-hospitalisation. In this sense, early signs of relapse can be alternatively conceptualised as 'at-risk mental states'. Such at-risk mental states are more common in the context of non-adherence or sudden abrupt and unplanned discontinuations of antipsychotic medication. This has led to interventions and treatments, which emphasise adherence or compliance with antipsychotic medication (e.g. Kemp & David, 1998). While these interventions are potentially powerful in reducing risk of subsequent readmission to hospital, at least when delivered to inpatients, many individuals do not accept traditional constructs of illness to explain their experiences. In addition, they are distressed by taking antipsychotic medication or have negative beliefs about and/or expectations of medication. Measures to enforce compliance with medication are likely to engender a greater sense of alienation in patients and an increased likelihood of non-engagement with services. Thus, these individuals will correspondingly become alienated or excluded from other potentially valuable interventions, such as family therapy, which have proven value in the prevention of relapse.

We therefore feel that there is an urgent need to develop an individually tailored psychological approach to staying well after psychosis. Such an approach may support individuals in reducing the overall burden of their antipsychotic medication. However, an alternative treatment strategy such as this also has to engage individuals who are at ultra-high risk of relapse. Viewed as a group, these individuals are often difficult to engage in services (Tait et al., 2003) and are likely to be non-adherent to medication (Robinson et al., 2002). Our treatment approach outlined in Parts II and III is complementary to the many excellent CBT approaches in psychosis, for example, Max Birchwood and colleagues, Tony Morrison and colleagues, and David Fowler and colleagues. The aim of this book is to describe a cognitive interpersonal approach to engage individuals who are *at risk* of relapse, to support the emotional recovery and adjustment after psychosis, to reduce psychological vulnerability to relapse, and to provide prompt and immediate support to individuals with at-risk mental states for relapse.

CHAPTER 2

ATTACHMENT THEORY, SELF-REGULATION AND PSYCHOSIS

INTRODUCTION

In the origins of the attachment context and attachment theory, John Bowlby formulated

> when the actual experiences they have had during childhood are known and can be taken into account, the pathological fears of adult patients can often be seen in a radically new light. Paranoid symptoms that had been regarded as autogenous and imaginary are seen to be intelligible, albeit distorted, responses to historical events. (1973, p. 210)

In writing a psychological treatment manual for recovery and relapse prevention following psychosis, we believe that it is essential to have a regulatory theory that provides an explanation of the interpersonal context of help-seeking and affective distress. The early stages of relapse are characterised by extreme affective reactions including fear, horror, helplessness, hopelessness, shame and depression. It is in this context we expect individuals to monitor signs of possible relapse and then seek help from a service that may not have provided effective help in the past. Therefore, relapse prevention starts with the person's emotional status after psychosis and their interpersonal response to emotional distress. For example, our experience has been that individuals with an avoidant style of recovery do not seek help in the context of increased risk of relapse. This narrows the window of opportunity for early detection and intervention. The impact of this avoidant strategy on families and mental health teams can lead to more coercive strategies of intervention. Coercive strategies such as involuntary hospitalisation are likely to reinforce avoidant self-regulatory strategies, increasing the probability of relapse and reducing the probability of emotional recovery. One theory that has already been developed to explain the link between emotional distress and help-seeking is attachment theory (Bowlby, 1969, 1973, 1980). Attachment theory is, in essence, a regulatory theory that is the basis for our developmental understanding of patterns of emotion regulation and proximity seeking. We aim to show in this chapter how early interpersonal experiences form templates for internalised interpersonal schemas which govern affect, relating, support seeking and support utilisation. We will show that this is closely related to service engagement and adaptive coping among individuals with psychosis. The following case scenario introduces some of the challenges associated with engagement, help-seeking and recovery following psychosis:

Gavin

Gavin came into our service following attendance at Accident and Emergency with a serious overdose. Following treatment in intensive care, Gavin was transferred under the Mental Health Act to an acute psychiatric ward. Gavin stated that he had been hearing voices for some months and had a monitoring device fitted into his arm. He also described feelings of persecutory paranoia. Gavin had the belief that people were generally trying to harm him for no good reason. He was suspicious of others' motives and was unable to travel outside without being accompanied. Gavin was experiencing both suicidal thoughts and homicidal thoughts. Following discharge from hospital, Gavin was then referred for help with persisting and derogating command hallucinations. He heard two voices; one he identified as his brother and one he identified as an unknown male. The voice of his brother told him to harm himself through cutting and other forms of self-harm, including abstaining from eating, and overdosing on medication. The voice also insulted him frequently. The second voice was more 'robotic' in nature, didn't have a clear identity, but like his brother was cruel and lacked emotion. In relation to the voices, Gavin felt controlled and overwhelmed. He felt that the voices were powerful and evil in their intentions towards him. Gavin described how he also felt angry in relation to his voices. Sometimes he felt that he wanted to kill his brother for his treatment of him.

Gavin hadn't seen his brother for some years. His brother was five years older. His relationship with his brother had always been difficult. Gavin remembers his father having a close relationship with his brother. He specifically recalls them spending time together going to watch football. Gavin couldn't understand why his brother wanted to do him harm. He had no other brothers or sisters. Gavin lived at home with his mum. He described their relationship as extremely positive and supportive. His evidence for this was that his mum didn't abandon him. Gavin hadn't seen his father in years. He said that his father had left when he was aged nine. He remembered little about his father other than remembering him angry a lot of the time and that he had been a drinker. Gavin was close to a maternal uncle between the ages of nine and 14. At the age of 14 his uncle died and following this he developed problems related to self-harm and drug misuse. Gavin sporadically attended school and found it difficult to establish confiding friendships. He reported feeling lonely, isolated and unlovable. He felt that, except for his mum, other people were untrustworthy.

Initially, Gavin appeared to develop good engagement with his key-worker and his psychologist. Despite being worried about readmission to hospital, he was able to discuss these fears. Gavin was particularly worried that if he discussed his symptoms he would be admitted to hospital. The psychiatrist, keyworker and psychologist worked closely with Gavin to allay his fears regarding this in order to help him develop a more open and collaborative stance. Gavin seemed keen to engage in psychological therapy to reduce the distress arising from his voices. However, his adherence with medication was sporadic. The apparent initial positive engagement gave way to increasing problems in attendance at all his appointments. Gavin started using drugs (mostly cannabis, speed and cocaine) on a regular basis and misusing alcohol. In this context, there was a growing instability of his affect, hallucinatory experiences and behaviour. Gavin was cutting regularly. His voices had increased in frequency and impact. In addition, Gavin had increasing suicidal and homicidal ideation. This culminated in his compulsory readmission to hospital.

This case scenario aids the illustration key developmental trajectories in relation to vulnerability to relapse. Gavin described problematic early relationship experiences characterised by early loss and unloving/rejecting behaviour from key attachment figures, difficulties in establishing a sense of self in the context of safe/positive peer relationships, and difficulties in regulating strong negative affect in the context of problematic coping strategies including substance misuse and self-harm. Such experiences provide a weakened platform to engage with others, and to integrate negative life events into his wider understanding.

PATTERNS OF ATTACHMENT

The fundamental tenet of Bowlby's (1969, 1973, 1980) formulation of attachment theory concerned the primacy of the human need for felt security – 'the secure base'. Infants can best explore and take an active interest in the world if they feel they have a secure base to which they can return if danger is perceived. Initially this base is provided by the attachment figure – the child's caregiver, usually the parent. As infants, we are extremely vulnerable and highly dependent on others. It is, therefore, an evolutionary necessity for infants to be able to secure the interests and attention of adults, and for adults to maintain the care and empathy for the infant. This describes a reciprocal control system. Therefore, when infants are separated from their caregiver, if their caregiver is unresponsive, or if an infant detects some threat (for example, the appearance of a stranger) and feels frightened or distressed, the attachment system is switched on (the infant seeks proximity to the attachment). The reciprocal aspect of this is the switching on of the caregiver's attachment system. The goal of the attachment system is protection and/or self-regulation. Once this goal has been achieved, the system switches off again. Attachment behaviours are those that increase proximity or maintain contact with an attachment figure.

The Strange Situation Test (Ainsworth et al., 1978) provides a laboratory-based procedure, which has been designed to capture the balance of attachment and explorative behaviour in infants. Mary Ainsworth and colleagues (1978), reporting on a substantial body of empirical research with infants, identified two main attachment styles: secure and insecure. Secure attachment strategies are observed when an infant can confidently rely on their caregiver for security. Insecure attachment styles can be further subdivided into avoidant and ambivalent patterns. In infants, these insecure behaviour patterns are attempts to maintain felt security in the absence of an optimal attachment situation (e.g. an inconsistently available or even rejecting caregiver) by either over-amplifying (ambivalent) or underplaying (avoidant) attachment behaviours. A subsequently discovered dimension yet to be categorised – disorganised/disorientated, – is characterised by bizarre or conflicted behaviour (Main & Solomon, 1986, 1990). It is often observed in infants who have experienced high levels of loss, separation, abuse or highly chaotic parenting behaviour (Lyons-Ruth & Jacobvitz, 1999). These categories of attachment in infancy are described in more detail below.

Attachment Classifications

Infants who are classified as *secure* use their mother as a base for exploration. When they are separated, the infant shows signs of missing the parent. When they are reunited, the infant actively greets the parent with a smile, vocalisation or gesture. If the infant is upset, it signals or seeks contact with the parent. The infant is comforted and returns to exploring. Infants who are classified as *avoidant* explore readily, show little display of affect or secure base behaviour. When infant and mother are separated, the infant responds minimally and shows little signs of distress when left alone. When reunited with the parent, the infant actively avoids the parent and often focuses on their immediate environment. When the infant is picked up, it may stiffen or lean away. Infants who are classified *ambivalent/resistant* are often fretful or passive and fail to engage in explorative behaviour or play. When separated, they become unsettled and distressed. When reunited, they may make alternative moves to make contact with signs of angry rejection and tantrums or appear passive and too upset to make contact. The parent does not comfort the infant's distress. Infants who are classified as *disorganised and disorientated* have behaviour that appears to lack an observable goal, intention or exploration. For example, the infant may show stereotypes, freezing, direct indications of fear of the parent, confusion and disorientation. There is a lack of a coherent attachment strategy at separation or reunion with the caregiver.

ATTACHMENT THEORY AND LATER PSYCHOPATHOLOGY

An influential framework for understanding attachment states of mind after infancy and childhood has been provided by Mary Main's work on adult attachment (Main et al., 1985; Main, 1990, 1999), operationalised in the Adult Attachment Interview (AAI). This conceptualisation of adult states of mind with regard to attachment provides analogous categories for infant attachment behaviour. Secure attachment in infancy is mirrored by an autonomous adult attachment state of mind; anxious/ambivalent infant attachment is paralleled by preoccupied/enmeshed adult attachment; avoidant infant attachment associates with an adult stance that is dismissing of attachment. Finally, disorganised infant attachment behaviour predicates a sub-category in adulthood of reflecting trauma with regard to loss and abuse (Hesse, 1999).

It is well established that early adverse experiences such as early loss and trauma are strongly linked to significant emotional and psychological problems in adulthood (Brown et al., 1986; Rutter, 2000; Hofstra et al., 2002). However, this association between early loss and/or trauma and later adult psychopathology is no longer understood as arising from a direct causal link or relationship between early adverse events and later psychopathology. A large proportion of those who experience significant adverse events in childhood *do not* go on to develop significant emotional problems later in life. Instead, the association between early life events and later psychopathology is viewed as being mediated by a number of factors relating to how these experiences are processed by the individual and incorporated into individuals' autobiographical narratives. Especially relevant in this context is John Bowlby's (1969, 1973) pioneering work on attachment theory and Margaret Mahler's experimental work (e.g. 1971, 1974) investigating children's early development of autonomy and independence through the process of primary separation and individuation, based on detailed longitudinal observations of mother–child and child–child interactions. Since these formative works, there have been numerous studies describing the impact of early attachment experiences on individuals' interpersonal functioning and emotional regulation (summarised in Fonagy, 1998; Fonagy et al., 2002), interpersonal relationships and trust, and identity formation (Cole & Putnam, 1992; Briere, 2002). Bowlby (1973) proposed that, over the period of normal childhood development, the experience of interactions with attachment figures becomes internalised and thus carried forward into adulthood as mental models, also known as *internal working models* or *core relational schemata* (Bretheron, 1985; Alexander, 1992; Pearce & Pezzot-Pearce, 1994). These implicit structures produce expectations about the self and others, and regulate responses in subsequent interpersonal interactions.

Early attachment relationships therefore come to form the prototype for interpersonal relationships throughout life, through the internal representation of models of the self and others (e.g. Styron & Janoff-Bulman, 1997). The development of mentalisation, reflective function and affect regulation also becomes intrinsically linked to the development of self-regulation through the context of close attachment relationships (Fonagy et al., 2002). Mentalisation is defined as the process by which we come to understand that having a mind mediates our experience of the world via the mental representation of psychological states. Mentalisation refers to 'mind mindedness'. Reflective function describes the processes by which mind mindedness is acquired. For example, in infancy this function is provided by the caregiver's appropriate mirroring of the infant's intentional and emotional expressions. For instance, the capacity to perceive and understand oneself, and others, in terms of mental states (thoughts, feelings, desires) arises in the context of sensitive caregiving, where the child recognises their own intentions (the 'intentional stance') in the appropriately reflective behaviour of the caregiver. In adults, reflective functioning is evidenced by an awareness of the nature, and opaqueness, of the mental states of others, where the adult shows an ability and commitment to understanding how mental states underpin the behaviour of others (Fonagy, 1998).

Security and Autonomy

Across the lifespan secure attachment is associated with the development of a range of capacities that depend on interpretive skills, such as explorative play, language ability, resilience and control, frustration tolerance and social cognition capacities. The caregiver's sensitivity towards the intentional and emotional states of the infant is one of the strongest predictors of secure attachment (e.g. Slade et al., 1999). The positive impact of attachment security on cognitive competence, emotion regulation and communication style is not mediated through the child's general security and self-confidence but because attachment security allows capacity for reflective function. Furthermore, it is documented that children with secure attachment are better at understanding negative emotion (Laible & Thompson, 1998) and perform better at theory of mind tasks (Fonagy & Target, 1997; Meins et al., 1998). Adults who have a secure or autonomous state of mind with respect to attachment are able to behave with flexibility and openness in relationships. They are able to reflect openly on and communicate information about their own state of mind without excessive distortions or censorship. They are more able to reflect on and attune to the mental states of others. Autonomous adults communicate an autobiographical narrative that is free-flowing, fresh, reflective, sensitive to context and collaborative with another person. Early experiences may thus play a formative role in generating internal working models and later social functioning through their robustness, rather than their representation of secure infant–caregiver interactions *per se*. These relational schemata that are formed through experience have a marked impact on the individual's capacity to form and maintain meaningful relationships with others (Briere, 2002), and also the regulation of negative and unwanted emotions (Alexander, 1992). In a positive attachment environment the child is able to experience uncomfortable internal states and, with the external security of a parent, develop strategies to tolerate and control negative affect. A model of the self as valued emerges through the scaffolding of a model of caregivers who are emotionally accessible, but also comfortable with the individual's autonomy in exploring the world.

Insecure Attachment

In contrast, a devalued model of self is implicated through a model construing caregivers as being rejecting, or disruptive of exploratory behaviour (Bretherton & Mulholland, 1999). Indeed, long-term reliance on behavioural strategies associated with insecure attachment increases vulnerability to later adult psychopathology (Bowlby, 1988). Securely attached children will experience anxiety but they know that they will experience safety and containment when they recover their attachment figure or when they can refer to the internalised working model of a secure base. Similarly, autonomous adults have developed the capacity to self-soothe. This is not the case for children and adults with insecure attachment patterns. In children, there is a lack of confidence that the attachment figure will be able to provide security. In adults there is a lack of capacity to reflect upon one's own experiences and emotions and provide the self with reassurance, warmth, security and self-soothing. In the context of attachment there are two key interpersonal strategies available to regulate affect and distress: either by minimising (avoidant strategies) affect or by exaggerating (ambivalent strategies) affect. In adults, an insecure state of mind with respect to attachment can therefore be understood from the point of view of a mainly *avoidant attachment organisation* or a mainly *ambivalent attachment organisation*.

Children who develop avoidant attachments adapt to often rejecting caregiving by downplaying or inhibiting feelings of need and dependency. Affect becomes over-regulated. Avoidant attachment patterns in childhood are mirrored by dismissing states of mind in adulthood. Dismissing adults minimise and avoid attachment-related experiences and therefore autobiographical memories related to attachment experiences tend to be under-elaborated. The dismissing adult's ability to reflect on his or her own affective experience, and attune to the minds, intentions and mental states of others, is reduced.

Children whose experience of their caregivers is inconsistent, under-involved, without necessarily being rejecting, are at higher risk of developing ambivalent attachment patterns. These children are preoccupied with their attachments and in an effort to harness parental responsiveness increase their distressed behaviour. In other words, they hyper-activate their attachment system. When the parent's attention is harnessed, the child is not reassured, but distrusts their parent's reliability. In this scenario the child will also resist being comforted and soothed. In adulthood this is mirrored by a preoccupied state of mind with respect to attachment, where the adult is often preoccupied by attachment experiences or figures, is valuing of attachment but is insecure, ruminative and distressed. Often adults with preoccupied states of mind are concerned with themes of abandonment and rejection.

Disorganised Attachment

Disorganised (or unresolved) attachment status is not an attachment pattern as such. It refers to the absence of a coherent attachment strategy or the collapse of a pre-existing attachment strategy due to unresolved trauma and/or loss. The description refers to infants most often parented by carers who are either frightening, frightened or both. For example, carers who are abusive, hostile, under the influence of drugs or alcohol, or carers who are highly distressed often by unresolved losses and trauma provide a disorganised and disorientating attachment base for an infant. The parenting strategies of those with unresolved and disorganised attachments include errors in mirroring and responding to affect, disorientated behaviour (e.g. confusion, panic and fear), negative intrusive behaviour (mocking and teasing of a child in distress), role confusion (where the parent seeks comfort from the child) and withdrawal (where the parent is distant and dissociated). In an effort to synchronise with a frightening and/or frightened parent, infant and child attachment strategies become disorganised and deregulated. Adults with disorganised and unresolved attachments patterns will characteristically show disorganisation of affect regulation, behaviour and the monitoring of narrative and discourse. This is characteristic of the approach avoidance conflict that we often see in adults seeking help for past trauma and abuse.

STABILITY OF ATTACHMENT ORGANISATION

Early attachment patterns are highly predictive of adult representational attachment styles, up to 77 per cent in the case of secure representations (Waters et al., 2000) and 94 per cent in terms of insecure representations when associated with subsequent negative life events (Weinfeld et al., 2000). Beyond that there is no clear prediction of adult psychopathology from insecure or disorganised attachment styles even though these seem to be over-represented in certain clinical groups. Therefore, it again appears that the association between early attachment experiences and adult interpersonal functioning (and consequently psychopathology) is mediated by internal working models, underlying processes of affect regulation, behavioural adaptation and reflective functioning.

In particular, the mediation of insecure or disorganised attachment to later maladaptive or pathological outcomes arises through the main variable of self-regulation and reflective functioning in combination with a number of external risk factors. In terms of known cognitive risk factors such as attentional processes, perceptual sensitivity and effortful control, it has been demonstrated that these are developmentally related to many of the sequelae of secure attachment, including social competency, empathy and low levels of aggression (Rothbart et al., 1994, 2000; Kochanska et al., 2000).

In light of this, both avoidance and resistance (frequently observed as coping strategies in psychosis) can be alternatively construed as self-protective strategies in intense interpersonal contexts. If the individual's internal working model is insecure, to avoid instability they might either withdraw from others, strengthening their self-representation relative to other representations (dismissive style), or protectively emphasise representations of others (preoccupied). Both strategies enable the separation of other representation from self-representation. Kobak and Sceery (1988) confirmed this theoretical association between attachment styles in adolescents and related strategies of affect regulation. Dismissive attachment was associated with denial of emotional distress, rejection of parental support and perception of others as hostile. Preoccupied attachment was associated with high self-report of distress and poor interpersonal skills. Adolescents classified as

having an insecure attachment style demonstrated a tendency to externalised coping styles and related use of aggression and alcohol and drugs.
In a study linking adolescents' state of mind in relation to attachment to
psychopathology, Rosenstein and Horowitz (1996) reported a strong link
between attachment strategies and differential vulnerability to psychiatric
symptoms. In their sample of 60 hospitalised adolescents, a dismissing
attachment organisation was linked to strategies minimising distress and a
rejection of the attachment figures. Mental states associated with denial or a
downplaying of distress occurred in the context of such dismissing attachment organisation. Adolescents using preoccupied attachment strategies
relied on a maximising of the attachment system and within that activated
mental states where negative affect was acknowledged and/or exaggerated.
In a related vein, Harrop and Trower (2001) contend that a key aspect of
adolescence is the struggle for autonomy from the parental base, and that
the premature development of autonomy or inability to achieve autonomy
is a potential risk factor for psychosis.

ATTACHMENT ORGANISATION AND PSYCHOSIS

Dozier and Kobak (1992) found that persons with schizophrenia (n = 21)
relied on more repressing attachment styles than those with affective disorder (n = 19). Repressing (avoidant) strategies were associated with lower
self-reported psychiatric symptoms compared to individuals who used
preoccupied strategies. Dozier and Lee (1995) investigated attachment
organisation in 76 adults with serious mental health problems, of whom 23
had a diagnosis of schizophrenia and 27 had a diagnosis of bipolar disorder.
Participants (n = 49) who relied on avoidant or deactivating attachment
strategies reported less symptoms and lower affect whereas those with
hyper-activating or preoccupied strategies reported greater affect and symptoms. In a later study (Dozier & Tyrrell, 1997), attachment organisation was
investigated in bipolar disorder (n = 7), schizo-affective disorder (n = 8) and
schizophrenia (n = 27). Using the three-way classification of attachment
organisation (autonomous, preoccupied and dismissing), most of these participants were classified as dismissing of attachment. Table 2.1 illustrates the
attachment classifications identified in this study. As shown in Table 2.1,
these data are illustrated by three-way and four-way classifications. The
three-way classification gives the organised attachment organisation as
assessed by the AAI. The four-way classification allows the fourth disorganised or unresolved dimension to be used. Dozier has argued two implications of these data. First, adult states of mind with respect to attachment
in the context of schizophrenia and bipolar disorder have the potential to
explain service engagement and treatment use. Second, Dozier states that

Table 2.1   Adult Attachment Interview classifications and diagnosis

	Three-way classification			Four-way classification			
	Secure	Preoccupied	Avoidant	Secure	Preoccupied	Avoidant	Disorganised
Diagnosis							
Bipolar disorder	0	0	7	0	0	3	4
Schizo-affective	1	1	6	1	0	5	2
Schizophrenia	3	0	24	1	0	16	12

these attachment states of mind have little to tell us about the psychological factors predisposing individuals to be diagnosed with schizophrenia. We will take each of these views in turn.

Treatment Use and Service Engagement

One important aspect of help-seeking and service engagement is the development of collaborative bonds with clinicians, therapists and case managers. The capacity to establish and organise collaborative bonds with others is highly likely to be mediated by the person's general state of mind with respect to attachment and their internal working models of self-representation and close interpersonal relationships. Optimal therapeutic relationships are likely to resemble those of secure attachment relationships, in that the therapist is a secure base for proximity seeking, the therapist acts to support the person in resolving distress in the context of a warm, friendly, accepting and soothing interpersonal stance. In addition, the relationship is a reciprocal one, characterised by collaboration and reflection in the context of security.

Dozier (1990) examined attachment organisation and use of treatment among 42 participants with schizophrenia (n = 12), bipolar disorder (n = 25), depression (n = 3) and 'atypical psychosis' (n = 2). Clinicians were asked to rate participants' compliance with required treatment, the extent to which clients sought or rejected treatment, the extent of self-disclosure and their acknowledgement of feelings. More secure attachment ratings were associated with greater compliance. Clients were more likely to show up for appointments and take medication. Individuals with avoidant attachment strategies were less likely to seek out treatment and more likely to reject treatment. Avoidance was inversely related to disclosure. Individuals with preoccupied attachment strategies were more likely to self-disclose and were more likely to seek help.

In a later study, Dozier et al. (2001) videotaped interactions between adults with schizophrenia or bipolar disorder completing two problem-solving tasks with either a family member (n = 17) or their case manager (n = 17). One task minimally involved interpersonal issues, for example, how to spend $100. The second task was interpersonally involving, for example, talking about three problems in their relationship. Clients with dismissing states of mind spent less time on task with their case managers and displayed more rejecting behaviour during problem solving. In relation to this, family members of dismissing clients felt greater sadness following problem solving. Therefore, we can see from this study that interpersonal interaction is clearly mediated by the person's organisation of their attachment model.

The development of a collaborative therapeutic bond is one that relies upon the development of reciprocity between the person seeking help and the treatment provider. Interestingly, in the Dozier et al. (2001) study, case managers were more likely to change the topic with their dismissing clients on the interpersonal task, apparently in response to subtle signs of the client's discomfort. The treatment provider's own state of mind with respect to attachment may therefore be relevant to the development of reciprocity and bond. Dozier et al. (1994) investigated the relationship between clinicians' attachment strategies and their ability to respond therapeutically to clients. Participants were patients with a diagnosis of schizophrenia (n = 16) or bipolar disorder (n = 9). Clinicians who were more insecurely preoccupied responded in greater depth to clients who were preoccupied and perceived preoccupied clients as having greater dependency needs in comparison to dismissing clients. These results show how clients' states of mind towards attachment interact with clinicians' own states of mind towards attachment. The attachment organisation of clinicians appears to have some importance in the development of reciprocity. Secure clinicians attend and respond to clients' underlying needs whereas clinicians who are more insecure 'respond to the most obvious presentation of needs' (Dozier et al., 1994, p. 798).

Unresolved Attachment

Dozier and colleagues state that unresolved or disorganised attachment status 'tell us little about factors predisposing to schizophrenia' (1999, p. 510). This is because disorganised status on the AAI is based on coded narratives where there have been lapses of reasoning and discourse. The AAI coding relies upon the unfolding of a coherent and collaborative discourse during discussion of attachment-related experiences and events such as loss and trauma that undermine the reflection on and communication of attachment representations. It is possible to draw a different conclusion in light of these findings. It may be that early adverse experiences contribute to the development of core predictors associated with the development of psychosis and the emergence of a negative trajectory of psychosis. This is characterised by problematic emotional and interpersonal adaptation, heightened sensitivity to interpersonal stress (e.g. criticism and emotional over-involvement), poor pro-social coping and help-seeking, social withdrawal and avoidant and/or conflicted coping styles, and impoverished reflective function and affect regulation. We now intend to examine the literature investigating predictors of poor emotional, symptomatic and quality of life outcomes among individuals with psychosis in light of our presentation of concepts central to attachment theory.

CHAPTER 3

PSYCHOLOGICAL FACTORS IN VULNERABILITY AND TRANSITION TO RELAPSE

INTRODUCTION

Prospective studies of the course and outcome following a first episode of psychosis have consistently shown that poorer outcome, as characterised by treatment-resistant symptoms or relapsing course of psychosis, is predicted by factors such as longer duration of untreated psychosis (DUP: Wiersma et al., 1998; Drake et al., 2000), poor pre-morbid social adjustment (e.g. Rabiner et al., 1986), early adolescent isolation (e.g. Robinson et al., 1999) and adolescent social anxiety (Jones et al., 1994). Of course, we need to remain mindful of the catch that developmental reasoning can pose for the transition of these findings into clinical work:

> so long as we trace the development from its final outcome backwards, the chain of events appears continuous, and we feel we have gained an insight which is completely satisfactory or even exhaustive. But if we proceed in the reverse way, if we start from the premises inferred from the analysis and try to follow these up to the final results, then we no longer get the impression of an inevitable sequence of events which could not have otherwise been determined.
>
> (Freud, 1917, p. 208)

Drake and his colleagues (2000) found that, after controlling for DUP, better levels of social integration predicted greater improvement in overall symptoms including psychotic experiences following a first or second episode of psychosis. These data suggest that early social/developmental factors and adolescent or adult interpersonal functioning are powerful potentiators of outcome in terms of recovery and relapse following the onset of psychosis. In particular, it appears that the quality of adolescent peer attachments and utilisation of social supports strongly predict longer-term outcomes and adaptation to psychosis. There is also extensive evidence from studies of schizophrenia that the interpersonal atmosphere is a key factor in relapse (Brown & Rutter, 1966; Leff & Vaughn, 1985). This demonstrates the continuing significance of interpersonal factors in the determination of course of psychosis. Furthermore, after a first episode of psychosis, the recurrence of psychotic experiences is often a highly significant, distressing and critical life event for individuals with psychosis (Birchwood et al., 2000), leading to problematic emotional adjustment and suicidal thinking.

In this chapter we will review the evidence for a range of individual psychological and interpersonal factors in the evolution of individual vulnerability to relapse. We highlight a range of interacting and unfolding factors including individuals' attachment organisation, their interpersonal environment, their wider social environment including life events, their interpersonal strategies and their appraisal of and affective response to the experience of acute psychosis. A number of studies have now shown that the way in which the early episodes of acute psychosis are experienced and processed by the person can have a significant influence on recovery and relapse. How the experience of psychosis is appraised has been linked to a variety of important emotional responses in individuals, families, carers and loved ones. Often these responses do not just relate to a person's current experience of a psychotic episode, but as we will argue, these responses are essentially reflections of particular early experiences, general developmental factors and their social context. Therefore, in this chapter we propose to broaden our focus to consider the wider context of recovery and staying well after psychosis.

THE INTERPERSONAL CONTEXT

One long-established interpersonal construct valuable in the study of the aetiology of psychosis is 'Expressed Emotion' (EE: Brown & Rutter, 1966). This construct has been consistently demonstrated to be implicated as a predictor of poor clinical outcome and relapse in a range of psychiatric conditions (see Butzlaff & Hooley, 1998; Wearden et al., 2000, for reviews). EE is a term that represents a set of mechanisms underlying interpersonal relationships and communication patterns. EE has three components implicated in the prediction of outcome. The first is emotional over-involvement (EOI) and a breakdown of the natural boundaries in the family. The second concerns critical comments, referring to the attitudes and condemnation of behaviours in the individual by carers. The third is hostility, involving a generalisation of criticism of the individual's personality and elements of rejection on the part of the carers. In addition, the EE construct can also include measures of warmth and positive comments.

Kavanagh (1992) reviewed 23 studies of the relationship between EE and relapse. These studies had followed up 1,707 participants and their families over a 9- to 12-month period. Only three of these studies failed to find a relationship between EE and relapse. A median relapse rate of 21 per cent was found for families characterised by low levels of EE, compared to 48 per cent for families living in an environment characterised by high levels of EE. Twenty studies found that relapse was greater in the high EE group, and 16 of these studies found this to be statistically significant. Four studies investigated relapse rate for up to two years after entry to the study. The median relapse rate for low EE families was 27 per cent compared to 61 per cent for high EE families.

In terms of specific EE constructs, criticism and hostility are strongly correlated, and hostility is rarely present in the absence of criticism. Indeed, hostility has been found to independently predict relapse (Leff et al., 1987). Warmth is negatively correlated with criticism to a moderate degree, and positively correlated with EOI. Brown et al. (1972) found that warmth in the absence of EOI was associated with a positive outcome. Brewin et al. (1991) found that relatives who had communication patterns characterised by hostility and criticism made more attributions to factors personal to and controllable by the person (e.g. 'he doesn't get up in the morning because he's lazy') than did relatives with marked EOI. These relatives made non-personal and uncontrollable attributions about the individual's behaviour (e.g. 'it's the illness, there's nothing he can do, it's not his fault').

Barrowclough and colleagues (1994) investigated the role of relatives' attributions for illness as a predictor of relapse in schizophrenia. Barrowclough and her colleagues proposed that critical and in particular hostile relatives would make attributions, which were more internal, personal and controllable to the individual, compared to relatives who display marked EOI and low EE patterns. They proposed that these latter relatives would make more external, universal and uncontrollable attributions to the individual. Relatives with high levels of EE had a higher rate of making causal attributions than did relatives with low EE. Compared to high EOI relatives, relatives high on criticism and hostility made more internal, personal and controllable attributions to the individual. In addition, these relatives invoked causal attributions attributing responsibility for outcome to the individual. Relatives high on EOI made more attributions of causality to external and uncontrollable causes, and indeed made most attributions to illness. Attributions of controllability and internality (e.g. it's your fault) were significantly related to relapse, even after controlling for EE status and intervention. In a further analysis of these data, Barrowclough et al. (1996) found a general lack of association between distress and relatives' attributions, except for a relationship between the tendencies for relatives who blame themselves to have higher levels of distress.

These studies demonstrate the importance of the role of attributions in the development of EE, the prediction of relapse and the development of distress among relatives. Indeed, this is consistent with the proposals of other investigators including Weiner (1985), who proposed that causal beliefs held about other people's problems would be instrumental in the development of distressing emotions. Barrowclough and colleagues (2003) explored the relationship between interpersonal environment, self-evaluation and positive and negative symptoms. Whilst it is well established that living in an emotional climate characterised by critical, hostile or emotionally over-involved attitudes and attributions is linked to increased risk of future relapse (Barrowclough & Hooley, 2003), the mechanism by which this might occur is as yet unclear, although increased physiological arousal has been proposed as one pathway (Tarrier & Turpin, 1992). Using an interview methodology with a group of 59 participants, Barrowclough and colleagues found that, consistent with previous research, family attitudes were associated with greater positive symptoms. In addition, participants' negative evaluations of self (NES) were associated with more positive symptoms. The relationship between family attitudes and positive symptoms disappeared when NES was included in the statistical model, and NES remained strongly

Alan

Alan is 24 years old and lives at home with his mother, his father and his younger sister. Alan experienced his first psychotic episode three years ago while studying mathematics at university. Alan had been living away from home when he experienced his first episode. Over the course of four months, during his third year at university, Alan became increasingly withdrawn and solitary. He was phoning home less frequently and coming home for weekends less often. His parents had interpreted this change in his behaviour as being preoccupied with university and his forthcoming examinations. However, during this period Alan had become preoccupied with mathematical formulae and religious thought. He also became increasingly taken with the idea that he was being followed by the secret service because of his knowledge of secret codes. Alan became very paranoid. He began telling his fellow students that satellites were interfering with his thoughts and that the secret service were trying to prevent him discovering impenetrable truths. His family arranged for him to be seen by a psychiatrist and shortly after he was admitted to a local hospital for two weeks. The family were understandably shocked, devastated and dismayed to discover Alan had been so distressed. They felt that they were to blame for his becoming ill and that they were bad parents.

Previously, Alan had quite a close relationship with his parents, particularly with his mum. They shared a lot of time together through the local church activities. Both his mum and dad had very high expectations of Alan. They were instrumental in helping him decide to study mathematics at university. His move to university created considerable anxiety in the family and Alan's mum was instrumental in arranging his accommodation and screening flat mates. Alan valued her support, but at times felt overwhelmed and unable to make decisions on his own.

After his first episode Alan rejected the notion of being ill and his parents' attempts to support him. He viewed his parents as stifling his development, and their services as marginalising his experiences. Although Alan seemed to recover rapidly from his psychotic experiences, he remained preoccupied with his experience of psychosis. He felt embarrassed and humiliated. He didn't want to talk about his experiences, and avoided contact with friends and fellow students. Over time his parents became increasingly exasperated. They felt that their attempts to help Alan were blocked. They complained to his psychiatrist that Alan refused to participate in any family therapy, he wouldn't return to university, he only partially adhered to his medication, he didn't attend appointments with his CPN regularly. Their sense of loss became intermixed with a sense of anger and frustration. Arguments began to develop in the home so much so that his younger sister left the house to live with her boyfriend. Shortly afterwards, Alan discontinued his medication. Eight weeks later he experienced a major relapse and readmission involving a return of his persecutory beliefs and a major overdose of paracetamol.

After his second episode Alan sought individual psychological therapy to explore his experiences. He reflected on his early adolescence, in particular, his perceived inability to form relationships and maintain conversations with peers. He described feeling lonely and isolated. He welcomed his parents' attempts to integrate him into the local church. On the other hand, he felt frustrated and restricted by his parental involvement. He resented them organising his accommodation at university. He described the sense of freedom that characterised his early experience of psychosis. He became more active, outgoing, began clubbing and meeting others. His social anxiety reduced and he felt greater clarity in his thinking. He felt devastated by his psychosis, how it had undermined his attempts to develop greater independence. He saw family therapy as stressful and overwhelming, he felt stifled and childlike, and was reminded of his dependence in his early adolescence. He saw help for his social anxiety, understanding his psychotic experiences and getting a girlfriend as his personal priorities for recovery.

associated with positive symptoms. Therefore, in this sample the impact of criticism on participants' positive symptoms appeared to be mediated by participants' own negative self-evaluation.

Figure 3.1 gives a diagrammatical illustration of the relationship between attributions, EE and the impact on the person's self-esteem and positive psychotic experiences.

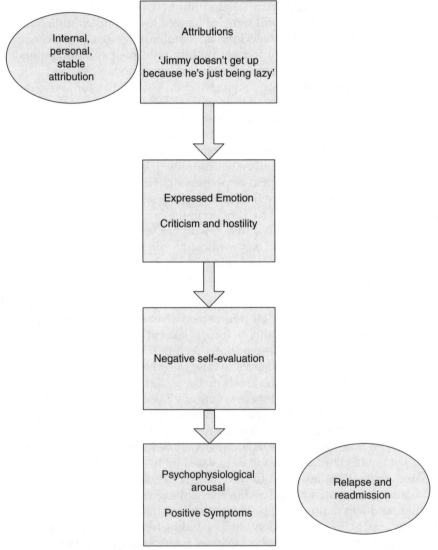

Figure 3.1 Attributional model of expressed emotion and negative self-evaluation

The Developmental Context of EE

Surprisingly, there has been little investigation into the separate developmental pathways of criticism and EOI for the purposes of early intervention and support. Patterson et al. (2000) have emphasised the importance of specialist family intervention in preventing the entrenchment of high EE. Family intervention studies have shown that if the frequency of critical, overinvolved and hostile interactions can be reduced, there is a secondary reduction in the risk of relapse over time (Birchwood, 1992, 1999). If one assumed that high EE was a stable factor, standard interventions could be directed on 'critical periods'. However, the evidence suggests that EE is unstable, particularly during the early phase of psychosis (Birchwood, 1992, 1999). It is therefore important to see EE not simply as a risk factor in itself, but as the outcome of a developmental process of adjustment and adaptation.

In a study by Scazufca and Kuipers (1996), changes in EE were linked to changes in the subjective burden and perception of a client's functioning. This supports the notion that EE is not a trait characteristic but varies according to patient–relative interactions at a particular point in time (Birchwood & Cochrane, 1990). Existing family intervention methods designed for use with families experiencing the effects of a longer-term psychosis in a relative appear to be less useful in first episode samples. One study of behavioural family therapy in first episode psychosis found no impact onrelapse and that for some families it actually increased distress (Linszen et al., 1996).

Patterson et al. (2000) suggested that the fluctuating nature of EE in first episode samples constitutes a critical period for adjustment before maladaptive response styles become entrenched. They followed up relatives of 50 individuals following a first episode of psychosis over nine months. Overall EE was unstable in 28 per cent of the sample over this period, with relatives mainly changing from high EE to low EE status. Relatives exhibiting high levels of EOI coupled with low levels of criticism reported significantly higher feelings of loss. Those whose EE status changed from high EOI to high criticism reported low levels of loss indicating that the evolution of criticism may be mediated by loss appraisals. At an emotional level, the emergence of criticism as a defence against the symbolic losses associated with a first episode of psychosis can be understood as the angry and rejecting responses frequently observed as part of the mourning process (Bowlby, 1980). At a behavioural level, it has been suggested that EOI and criticism are strategies used in order to exert a degree of control over the home environment (Hooley, 1985). Furthermore, according to Bowlby (1982), criticism functions as an adaptive mechanism to coerce and discourage a family member from 'deviant' or problem behaviour. In this sense, the evolution of criticism in the context of first episode psychosis may serve a similar function.

EOI is seen more often in parents and has been linked to the individual's poor pre-morbid functioning and burden (Miklowitz et al., 1983). Miklowitz and colleagues (1983) found that over-involved family members tended to have relatives with poor pre-morbid histories and many residual symptoms in comparison to both critical family members and low EE family members. Cook and colleagues (1989) found that adolescents interacted with high EE mothers more problematically than adolescents with low EE mothers. High EE mothers then tended to reciprocate negative affect of their adolescents' interactional style. In this sense we can understand the evolution of EE as a reciprocal process in the context of adolescent development.

Dozier and Kobak (1992) have suggested that the attachment strategies of individuals themselves may be important in eliciting characteristic EE responses from their family members. They investigated attachment organisation and EE of family members of 40 participants with schizophrenia (n =21) and affective disorders, mainly bipolar disorder (n = 19). More extreme use of avoidant or preoccupied attachment strategies was associated with higher levels of EOI of family members. It may be that greater reporting of distress and neediness which is characteristic of a preoccupied attachment style may elicit more caring behaviour by family members. Avoidant strategies tended to be associated with lower symptom reporting and self-reported distress. Dozier and colleagues noted that this strategy may be unconvincing to family members, and therefore families sense the need to provide care. EOI strategies may then perpetuate problematic attachment strategies either by reinforcing feelings of neediness and vulnerability in preoccupied persons or by driving greater withdrawal and avoidance in individuals who use avoidant attachment strategies. These findings highlight the importance of working with individuals' interpersonal and attachment strategies in the context of living in a high EE environment. This may be particularly useful in scenarios where patients and/or relatives decline to participate in family-based interventions.

THE WIDER SOCIAL CONTEXT OF PSYCHOSIS

We need to look beyond the interpersonal processes involved in the immediate environment of caregivers, loved ones and the family. It is important to consider the impact of the wider social context (and events within this context, e.g. trauma and loss) in the aetiology of psychosis. These factors have ramifications for engagement and recovery. Social anxiety and poor early adjustment have also been shown to be elevated among individuals who go on to develop psychosis (Pilkonis et al., 1980; Jones et al., 1994; Olin & Mednick, 1996; Malmberg et al., 1998). In a cohort study of 50,054 Swedish army conscripts, Malmberg et al. found that a combination of interpersonal problems including difficulty mixing in groups, having few friends, feeling more sensitive than others and not having a girlfriend were associated with an increased risk of developing schizophrenia. Jones and colleagues (1994), in the 1946 UK birth cohort study of 4,746 individuals, found that self-reported social anxiety at age 13 and teacher-rate social anxiety at age 15 were associated with an increased risk of developing schizophrenia in adulthood.

Urbanicity, Migration and Discrimination

In a five-year prospective study of 2,548 adolescents, Spauwen et al. (2004) found that 17.3 per cent had at least one psychotic experience. They found that growing up in an urban area was associated with an increased risk of expression of psychosis or mania even after controlling for gender, socio-economic status, family history of psychosis and any adolescent psychiatric diagnosis. In a three-year study of the total Swedish population aged between 25 and 65 (4.4 million), Sundquist and colleagues (2004) found an incidence of 6,163 cases of first episode psychosis. They found that increasing levels of urbanisation were associated with increased rates of psychosis. Those living in the most densely populated areas had a 66–77 per cent increase in risk of developing psychosis. Van Os et al. (2004) found that in a population-based Danish cohort study of 1,020,063 persons, the effect of family history on later risk of schizophrenia increased with the level of urbanicity; that is, between 20–35 per cent exposed to both factors had developed schizophrenia because of the interaction of these two causes. Van Os (2004) argues that individuals with increased genetic liability to psychosis may have less opportunity to modify unusual or psychotic experiences in an (urban) environment with high levels of social fragmentation and low levels of social control, in combination with the lack of perceived safety and increased social stress associated with living in inner city environments.

A related possible risk factor is the effect of minority group migration, particularly where the incoming group is emigrating for economic reasons, and is therefore faced with the challenge of successfully integrating into a pre-existing cultural climate. Selten et al. (2001) found increased incidence of psychotic disorders, relative to the established population, in several migrant groups to the Netherlands. In particular, ratios for immigrants from Morocco, Surinam, Netherlands Antilles and other non-Western countries were elevated, whereas ratios for Turkish and other Western migrants were not sufficiently increased. The authors rejected the hypothesis that increased ratios were caused by selective migration of those at risk of psychosis (further supported by a case note comparison with a time-matched comparison in Surinam; Selten et al., 2005). It seems plausible that the need to integrate into an unfamiliar culture, and the additional social pressure of being a member of an outgroup, could have similar stressful effects to urbanicity, if not an interaction with this factor via economic forces. Indeed, in relation to the above environmental factors of safety and threat, Janssen and colleagues (2003) found that perceived ethnic discrimination was linked to the subsequent development of delusional persecutory ideation in a three-year study of the Dutch general population (n = 4,076).

SIGNIFICANT LIFE EVENTS

It is well established that stressful life events increase the risk of relapse in psychosis. In a retrospective study, Brown and Birley (1968) first established that individuals suffering from schizophrenia reported an increased frequency of stressful life events that were independent of the patient's illness in the three-week period just prior to the onset of an episode. Some 46 per cent of individuals in that group reported an independent life event in the three-week period just before a psychotic episode, compared with 14 per cent of a sample of community controls for a similar period. In addition, except for the three-week period prior to an episode, the life-event rates of the two groups did not differ significantly. Brown and Birley concluded that life events play a role in *triggering* the onset or relapse of psychotic symptoms in schizophrenia sufferers.

The role of stressful life events has since been established in a number of studies (Lukoff et al., 1984; Bebbington & Kuipers, 1998, for reviews) and precipitated the formulation of the misguided vulnerability stress hypothesis in psychosis. Furthermore, this work has also generated hypotheses about the salutogenic effects of social environments on these vulnerabilities and the resulting stress reactivity. In addition, the effect of severe life events has also been implicated in the onset of bipolar episodes. Postulated mechanisms for this link have included loss of family members through death (Kessing et al., 2004) and social rhythm disruption (Malkoff-Schwartz et al., 1998). However, the majority of studies in this area are based on retrospective accounts of events prior to an episode and the onset of the key episode. Thus, it is not possible to differentiate effectively between stressful events independent of residual symptomatology or possible prodromal signs, and events that may have been a result of the negative consequences associated with a psychotic episode.

Hirsch and colleagues (1996) followed up 71 individuals with a diagnosis of schizophrenia for 48 weeks and assessed on the Life Events and Difficulties Schedule. Half of this group were treated with regular antipsychotic medication and half had been recently withdrawn from medication. The risk of relapse increased in proportion to the number of life events but there was no interaction between medication status and events, that is, life events were not more closely associated with relapse on medication than off medication. The authors concluded that the contribution of life events to the risk of relapse in schizophrenia was confirmed by this study but the hypothesis that life events trigger relapse was not supported, nor was the hypothesis that life events are more relevant to relapse in persons on maintenance anti-psychotic medication than in those off medication.

Castine et al. (1998), studying a sample of 32 Vietnam veterans, reported a negative correlation between negative life events and psychotic episodes. That is to say, recent life events had a greater association with early episodes of schizophrenia than those with a more chronic presentation. These findings were also consistent with those of Bebbington et al. (1993) who found an increase in the number of life events in the six months before relapse, and not just in the few weeks before. Therefore, it is likely that the relationship between life events and relapse may be mediated though other factors such as coping and self-efficacy (Pallanti et al., 1997; Ventura et al., 2004), social integration (Hultman et al., 1997) or emotional reactivity (Myin-Germeys et al., 2003).

Hultman and colleagues investigated social support and general coping style in 42 individuals for up to four years. In a second part of the study, a sub-group of the patients were interviewed using the Life Events and Difficulties Schedule, nine months after discharge or at relapse. Patients contented with low social integration had a higher relapse rate over four years. There was also an excess of life events three weeks before relapse compared to events reported in the non-relapsing group. The time between a life event and relapse was significantly extended among patients with a high availability of attachment and a coping strategy characterised by active support seeking.

Myin-Germeys and colleagues (2001, 2003) investigated whether previous exposure to stressful life events affects: (1) the subjective stressfulness; and (2) emotional reactivity to life stress. In a sample of 42 people with psychosis using the Event Sampling Method, prior life events did not influence the perceived stressfulness of daily life stresses, rather it was the person's emotional reactivity to these events that was modified. Therefore, life events may contribute to relapse via an interactive process involving increased emotional reactivity, coping and availability of important social supports and attachment figures. In light of this, it would be valuable to explore the nature and significance of life events with regard to the individual.

TRAUMA

Early Childhood Trauma

Morrison and colleagues (2003) have argued that rates of childhood trauma are elevated among individuals with psychosis. This is based on several lines of evidence. First, studies have demonstrated that there is a high rate of trauma in the lifetimes of those individuals who have established psychosis. For example, in a casenote review of 200 individuals, Read and colleagues (2003) found that those who had experienced sexual abuse were more likely to report psychotic symptoms. Scheller-Gilkey and colleagues (2004) found that individuals with a diagnosis of schizophrenia and concurrent substance use (a risk factor for relapse) had a higher frequency of childhood traumatic events, greater post-traumatic stress disorder (PTSD) symptomatology and higher depression scores. Second, studies have demonstrated that childhood sexual abuse is linked to co-occurring hallucinations and delusions in other diagnostic populations. For example, Hammersley and colleagues (2003) have shown an association between childhood abuse and hallucinations among individuals diagnosed with bipolar disorder. Third, epidemiological studies have shown a link between childhood trauma and psychotic experiences. Bebbington et al. (2004) identified psychiatric disorders among 8,580 individuals living in the UK. Compared to respondents with other psychiatric disorders, the prevalence of lifetime victimisation among people with definite or probable psychosis was elevated. These experiences included sexual abuse, bullying, local authority care, running away from home, or being a victim of assault. After controlling for the possible interrelationship between events, sexual abuse, running away from home, being in a children's home, expulsion, homelessness and assault all remained significant predictors of psychosis. Controlling for current levels of depression, childhood sexual abuse remained the most significant and powerful risk factor for psychosis.

Finally, after controlling for both depression and the inter-dependence of events, sexual abuse, being expelled from school and experiencing assault were predictors of having psychosis. What is apparent from these data is that severe disruption in early attachment and bonding experiences increases individuals' vulnerability to developing psychosis. In a general population sample of 4,045 participants, who were followed up over two years, Janssen and colleagues (2004) found that experience of childhood sexual abuse was associated with psychosis. This relationship remained despite different types of measurements of psychosis. In addition, more frequent sexual abuse was associated with greater risk of developing psychosis and having need for care.

Psychosis as a Traumatic Event

There is growing evidence that psychosis is experienced as a traumatic event. Eight studies have investigated the prevalence of PTSD symptomatology following psychosis (McGorry et al., 1991; Shaw et al., 1997; Priebe et al., 1998; Meyer et al., 1999; Frame & Morrison, 2001; Kennedy et al., 2002; Neria et al., 2002; Jackson et al., 2004). These studies reported that between 11 per cent and 67 per cent of individuals meet criteria for PTSD following an acute episode of psychosis, although the prevalence of trauma-related symptom clusters such as recurrent intrusive memories is considerably higher in some studies (e.g. Meyer et al., 1999). Most studies indicated that the experience of the psychotic symptoms themselves was primarily responsible for patients' trauma (Meyer et al., 1999; Frame & Morrison, 2001; Kennedy et al., 2002; Shaw et al., 2002); however, some studies have suggested that the methods used to treat psychosis may also be partly responsible (McGorry et al., 1991; Frame & Morrison, 2001). Although the methodology of these studies has been criticised (Morrison et al., 2003) and despite the fact that acute psychosis is not formally recognised as an event which fulfils DSM-IV (American Psychiatric Association, 1994) criterion A for PTSD, the findings still appear to indicate that many patients experience significant PTSD symptomatology, which arises following the treatment and experience of acute psychosis. Participants in these studies reported intrusive recollections of stressful hospitalisation events such as police involvement, or symptom-based experiences including uncontrollable auditory hallucinations, persecutory paranoia, thought broadcasting and passivity phenomena. Individuals with a 'sealing over' recovery style were more likely to report fewer intrusions and greater avoidance when assessed using the Impact of Events Scale (Jackson et al., 2004). Those participants with greater levels of peri-traumatic depersonalisation derealisation and numbing also had greater levels of intrusions and avoidance (Shaw et al., 2002). Shaw et al. (1997) found that experiences representing loss of control were rated the most distressing by individuals. These 'loss of control' experiences, which included enforced seclusion, experiencing the self being controlled by external forces, visual hallucinations and thought insertion, were associated with the highest levels of distress. Frame and Morrison (2001) found that having controlled for symptom severity, experience of psychosis accounted for a substantial proportion of the variance (24 per cent) in PTSD symptoms, whereas experience of hospitalisation only accounted for 7 per cent of the variance. Therefore, it is possible that certain internal processes and events such as particular symptoms or configurations of symptoms cue intrusive vivid visual memories of previous relapses or events that are associated with psychosis.

INTERPERSONAL COPING

Having established both the interpersonal context and the effect of the wider social environment on vulnerability to psychosis, we now consider the impact of these factors upon an individual's ongoing interpersonal interactions – both in general and with regard to psychosis. Following the evidence of the above discussion, the connection between attachment styles, interpersonal functioning and utilisation of social supports seems clear. Sarason and colleagues (1990, 1991) investigated the link between perceived social support and adult attachment styles. They noted that avoidant individuals hold representations of self and others that make them prone to encoding and recalling instances of helpful behaviours as less supportive. In a similar vein, Blain et al. (1993) showed that higher levels of perceived support occurred among secure individuals. Ognibene and Collins (1998) also found higher support perceptions among secure individuals and significantly lower levels among fearful avoidant persons. On another dimension, social support and attachment styles also seem to be related in terms of the utilisation of available supports and the search for support. Wallace and Vaux (1993) found that individuals with an insecure attachment representation hold a more negative support network orientation. Mikulincer et al. (1993) demonstrated that individuals with a secure attachment style use social support seeking to a greater extent than insecure ones. Mikulincer and Florian (1997) further found that attachment style was a mediator for the impact of social support. In an experimental task they determined that conversing with a close other about the emotional and instrumental aspects of a stressful and distressing event reduced negative affect among secure individuals whereas avoidant individuals appeared to benefit only from instrumental support in the same condition and anxious/ambivalent individuals showed increased negative affect in the condition of emotional support being offered.

On the other hand, an alternative set of possible models for the effect of social support on emotional health, particularly in the presence of stressful life events, has centred on direct effects and so-called indirect or buffering effect of social supports (for reviews, refer to Alloway & Bebbington, 1987; Landerman et al., 1989). In terms of a direct social support effect, low levels of social support and impoverished or absent confiding relationships are associated with poor emotional health and a significant vulnerability to mental disorders (for an overview, see Cohen & Willis, 1985). The so-called 'buffering hypothesis' of social support proposes that social support has a protective function in the face of stress and that, in the absence of high levels of stress, social support will show no relationship to mental health (e.g. Brown, 1989; Parry et al., 1989). The model of social support proposed by Brown and Harris (1978) is the principal example of a 'buffering' model and has been replicated in numerous studies, including longitudinal investigations of the impact of early negative experiences and the effect of social support over long developmental time frames (Champion et al., 1995). The main vulnerability factor emerging from this research is the lack of a supportive network and particularly the lack of an intimate or confiding relationship.

It is known that social support from family and friends can act as a bulwark against psychosocial stressors and enhance functioning among individuals with an experience of psychosis. A number of studies demonstrated that individuals suffering from a bipolar disorder experience less positive social support and that low social support is associated with affective relapse (Romans & McPherson, 1992; Kulhara et al., 1999; Beyer et al., 2003). In two prospective studies, Johnson and colleagues (Johnson et al., 1999, 2000) found that poor social support predicted a higher number of relapses and longer time to recovery; the main mediators for relapse were higher depressive symptoms and low self-esteem. However, social support and social stress are not innovative concepts or concepts particular to psychosis; like 'parenthood', these are inherent to human sociability, and associations between mental well-being and social connectedness has been stressed by early authors (e.g. Burton, 1621). In that respect we are not faced with a unitary concept; rather, any consideration of social or developmental risk factors depend on their context and on their given operational definitions.

In an attempt to better understand the processes by which social support exerts its effects on emotional health, a number of mechanisms need to be considered. In particular, it is important to consider the likelihood of confounding effects in the measurement of social support and the assessment of stress. Sources of support are often also sources of stress; and the perception of stress does not occur independent of the perception of support. Significant stressors can directly change the availability of supports or the utilisation of existing supports. Schuster et al. (1990) pointed out that most relationships involve positive and negative aspects and that close interpersonal networks are most likely to be sources of stress. The processes by which negative aspects of close relationships and networks exert their effects on the emotional health of individuals are likely to be equally complex, and negative aspects are likely to have direct and indirect effects. Some of the investigations in the negative aspects highlighted that the negative effects of social networks might outweigh the positive ones in terms of their influence on mental health (e.g. Schuster et al., 1990). It is predominantly qualitative aspects of interpersonal relationships that seem to have significant effects, such as experiences of being let down (Brown et al., 1986) and lack of reciprocity in relationships, both in terms of not receiving sufficient support from close others but also significantly in terms of building up 'caring debts', the feeling of not being able to reciprocate received support (Pearlin, 1985).

Individuals suffering from a psychotic disorder or schizophrenia might be especially vulnerable to the particular interactions associated with high EE, such as increased criticism or emotional involvement. It appears to be a connected characteristic that individuals suffering from psychosis tend to have very small social networks which are usually also very dense in terms of the interconnectedness of network members and consist mainly of relatives and professionals (Cohen & Kochanowicz, 1989). However, for this group smaller networks are often associated with increased satisfaction with the available support (Schwannauer, 1997).

Macdonald and colleagues (1998) made a preliminary investigation of the effects of social skill on social support with 46 psychotic participants. When compared to multiple episode participants, first episode participants were identical in terms of social skill, social networks and support, but when age was factored into the model, younger first episode patients had greater degrees of social skill, and larger social support networks. The authors use these results to support the need for multiple discipline interventions for first episode psychosis. Throughout the research literature looking at the specific effects and functions of interpersonal relationships on emotional well-being, social support is conceptualised as an external and mainly structurally stable component. This can be misleading as it underestimates the dynamic and changeable nature of most interpersonal relationships and the active role that individuals play in creating and maintaining most of their significant relationships. Social support and the positive and negative effects of significant interpersonal relationships need to be understood from a developmental and dynamic perspective which will also shift the focus on the inter-relationship between stressful life events and support. In a long-term follow-up study, Champion (1995) found that a lack of emotional support was associated with an increased rate of negative events.

APPRAISALS OF PSYCHOSIS AND EMOTIONAL DISTRESS

Finally, in this chapter, to complete the jigsaw of factors implicated in staying well after psychosis, consideration needs to be given to the individual's cognitive and emotional response to the experience of a first episode of psychosis. In particular, the appraisal of psychosis has been strongly linked to depression subsequent to the abatement of acute psychotic symptoms. First, Birchwood et al. (1993) showed that depression following an acute episode of psychosis was associated with individuals' perception of being unable to prevent or control relapse (e.g. 'I am powerless to influence or control my illness') or the fear of psychosis itself (e.g. 'My illness frightens me'). Rooke and Birchwood (1998) followed up this group of patients two and a half years later. In this group, levels of depression were persistent over time, as were appraisals of entrapment (inability to control or escape from psychosis), loss of social role and self-blame. Individuals who were depressed felt greater entrapment and loss in relation to their psychosis. In addition, there was evidence that these appraisals were consistent with participants' personal experiences of psychosis. For example, participants with depression were more likely to have experienced more compulsory admissions and loss of, or drop in, employment status. Theoretical perspectives derived from evolutionary psychology as exemplified by social ranking theory (Gilbert, 1992) provide a theoretical framework to explain these findings. A person's perception of their social attractiveness and acceptability to others confirms their sense of rank, importance and place within their social and interpersonal environment. Therefore, life events that evoke feelings of loss (e.g. loss or disruption in important attachments or friendships) or events that threaten an individual's social ranking or importance (e.g. feeling humiliated by an episode of psychosis) are depressogenic via their impact on the lowering of perceived self-esteem and social status.

In relation to people with a diagnosis of schizophrenia, these processes can be observed in two important recent studies. Birchwood et al. (2000) found that, in a sample of 105 individuals, a proportion of 36 per cent developed post-psychotic depression (PPD) without concomitant changes in positive and negative symptoms. Participants who developed PPD were more likely than their non-PPD counterparts to attribute the cause of psychosis to themselves (self-blame), perceive greater loss of autonomy and valued role, and perceive themselves as entrapped and humiliated by their illness. In addition, individuals with and without PPD aspired to similar social and vocational roles. However, consistent with the predictions of social ranking theory, those who developed PPD saw their future status as lower. These participants also had greater insight into having a psychotic illness. Therefore, psychosis can be conceptualised as a life event that triggers depression via awareness of its social, interpersonal and affiliative implications. Individuals who develop depression following psychosis appraise this life event as representing a humiliating threat to their future status, leading to the loss of valued social roles, from which escape is blocked due to actual or feared relapse, or indeed persistent symptoms.

CONCLUSIONS

We have presented a multi-factorial account of the individual psychological, developmental, environmental and interpersonal factors linked to the evolution of problematic recovery and vulnerability to relapse following psychosis. Any account of vulnerability to the development of psychosis and the evolution of a chronic or problematic relapsing course needs to account for these interacting factors over time and in the individual's particular cultural and socio-economic context. First, we see the evolution of individual cognitive vulnerability through the development of negative cognitive interpersonal schemata. This has been suggested by the findings showing that early adolescent social anxiety and low self-esteem heighten risk for the development of psychosis. Second, we see the emergence of individuals' interpersonal vulnerability via their experience of core attachments, peer relationships and the successful utilisation of social supports and networks. This is suggested by the evidence for the role of early adolescent social isolation and high sensitivity to negative interpersonal environments and stressful life events. Third, we see that those who develop psychosis are at heightened risk of experiencing a range of traumatic events including sexual abuse, which have the capacity to undermine core attachment experiences. We also see the importance of increased risk arising from living in an urbanised and fragmented social environment where themes of interpersonal mistrust and fragmentation may mesh with existing negative cognitive interpersonal schemata. It is in this context that psychosis itself provokes major affective responses in both individuals and their social environments. These affective reactions are mediated via appraisals of danger, loss, entrapment and humiliation. This may occur in the context of an already weakened platform for the regulation of affect conferred by the experience of a range of pre-existing adverse social events and/or social isolation.

PART II

OVERVIEW OF STRUCTURE, STYLE AND ORGANISATION OF THERAPY

CHAPTER 4

OVERVIEW OF PRINCIPLES AND PROCEDURES

INTRODUCTION

This chapter provides an overview of the basic principles, procedures and structure of *Staying Well After Psychosis*. In particular, we will demonstrate how the principles of cognitive behavioural psychotherapy can be applied to support individuals who are recovering from psychosis. We emphasise how a number of tensions, including the engagement of the person following psychosis, the importance of a co-ordinated and multi-disciplinary team-based approach focused on emotional and interpersonal recovery, and the maintenance of a compassionate and vigilant attitude to staying well, need to be carefully considered in the design of services and treatment. In this context the importance of prioritising problems related to risk, therapeutic alliance, specific problems and valued goals, and underlying schemata is also considered.

PRIMARY AND SECONDARY OUTCOMES

In his editorial for the *British Journal of Psychiatry*, Max Birchwood (2003) emphasised the importance of emotional recovery as the much-neglected cornerstone of psychological research and psychotherapies for people with distressing psychotic experiences. Here emotional distress is considered as a psychological reaction to psychosis, where the person experiences strong feelings of shame, loss and trauma. Crucially, from this position, the conceptualisation of relapse must capture critically important elements of the person's sense of entrapment and inability to escape from a stigmatising experience. In this context, our focus is therefore on two co-primary outcomes: (1) emotional recovery; and (2) relapse prevention. These two co-primary outcomes are encapsulated by the term 'staying well after psychosis'. We hypothesise that staying well after psychosis is achieved by addressing negative beliefs about psychosis, improving interpersonal functioning, insight and self-reflectiveness, and increasing overall engagement with services. Changes in psychotic symptoms *per se* are secondary out-comes. In staying well, it is the specific personal meanings attached to psy-chotic experiences which signify emotional and interpersonal distress that are of greatest importance.

ASSESSMENT

In addition to a comprehensive clinical assessment, including consideration of the developmental and interpersonal context of psychosis, there are areas of psychological functioning that can helpfully be supported by a range of formal assessments and self-report measures.

Emotional Distress

It is helpful to have a measure of emotional distress. For example, this can be measured using the Beck Depression Inventory (BDI: Beck, 1967), an extensively validated 21-item self-report scale for depression. In addition, the Calgary Depression Scale for Schizophrenia (CDSS: Addington et al., 1993) is an interview-based measure of depression developed specifically to avoid the overlap between depressive and negative symptoms. This is also a useful measure. Both measures are highly correlated with each other to almost unitary ($r = 0.91$: Shahar et al., 2004).

Psychotic Experiences

It is important to assess psychotic experiences from a multidimensional per-spective. For example, the Psychotic Symptoms Rating Scales (PSYRATS: Haddock et al., 1999) is an interview-based measure with two subscales: auditory hallucinations and delusions. The auditory hallucinations subscale is an 11-item scale that assesses frequency, duration, severity and intensity of distress and also symptom-specific dimensions of controllability, loud-ness, location, negative content, degree of negative content, beliefs about origin of voices and disruption. The delusions subscale is a six-item scale, which assesses dimensions of delusions including preoccupation, distress, duration, conviction, intensity of distress and disruption. The scale shows good inter-rater reliability and validity with other measures of psychotic experiences. Compared with traditional observer-rated symptomatic rating scales in psychosis such as the Positive and Negative Syndrome Scale (PANSS: Kay et al., 1987), this scale highlights the subjective experiences related to psychotic phenomena rather than being restricted to a description of the presence/absence and relative severity of symptoms.

Beliefs about Psychosis

The meaning attached to the experience of psychosis is important to our understanding of the person's emotional reaction to psychosis. For example, a person's appraisal of their psychosis can be assessed using the Personal Beliefs about Illness Questionnaire (PBIQ: Birchwood et al., 1993). The PBIQ is comprised of 16 items rated on a four-point scale and assesses individuals' beliefs in five domains: loss, humiliation, shame, attribution of behaviour to self or to illness, and entrapment in psychosis. The scale has been demonstrated to have good reliability and validity with people who are diagnosed with schizophrenia. However, to date, the PBIQ lacks a confirmed factor structure for the subscales hypothesised to underpin the particular items. That said, at an item level, the PBIQ is an excellent measure for identifying problematic themes in relation to a person's cognitive appraisals of psychosis. There is a consistent relationship between scores on this measure and level of depression (e.g. Iqbal et al., 2000).

The Fear of Recurrence Scale (FoRSe, Appendix 1: Gumley et al., in preparation) is a 23-item self-report questionnaire that provides a measure of idiosyncratic negative beliefs and appraisals, which are hypothesised to play a causal role in the acceleration of psychotic relapse (Gumley et al., 1999). The measure has three subscales: Fear of Relapse, Heightened Awareness and Intrusive Thinking. The measure has excellent internal consistency ($\alpha=0.93$) and good test–retest reliability ($r=0.71$). Higher total scores on this scale are associated with higher scores on the Early Signs Questionnaire (ESQ: Birchwood et al., 1989) ($r = 0.70$, $p < 0.001$), more positive symptoms ($r = 0.59$, $p<0.001$), more general psychopathology ($r=0.52$, $p<0.001$), more negative illness beliefs (PBIQ) including loss ($r=0.31$, $p<0.001$), entrapment ($r = 0.32$, $p<0.001$), shame ($r=0.18$, $p<0.05$) and self-blame ($r=0.18$, $p<0.05$).

Interpersonal Functioning

The Adult Attachment Interview (AAI: Main et al., 1985) is an hour-long semi-structured interview consisting of 18 questions assessing adults' state of mind with respect to attachment. The interview asks respondents for descriptive adjectives of attachment figures during childhood, alongside specific autobiographical memories supporting respondents' choice of adjectives. Specific questions are asked about what respondents did when emotionally upset, physically hurt or ill and how their attachment figures responded. Respondents are asked about experiences of separation, loss, rejection and abuse. Respondents are also invited to reflect on how their early experiences have affected their adult development. Importantly, the interviewer is required to be relatively non-directive. Hesse (1996) has defined the central task within the AAI as the challenge to generate and reflect upon memories related to attachment while simultaneously maintaining a coherent discourse. The interview is transcribed and coded according to well-established criteria (Main et al., 2002). Coding of uncomplicated transcripts may take about five to six hours. In the overall system of analysis, transcripts are judged to reflect secure/autonomous, dismissing, preoccupied and unresolved/disorganised classifications (see Figure 4.1). Given the emphasis in the coding to the maintenance of coherent discourse, application of the AAI in the context of psychosis and other adult psychological disorders requires care. In addition, coders require extensive training before being classified as reliable, making the AAI an interview that is potentially unsuitable for administration in routine care.

Alternatively, the Attachment Style Questionnaire (ASQ: Feeney et al., 1994) is a 40-item self-report scale, measuring adult attachment styles. It yields various solutions, including a three-factor solution based on Hazan and Shaver's (1987) attachment prototypes: secure, anxious/ambivalent and avoidant. This is similar to the AAI classification of secure/autonomous, dismissing, preoccupied states of mind respectively. It is suitable for use with adolescents and young adults who have limited experience of romantic relationships. The ASQ has good test–retest reliability and internal consistency. One major difficulty in using self-report measures of attachment style is that those with dismissing/avoidant states of mind tend to report 'optimal' parenting experiences during the AAI and secure/autonomous states of mind on self-report measures. Dozier and Tyrrell (1997) found that the transcripts of adults diagnosed with schizophrenia tend to be classified as dismissing.

The Inventory of Interpersonal Problems (IIP-64: Horowitz et al., 1988) is a 64-item self-report questionnaire. From this, a shorter 32-item version of the questionnaire (IIP-32: Horowitz et al., 2000) has subsequently been developed. The scale provides a measure of underdeveloped and overdeveloped interpersonal strategies. Underdeveloped strategies are measured by eight items preceded by the phrase 'It is hard for me to . . .' (e.g. '. . . tell a person to stop bothering me', '. . . show affection to people'). Overdeveloped strategies are assessed by 14 items describing interpersonal behaviours a person perceives that they do too much (e.g. 'I try to control other people too much', 'I am too suspicious of other people').

Engagement, Alliance and Bonding

Examples of measures that can be used to assess engagement, alliance and bonding are given below. The Service Engagement Scale (SES: Tait et al., 2002) is a 14-item measure consisting of statements which assess a person's overall engagement with a service. Key workers complete the scale. Each item is on a four-point scale anchored by 'not at all or rarely' and 'most of the time'. Items assess four subscales including availability ('When a visit is

Secure/autonomous

Coherent and collaborative discourse. Valuing of attachment, but seems objective regarding any particular event/relationship. The description and evaluation of attachment-related experiences are consistent whether experiences are favourable or unfavourable.

Secure

Explores room and toys with interest in pre-separation episodes. Shows signs of missing parent during separation, often crying by the second separation. Obvious preference for parent over stranger. Greets parent actively, usually initiating physical contact. Usually some contact maintaining by second reunion, but then settles and returns to play.

Dismissing

Not coherent. Dismissing of attachment-related experiences or relationships. There is an implicit claim of strength, normality and/or independence and highly positive generalised representations of parents or attachment figures tend to be unsupported or actively contradicted by episodes recounted. Potential negative effects of parenting or other untoward experiences are denied or minimised, or (rarely) attachment figures are derogated. Organisation of attachment representations permits attachment to remain relatively deactivated.

Avoidant

Fails to cry on separation from parent. Actively avoids and ignores parent on reunion (e.g. by moving away, turning away or leaning out when picked up). Little or no proximity or contact seeking, no distress and no anger. Focuses on toys or environment throughout procedure.

Preoccupied

Not coherent. Preoccupied with or by past attachment relationships/ experiences, speaker appears angry, passive or fearful. Descriptions of early relationships may seem vague and uncritical, or else angry, conflicted and unconvincingly analytical. In rare cases, some seem fearfully preoccupied with or overwhelmed by traumatic experiences.

Resistant or ambivalent

May be wary or distressed even prior to separation, with little exploration. Preoccupied with parent throughout procedure; may seem angry or passive. Fails to settle and take comfort in the parent on reunion, and usually continues to focus on parent and cry. Fails to return to exploration after reunion.

Unresolved/Disorganised

There are marked lapses in metacognitive monitoring or reasoning or discourse during the discussion of loss or abuse experiences. For example, the person may briefly indicate that a dead person is still alive in the physical sense. The individual may lapse into prolonged silence or eulogistic speech.

Disorganised/disoriented

The infant displays disorganised and/or disoriented behaviours in the parent's presence, suggesting a temporary collapse in the parent's strategy. The infant may freeze with a trance-like expression, hands in air; may rise at parent's entrance then fall prone, then huddle on the floor; or may cling, cry hard and turn away.

Figure 4.1   Adult Attachment Interview: classifications of states of mind to attachment alongside corresponding patterns of the Infant Strange Situation Test

arranged, the client is available'), collaboration ('The client actively participates in managing their illness'), help-seeking ('The client seeks help to prevent a crisis') and treatment adherence ('The client refuses to co-operate with treatment'). The scale has good reliability and discriminant validity. The scale is also sensitive to individuals with a predominantly sealing over versus integrating recovery style.

The Service Attachment Questionnaire (SAQ: Goodwin et al., 2003) is a 25-item measure developed using grounded theory methods to record individuals' perceptions of the service in terms of: (1) being attended to and listened to; (2) being there – consistency and continuity; (3) being given enough time – ending and leaving; (4) safe environment; (5) relationships which enable helpful talking; and (6) human contact and comfort. Each item is assessed on a four-point Likert scale anchored by 'not at all' and 'always'. The factor structure suggests one underlying construct accounts for 72 per cent of the variance.

The Working Alliance Inventory – Short Form (WAI-SF: Tracy & Kokotovic, 1989) is a client and therapist self-report measure based on 12 statements rated on a seven-point scale ranging from 'never' to 'always'. The scale is based on Bordin's (1979) conceptualisation of therapeutic alliance as being rooted in three components: (1) therapeutic bond; (2) client and therapist agreement on goals; and (3) client and therapist agreement on tasks. In a large Danish study reported by Valbak et al. (2003), the WAI was predictive of adherence to psychotherapy among 72 first episode psychosis participants.

Insight and Self-reflectiveness

Another important area is the person's stance with respect to an illness-based model of their experience. The Birchwood Insight Scale (BIS: Birchwood et al., 1994) provides an eight-item self-report measure of three hypothesised underlying constructs: (1) perceived need for treatment; (2) awareness of illness; and (3) re-labelling of symptoms as pathological. Trauer and Sacks (2000) have confirmed the factor structure for this scale. In contrast, the Beck Cognitive Insight Scale (BCIS: Beck et al., 2004) is a 15-item self-report scale with two subscales: self-reflectiveness and self-certainty. Self-reflectiveness refers to the person's metacognitive ability to reflect upon, correct and re-evaluate their beliefs and interpretations. Self-certainty refers to the person's confidence in their own beliefs and judgements. Reduced self-reflectiveness as measured by the BCIS was associated with more severe hallucinations, delusions and thought disorder.

The scales described above are not exclusive but are given as examples to indicate the importance of assessing these spheres of functioning.

STRUCTURE OF THERAPY

Cognitive interpersonal therapy is a structured, focused and collaborative approach to psychotherapy. When employed by individuals with complex and enduring psychological problems, there are a number of adaptations to the conventional style of cognitive therapy as described for psychological problems, such as depression or anxiety. This is summarised in Table 4.1.

Cognitive interpersonal therapy for staying well is designed as a 25- to 30-session intervention, which is conducted over 9–12 months. It is divided into three distinct but overlapping phases: (1) engagement and formulation; (2) transforming beliefs and problematic interpersonal strategies; and (3) end phase and closure. Over these phases the frequency of therapy is variable with frequent sessions (one per week) at the beginning of therapy when the therapist is focused on the development of a shared formulation, alliance

Table 4.1   Characteristics of cognitive interpersonal therapy

	Clinical disorders	Recovery and staying well
Length of treatment	3–4 months	9 months or more
Pace of treatment	Brisk	Variable
Problem timescale	Here and now	Here and now and lifetime
Therapeutic relationship	Collaborative	Collaborative, empathic, responsive, stable and activating of bonding
Problem content	Client's world, present and future	Client's world, past, present, future, interpersonal relationships and therapeutic relationship
Problem focus	Behaviour, cognition and emotion	Interpersonal coping, therapeutic relationship, cognition, emotion and behaviour
Emphasis in intervention	Automatic thoughts	Schema, behaviour and interpersonal coping
Homework	Automatic thoughts data collection	Behavioural and interpersonal data and strengthening of new beliefs and strategies
Scientific method	Experimental	Experimental, reflective exploration
Learning model	Maladaptive learning	Experiential understanding and self-reflection
Openness	Explicit	Explicit and transparent

and mutuality of goals and tasks, less frequent in the middle phase (one per fortnight) allowing for greater reflection and exploration of predominant cognitive themes and interpersonal strategies, then more frequent in the end phase to enable issues such as loss, separation and dependency to be addressed. For some individuals who engage well in psychotherapeutic work and who might focus on particular areas of interpersonal functioning, it can be important to keep the therapeutic frame stable and to keep the regularity of weekly sessions throughout the treatment.

Contracting such a long period of therapy can be difficult for many individuals. Therefore, therapy may be contracted in blocks of sessions determined by agreement between client and therapist. For example, initial sessions may be contracted to explore whether therapist and client get along with each other and whether goals can be a formulation suitable for psychotherapeutic work, whereas later sessions may contract work on specific problems. Just as the frequency of therapy is variable, so is the pacing of sessions. Therapists need to be mindful of exploring experiences and cognitive themes that are associated with strong affect. High levels of affect can overwhelm clients' ability to reflect on their own experiences and to mentalise the beliefs and intentions of others. It is important at this juncture that a therapeutic relationship is established that allows clients to explore difficult emotional content or particular experiences within a containing and safe interpersonal context.

In working with this client group, therapists often need to model the expression of tensions and uncertainties in the room and allow for these anxieties to be verbalised as they can often become roadblocks in the interpersonal context of therapy and therefore prevent an open exploration of emotions attached to psychotic experiences. For example, in our qualitative research with individuals who experience paranoia, respondents often express the evidential and experiential basis of their threat appraisals as being their own feelings of vulnerability and conspicuousness. For example, 'I know other people want to hurt me because I sense it'. We also find this clinically during therapy. Therefore, therapists need to be careful to slow the pace of therapy during exploration of affect-laden autobiographical memories, images and cognitions. Roadblocks in the expression of emotionally salient material can be a constructive guide to reflect on associated factors or experiences that make this process difficult.

An important aspect of staying well cognitive interpersonal therapy is the availability of additional targeted sessions provided during periods where the client experiences increased vulnerability or during periods suggesting increased risk of relapse (as determined by the formulation). This is a flexible but intensive phase, which may involve up to three to four sessions per week. This form of flexibility also characterises the therapy as a whole with sessions carried out in environments acceptable to the client. For example, during the initial phase, reluctance to engage may, and usually does, neces-sitate domiciliary visits or arranging sessions in other places acceptable to the client (e.g. a local café). However, even though the therapeutic context is characterised by flexibility and remains sensitive to each individual client's needs, it will still be important for therapists to provide a stable and consis-tent therapeutic environment and to work thoughtfully with therapeutic boundaries so that the therapy is experienced as containing, able to with-stand crisis and interpersonal challenges.

STYLE OF THERAPY

Problem List

Therapy and therapist activity are licensed by the client's problem list and their valued goals. The role of the therapist in the early stages of engage-ment is to focus on the identification of clients' overt problems alongside their cognitive, affective, interpersonal and developmental dimensions. Careful descriptive characterisation of clients' problems enables the evolu-tion of a micro-level formulation describing the nature of the difficulties. Careful problem analysis also drives the development of shared goals. The relationship between clients' problems and their goals facilitates the nego-tiation of the key tasks of therapy. This mutuality between goals and tasks is central to the development of a strong, but fluid, early working alliance.

Formulation

Case formulation is tailored according to the function of case formulation within the therapeutic progression, the client's interpersonal and recovery style, and the timing or phase in therapy. Case formulation evolves through-out therapy and is seen as a live, creative and ongoing process. It is not an event that is delivered to the patient by the therapist in a static or one-dimensional manner. Case formulation during the engagement phase is designed to capture the client's valued goals, important emotional meanings and to facilitate the development of a therapeutic working alliance. Coher-ent narrative is emphasised as a means of capturing important meanings and overcoming paranoid states of mind or an avoidant/sealing over recovery style. In this sense, the therapist is attempting to activate the client's own attachment system by providing meaningful representations of the client's experience, and which capture implicational/emotional rather than intellec-tual levels of meaning (Teasdale & Barnard, 1993). Case formulation is also sensitive to linking information together on an 'as required' basis. For example, when working on alliance, the therapist will attempt to incorpo-rate meanings that are relevant to alliance, whereas when working with interpersonal schema, the formulation will connect the client with relevant experiences (e.g. early trauma) and interpersonal responses (e.g. compliance and subjugation). This layering of formulation throughout the process of therapy is central to tracking client progress and recovery, appropriately pacing therapy and timing specific interventions. The emphasis on narrative formulation corresponds to important exercises during therapy, which focus on the development of an integrated and coherent self-reflective stance, and the crafting of a revised and self-accepting narrative.

Compassionate and Rational Mind

In staying well therapy, the therapist combines and utilises both rational mind and compassionate mind perspectives as described by Gilbert and others (2005). The characteristics of rational and compassionate mind are described in Table 4.2. Staying well therapy requires both approaches. A compassionate mind captures emotional meanings, and is nurturing, kindly, empathic and warm. A compassionate mind engenders a resonance for positive interpersonal experiences to remembered and developed. In addition, a compassionate mind creates a feeling of security within which the client can explore negative interpersonal experiences. It also creates the opportunity for clients to learn self-soothing approaches to responding to negative self-critical internal narratives. This presents an accepting challenging of self-destructive appraisals and beliefs. In contrast, a rational mind encourages an experimental, objective, logical and measured approach to judgement and appraisal. This is the mind most often associated with traditional cognitive therapy. The rational mind encourages individuals to reflect on their reasoning processes and therefore fosters greater mind mindedness.

Therapeutic Relationship

The therapeutic relationship is central to cognitive interpersonal therapy, whereby the development of a collaborative working alliance is central to achieving client goals. In the context of staying well therapy, the therapeutic relationship becomes an important scaffold to facilitate the development of clients' understandings of their own experience and their understanding of the beliefs and intentions of others. Process factors within therapy, such as those expressed in concepts derived from psychodynamic therapies (e.g. transference and counter-transference), are embraced within therapy. These are important constructs, functioning to allow the therapist to mentalise how their own affective, cognitive and interpersonal responses within therapy may facilitate or interfere with recovery. The establishment of a containing and reflective therapeutic relationship will enable therapeutic change to take place within an interpersonal context that can in itself provide an essential

Table 4.2 Characteristics of the rational mind and the compassionate mind

The rational mind	The compassionate mind
The rational mind likes to look at the evidence. It is a scientist or detective and treats ideas and thoughts as theories that can be proved incorrect.	The compassionate mind has empathy and sympathy for those who are in pain and suffering.
It does not settle for simple answers; like Sherlock Holmes, it observes carefully and wants to know as much as possible before coming to a decision.	It is concerned with personal growth and helping people reach their potential.
The rational mind likes to have several alternatives to choose from. It does not like to have few choices because it tends to assume that there is always more than one way of seeing things.	It is concerned with healing, supporting and listening to what we and what others need.
The rational mind likes to test things and run experiments.	It listens and enquires about problems in a kind and friendly way.
The rational mind does not like being overly influenced by emotional appeal or hasty conclusions.	The compassionate mind is quick to forgive and slow to condemn.
The rational mind knows that knowledge develops slowly. Things become more complex as we know more, and this is a source of fascination and deepening understanding.	It does not attack, but seeks to bring healing, reunion and repair.
The rational mind knows that we learn most from trial and error – that, in fact, we often learn more from our errors than we do from our successes.	The compassionate mind recognises that life can be painful and that we are all imperfect beings.
The rational mind will attempt (if given a chance) to weigh the advantages and disadvantages of a particular view or course of action.	It does not treat ourselves or others simply as objects with a market value. Self-worth and self-acceptance are not things to be earned; they are not conditional or based on fulfilling contracts.
The rational mind likes to take a long-term view of things and recognises that we often get to where we are going step by step. It realises that it is our long-term interests that are important, regardless of short-term setbacks or benefits.	

corrective emotional experience. Within the structure of a stable and consistent therapeutic relationship, interpersonal problems and ruptures can be detected and explored that might not otherwise be volunteered or raised by the client. This is important when considering that the client may be highly avoidant and unaware of possible problems. Alternatively, for some clients, there is a lack of emotionally close or confiding relationships, thus underlying interpersonal problems never overtly are expressed.

Narrative Style

Cognitive therapy has emphasised the importance of the therapist's use of Socratic questioning in guiding the person's discovery. Socratic questioning, as defined by Padesky (2003), is a therapeutic process that involves asking the client questions, which the person has the knowledge to answer. Questions draw the client's attention to information which is relevant to the issue being discussed, but which may be outside the client's current focus. Questions generally move from the concrete to the more abstract so that in the end the client can apply new information to either re-evaluate a previous conclusion or construct a new idea. This is a goal-orientated approach to therapeutic discourse. After new information has been discovered, idiosyncratic meanings have been heard and explored, and a summary has been constructed, the therapist completes the guided discovery process by asking the client a synthesising or analytical question, which applies this new information to the client's original concern or belief. This is one means by which cognitive psychotherapy can foster a dialogue that develops the person's sense of agency and explorative self-reflection. This is constructed through the development of the therapeutic processes and interactions.

In particular, we are concerned with how therapists encourage clients to engage in therapeutic dialogues which foster and heighten their ability to reflect on their construction of meaning in relation to their sense of agency and self. This is a process that is active and participatory rather than passive and observed. This, we feel, is the essence of personal recovery and staying well. Therefore, throughout this text we will illustrate the importance of narrative discourse as a source of reflection for therapists and clients. In addition, Greenberg and Pascual-Leone (1997) and Greenberg et al. (1993) have also suggested that a pivotal task of therapy is, in the context of a safe therapy relationship, to increase awareness of emotion by focusing attention on emotional experiences, and the development of a narrative enabling symbolic self-reflection on the fundamental experiential meanings embedded in personal experience. In their process experiential approach to psychotherapy, Greenberg et al. (1993) have emphasised therapeutic tasks facilitating experiential rather than conceptual processing of events. The therapeutic narrative gives an indication of the levels of processing and understanding achieved by the client and can be used to focus therapeutic discourse. For example, when discussing trauma, it is not unusual for narrative to become fragmented, difficult to follow and impoverished. This acts as a signal to the therapist of the presence of problematic or unresolved experiences.

BASIC ELEMENTS OF THE THERAPEUTIC STANCE

Siegel (1999) proposes five basic elements of how caregivers can foster a secure attachment in the children under their care. These elements also form the basic elements of any therapeutic discourse.

- *Collaboration.* Secure relationships are based on collaborative and carefully attuned communication. Collaboration is developed through the careful negotiation of clients' problems and goals within therapy, and the therapist's encouragement of the client to develop an active, enquiring and explorative approach to understanding and resolving emotional distress.
- *Reflective dialogue.* There is a focus on the person's internal experience, where the therapist attempts to make sense of client narratives and then communicate their understanding in such a way that helps the client create new meanings and perspectives on their emotions, perceptions, thoughts, intentions, memories, ideas, beliefs and attitudes.
- *Repair.* When attuned communication is disrupted, there is a focus on collaborative repair allowing the client to reflect upon misunderstandings and disconnections in their interpersonal experiences.
- *Coherent narratives.* The connection of past, present and future is central to the development of a person's autobiographical self-awareness. The development of coherent narratives within therapy aims to help foster the flexible capacity to integrate both internal and external experiences over time.
- *Emotional communication.* The therapist maintains close awareness not only of the contents of narrative but also of clients' emotional communications. In focusing on negative or painful emotions within sessions, the therapist communicates and encourages self-reflection, understanding, acceptance and soothing.

GENERAL OUTLINE OF THERAPY SESSIONS

Psychosis is a powerful event characterised by severe and distressing changes in thinking and experiences that are unified by a pervasive sense of powerful interpersonal threat, dominance and paranoia, combined with a sense of personal vulnerability. While psychosis, as a disorder, signifies stigmatising negative life trajectories generating feelings of hopelessness or triggering defensive denial and sealing over, the symptoms themselves have the potential to undermine basic assumptions of safety, interpersonal security, intimacy and attachment.

The therapist's orientation throughout therapy is the collaborative development of a coherent client narrative that optimises the evolution of their self-reflectiveness, the crafting of alternative helpful beliefs and appraisals, and the development of adaptive coping and interpersonal behaviours. Through the discourse of psychotherapy, the focus on narrative and the use of cognitive and interpersonal techniques, the therapist supports the client in meshing behavioural and cognitive change. Underpinning this process, the therapist carefully nurtures the therapeutic alliance and provides the client with a secure base from which to explore difficult issues.

Engagement and Formulation (Sessions 1–10)

The initial sessions over the first three months (sessions 1–10) focus on developing the therapeutic alliance and bond, and mutual tasks and goals. During this phase the therapist and client collaboratively develop and prioritise a problem list from the client's perspective. The therapist needs to listen carefully and feed back their understanding of the client's experiences, interpretations and problems in their own words. During the early engagement sessions (sessions 1–4) the focus tends to be on the client's immediate problem list and goals before exploring more difficult and affect-laden experiences. Where relevant, negative experiences of treatment are explored sensitively and the therapist encourages the client to reflect on the implications of these experiences for the therapeutic relationship. In this way the therapist can begin to develop an understanding of the synchrony between clients' specific autobiographical memories and their beliefs, attitudes and expectations of treatment. Negative experiences of psychosis are also explored. Again the therapist attempts to maintain a fresh and open dialogue by attending to specific examples of clients' descriptions. This process allows the therapist to develop further hypotheses about the nature of the clients' idiosyncratic appraisals of psychotic experiences and how these are likely to shape recovery and determine emotional and behavioural responses to the threat of relapse, should early signs of relapse occur in the future. During narratives exploring experiences of treatment and psychosis the therapist needs to maintain sensitivity to the client's trauma by being aware of changes in voice tone, eye contact and body posture. These changes often signal changes in affect and the occurrence of intrusive thoughts or images.

Such changes are thus important opportunities to help develop the client's own self-reflectiveness and their awareness of the importance of their experiences and interpretations in mediating their adaptation and adjustment to the experience of psychosis. However, in doing this, the therapist needs to be careful to support clients in regulating the affect within sessions by carefully timing exploration of these sensitive areas. The therapist can calibrate their timing by reflecting on the strength of the therapeutic alliance, and the client's resilience and/or access to coping skills and interpersonal resources. In addition, the therapist can structure sessions in such a way to enable exploration of more difficult issues during the middle phase of sessions, thus allowing the session to shift focus onto other matters towards the end. The use of agenda setting and item prioritisation can support this process. Formulation during this phase is tailored to the person's recovery style, the level of alliance and the nature of goals and tasks, which have been agreed. Therapists often make errors in using formulation to explain clients' problems at a level that is important to the therapist (in terms of guiding treatment, looking for barriers, etc.) but have less relevance for the client.

For example, it is often important for the therapist to understand how beliefs have evolved from very early childhood experiences. However, the client may see such an approach to formulation as a stereotypical attribution of adult problems to childhood experiences (e.g. 'you mean, it's all to do with my childhood!'). The client may connect problems to experiences in a way that activates strong (and potentially overwhelming) negative affect, or the client may be attempting to seal over and isolate their psychotic experiences from other aspects of their life history. This latter strategy may be an attempt (consciously or otherwise) to avoid strong affect or to prevent contamination of the traumatic experiences into other aspects of their life. An example of a written formulation is given below. Readers will note that the formulation emphasises those core components of therapeutic alliance, bonding, mutual goals and shared tasks. The engagement phase determines that the function of formulation at this stage is to support the development of alliance, client self-reflectiveness and accurate mentalisation of the therapists' beliefs and intentions.

Dear Michael,

Over the last number of weeks we seem to have developed a good relationship . . . [REFLECT ON RELATIONSHIP] Your goals have been to . . . [GOALS]. For you, being admitted to hospital has been a terrifying and humiliating experience that has left you feeling dejected and shamed . . . In an effort to restore a sense of security and control, you have developed a number of important ways of coping. You work hard to show people that you are friendly and likeable but sometimes this means that you can't tell them how you feel. [VALIDATION,

BONDING] This means that you often feel like you must cope on your own and other people do not understand you. You feel strongly that other people have misunderstood your experiences during admission to hospital, blaming your thoughts and feelings on your use of alcohol and on having an illness. You have fought hard not to accept these views of your difficulties, but at the same time have been unable to help people make sense of your experiences. [FORMULATION] Perhaps an important task for you is therefore to find a way to help others accept your views [THERAPY TASK].

A Therapist

Transforming Beliefs and Problematic Interpersonal Strategies (Sessions 11–20)

This middle phase of therapy tends to be conducted over sessions 11–20 and focuses upon the development of a more careful understanding of how clients' experiences have led to the development of their problematic beliefs about themselves, others, the world and the future. Within a compassionate framework (Gilbert, 2000) the therapist explores with the client how helpful (and unhelpful) their specific beliefs and appraisals are in terms of achieving their specific goals. For example, a client may describe feeling lonely and isolated and want to develop more meaningful relationships with others. However, based on their experiences prior to their first episode of psychosis, they believe other people are intrinsically untrustworthy. Often individuals also have an extremely limited experience of confiding and trusting peer relationships. Furthermore, in many cases they might not have had a chance to develop these as their first episode of psychosis interrupted the development of appropriate interpersonal skills and social integration. Therefore, in order to reduce their sense of vulnerability, they often avoid contact with others.

In this scenario, the functional significance of avoidance can be validated, and the negative consequences for the person explored. In addition, the therapist maintains a mindful awareness of a number of key dimensions or themes relevant to staying well after psychosis, including: (1) emotional distress; (2) interpersonal trust and intimacy (encompassing the ability to interpret and predict the responses of others); (3) feelings of entrapment, shame or humiliation in psychosis; (4) clients' sense of hope and optimism for recovery; and (5) help-seeking in the context of distress and self-experienced vulnerability to relapse. The therapist helps the client mesh their negative beliefs with functional aspects of their coping and interpersonal behaviours in order to create opportunities for the client to consider developing new or underdeveloped interpersonal strategies. For example, a client may describe his parents as critical and intrusive and feel angry when they complain about his behaviour at home. In response to this, the client shouts at his parents, leaves the room and avoids speaking to them. While it is important for this client to maintain his sense of autonomy and independence and to avoid being treated like a child, the costs of this strategy for the client are increased distress, rumination, negative reactions from his parents and an increase in feelings of suspicion and paranoia. The therapist might work with the client to develop alternative strategies including assertiveness and anger regulation, combined with developing a compassionate mentalisation of his parents' anxieties, worries and concerns for his well-being. This latter strategy allows him to develop a reassuring communicative style with his parents.

The development of new or underdeveloped interpersonal strategies provides an important opportunity for the therapist and client to craft alternative accounts of the client's experiences, enabling the development of alternative beliefs. For example, on reflecting on his parents' behaviour, this client considered how their anxiety and worry reflected their parental feelings towards him, and how they had valued his development. This was particularly so given their harsh upbringing in the shipbuilding areas of Glasgow. Their expectations had been devastated by his first psychotic episode, and they had thought that he would never work again. This client valued his independence and autonomy, and saw an important aspect of this transition as reducing their anxiety about his well-being.

The therapist further fosters clients' recognition of the presence of existing strengths and skills that enable them to survive and endure traumatic and distressing experiences and adverse life circumstances. We feel it important that a formulation at this stage incorporates both negative and positive aspects of existing strategies in order to develop meaning-making that incorporates positive life experiences without the minimisation of negative life events. In this sense the therapist encourages a model of complex affect, encouraging the integration of both positive and painful emotions. In this way, the therapist helps the client not to disregard or avoid negative emotions in association with their psychotic experiences.

End Phase and Closure (Sessions 21–30)

The end phase of therapy from sessions 21 to 30 focuses on the continued meshing of interpersonal and cognitive change, on issues arising from closure and ending of therapy, and the rehearsal of a formulation-driven approach to detection and response to at-risk mental states for relapse. In order to address issues of separation and dependency that may have arisen during therapy, the frequency of sessions may be increased during this phase to one per week. Therapist and client collaborate on the development of both a narrative-based and diagrammatical formulation of relapse. This formulation lays down the basis for planned interventions in the event of an at-risk mental state for relapse. These interventions may involve targeted cognitive behavioural therapy (Gumley et al., 2003), key worker interventions or changes in prescribed medication (depending on the client's choice). It is vitally important that the end phase of treatment acknowledges the ending of the therapeutic relationship and the negative emotions associated with this. Often individuals in this client group are socially isolated and have had a number of negative interpersonal experiences. They therefore can be particularly vulnerable to feelings of loss and perceived rejection. It is essential, therefore, for the feelings and attributions associated with this loss to be recognised and dealt with within the therapeutic discourse.

SERVICE MODEL

Staying well therapy requires a co-ordinated multi-disciplinary response to clients' needs in relation to recovery, relapse detection and relapse prevention. It also seems to us to be unreasonable to work with a client to encourage and develop their help-seeking behaviours if the help that they receive isn't the help that they were seeking in the first instance. Designing services to best meet the needs of emotional recovery and staying well is an important but complex task. An important characteristic of our treatment protocol is that it is incorporated into a multi-disciplinary context. This requires a coherent and co-ordinated approach supporting clients' recovery and, importantly, to responding to crises. In relation to this, Goodwin et al. (2003) propose that a key function of multi-disciplinary teams is to facilitate a 'secure base' by providing continuity and consistency of care during acute and recovery phases, by providing sensitive and appropriate responses to affective distress, and by providing emotional containment during times of crisis. It is important to strike a balance between providing a reassuring supportive environment with encouragement to explore.

Desynchronous approaches to recovery, relapse detection and prevention have the potential to produce ruptures in therapeutic alliance. For example, the basic approach of staying well is the development of an accepting compassionate model of psychotic experiences. Catastrophic or anxiogenic responses by staff to the re-emergence of low-level psychotic experiences are therefore considered desynchronous within our approach to staying well therapy. An integral component of staying well is the provision of team-based multi-disciplinary training aimed at encouraging staff to reflect on their own beliefs, attributions and assumptions about recovery and relapse. Training focuses on helping staff identify and reflect on their own beliefs about psychosis, how they make attributions about clients, particularly during periods of high stress, how these attributions influence their own emotional and behavioural responses to relapse, and how these attributions interact with clients' beliefs, expectations and responses during periods of crisis. Training also focuses on providing key workers with the basic techniques and strategies described in this treatment manual. In particular, the aim here is to support the key workers' role in supporting the client particularly in the context of crises or at-risk mental states for relapse. Chapter 12 will focus on the role of the therapist, the client's key worker and the psychiatrist and others in delivering a co-ordinated, consistent approach to recovery.

CHAPTER 5

STRATEGIES FOR ENGAGEMENT AND FORMULATION

INTRODUCTION

Within all psychotherapeutic schools a positive therapeutic relationship is the cornerstone for the development of a constructive, kindly and empathic understanding of the key problems that have led to a person seeking help. This kind of understanding is also a prerequisite for the subsequent development of a meaningful collaborative working alliance, both for future positive change and problem resolution. For individuals who are experiencing or recovering from psychosis, the basis for this constructive and empathic interpersonal framework can be challenged, undermined and/or ruptured by (1) the surrounding mental health services and treatment context; (2) negative or traumatic experiences linked to psychosis or interactions with those mental health services; or (3) the interpersonal nature of particular psychotic experiences, particularly in terms of possible paranoid beliefs, suspiciousness or delusional thought content.

ATTACHMENT ORGANISATION, RECOVERY AND DISTRESS

It is also well documented that individuals with psychosis can be particularly difficult to engage in mental health services. Therapeutic engagement is particularly important given that following a first episode of psychosis there is a need for ongoing support and interventions in order to facilitate recovery and maintenance of well-being. However, even before contact with any mental health service, individuals often find that it is difficult for others to accurately understand their difficulties. They may have frequently found themselves faced with a lack of understanding and suspiciousness from others. For example, in a study looking at the mutual engagement of persons experiencing psychosis and general practitioners, McCabe et al. (2002) found that patients actively attempted to talk about the content of their psychotic symptoms in consultations, but in response their general practitioner often hesitated, responded with a question rather than with an answer, and smiled or laughed (when informal carers were present), indicating that they were reluctant to engage with patients' concerns about their psychotic symptoms.

A further challenge that arises following the initial resolution of an acute psychotic episode is that individuals are often found to withdraw from services and active treatments. Perhaps this arises from a wish to leave behind very painful and negative experiences, that the experiences themselves are emotionally overwhelming, or the person is attempting to escape from being a patient labelled with a mental illness. Linda Tait and her colleagues (2003) have explored this phenomenon among 62 persons recovering from acute psychosis. Strikingly, sealing over and integrating recovery styles were unstable over the medium term. Over six months there was a tendency for individuals to move from a predominantly integrating stance to a sealing-over position. Importantly, sealing over was not found to be related to psychotic symptoms or to insight. Tendency towards sealing over or the avoidance of the personally painful and difficult experiences linked to psychosis was predictive of subsequent levels of engagement at six months. Indeed, as symptoms and insight improved, individuals tended to become more sealing over.

This may suggest that as the person begins to reflect upon their experiences of psychosis, and the associated painful emotions or catastrophic life implications, they adopt a psychological and interpersonal strategy aimed at limiting, curtailing and encapsulating those experiences. In a subsequent analysis of these data, Tait et al. (2004) explored the hypothesis that individuals who seal over have greater psychological vulnerability and lowered resilience, defined by more negative beliefs about themselves, more problematic early parenting experiences and a less secure self-reported attachment attitude. Compared to integrators, individuals who sealed over had more negative views of themselves, felt more insecure, and rated their mothers and fathers as less caring and more abusive. In addition, individuals who used a sealing-over recovery style described their attitudes to attachment as less close, less dependable and rated themselves as having greater fear of rejection by others. Insecure attachment attitude was related to service engagement; that is, those who felt less close, had greater fear of rejection and saw others as less dependable were less engaged with services. Attachment attitudes correlated with parental bonding, where insecure attachment attitudes were related to more perceived parental abuse and less perceived parental care.

These data provide a helpful framework from which to view engagement, whereby individual attitudes to adult attachment (derived from early parental (attachment) experiences) mediate how individuals cope with their psychosis and engage with services. Consistent with this, John Gleeson and his colleagues (2005) found that agreeableness as measured by the NEO Personality Inventory – Revised (NEO-PI-R: Costa & McCrae, 1992) was predictive of staying well after psychosis. That is, individuals who were more sympathetic to others, more prepared to offer help and believed that others were more likely to reciprocate, remained stable and remitted following a first episode of psychosis. The reciprocal of this is that individuals rated low on agreeableness were more likely to be readmitted to hospital.

However, interpretation of these data on the relationship between engagement, sealing over, parental bonding and attachment attitudes can be problematic. Insecure attachment is not a single construct and those who use sealing over may have very different and contrasting states of mind with respect to adult attachment. Those with an insecure attachment organisation may be preoccupied with attachment relationships or, in contrast, dismissing or minimising of attachment. Each of these subgroups acknowledge and respond to distress in quite different ways. Individuals who are securely attached develop metacognitive knowledge that emotions can be experienced and safely regulated, and indeed have greater competence in regulating emotion. However, individuals who are insecurely attached tend to have experienced inconsistent or rejecting responses to their negative emotions. These experiences interfere with the development of metacognitive knowledge and emotion regulation competencies. Individuals with preoccupied attachment styles tend to have experienced inconsistent or rejecting experiences that would draw a child's attention towards attachment. Those with a dismissing or avoidant attachment style avoid close relationships, and minimise or deny emotions and distress. Often, these individuals will have learned that seeking out others during times of distress has been ineffective.

Dozier and Lee (1995) investigated 76 individuals who were diagnosed with schizophrenia or bipolar disorder in order to examine how attachment organisation as measured by the Adult Attachment Interview (AAI: Main et al., 1985) was associated with individuals' self-report of psychiatric symptoms and quality of life. Those individuals with preoccupied styles tended to report more symptoms and greater distress than those with dismissing/avoidant styles. However, in contrast, raters reported those with dismissing styles as more symptomatic (i.e. more delusional and more likely to hear voices) than those with preoccupied styles. The desynchrony between experience and expression of distress has important implications for recovery style and engagement. It may be that there are two (or more) sub-groups of individuals who seal over. One group may seal over because they are anxious and fearful and experience attachment as potentially threatening via fears of rejection. This group is likely to report greater distress but be less likely to seek help and engage. Another group may seal over because they are dismissing and avoidant of attachment and regulate distress by minimising or avoiding others. This group is likely to report not being distressed despite appearances to the contrary, and will be more likely to resist engagement.

Dozier (1990) found that this group of dismissing individuals were more rejecting of help and less disclosing of problems. Indeed, it is very interesting that clinicians with heavy caseloads report their dismissing clients as less problematic than their clients who are rated as preoccupied (Dozier, 1990). Therefore, during the process of engagement and formulation, it is important that the person's probable state of mind with respect to adult attachment is considered in the context of recovery style; and that the engagement process is calibrated to be responsive to this. For example, clients who are dismissing become distressed when they are unable to distract discussion away from interpersonal issues (Dozier & Lomax, 1994), yet present a mask of invulnerability. The process of engagement, the development of a problem list and the focus on affect need to be carefully calibrated to optimise engagement. It is important for the therapist to be aware that attachment is an outcome and the processes of careful engagement can enable an optimal therapeutic attachment, bonding and alliance to be achieved.

This interplay between individuals' models of self, models of others and dependence on, or avoidance of, others has been conceptualised by Bartholomew (1990) (Figure 5.1). This is a helpful system for therapists to think about their client's state of mind with respect to adult attachment and the kinds of challenges that may be implied for engagement and formulation. These working models of self and others define four styles of attachment, which include two avoidant styles: dismissing and fearful. Dismissing individuals emphasise self-reliance at the expense of trust and intimacy, whereas fearful individuals desire intimacy but distrust others; they avoid close relationships because they may lead to loss and rejection.

Of course, practising psychotherapy using an attachment paradigm is not new (Harris, 2004), but for the purposes of this therapy manual, attachment theory is valuable in enabling therapists to rise to the challenge of engage-

		MODEL OF SELF (Dependence)	
		POSITIVE (Low)	NEGATIVE (High)
MODEL OF OTHER (Avoidance)	POSITIVE (Low)	SECURE	PREOCCUPIED
	NEGATIVE (High)	DISMISSING	FEARFUL

Figure 5.1   The four attachment styles defined by Bartholomew in terms of working models of self and others

ment following psychosis and incorporating a formulation of avoidant recovery strategies within the context of the therapeutic relationship. Tirril Harris (2004) helps us reflect on the relevance of attachment theory as a basis for understanding inner and outer worlds, and how individuals' internal working models (IWMs) interact with the responses of others in the external world (Figure 5.2). This helps us to reframe our roles as psychotherapists to reflect our position as agents occupying clients' outer worlds, from which we can help begin to influence clients' IWMs. The most outstanding example of this in cognitive psychotherapy for individuals with psychotic experiences is the impact of the befriending condition in Sensky and colleagues' (2000) randomised controlled trial of cognitive behavioural therapy (CBT) for drug refractory schizophrenia. Befriending produced clinical changes over nine months of the same magnitude as CBT. However, once befriending was withdrawn, those clinical changes were reversed.

A number of authors, including Jeremy Holmes (2003), Tirril Harris (2004) and Robert Leahy (2005), have emphasised the importance of tailoring therapy style to attachment style in the first few months of therapy. Our clinical experiences have led us to feel that such an approach is extremely helpful in supporting recovery from psychosis. In this context, there are two central therapeutic processes involved in the development of engagement and therapeutic alliance: *validation* and *formulation*. It is via the process of combining validation and formulation that the framework of therapeutic bonding, agreement of personal goals and mutuality of tasks (to enable the person to reach those goals) evolves. As stated in Chapter 4, the process of formulation is layered: the formulation evolves in step with the therapeutic bond

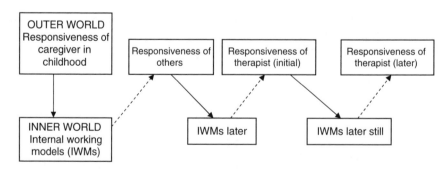

Figure 5.2 Interaction between inner and outer world

Note: Dotted line: impact of inner world on outer world; continuous line: impact of outer world on inner world.

Source: From Harms (2004). Chef or chemist? Practicing psychotherapy within the attachment paradigm. *Attachment and Human Development*, 6(2), 191–207.

priorities and the evolution of the person's goals. For example, during the initial stages, formulation is used to strengthen therapeutic bonding, whereas, later, formulation might be used to highlight important therapeutic tasks or to identify the relationship between historical events and current problems, which was also highlighted in the therapeutic relationship itself.

VALIDATION

Validation has been defined as 'finding the truth in what we feel and think – [it] stands as the fulcrum between *empathy* (where we recognise the feeling that another person has) and *compassion* (whereby we feel with and for another person and care about the suffering of that person)' (Leahy, 2005, p. 195). Leahy (2005) has recently described a social cognitive model of validation, constructed within a context that incorporates an understanding of therapeutic alliance in the context of the person's attachment organisation (see Figure 5.3).

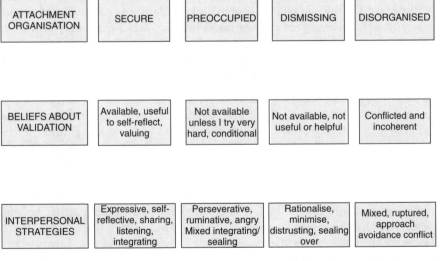

Figure 5.3   Relation between attachment organisation, beliefs about validation and interpersonal strategies

Source: Adapted from Leahy (2005). A social-cognitive model of validation. In P Gilbert (ed.), *Compassion, conceptualisations, research and use in psychotherapy*. London and New York, Routledge, pp. 195–217.

The above model is predicated upon the basis that from our early parenting and attachment experiences we develop emotional schemata (Leahy, 2005). It is hypothesised that emotional schemas are characterised by a number of dimensions including beliefs about *validation by others*, *comprehensibility* of emotions, *guilt* about negative emotions, beliefs about *conflicting emotions* (*simplistic views of emotion*), *uncontrollability of emotions*, and *acceptance of feelings*.

Attachment systems are designed to facilitate proximity seeking, protection and care, and emotional validation: the basis of any explorative behaviour and productive self-reflection. Difficult attachment experiences may lead to the development of problematic interpersonal styles where the seeking or avoidance of validation may result in the maintenance of emotional distress, increased self-focus, or even rejecting behaviour from others. In this context, coping strategies have important interpersonal consequences. Therefore, particular interpersonal coping styles may be problematic for the person (see Figure 5.3). Optimal psychological development, via a secure attachment organisation, will enable a person to develop positive beliefs about their positive and negative emotions being comprehensible, meaningful and valid. These positive beliefs about emotions facilitate greater expression, learning, greater sense of control and reduced duration of painful emotions (Leahy, 2002). In contrast, those with preoccupied or avoidant attachment organisations view their emotions as problematic, negative or unacceptable, thus leading to difficulties in responding to and regulating emotion. For example, a person with an avoidant state of mind towards attachment may seal over, minimise, use substances or be more prone to dissociation. Conversely, a person with a preoccupied state of mind towards attachment may adopt worrying and rumination as strategies to manage difficult emotions.

Peter Fonagy and colleagues (2004) have argued that the capacity to mentalise is a key determinant of self-organisation and affect regulation, and this capacity to mentalise is acquired in the context of early social and attachment relationships. Fonagy and colleagues have operationalised mentalisation, that is, the capacity to interpret one's own and others' behaviour by attributing mental states, as reflective function. Reflective function refers to an intentional stance characterised by an interpersonal awareness that experiences give rise to certain beliefs and emotions, and that particular beliefs, desires and intentions tend to result in certain kinds of behaviour. This stance is essential in the creation of a continuity of self-experience, forming the underpinning of a *coherent* self-structure. Reflective function has its roots in the development of children's mental states. It then is developed within an interpersonal environment that is characterised by a network of complex and often emotionally charged relationships. In this context, self-reflective capacity becomes essential to the development of metacognitive thinking and affect regulation. Validation is important in the development of self-reflective functioning, as the child's representation and regulation of affect evolves via dynamic attachment interactions. This is termed representational mapping; meta-representations of self-experienced affect and the emotions of others, coupled with the exchange of affect during interactions, provide a unique source of information to the child regarding their own mental states and the mental states of others. As an illustration of this dynamic process, Fonagy et al. (1995) found that mothers who soothe their distressed infants following an injection rapidly reflect their child's emotion using more complex and incompatible affects (for example, smiling and questioning), thus producing analogous *but not identical* emotions.

These important theoretical developments provide important insights into the use of validation, and the development of self-reflection within a developing therapeutic alliance following psychosis. It is particularly striking that psychosis provokes appraisals of loss, and is experienced by many as traumatic. Therefore, when engaging the person following psychosis, the therapist needs to appreciate the person's social and developmental experiences, in combination with the specific meanings linked to psychotic experiences. The robust establishment of reflective function promotes resilience whereas fragile reflective function predicts greater vulnerability. For example, early trauma, impoverished social development and relationships, which may include emotional neglect, may mean that the social scaffolding necessary for the development of reflective function or coherent emotional schemata has been largely absent. In these contexts, the person may be more vulnerable to the development of negative or persecutory appraisals of the mental states of others in the context of an impoverished sense of one's own self-worth.

The experience of psychosis and the negative interpersonal nature of psychotic experiences (e.g. persecutory paranoia or command-type hallucinations) reflect underlying negative interpersonal schemata, and thus psychosis is processed as a life event that is confirmatory of earlier life experiences. In contrast, social and psychological development in the context of optimal circumstances, where the caregiver(s) and other important social relationships provide an optimal or indeed 'good enough' sensitive reflection (enabling the development of an explorative, secure and self-reflective self), is likely to provide the individual with a resilience to adapt to the psychological, emotional, social and interpersonal demands of psychotic experiences. However, it may be that the severity or consequences of psychosis serve to undermine the person's beliefs about the self, world, future and others or rupture important dimensions of emotional schemata. Two contrasting case examples illustrate these points:

Bill

Bill was referred during his second episode of psychosis. He was living in an acute psychiatric ward, detained under the Mental Health Act, and was described as having persisting persecutory paranoia characterised by a persisting hostile and angry attitude towards staff and particularly his psychiatrist. He was described as having persecutory delusions where the government, the police, social services and mental health services were conspiring to cause him psychological harm. He had been involuntarily tranquillised on two occasions. Nursing staff felt threatened by him. Bill denied having any difficulties concerning anger, hostility and paranoia. When challenged, he would become increasingly paranoid, extremely angry and threatening to staff and others that he perceived as being involved in his persecution.

Engagement began with a suggestion to carefully explore his experiences, with the explicit aim of developing a shared understanding. During the initial session the therapist carefully explored Bill's feelings of being traumatised, humiliated and trapped on the ward. At the end of the first session, his crisis of being detained on the ward was framed as an impasse leading to feelings of entrapment and humiliation. The therapist expressed the wish to explore in greater detail the events leading up to his detention in hospital. Bill agreed to meet over three further occasions. During these sessions the therapist worked carefully with Bill to build and elaborate the story of the events leading to his second admission to hospital. The therapist carefully encouraged self-reflection on these events, their impact on his thoughts, feelings and behaviour, and the impact on others' thoughts, feelings and behaviour. This gave rise to opportunities for the therapist to validate his emotional experiences and support his reflection on painful emotional events. Bill was able to begin to reflect on long-standing painful feelings of loneliness and social isolation, whether at home or at school, in particular, the absence of key attachment figures and peer relationships. As the sense of trust and openness began to evolve, the therapist began to encourage Bill to reflect on the development of therapeutic alliance, bonding and trust. This was helpful in encouraging Bill to reflect upon contrasting different and inconsistent interpersonal experiences. Bill and the therapist began to consider how they could use their alliance to help Bill communicate more effectively with others, particularly ward staff and his family.

Patricia

Patricia contacted her therapist six months after completion of a phase of cognitive therapy following her first episode. Patricia had noticed feeling greater levels of depression, pressured thinking, inability to concentrate and feelings of suspiciousness, including ideas of reference. Patricia attributed these experiences to the possibility of a relapse and return of her voices. She felt that she had taken her 'eye off the ball', and had started drinking and clubbing too much. She felt that she was mentally ill and had an image of seeing herself in the future alone and dejected. Her speech was pressured, confused, ruminative and preoccupied. Over the initial three sessions, the therapist encouraged emotional expression, reflection on feelings and their connections to events. A key theme was her sense of pressure to achieve on behalf of her family. She then began to talk of the loss of her mother three months earlier. The therapist worked carefully and gently with Patricia to consider the relationship between her feelings of loss, feelings of depression and her pressure to achieve. Patricia began to reflect on how the loss of her mother had placed on her a sense of responsibility for the care of her father and the necessity for her not to tolerate or accept negative emotions. With this construction of the complex interplay of affects, Patricia's pressure of speech and incoherence of narrative began to subside.

THE EVOLUTION OF THERAPEUTIC DISCOURSE

During the process of engagement, and indeed throughout therapy, the therapeutic discourse aims to attune to the person's emotional experience and to support the person in experiencing emotions and developing a self-reflective personal narrative. Within this narrative, the therapist and client can explore the development of a sense of the client's own personal agency and control. The speed at which this process proceeds will depend on a number of factors including the therapeutic alliance, the person's ability to attune to negative affect, the degree to which the person has been traumatised by their psychosis and the possible presence of other traumatic and loss-related events if these refer to present complaints. Trauma and loss can disrupt the development of a coherent narrative and care should be taken in accessing strong negative affect. The therapist needs to work conscientiously with the client, and to carefully consider the client's ability to regulate strong negative affect in the context of the therapeutic relationship. Therefore, during the engagement phase therapist and client may prioritise working with the client's appraisals and response to emotion.

Cognitive therapy has traditionally focused on the content of the client's discourse, such as a person's expression of the idea that they are unloved and that others are untrustworthy. The therapeutic discourse then focuses on how these beliefs have evolved over time and the psychological, interpersonal and environmental factors that maintain these beliefs. This process of exploration is helpful in the crafting and development of alternative explanatory models of experience. However, the *construction* of the client's discourse is also of importance. The construction of discourse describes how narratives develop during therapeutic interactions, the form and structure of the expression of ideas. This would also include the way in which difficult aspects of client narrative are approached by the therapist. Consider the following example where a client is encouraged to reflect on the quality of their peer relationships prior to the development of psychosis:

Th = therapist; *C* = client

Th: Tell me more about those friends you had at college.
C: They all had an easy time, they could laugh and joke about others around them and they would always find it easy to do their work and have a good time. They asked me out all the time, and would always wonder why I was quiet.
Th: How did you get to know them?
C: They were the cool people in the class and they had a lot of fun.
Th: They seem to be an interesting bunch. Did you speak to them when you joined that class?
C: No, I couldn't. I was put into the same study group . . .

Reflecting on this short discourse, we notice how the person makes negative comparisons between themselves ('I was quiet') and their friends ('they had a lot of fun'). In so doing, their relative lack of sense of personal agency is reflected in the statement 'They asked me out all the time'. It is interesting that the person then makes a negative self-evaluation. Rather than focusing on the cognitive contents of this evaluation, the therapist pursues their sense of agency by asking 'How did you get to know them?' Again, the person responds by giving a positive evaluation of others, perhaps avoiding focusing on the self. This is further reflected in the form in which the narrative unfolds between the individual and the therapist. There is little sense of a consistent and flowing recollection. Rather, it appears a stilted and incomplete account. The therapeutic task at hand is perhaps to pursue the development of a fresh reflective autobiographical narrative:

Th: Can you remember the first time you spoke to them?
C: No . . .
Th: Try to think of the first time your study group met together and you were in the same room.

C: . . . I wasn't sure what to say. I can't remember what we were working on but didn't know how to start. They seemed confused too. They laughed about the lecturer and his polo neck jumper. I thought they were funny, but I felt nervous too . . .

It is helpful at points like this to persevere with particular situations and support the unfolding of a more active account where the focus is on the person as an agent in the situation, which will ultimately aid development of a more coherent narrative of themselves.

CASE FORMULATION

General Principles

The development of an individualised formulation of a person's problems, their emotional distress and interpersonal difficulties lies at the core of cognitive therapy. Rather than being a closed and final explanation of the origins and maintenance of a particular problem or series of problems, the formulation is an open, collaboratively developed working model of the person's adaptation to, and recovery from, the distressing experiences of a psychotic episode. The formulation is functional in that it helps the person and their therapist to agree the goals and tasks for therapy. In this sense, therefore, an active and dynamic formulation drives the evolution of psychological therapy and develops as the treatment unfolds. New and emerging information is added to and incorporated within the collaborative working model. In this way, over time, a comprehensive formulation should help to make sense of an individual's difficulties at different levels of their functioning, their problematic interpersonal strategies and interactions as well as their symptomatic and emotional experiences.

Understanding the antecedents to and circumstances at the onset of psychotic experiences can be invaluable in establishing the origin of the personal beliefs and convictions that might have developed subsequently. Developing a narrative incorporating the individual's personal history and experiences throughout the lifespan can aid the discovery of relevant factors and possible precipitators. This process seeks to actively engage the individual in the development of an understanding of their difficulties. Case formulation provides a conceptual framework to represent individuals' psychological difficulties and provides the basis for assessment and therapy planning. Persons (1989) conceptualises psychological problems as occurring at two levels: *overt difficulties* and *underlying psychological mechanisms*. Overt difficulties are the problems that clients present with such as depression, interpersonal problems, procrastination, social anxiety or body image. Overt difficulties can be broken down into their component parts including: specific emotions (e.g. embarrassment, fear and shame), behaviours (e.g. pleasing others, avoidance, passivity) and thoughts (e.g. views of self, others, world and future). Underlying psychological mechanisms are the hypothesised psychological structures, processes or difficulties that underlie and cause overt difficulties. In this way, the case formulation can help make problems appear more cohesive and coherent in that an understanding of the underlying processes can help to synthesise a number of problems in a few problem areas with a common underlying mechanism. The formulation can further highlight the connection between these problem areas and, in particular, a developmental case formulation regarding the genesis of particular difficulties can provide a comprehensive and manageable framework for the understanding of complex difficulties that might appear extremely overwhelming and all-engulfing.

Another important constructive component of any case formulation is the clear implication for treatment and specific intervention strategies and techniques. Case formulation aims to help a person to prioritise what feels most important or essential at the time. It will also highlight connections and interdependence between emotions and certain interactions or behaviours that will help to prioritise certain areas for intervention. It will often appear that treatment progress is not being achieved within an anticipated time frame or that patients might find it a lot harder than expected to make certain agreed changes or to implement particular strategies. These roadblocks are important way markers to refine and re-evaluate both formulation and the related intervention strategies.

Paul Chadwick and his colleagues (2003) investigated the impact of case formulation in psychosis. The case formulation was comprised of a diagram and an accompanying letter. The diagrammatic formulation contained an analysis of problem maintenance (that is, the links between thoughts, feelings, physiology and behaviour), triggers to the current problem, the onset of the current problem (or critical incidents), underlying assumptions, core beliefs and key formative experiences. The accompanying letter described the case formulation using, as far as possible, the person's own words. It described possible targets for therapy, raised the idea that the person's delusional beliefs were not factual but were ways of making sense of experience, and finally identified possible risks to the therapeutic alliance. Case formulation did not improve self-rated therapeutic alliance (as measured by the Helping Alliance Questionnaire: Alexander & Luborsky, 1986), although case formulation had a significant impact on the therapist's rating of alliance. Case formulation did not reduce anxiety or depression. Of the 18 participants, 9 found the case formulation helpful, 6 felt reassured, encouraged and more hopeful and 3 felt that their therapist understood them. Six participants reported negative emotional reactions, particularly in response to seeing the duration, chronicity and origins of their problems. While case formulation did not produce changes in those variables measured, this does not mean that case formulation has no value. In fact, we need to think in functional terms about the role of case formulation in achieving a number of different tasks, over the course of therapy, tailored to the person's state of mind with respect to attachment. This is the governing principle of case formulation in this therapy manual.

CASE FORMULATION IN SWAP

In the development of case formulation, therapists need to reflect on a number of important questions. For example, what purpose does case formulation serve at this point in therapy? What elements of the case formulation are important to emphasise? What are the potential positive and negative reactions that could be evoked by the formulation? Should I use a diagrammatical formulation or a formulation letter? These questions encourage the therapist to think about the strategic importance and the interpersonal context of case formulation. During the early stages of engagement, which may take place over a period of three months, a key strategic goal of case formulation is to underpin alliance and engagement. In order to achieve this important goal, there are a number of core features of case formulation that should be considered:

- *A statement of the person's problems and their associated goals.* This should be written as much as possible to reflect the person's own language and narrative using quotations derived from the therapeutic discourse.
- *Validation of the person's distress.* The therapist takes the opportunity to attune to the person's distress and contextualise their experience. The therapist's role here is to communicate a compassionate interpretative framework. This is important because individuals may frequently use their problems as evidence for their negative self-evaluation. For example, notice the contrast between the appraisals 'my depression is a sign of my defectiveness' versus 'my depression has evolved as an understandable reaction to being hospitalised'.
- *The therapist's hypothesis about the underlying psychological mechanisms.* Consistent with Persons (1989), the case formulation contains a statement hypothesising what the underlying psychological mechanisms are that are maintaining the person's problems, blocking recovery or increasing vulnerability to relapse. The focus of the formulation is attuned to the client's recovery style, attachment organisation, and their ability to regulate affect. As an example, for clients who use a sealing-over recovery style and who are fearfully preoccupied or avoidant of their attachments, the therapist takes care in judging the amount of affect that may be generated by hypothesising that problematic early childhood relationships that underpin their current problems. Clearly such a formulation is likely to draw the client's attention to attachment relationships in a way that

generates negative affect. Drawing a client's attention in this way early in the process of engagement may counter-productively lead to increased fearful preoccupation with attachment figures, including the therapist.

- *Valuing the alliance.* This is a statement which draws the client's attention to the value of the therapeutic relationship. This may simply be a statement of the therapist's value of the alliance, or a reflection of discourse that has taken place within therapy.

- *A statement of tasks.* This is a further statement, which sets out the proposed tasks of therapy. These may be planned for the short, medium or longer term. These tasks are licensed by the interplay between the client's problems and goals and the therapist's hypothesis of the underlying mechanisms.

Case Example

An example of the formulation letter sent to Bill is given below. During the therapeutic discourse, the therapist noted how Bill idealised members of his family but at the same time he was simultaneously derogating of them and of others. She noted how Bill had long-standing difficulties forming relationships with others. Furthermore, she noted Bill's extreme feelings of anger, humiliation and suspiciousness, although Bill himself would not accept that he felt angry or suspicious of others. The therapist wished to strengthen the therapeutic alliance and promote the idea of a shared approach to recovery. Thus the key elements of formulation were: (1) validation and contextualising distress; (2) communication of a compassionate understanding of Bill's distress; and (3) development of a shared task agenda.

Dear Bill,

Recently we have talked more about what it feels like for you to be on the ward. You described feeling upset, angry and stuck. You described your main problem just now as being sectioned, having to take medication, being stuck on the ward. You also feel strongly that your key worker and doctor won't listen to you. The most distressing problem is being stuck on the ward. You often feel overwhelmed especially when you think about how you got into hospital and being jagged against your will. You get overwhelmed at your weekly review meeting. So many thoughts and feelings have been running around in your mind. This makes it difficult for you to communicate clearly with others. You have told me how you had fallen out with your advocate because they hadn't understood your viewpoint. It seems to me that we have been able to talk about some of your experiences and I feel we get on well. I wondered whether an important task for us to consider is to work together to learn how to help you to keep your cool and let other people know what you think, even when other people might disagree with you, such as your doctor.

A Therapist

Diagrammatical Formulation

The therapist may or may not decide to use a diagrammatical formulation illustrating the proposed mechanisms underpinning the evolution and maintenance of problems. It is useful for the therapist to rehearse the advantages and disadvantages of using basic/maintenance formulations versus historical formulations. Basic/maintenance formulations describe how psychological factors such as beliefs and behaviours maintain emotional distress or prevent disconfirmation of the person's beliefs. An example is given in Figure 5.4 showing how the person's interpretation of her voice-hearing experiences leads to feelings of fear and anger, and how her behavioural responses might inadvertently maintain her belief that she is powerless and must comply or, at least in this case, partially comply with the voice requests.

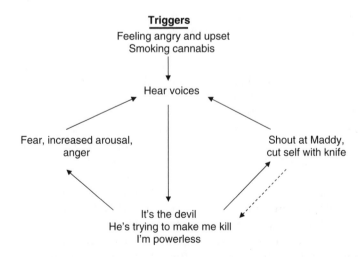

Figure 5.4   Example of maintenance formulation
Source: From Morrison (2001). The interpretation of intrusions in psychosis: an integrative cognitive approach to hallucinations and delusions. *Behavioural and Cognitive Psychotherapy*, **29**, 257–276.

Advantages of basic diagrammatic formulation are that it is focused in the here and now, makes processes involved in the maintenance of distress explicit and breaks down a problem into its component parts. Historical formulations, in contrast, provide greater and more complex information, and identify underlying, possibly long-standing difficulties. On the other hand, historical formulations can be overwhelming, re-open issues that have been previously closed, generate substantial affect, but also may be experienced as reductionist and over-simplifying.

Our experience is that keeping the formulation faithful to the agreed problem and goals and specifying the tasks of therapy in that context is most beneficial. In this sense, importing earlier experiences into the formulation is licensed by the client's reference to that as a relevant factor in therapeutic progress, rather than attempting to formulate the whole of the complex presentation and history which might make the client's difficulties appear intangible within the therapeutic context. In saying this, it is useful if the therapist is mindful of the impact of earlier experiences on the evolution of the therapeutic discourse and the client's interpersonal stance. This aids the therapist in tailoring engagement, reflection and emotional discourse during therapy.

CONCLUSIONS

The key aim of engagement and formulation is the development of a shared and collaborative discourse that is carefully attuned to the client's emotional experiences. During this discourse the therapist carefully crafts the engagement process to be sensitive to the interplay between recovery style, attachment organisation and the therapeutic relationship. It is critical here to explore the nature of the client's problems, their goals and to communicate a compassionate and validating working model. In facilitating such a discourse, the therapist can then begin to provide the necessary scaffolding to enable the evolution of a self-reflective narrative that enables the development of a client's sense of agency, control and hope. This narrative is a self-accepting one where negative affect allows therapist and client to collaborate on the development of experiential meanings. In this sense, cognitive interpersonal therapy does not seek to dispute, rationalise or disconfirm the client's beliefs and interpersonal behaviours. This can be fundamentally invalidating. Rather, the development of a shared, compassionate, self-reflective formulation embedded in the client's experiences provides a platform for the client to choose and strengthen alternative perspectives and interpersonal coping. In this text we propose to illustrate the therapeutic techniques through the description of four therapeutic scenarios. Each are described below.

PART III

SPECIFIC COGNITIVE AND INTERPERSONAL STRATEGIES FOR RECOVERY AND RELAPSE PREVENTION AFTER PSYCHOSIS

CHAPTER 6

REORGANISATION OF THE SELF IN RECOVERY: WORKING WITH HUMILIATION, ENTRAPMENT AND LOSS

INTRODUCTION

> The effect of powerful and oppressive experiences (or shattering life events, such as psychotic illness) . . . initiates an internal defensive mechanism that forces the individual to 'down-rank' and yield to others, particularly if escape is blocked (entrapment). This mechanism may be accompanied by cognitions that are 'self-attacking' leading to feelings of inferiority and self-blame. (Birchwood et al., 2000b)

Birchwood and colleagues (1993, 1998, 2000a, 2000b) have successfully established the importance of life event dimensions in emotional adaptation to psychosis. In the case of Post-Psychotic Depression (PPD), Birchwood and colleagues (2000a) have shown that PPD occurs independently of changes in other problems associated with psychosis including positive and negative symptoms. In addition, development of PPD is linked to negative appraisals of shame, humiliation, entrapment and loss arising from the experience of psychosis (Birchwood et al., 1993; Rooke & Birchwood, 1998; Iqbal et al., 2000b), higher levels of insight (Iqbal et al., 2000b) and lowered self-esteem (Birchwood et al., 1993; Iqbal et al., 2000b). Gumley et al. (2004) reported that individuals with social anxiety disorder in the context of psychosis have greater feelings of self-blame, entrapment, shame and lowered self-esteem. Gumley and colleagues (Karatzias et al., in submission) have also investigated the incidence of co-morbidity in a group of 144 individuals with psychosis using the Structured Clinical Interview for DSM-IV (First et al., 1997). Of this group 47.2 per cent were experiencing either an anxiety disorder (e.g. obsessive-compulsive disorder (OCD), generalised anxiety, panic, social anxiety) or an affective disorder (e.g. major depression). In this group, lowered self-esteem and a heightened sense of entrapment were both associated with the presence of a concurrent psychological disorder.

LIFE EVENTS AND THEIR DIMENSIONS

This line of research has its theoretical origins in the life events tradition (Brown & Harris, 1978, 1995). Drawing on both the life events and social ranking literatures (e.g. Gilbert, 1992; Brown et al., 1996; Kendler et al., 2003), the key dimensions of stressful life events appear to be related to loss (Brown & Harris, 1978), humiliation (Farmer & McGuffin, 2003; Kendler et al., 2003), entrapment (Harris et al., 1987) and danger (Kendler et al., 2003). Furthermore, implicit within the definition of a 'severe life event' is the understanding that there is a degree of perceived threat inherent within the event. We will now address the conceptualisation of each of these dimensions in turn.

George Brown and colleagues (1995) have extended the concept of loss outwards from death and separation only to embrace loss of role (e.g. worker, partner, parent) or loss of a cherished idea (e.g. partner in a stable relationship). Loss, according to this definition, is a 'diminution of a sense of connectedness or well-being potentially covering every aspect of life' (quoted in Kendler et al., 2003). Indeed, the utilisation of this wider definition of a 'loss' experience has been successfully shown to illustrate the depressogenic quality of stressful life events (Brown et al., 1995; Kendler et al., 2003). In the context of psychosis, loss may involve loss of friendships and relationships, perceived current and future status, or loss of role.

Danger relates to a prospective dimension, which hinges on an individual's perception that with the occurrence of an event there is an accompanying likelihood of recurrence. Alternatively, the event can also signal the beginning of a series of consequences that are unpleasant or threatening to the individual (Brown & Harris, 1996). In psychosis, fear of relapse and recurrence are often associated with high levels of anxiety and avoidance. On the other hand, the stigmatising nature of psychosis can mean that the person becomes fearful that friends, family, employers and work colleagues will discover that the person has experienced psychosis.

Within a life events framework, humiliation has been defined as a feeling of being devalued or 'put down', with consequential negative effects upon the self-concept (Brown, 2002). Inherent within this construct is an interpersonal evaluation. In the context of psychosis, humiliation may arise from events such as compulsory admission, the feeling that neighbours and others are judging the person critically, or perhaps through the experience of specific symptoms such as voices.

Entrapment is defined as an appraisal of a situation or event as having ongoing negative consequences or ramifications that will, at best, persist, and may well deteriorate. In the context of psychosis, feelings of entrapment are likely to arise from the experience of repeated relapse/re-hospitalisation or persisting psychotic experiences.

These dimensions can also be considered with reference to evolutionary theory, particularly as expressed in Paul Gilbert's social ranking theory (Gilbert, 1989, 1992). For instance, loss, be it of a significant other, via death or separation, or of a cherished idea, may well have a social consequence in terms of diminution of 'Social Attention-Holding Power' (SAHP: Gilbert, 1989). This evolutionary construct refers to the way in which individuals need to present an outward façade of the self as desirable and attractive to others (both in the physical and social sense), the aim being to persuade other people to invest in us. The consequences of positive SAHP include being perceived as having social status or being liked, valued, respected and wanted (Gilbert, 1997; Sloman et al., 2003). Conversely, the consequences of perceiving that one has low SAHP include low self-esteem, withdrawal and avoidance; one feels of little or no social value.

Second, events or difficulties can directly attack one's sense of self by forcing the person into a subordinate position. For example, an abusive relationship often entails the abused individual being forced to submit and subjugate to a more powerful other. This sense of disempowerment has a direct impact on self-esteem (Gilbert, 1989, 1992).

Third, entrapment can be explained in social ranking terms as a 'blocked escape' (Gilbert, 1989). The dimensions of the event are such that the individual is 'confined' by it. The sense of confinement or restriction relates to being stuck in a socially marginalised and subordinate role. This often results in the person's perception of having fewer internal resources available to escape from this situation or to alleviate distress. In addition, their reduced perceived relative attractiveness to others means that there is a concomitant loss of interpersonal resources available to assist escape.

Influential though these dimensions are individually, there is also considerable interaction between them. Brown and colleagues (1995) proposed that although all of the above dimensions encompass a socio-interpersonal defeat, the depressogenic effect is more marked where the dimensions overlap or accumulate. Often a severe negative life event will encompass several dimensional boundaries. For example, loss of employment through dismissal encompasses feelings of loss of a valued role and the loss of relationship with others, danger via financial, social and interpersonal repercussions, and humiliation due to being subject to the undesired decisions of powerful others. Indeed, they go on to propose a hierarchy for the dimensional meaning of an event. In this hierarchy, humiliation, via other-initiated separation, others' delinquency or 'put down', is given primacy, followed by entrapment, loss and finally danger.

The key role of humiliating or entrapping severe life events in depression has been confirmed by Brown et al. (1995). In this sample, 85 per cent of those who developed depression had a severe life event in the six months preceding onset, with three-quarters of those experiencing an event that was humiliating or entrapping. These events often encapsulated loss. Similar results were recorded in a patient series already receiving treatment for depression. A loss event via death or separation without associated humiliation or entrapment was involved in 22 per cent of depressive episodes. Finally, results also suggested that many events involved a loss of an individual's sense of control. In a study of 7,322 twins, Kendler and colleagues (2003) investigated life event dimensions as predictors of major depression, generalised anxiety and mixed episodes of anxiety and depression. High threat events were significantly associated with the onset of any emotional distress. Risk of developing depression or mixed anxiety and depression was higher in the context of loss- and humiliation-related life events. One month following the life event occurrence, ratings of entrapment and danger predicted the onset of mixed anxiety and depression. Risk of developing generalised anxiety was higher in the context of loss and danger life events. Three months following the life event occurrence, generalised anxiety was only predicted by ratings of danger. Therefore, in understanding the onset of anxiety and depression, we need to consider: (1) the overlap of dimensions within life events; and (2) the depressogenic and anxiogenic potential of ratings of loss, entrapment, humiliation and danger.

We now must ask whether life event dimensions map onto psychosis. Birchwood and colleagues (1993, 1998, 2000), investigating psychological mechanisms underlying the development of PPD, re-conceptualised psychosis as a severe life event, the appraisal of which precipitates a depressive reaction. In the original (1993) cross-sectional sample, 29 per cent of patients diagnosed with schizophrenia had co-morbid depression. The key discriminating factor between depressed and non-depressed psychotic patients was perceived control over illness, with lack of control over illness being linked to depression. This was later re-labelled as entrapment in subsequent studies. This is entirely consistent with Beck's (1976) conceptualisation of hopelessness relating to an external locus of control, whereby the individual perceives himself or herself to have no control over external events. On a methodological note, in contrast to the objective rating of the severity and dimensions of life events by Brown and Harris (1978), the cited psychosis studies relied on the participant's self-report of appraisals of psychosis in general rather than relating to a specific situation or event.

A subsequent follow-up analysis, involving 47 of the original 49 participants, further expanded the notion of psychosis as a severe life event (Rooke & Birchwood, 1998). The results suggested a consistent stable prevalence of depression in the psychosis sample. Moreover, in depressed psychosis patients there was also stability in self-report of loss of social role and autonomy and in locating responsibility for psychosis within the self (self-blame). Entrapment (in the sense of lack of control over psychosis) was predicted by entrapment rating at baseline, plus compulsory admission status. The authors attribute these results to the secondary social 'knock-on' effects of experiencing a psychosis, such as compulsory admission, loss of employment, status and stigma. They also emphasise the capacity that psychosis has to seriously limit both personal and interpersonal achievements.

Further work in a larger (n=105) longitudinal sample (Birchwood et al., 2000; Iqbal et al., 2000) replicated these results, and also linked low self-esteem to PPD. Iqbal and colleagues suggest that a social ranking model (Gilbert, 1992) explains these findings, through conceptualising psychosis as an overpowering event, forcing down-ranking and submission, which then becomes entrapping via the 'knock-on' effects mentioned above. They also refer to Lazarus and Folkman's (1984) proposal that highlights the initial emotional reactions which accompany catastrophic life events such as anger, disbelief and depression. Individuals' emotional reactions to psychosis can be conceptualised as a process of mourning and grief as outlined by Bowlby in 1980.

BOWLBY ON LOSS

Originally, Bowlby described permanent loss as an extended version of the infant's normative reaction to separation (as documented by Ainsworth et al., 1978). The process of mourning postulated by Bowlby is divided into four stages: (1) numbing; (2) yearning, searching and anger; (3) disorganisation and despair; and finally, (4) reorganisation (Holmes, 1993). Initially, numbing serves to block off emotional responses to bereavement, a short-term strategy until it is 'safe' to give vent to emotion. The second stage is similar to the 'protest' of a separated infant, the yearned- for figure is searched for, as is information that would disconfirm the loss. Finally, the permanence of the loss is faced in the disorganisation and detachment stage. Here the individual is faced with the reality that the bond has been severed, and must begin to reorganise their internal working models (IWMs) or schemata pertaining to this relationship in order to carry on with everyday life. These phases may all play a role in the genesis of atypical mourning (Bowlby, 1980; Shaver & Fraley, 1999). Additionally, at this juncture it is valuable to remember that the four phases of mourning are not inevitably sequential, and can fluctuate; the reaction to loss is thus a fluid process.

This paradigmatic description of the mourning process evolved from the separation of an attachment figure and generalised to the loss of a close other. Similar processes are involved in symbolic or indirect losses which may be expressed through other types of life events. For example, the loss of employment or educational opportunities, loss of social status, the loss of future self–other ideals engender a sense of grief and prompt a need to reorganise personal beliefs, interpersonal schemata and future expectations. Psychosis often triggers a series of other related life events that limit the individual's ability to reorganise as societal and interpersonal expectations readjust and predominantly limit vocational, educational and financial opportunities to support escape and recovery. A normative response to such a loss enables a person to compartmentalise and devalue certain life dimensions in favour of others which has a compensating effect. For example, a person may come to see it as not important to achieve high marks in exams and will increase value attached to their athletic performance. The additional difficulties attached to psychosis as a life event limit the ability to compartmentalise as all aspects of one's life can be affected to a significant degree. This pervasive quality therefore limits the process of recovery and adaptation engendering a sense of self as overwhelmed, defeated and unattractive.

Atypical Mourning

Responses to bereavement that are held to be atypical fall into two distinct areas, on a continuum ranging from chronic mourning to prolonged absence of mourning (Middleton et al., 1993). In attachment terms, the absence of grief mirrors the dismissing/avoidant individual. Bowlby (1980) saw this to be indicative of 'defensive exclusion', an internal mechanism of downplaying the emotional impact to minimise distress to the self. This strategy was hypothesised to leave fragmented shards of 'raw' memories and feelings about the loved one. When such memories are triggered by events or experiences, e.g. an anniversary, there is a 'suppression rebound', which impacts on the individual with a frightening intensity (Shaver & Fraley, 1999).

In contrast, the chronically mourning individual mirrors the behaviour of an anxious/ambivalent infant undergoing separation. As a response to inconsistent caregiving, the anxious/ambivalent infant develops a hyperactivating strategy to maintain contact with and attract the attention of the caregiver (Kobak et al., 1993). The loss of an attachment figure will then lead the individual to make persistent attempts to retain proximity or attention of any attachment figure as part of a pervasive and enduring interpersonal schema. This accentuates the feelings of anxiety, distress and disorganisation associated with any loss or separation (Parkes & Weiss, 1983; Parkes, 1985; Fraley & Shaver, 1999).

In summary, the Bowlbian delineation of loss and bereavement provides a process model of long-term adaptation to loss, which can be utilised when considering bereavement, and also the effects of loss due to severe life events such as psychosis. In relation to psychosis, the framework of loss and grief provides a helpful clinical and theoretical context to consider emotional adjustment to psychosis. At one end of the spectrum, we observe how individuals attempt to block off, minimise and deny the occurrence of psychosis.

This group uses a sealing-over strategy to aid recovery. This group has difficulty engaging with services (Dozier et al., 2001; Tait et al., 2004). As noted by Dozier and colleagues, individuals with dismissing states of mind are more likely to 'avoid therapeutic activities or drop out of treatment' (2001, p. 74). These dismissing/avoidant strategies may, on the one hand, be adaptive in the short run via minimising the awareness of the negative social, cultural and interpersonal meanings and consequences of psychosis. On the other hand, dismissing/avoidant strategies may be maladaptive in the longer run by preventing the emotional processing and personal readjustment or reorganisation to psychosis. At the other end of the spectrum, individuals may become enmeshed in a chronic ruminative mourning process characterised by persisting preoccupation, depressed mood, fearfulness and anxiety. This chronic pattern of mourning might be observed in those with greater insight and awareness of the social, cultural and interpersonal consequences of psychosis.

Constructs of loss may also have wider implications for people with psychosis. For example, Roy et al. (1983) found that early parental loss was a predictor of depression and suicide in people with a diagnosis of schizophrenia. Friedman et al. (2002) found, in comparison to panic, anxiety and major depression, individuals with schizophrenia were more than twice as likely to have experienced maternal separation and loss in childhood. These data make us aware of how loss issues arising in the context of psychosis may resemble and activate earlier loss events arising from bereavement and separation, but can also mirror normative patterns of adjustment to separations as conceptualised in the attachment literature.

CLINICAL INTERVENTIONS AND TECHNIQUES

During the process of supporting individual adaptation and reorganisation following psychosis we have identified a number of key therapeutic domains. This therapeutic work is driven by the client's problem list and personal goals as discussed at the beginning of therapy. We will now describe a number of interventions to support individuals in the process of reorganisation and adaptation to the experience of psychosis. Importantly, as part of this process, we want to emphasise the development of a normalising, accepting and compassionate understanding of psychotic experiences. We emphasise the importance of gently encouraging helpful self-reflection and the processing of important aspects of individuals' psychotic experiences. This process of adaptive self-reflection is compromised by avoidant or ruminative/preoccupied cognitive emotional strategies that require an adaptation of therapeutic strategies. During this process in therapy we also attempt to orientate individuals to a positive regard for and an understanding of their strategies for dealing with the painful emotional aspects of psychosis.

In the next section of this chapter we are going to explore a therapeutic discourse that is developed from working with Gavin.

Gavin

Gavin has had two episodes of psychosis, both associated with compulsory admission to hospital. Gavin experienced his first episode at the age of 21. He came into contact with services following an overdose of paracetamol. He was detained under the Mental Health Act and admitted to an acute psychiatric ward for a period of five weeks. On admission Gavin gave a three-month history of persisting derogating command hallucinations and persecutory paranoia. He also believed that he had had a microchip planted into his body. He was unsure of the reason for this. Gavin described two male voices, one belonging to his brother, and one belonging to an unidentified person. They conversed about Gavin. They told him that he was a smelly, ugly, fat, disgusting slob. His brother told him when to eat, drink and wash. His brother also told him to cut himself, and overdose. He partially complied with the voice of his brother most days. He believed that his brother was trying to harm him by getting him to commit suicide. In relation to this, he felt angry, fearful and panicky. He would experience homicidal thoughts in relation to his brother. The other voice was detached, cold, emotionless and cruel. It would mirror the commands of his brother's voice. Gavin felt disgusted and uncomfortable in response to the voice.

Gavin initially stated that he had a great upbringing, that everything had been fine and that he and his mum were great friends. However, he stated that his father was a 'useless dickhead' who had left him at the age of nine. He recalled his father being drunk and assaulting his mother. He also recalled his father never turning up at football practice despite repeated promises to do so. He said his mum was loving, loyal and fun. In relation to this, he stated that his mum had never rejected him. He spoke little about his brother who was five years older. He said that they never got on and were always fighting. He never had his own room or space to be alone. His brother was often intrusive in that he teased Gavin when he was playing with other kids in the neighbourhood. During adolescence, Gavin developed problems related to drug misuse and repeated self-harm and self-mutilation. Six months prior to his first episode his maternal aunt died. In relation to his aunt and uncle, Gavin would freely describe specific memories of feeling safe and loved when with them.

Exploring Loss, Humiliation and Entrapment

In this part of the intervention we want to provide a reflective space and opportunity for clients to explore their specific autobiographical memories of psychosis and their emotional reactions to the event. Commonly we would see emotions such as shame, embarrassment and humiliation. These emotions are often associated with the aftermath of psychosis, the consequences of psychotic experiences or diagnosis itself, and can include the reactions of others. Clients often experience difficulty reflecting on these specific memories because of the strong associated emotions and interpersonal nature of their experiences. Therefore, the therapist needs to consider a sensitive way to facilitate this process. This might involve techniques that help to de-centre the individual from the immediacy and emotional intensity of a recalled event. Such techniques are also important in the development of a coherent autobiographical narrative that incorporates past events, current appraisals and future expectations. For example, with younger adolescents the therapist might invite the young person to create a storyboard or a comic strip; with an adult the therapist may invite the person to write or tell their story. Alternatively, the therapist might ask the client to focus on a specific autobiographical event and use questions to support the client in developing greater context and elaborate associations with other autobiographical events:

Th: You were telling me how being admitted to hospital was particularly upsetting for you. Can you tell me more about that?

C: Aye, it was really hard like. They arrived in the afternoon, I just came home from school; the other kids were still going home, everybody was watching, I am sure.

Th: What happened next?

C: Well, they'd already been in talking to Mum and Dad, so they already knew I trashed my bedroom the night before – it's like Mum and Dad had told them everything.

Th: That sounds really horrible.

C: It was terrible. I was so embarrassed. They started asking me all these questions, if I had been OK at school, whether I had a girlfriend, whether I was hearing voices, and really stupid stuff, like, did the TV talk to me? I mean, how daft is that? Then they asked me if I was paranoid, if I wasn't then, I fucking was now! They're standing there, outside the house, and I just lost the plot! . . .

Th: Take me back, when you lost the plot, how did you feel inside?

C: I felt really angry; I mean, how could they do that? I was so embarrassed, I felt like everybody was looking at me and thinking: 'Ah, look; there is "mad Pete", he's off his head.'

The above therapeutic discourse gives an example of a therapist who focuses on a specific event to facilitate an enriched memory linked to important personal appraisals of self and others and salient emotional responses. This provides a platform to validate and explore clients' personal experiences of psychosis. Similarly, during exploration of loss-related dimensions of psychosis, it may be helpful for the therapist to describe individuals' common reactions to psychosis in terms of normative loss and grief reactions, for example, shock, anger, despair, disbelief and searching. This narrative provides the opportunity to scaffold the development of the client's discourse and provide them with a window to reflect on the importance of their understandable and normative emotional reactions to stressful and severe life events such as psychosis. This process also highlights the opportunity for the client to express their feelings of loss that they may have been experiencing but have been unable to verbalise or articulate. For example, this allows clients to talk about their experience of loss arising from their experience of psychosis or the withdrawal of friends and the impact this had on their sense of status, agency and acceptance:

Th: How were things after you came out of hospital?
C: I don't know, it's like everything was unreal. I couldn't believe what had happened to me. It's like, how could this have happened to me?
Th: How does that feel?
C: Unreal, it's like things are happening to me and I'm just watching, it's like I'm not part of things, everything was unreal, like it was happening to someone else.
Th: Did you feel distressed?
C: No, that's the funny thing. I felt fine. I'd had this odd episode and it was over. But then, it was like, it was like not the, I don't know . . . [12-second pause] it was like it hit me . . . [7-second pause] my friends were OK, they're OK, the, no, I mean, one friend didn't want to, I'm not sure. People seemed different somehow.

In this narrative we observe the client describing their sense of numbing and disbelief in response to psychiatric hospitalisation. The therapist might consider opportunities to describe such feelings as understandable and common, albeit distressing emotional responses to psychosis. However, in this discourse the client's speech becomes fragmented and difficult to follow as they begin to describe their growing awareness of the changed responses of others. During this process the therapist is sensitive to breaks or fragmentation within the developing narrative of the client. These may indicate areas where unresolved emotion or partial and under-elaborated processing of events has occurred. It might be helpful for the therapist to slow down the pace of the session and to gently enquire as to how the client is feeling or what the client is thinking or remembering at that point in the session.

This provides a grounding for the client's emotions. It also provides an important opportunity for the client and the therapist to explore these important emotion-laden thoughts and memories that are relevant to blocking adjustment and emotional recovery. Note the following discourse that picks up the client's reactions during the description of their friends' reactions following psychiatric admission:

Th: How are you feeling just now?

C: Really strange, I'm not sure.

Th: Tell me, what were you thinking when you were talking about your friend's reactions?

C: . . . [7-second pause] one friend seemed strange with me. He didn't say much so I asked him, 'What's up with you?' He said, 'My aunt has a mental illness. She cannae get out of the house and all my family think she's really weird . . .'

Th: What did you feel?

C: I felt different . . .

Th: In what way?

C: Like something had changed . . . [8-second pause]

Th: What are you thinking just now?

C: I don't know, like, it's awful. I've had this mental illness and I'm stuck with it maybe, maybe I'm going to end up like one of those old guys you see in the street.

Th: What do you mean?

C: Like, I can see it now, me dribbling like some fucking idiot . . .

In this scenario the client's awareness of the stereotypical societal views and expectations of mental illness are brought home to him through conversation with his friend. During the therapeutic discourse, the client experiences a powerful humiliating and shaming image of a future self as defeated and entrapped by mental illness. It is these kinds of appraisals, whether in the form of verbal statements or visual imagery, that are important in order to develop an understanding of the person's psychological adaptation to the experience of psychosis. Such strong and emotionally salient images can act somewhat like intrusive images in the context of the processing of traumatic material in that they become more entrenched by developing strong associations and links with core beliefs about self and with memories of events and the meaning structure of past experiences that carried similar emotions.

In the brief example above, the image of having seen somebody in the street who looked like he had a mental health difficulty was triggered by the interpretation of his friend's response, and is subsequently associated with feelings of humiliation and shame, but also with past experiences when shame and humiliation were experienced in a different context which now becomes associated with the fact that he had been admitted to a psychiatric hospital, and what that might entail in terms of future expectations. Salient negative emotions are thus strengthened by multiple associations with numerous events and memories that carry similar emotions and by an expanding meaning structure that developed from the varied outcomes of these past events.

Working with Idiosyncratic Appraisals

Novice, new therapists in cognitive therapy often find themselves attempting to modify a particular thought or image too quickly without adequate exploration and formulation. Clients' construction of their psychotic experiences often spans a number of key psychological dimensions such as humiliation, entrapment, loss and danger. Humiliation appraisals encompass feelings of self-attacking shame ('I am a dribbling idiot') and other attacking shame ('People see me as a dribbling idiot'). It is therefore important to adequately explore the client's perspective and to provide an integration of these specific thoughts or images with the overall individual style of appraisals. In addition, it is important to take account of the meaning-making and reasoning behind them and the emotional resonance these thoughts or images carry with other experiences. This then provides an opportunity to help the client reflect on the wider affective, physiological and interpersonal consequences of their appraisals. Returning to the client above, later on the therapist further explores the client's intrusive image:

Th: I'd like to take some time with you now to explore the image that you just described. I think that this might help us understand more clearly the upsetting feelings that you have been experiencing since coming out of hospital. Could you tell me what you see in that image?

C: Yea, OK, well. It's just me standing there. I can't see my face properly but I can see that I'm sort of stooped. I look untidy, awkward and lonely too. I don't look normal.

Th: Can you tell me what the most difficult thing about this image is?

C: It's like, it's me and there's nothing I can do about it. I'm alone. I look repulsive.

Th: Is that how you see yourself now?

C: Maybe not as strong as that, but yeah. I feel kind of ugly, like an unpleasant person to be around. I feel sort of weak. That I'm not as good as other people now.

Th: How does that make you feel?

C: Embarrassed, awkward. I don't want to talk to people; I kind of want to hide away. I don't want to answer the phone or talk to my friends. I feel really 'para' when I go outside. I think that's my illness. That's just me now, how it's going to be.

Th: What do you mean?

C: Well, I kind of feel that I need to accept it. I've got this illness and I have to put up with it.

We see in this discourse a number of key themes surrounding humiliation ('I feel kind of ugly, like an unpleasant person to be around. I feel sort of weak. That I'm not as good as other people now') and entrapment ('Well, I kind of feel that I need to accept it. I've got this illness and I have to put up with it'). Pivotal to this personal adaptation is the presence of humiliating, self-attacking imagery that drives feelings of shame and embarrassment, alongside interpersonal responses including withdrawal and social avoidance. This provides a platform for the therapist to work with the client to build a preliminary formulation of her client's problems and goals, focusing on the importance of self-attacking imagery in the development of psychological distress and interpersonal withdrawal. It may be important in that context to also explore the individual's reactions to such emotions and images as their response style often indicates styles of dealing with emotional distress and beliefs about coping ('Other people will only accept me if I can deal with things by myself').

The therapist might employ a range of techniques to support clients who are experiencing such intrusive and unwanted thoughts and images. It is therefore difficult to be prescriptive in a treatment manual. However, it is important for the therapist to work within the client's problem list and goals, and their formulation of the key underlying psychological processes and relevant therapy tasks. The therapist might consider working with self-stigmatising beliefs by providing normalising non-pathological information about psychotic experiences. On the other hand, the therapist may contextualise the client's problems by identifying normative adaptation patterns following psychosis, including communicating the relatively high frequency of depression or social anxiety following the illness. The therapist might consider selecting cognitive and behavioural strategies and techniques used to alleviate depression. On the other hand, the therapist may consider employing strategies aimed at alleviating social anxiety. These strategies may include techniques such as verbal reattribution of anxiety to intrusive images of the social self, behavioural experiments designed to modify intrusive images and thoughts via modifying safety-seeking behaviours, strategies to address anticipatory processing or strategies to address post-event processing and ruminative thinking.

There is good clinical evidence for these techniques with people suffering from low mood or intense anxiety. We do not see any reason why these techniques should not be employed with individuals recovering from psychosis. The only adaptations to consider are the special context that psychosis gives to how depression and anxiety become manifest, particularly via the cultural context of societal and stereotypical beliefs, attitudes and behaviours towards people with a mental illness.

Whichever route the therapist takes, a therapeutic priority is the development of a warm, self-soothing and compassionate narrative that counters the self-attacking, shaming feelings that can arise from thoughts and images linked to feelings of humiliation, loss and entrapment (Gilbert & Irons, 2005). The therapist might work with such thoughts and imagery in a number of ways. The therapist might explore the development of alternative imagery and/or appraisals within sessions (e.g. Hackmann, 1998), use writing techniques to evolve a self-accepting narrative, and develop helpful coping strategies to strengthen underdeveloped alternative beliefs and schemata. In light of the salience of emotions and associated memories and meanings, it can be valuable to explore these emotional resonances and associated experiences as these might often carry clues about the origins of particular negative self-conceptions (e.g. 'People make fun of me if I show my emotions or if I allow myself to become upset'). This can be achieved by asking the client what he feels reminded of when feeling sad or humiliated or whether he can think back to a time when he first experienced that emotion.

Development of Alternative Imagery/Appraisals

There are a number of important stages in exploring unwanted thoughts and images and developing alternatives. Gilbert and Irons (2005) have noted that rational or intellectual responses may not enable the person to achieve emotional change. Max Birchwood and colleagues (e.g. Tait et al., 2004) have also established that insecure attitudes to relationships may predispose individuals to problematic adaptation to psychosis. In addition, there is some developing evidence that insecure attitudes to early parental relationships may predispose individuals to develop post-psychotic social anxiety problems (Birchwood, personal communication, 2005). An important element of an individual's attachment security is the development of a self-soothing and accepting self-narrative. Not only is this an important part of the process of therapeutic engagement, but it is also an important aspect to the client's emotional recovery and adaptation to psychosis. We would like to emphasise that these emotional responses develop over time and find their origin in the context of early attachment relationships and experiences. These responses therefore emerge in a dynamic and evolving fashion over a variety of emotional and developmental domains. Their emergence within the context of adaptation to psychotic experiences is therefore embedded in the individual's pattern of responding and their developing cognitive interpersonal schemata.

Working with Meaning and Narrative

Therefore, it is important to support the client in exploring the central and core meanings and resonances responsible for their emotional distress. In so doing the therapist gently supports the client in understanding the emotional, cognitive and sensory elements of a particular appraisal or image. In addition, the therapist explores the occurrence of other images and appraisals and, in particular, attends to the emergence of autobiographical material. This material often emerges in fragmented and loosely associated forms. Therefore, therapists need to be careful not to provoke premature 'eureka' moments by closing and summarising developing narratives too quickly.

C: I remember when I was first on the ward, seeing this old guy. He was sitting there smoking . . . no teeth . . . his shirt was stained and dirty . . . everybody avoided sitting next to him.

Th: How do you feel just now thinking about that moment?

C: I feel disgusted . . . and bad for thinking that . . . is that going to be me?

Th: Describe to me what that feels like just now.

C: Oh, man, . . . it feels kind of dirty and upsetting. I feel so alone with this . . . I did not want to talk to him either.

Th: Thinking about that right now, what does that mean to you?

C: Is that how people feel about me?

Th: Is this the first time you have felt like this?

C: . . . I don't know . . . I remember being at school and always getting picked last. I did feel kind of odd, awkward; like people did just not take me seriously. It's like I stuck out, like I was the wrong shape or something. Girls didn't want to talk to me either.

By identifying the key emotional meanings, the therapist is able to extract the core meanings and qualities of an image. Through the explorative dialogue the therapist and client are able to express and reflect upon these images and meanings in an externalised verbal format. This enables the therapist and, most importantly, the client to mould and reshape new meanings. One way that this can be addressed is through a process of encouraging the client to take a reflective stance on their personal meanings and become aware of their origins and their restrictive qualities. Such a stance encourages the client to develop a curious and questioning approach to their own thinking and emotional experiences. The therapist actively encourages this curious yet non-judgemental attitude to their narrative.

Furthermore, the therapist might encourage the client to think about how they would like to portray themselves within an image specifically focusing on the desired emotional meanings and resonances. For example, the client may wish to explore feelings of agency and control. Therefore, the therapist might help the client recall specific autobiographical evidence and memories consistent with a sense of agency and control. On the other hand, clients might want to wish to explore feelings of attractiveness and desirability. Similarly the therapist will work with the client to draw upon autobiographical memory and alternative imagery that are consistent with these adjectives. Essentially we are describing a process where therapists use clients' adjectives and descriptors in different contexts or narratives to re-associate new meanings and further emotional resonances.

Th: Given how you described yourself in these situations (at school), how would you like to see yourself?

C: Do you mean now?

Th: Well, take yourself back to that time in your life and think about an event when you had fun and you felt included and comfortable.

C: Aw, right. I was really good at art and that meant I helped out every year at the school play. We always had a party at the end and people had lots of fun, I had a good time and stuff.

Th: Tell me what that felt like.

C: Just alright. I did not feel odd then.

Th: I think this is really important, let's focus a bit on what that felt like. Can you remember a specific example of having lots of fun at the party?

C: OK, let me think. There was this girl I really fancied. My friend came up and said she wanted to dance with me. I felt, like, really shy, like, but got it together and asked her to dance. She did! It felt so cool and buzzing. I felt really good, like I was somebody.

Th: As you think about that moment, can you see yourself in your mind's eye now?

C: Aye.

Th: Tell me what that feels like right now.

C: It's kind of weird, but it also feels alright.

Th: Can you attend to how it feels and describe those feelings to me just now?

C: It is nice to remember that, I forgot all about that before. I feel kind of good, it's like it is kind of part of me, part of me knows that I can feel OK. It feels like maybe something like that can happen again.

Within the session the therapist would stay with this alternative image for a while and explore all aspects of that memory and its associated resonances. This process allows the development of alternative verbalised meanings such as 'my friends like me', 'I'm good at putting things together and chatting to people', 'I am approachable', and 'I had a really difficult time that I am recovering from', 'being upset is not the same as being mentally ill'. This allows for alternative appraisals to be grounded in the client's narrative and linked to their lived past, either specific events or valued goals:

Th: Remember those feelings and take yourself back to when you met your friend after you came out of hospital.

C: What? What do I take where?

(Therapist blushes intensely.)

Th: OK, you got me there. Can you see yourself with your friend when he was talking about his aunt being mentally ill?

C: OK, I can see that.

Th: In that situation, can you hold on to that feeling of being accepted by your friend?

C: OK. Maybe, it's kind of hard. I can see myself and part of me thinks I am like his aunt, but there is another part of me, I kind of know that my friend cares for me and he was really worried about me and he came and visited me all the time and he, like, gave me these pictures from when we went camping in the spring. And we still talk about that now.

Th: Thinking about that now, how does that feel?

C: It's kind of comforting, he is there for me and I am just thinking I need to see more of him.

The therapist then invites the client to reflect on this process, to think about how he came to see different aspects of how he saw himself and his friend in that situation. The client becomes aware in this that past experiences influence how he reacted in that situation and he was able to apply multiple meanings and perspectives to his friend's comments. The therapist highlights the importance of developing a warm accepting self-narrative as a means to respond to painful moments and situations. This can be supplemented by encouraging the client to keep a diary of thoughts and images that accompany distressing emotional experiences and use these as opportunities to develop alternative understandings. In addition, the therapist can encourage the client to record evidence supporting positive self-appraisals generated within the session. This is akin to keeping a positive data log. The therapist may also work with the client to devise behavioural experiments to test out alternative compassionate forms of thinking. It is important that the reader is aware that the process of therapy does not attempt to directly challenge negative thoughts or imagery but to craft, sculpt, rehearse and elaborate client-derived alternative appraisals and narratives of the self and others.

One further technique to recreate an autobiographical narrative from clients' experiences and their meanings is to use storyboards, comic strips or letter writing, depending on the person's developmental contexts. Working with young people who often have not fully developed a compartmentalised role understanding that allows them to become easily self-reflective within a therapeutic context, or individuals who have low emotional awareness and reflexivity, can be challenging. More tangible and playful techniques can be helpful in facilitating similar explorative processes and in developing metacognitive skills in monitoring and reflecting upon thoughts, memories and feelings. One example would be the use of storyboards or comic strips where the person is invited to take a specific experience or situation and create a story that then becomes the focus for exploration. For example, clients are invited to choose a particular character or episode in which they can translate their experience.

Therapist and client would then work together in exploring that situation in similar lines to the above description but using the development of a comic strip or story to explore the client's feelings and reactions. One client devised a story based on 'South Park' where the client is a new character, for example, Kyle's new friend and the story would unfold using the known characters. For example, Cartman could be a derogating critical peer who tells the client that they are defective and mentally ill ('You suck, dude, you should be in an institution'). The story then becomes a vehicle through which the client explores their responses to derogating criticism but also explores how to seek out interpersonal alliances and support from other characters and practises assertive responses to criticism.

Another example of exploring narrative is through letter writing, where the client is encouraged to write an account of their experiences but construct the account in such a way that facilitates communication of self-accepting, warm and empowering self-perspectives. Again, the therapist works with clients' verbatim accounts to evolve an elaborated narrative that incorporates the rehearsal of new cognitive, emotional and interpersonal responses to adversity. Even though it remains emotionally salient, this allows exploration of perspectives in a way that can be emotionally less overwhelming for clients. This allows some clients to explore and begin to develop a language and meaning-making from their experience. For example, some clients may find the process of labelling emotional experiences challenging. This process facilitates a discussion and exploration of a narrative structure that best communicates the client's experience in manner that aids reflection and integration.

CONCLUSIONS

In this chapter, what we have attempted to do is to describe some of the major obstacles for adaptation in psychosis, in particular focusing on meanings associated with humiliation, entrapment and loss. In the context of an evolving formulation the therapist aims to construct a narrative account that allows the client to explore new meanings and resonances, embedding these as fully as possible within the client's autobiographical memories. One of the main challenges in achieving this is working with clients who lack specific positive autobiographical memories. For these challenges in therapy we describe a schema-focused approach in Chapter 10. Most clients with an experience of psychosis face significant interpersonal difficulties either as part of or as a consequence of their psychosis. In Chapter 11 we describe techniques relating to these interpersonal aspects and difficulties. For other clients the appraisals relating to psychosis are dominated by feelings of danger or intrusiveness that inhibit the development of self-reflectiveness and exploration. We explore these issues in Chapters 8 and 10 of this manual. We are also keen to remind therapists that there is a range of evidence-based techniques that have been developed to alleviate anxiety and low mood with populations of clients who have not experienced psychosis. Within the context of clients' problem lists and goals we fully support the incorporation of these techniques while attending to the particular qualities and problems associated with the experience of psychosis.

CHAPTER 7

WORKING WITH INTERPERSONAL DISTRUST: DEVELOPING A CONCEPTUALISATION OF THE PARANOID MIND

INTRODUCTION

One significant obstacle to recovery and to vulnerability to recurrence of psychosis is the presence of continuing low-level feelings of paranoia, vigilance, suspicion and interpersonal threat appraisal. There is a need to explore, understand and narrate the person's experiential framework, which guides their awareness, interpretation and response to interpersonal situations. In this context paranoia might be conceptualised as an evolutionarily adaptive state of mind designed to favour survival. However, this goal may be achieved at the cost of affiliation, proximity seeking and kinship. We refer to this as the 'paranoid mind'. Our aim in this chapter is to describe an approach to paranoia that facilitates the process of individual mindful awareness of the interpersonal context of paranoia and their own cognitive, affective and behavioural responses to the appraisal of interpersonal threat.

PARANOIA AS AN INTERPERSONAL THREAT RESPONSE

Here paranoia, like social anxiety, is conceptualised as a response to perceived interpersonal threats to the self. For example, Kinderman (1994) found that individuals with persecutory delusions have a specific attentional bias for information relating to self-concept. A key characteristic of persecutory delusions is highlighted by the work of Trower and Chadwick (1995) who argue that the sources of threat are a solely interpersonal negative evaluation. In a similar vein, people with social phobia (which can be conceptualised as extreme social anxiety) display an attentional bias to socially threatening information and hypersensitivity regarding others' evaluations of them (Hartman, 1983; Hope et al., 1990). Thus both groups display what can be termed as a 'self as target' bias, where appraisal of threats related to the self is of paramount importance. Gilbert (2001) describes the threat focus and defensive strategies associated with paranoia and social anxiety. Social anxiety is concerned with loss of status or rejection resulting from displaying socially unattractive behaviour (for example, being seen as incompetent by others). Social anxiety is then associated with defensive strategies including vigilance for one's own behaviour and its impact on others, particularly those within the social group (e.g. a student giving a presentation to other students), social avoidance and socially inhibited behaviour. In contrast, paranoia is linked to perceived threat from hostile groups or alliances. This is defended against, using vigilance, distrust, avoidance of or aggression towards those identified as belonging to the (outside) group. Gilbert et al. (2005) found that social anxiety was associated with submissive behaviour, lower social power and negative social comparisons. In this group, paranoia and social anxiety were highly correlated, indicating that both might be related to social rank perceptions, power and submissive behaviour.

The Paranoid Mind Is Concerned with External Personal Threats

Individuals with persecutory paranoia attend to interpersonal threat-related stimuli (Bentall & Kaney, 1989; Fear et al., 1996), recall more threat-related information (Kaney et al., 1992; Bentall et al., 1995) and tend to view not only themselves as vulnerable to threat but also see others as vulnerable to threat (Kaney et al., 1997). When making inferences about positive and negative events, individuals attribute the cause of negative events to other people, whereas depressed patients attribute cause to the self (reviewed by Bentall et al., 2001). Such attentional and inferential biases are consistent with a model of paranoia as a state of mind designed to be sensitive to the detection of interpersonal threat.

The Paranoid Mind Makes Decisions Quickly

Numerous studies have shown consistently that individuals with persecutory paranoia have a reasoning style characterised by 'jumping to conclusions' (reviewed by Garety & Freeman, 1999; Dudley & Over, 2003). Generally, individuals with delusions come to decisions more quickly and do so on less evidence compared to controls. Such biases in data gathering and decision-making have been reported in spider phobics (de Jong et al., 1997) and individuals who are anxious about their health (de Jong et al., 1998). Dudley and Over (2003) have argued that heightened levels of threat awareness increase the sense that a threat exists. The tendency to engage in confirmatory reasoning and jumping to conclusions is therefore likely to be protective. Disconfirmatory reasoning, while more effective in decision-making, takes longer and is an inefficient strategy to deal with threat. In other words, better to jump to conclusions that a threat exists and react even if this means getting it wrong, than come to a considered and logical decision that there is no threat, and get that wrong. False positives are therefore less costly in terms of survival than false negatives.

THE PARANOID MIND IS STRATEGICALLY DEPLOYED

It could be argued that paranoia represents a strategic cognitive response to the perception of interpersonal threat. In a factor analytic study, Morrison et al. (2005) investigated beliefs about paranoia. Using a 31-item questionnaire, in a sample of 317 undergraduates, they found four empirically distinct constructs: (1) beliefs about paranoia as a survival strategy; (2) positive beliefs about paranoia; (3) normalising beliefs about paranoia; and (4) negative beliefs about paranoia. Beliefs about paranoia as a survival strategy are exemplified by the following examples: 'paranoia is useful for avoiding trouble' or 'being paranoid or suspicious keeps me safe from harm'. Survival beliefs were associated with more frequent paranoid thoughts and negative beliefs were associated with the distress arising from delusional ideation. These findings help us reflect on how individuals' survival beliefs might be activated by an interpersonally threatening situation. Thus being in a threatening situation (e.g. meeting a friend in an unknown pub) activates survival beliefs (e.g. watch out for untrustworthy people in strange situations), thus generating vigilance for threat and heightened self-awareness. Consistent with this, Fenigstein and Vanable (1992) have previously proposed that it is not just beliefs about the self that are of importance in paranoia, but beliefs about the 'self as target'. Fenigstein and Vanable (1984) have argued that, as a result of increased self-awareness, an individual may come to think that *others* are also directing attention towards them.

ATTACHMENT AND PARANOIA

Little is known about the relationship between attachment status and persecutory paranoia. While the work of Dozier and colleagues shows that insecure (avoidant) states of mind are common in the context of individuals diagnosed with bipolar disorder and schizophrenia (e.g. Dozier et al., 2001), it is unclear how attachment states of mind relate to specific symptoms such as paranoia. It is also unclear whether attachment states of mind may be a vulnerability factor in the development of persecutory paranoia, or whether persecutory paranoia might undermine the person's internal representations of attachment relationships.

Irons and Gilbert (2005) have noted that, among adolescents, social rank concerns mediated the relationship between insecure attachment status and depression/anxiety. In this study, insecure attachment appeared to sensitise individuals to be focused on competition and the power of others to shame, hurt or reject. Sloman et al. (2003) have argued that insecure attachment status and social rank behaviour underpin the evolution of depression. Benn et al. (2005) found that students who recalled a secure parenting environment compared themselves favourably with others and had greater interpersonal trust. Conversely, recall of rejecting parenting was associated with more negative social comparisons and lower interpersonal trust. In particular, those who recalled rejecting parenting were more likely to have difficulty coping in social situations, lower social intimacy and greater difficulty in disclosing to others. These data tentatively suggest that the relationship between attachment status and paranoia/interpersonal distrust might be mediated by the person's use of interpersonal strategies such as submissiveness/subordination or dominance (Sloman et al., 2003). In Trower and Chadwick's (1995) conceptualisation of two types of paranoia – 'poor me' and 'bad me' paranoia – one might expect to see contrasting defensive strategies in line with the differentiation of beliefs relating to self in those two types of paranoia. In 'bad me' paranoia, the paranoia is seen as arising from negative beliefs about the self (e.g. I am bad and evil) and the persecution or punishment by others is experienced as justified. In this case, we would expect to see interpersonal strategies characterised by submissiveness and subordination to others. In contrast, we might expect to see greater use of dominance strategies among those individuals who see their persecution as undeserved ('poor me' paranoia).

If one does accept that paranoid thinking might be underpinned by experiences of insecure or rejecting attachment experiences and mediated by the individuals' interpersonal behaviour, then early attachment experiences may also explain vulnerability to paranoia via limitations in mind mindedness or mentalising ability. There is evidence that persons who are experiencing acute persecutory paranoia have difficulties understanding the intentions and motivations of others, in other words they have a theory of mind or mentalisation difficulty (Corcoran et al., 1995; Frith & Corcoran, 1996; Corcoran et al., 1997; Pickup & Frith, 2001; Herold et al., 2002; Langdon et al., 2002; Craig et al., 2003; Randall et al., 2003).

In working with interpersonal mistrust it is important for therapists to remain mindful that the paranoid mind is experienced and largely becomes problematic in the process of establishing close and trusting relationships. When problems relating to the paranoid mind are directly explored and addressed within the therapeutic relationship, this can provide an important mirror of how particular cognitive styles and compensatory strategies can impede an open and accepting engagement. Rational-didactic and cognitive techniques, therefore, would need to be relative to the level of engagement and the reflective flexibility of the therapeutic relationship.

PROBLEMS WITH THE TERM 'PARANOIA'

It is important to agree terms with respect to how the term 'paranoia' is understood. We have found it extremely useful to explore the meaning of the term with the person. The process of exploring the meanings attached to the term 'paranoia' can lead to the development of a rich narrative. Often individuals have described associations with the drug-using culture (e.g. 'being para'), associations with mental illness or more idiosyncratic associations with weakness or defectiveness. Indeed, depending how an individual responds to the question 'What do you understand by the term "paranoia"?', this can have a marked influence over the structure of the unfolding discourse. For example, the following transcript is taken from a conversation exploring the meaning of paranoia:

Th: What do you understand by the term 'paranoia'?
C: Well, it's a sign of weakness, isn't it? I've never had it myself, but if you let anyone see that you're paranoid, you're buggered, aren't you? They'll be straight in there!
Th: Can you tell me what you mean by 'straight in there'?
C: They'll have you; you'll get a right good kicking.
Th: OK, so you've said paranoia is a sign of weakness. Can you tell me anything else about what you understand by the word?
C: Well, put it this way. If you are, like, in a group like a motorcycle gang or something, and you do something wrong and then they chuck you out, and then you are on the outside and you don't feel cocky any more, and they can attack you because, like, you're on the outside of the group now, and that is what paranoid is, eh?

So in this more extreme example of the beginnings of a discourse on paranoia, the client creates an edifice of paranoia as a sign of weakness and therefore vulnerability to attack, and a sign of being on the outside and a loss of confidence. In creating such an edifice it then becomes difficult for the client and therapist to maintain a collaborative discourse, given that the current meaning framework compels the client not to accept the term in relation to their own life experiences. Instead the therapist may explore experiences of interpersonal threat and how the person has maintained resilience and strength in the face of adversity. In so doing, the therapist may work carefully to develop a developmental and life history view of interpersonally threatening events alongside a careful description of the cognitive, emotional and behavioural consequences of these events. In this sense the therapist always maintains the stance that specific meanings in relation to interpersonal threat are products that have arisen from the complex interplay of life events, interpersonal relationships and interactions accounting for how the person and significant others have interacted within that framework over time and what meanings have been constructed by the individual to make sense of these interactions. The short transcript illustrated above is contextualised by the following case description:

Bill

Bill is 20 years old and grew up in a small tenement flat in the centre of Glasgow in a large family of eight. Bill never met his father. His mother had to work long hours and he does not report many positive memories of loving or caring behaviour. One older sister living in the house brought him up. He had four older brothers, three of whom have long-standing drug problems. He has one younger sister and one younger brother. A family friend, who has since been imprisoned, sexually abused Bill until his mid-teens. During this period Bill developed a number of problems in terms of poor school attendance, drug using and antisocial behaviour. Bill left home at 16 years old and over the past four years has spent much of his life homeless. During that period Bill learned to be suspicious of the motives of others and has maintained a hostile approach to others he doesn't know. Over this period, he has never discussed his experiences or his feelings with others. In the year before referral to the service, Bill had his first stable relationship and his girlfriend became pregnant. Bill was referred following an episode of persecutory paranoia characterised by beliefs that Mafia gangs were trying to kill him and his girlfriend, and that information about him was being communicated on the TV and radio.

WORKING WITH THE PERSONAL DISTRESS OF THE PARANOID MIND

Given this conceptualisation of paranoia, the therapist aims to work carefully with the person to help them become aware of the attributes of the paranoid mind. The therapist can explore the advantages and disadvantages of the person's use of paranoia as a strategy. The therapist may focus on ways in which paranoia has been helpful in the person's life and the life situations or interpersonal relationships that have prompted this response. In doing this, the therapist begins to chart the relationship between life events, interpersonal relationships and the development of a paranoid state of mind. This allows the therapist and client to identify specific situations in which the development of a paranoid state of mind made sense. In so doing the therapist encourages the client to reflect upon their experiences and to consider the strategic or survival value of paranoia in their social and emotional context. This provides the therapist with a valuable opportunity to validate the person's experience but also to provide a normalising and accepting narrative of the development and context of paranoia.

It seems important to highlight the open and transparent exploration necessary for this therapeutic step, which is best facilitated within a positive therapeutic alliance where trust, understanding and compassionate acceptance are modelled. In the context of reconstructing meaning from past interpersonal situations of these experiences, the therapist has to feel able to reflect on the impact on the therapeutic relationship and to openly address any feelings of mistrust or misconception. In doing this the therapist is attempting to encourage the development of a metacognitive stance: that is, the ability to reflect on and judge one's own thinking and feelings. In this way the therapist can then gently encourage the person to consider the negative consequences of paranoia in terms of their own emotional well-being, their feelings of closeness, warmth and affiliation with others, and their ability to trust and understand others. In this way the interplay between events (e.g. being bullied at school), beliefs (e.g. people are untrustworthy), emotions (e.g. fear, anxiety, embarrassment) and interpersonal coping behaviours (e.g. avoidance, suspiciousness and vigilance, jumping to conclusions) can be formulated and understood. Figure 7.1 is a diagrammatical formulation of the maintenance of the paranoid mind using Bill's experiences as an example.

In this way the therapist is able to illustrate how the person's beliefs about others as characterised by mistrust, danger and exploitation are embedded in important and emotionally salient life experiences and how these may have been shaped over time in the context of confirmatory experiences and in contradiction to other aspects of self-understanding, such as the longing to be accepted. This is an important part of the process of validation and support. The therapist is also able to help communicate a warm, compassionate and kindly understanding of the evolution of paranoid beliefs. This is an important step in helping the person towards a similarly non-critical, kindly and warm attitude and mentality that may be useful in communicating with the paranoid mind. In addition, the interplay between beliefs and interpersonal coping gives the person the opportunity to explore how interpersonal strategies have become overdeveloped or underdeveloped and how these strategies may unintentionally distort interpersonal experiences, prevent the development of trust and maintain feelings of loneliness, isola-

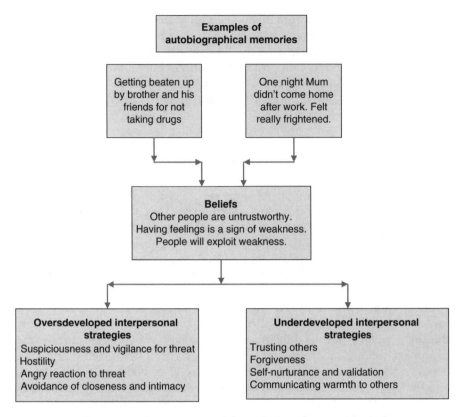

Figure 7.1 Diagrammatical formulation of paranoid mind

tion, vulnerability and threat. In undertaking this process of formulation, it may be important to attune to the developmental context of paranoia, particularly the person's caregiving environment, trauma, abuse and peer attachments.

The therapist might then consider a range of possible strategies to support the person in developing trust and reducing vulnerability. For example, a therapist can work to craft new beliefs with the person such as, for example, 'Some people might be trustworthy', 'I can cope with threats from others', 'I can look after my girlfriend'. These new beliefs might be investigated and strengthened by a range of evidence-based strategies such as historical testing of old and new beliefs, use of continuum, the use of behavioural experiments to strengthen new beliefs, notebooks to collect evidence for and against old and new beliefs, monitoring interpersonal strategies such as jumping to conclusions (while noting both costs and benefits to self and others), and addressing traumatic imagery or memories that maintain negative interpersonal schemata. In addition, this approach to conceptualising paranoia opens up important possibilities in exploring the use of compassionate mind training to support the development of an accepting, compassionate caregiving mentality to address persecutory states of mind (Gilbert & Irons, 2005). Specific strategies for working with continuing feelings of interpersonal mistrust and paranoia are detailed below.

AWARENESS OF THE PARANOID MIND

It is helpful for the therapist to focus on a specific situation involving a detailed description of the person's reaction to perceiving an interpersonal threat. The therapist works to encourage a mindful and curious exploration of the person's emotional, physiological, cognitive and behavioural responses within that situation. In addition, the therapist might encourage the person to explore and reflect upon the reactions (including internal as well as behavioural) of others. Obstructions and blocks during this therapeutic discourse might involve the person not being able to remember their own or others' reactions in sufficient detail. The therapist might respond to this by checking the vividness of the imagery experienced during the account, checking other specific situations or encouraging self-monitoring between therapy sessions. The therapist may also reflect on the discourse and the therapeutic interaction in sessions, as feelings about the therapist or the relative sense of exposure provoked by an open and transparent communication may conflict with the client's sense of felt security and hinder their ability to fully explore their experiences. The aim is to develop a greater sense of awareness of internal and external events within interpersonal situations, to develop a greater reflective and metacognitive awareness of changes in thinking, perception and emotion, and to encourage a mindful, curious and non-judgemental attitude towards the self. The narrative below illustrates this approach to development of awareness:

C: I came out of the flats and there were these wee guys, right, you know, hanging about. Four of them. I knew they were looking at me. Sizing me up, like. Going to give me a kicking.

Th: What happened?

C: I put my head down, carried on walking. I heard one of them say, 'That guy's a fruitcake.' I thought, 'Wee bastard, I'm going to give him a kicking.' I turned around and headed over to them. They just started shouting at me and ran off. I couldn't be bothered chasing after them.

Th: Thinking about that now, what was the worst thing about that?

C: Well, it's constantly feeling that you are on guard, people are just going to 'take the mick' if you let them, if you give them an inch.

Th: I'd like to focus on that with you. In thinking about this situation, I'd like you to reflect on your reactions to these guys. Perhaps you could begin with when you were heading out of the flats?

C: OK, well, I hate going out. I'm always uptight, looking about me, you know. Some guy got stabbed last week on the stairs at the bottom. I came out. I saw them standing there kicking their ball about. One guy was really big, had a Glasgow Rangers top on. I've seen him before. The others I didn't recognise.

Th: So, what were you thinking at that moment?

C: They're gonna give me a hiding. They're going to start a fight with me.

Th: What did you do?

C: I put my head down, I felt really 'para', but I kept my eyes on them. I could see them out of the corner of my eye. They were looking at me. That's when I heard them say I was a fruitcake. I was mad.

Th: What did you think when they said that?

C: That they were 'taking the mick', you know, because I've been in hospital and that.

Th: How did that make you feel?

C: Really bad, I just wanted to go for the big one and take him out. I was raging.

Through this discourse the therapist is able to observe and identify key attributes of the client's response to interpersonal threat including vigilance and monitoring, distrust of others, selective attention, rapid decision-making, personalisation and aggressive reaction to threat. This gives the therapist an opportunity to begin to characterise and draw the client's attention to their cognitive, emotional and behavioural responses to threat (see Table 7.1).

DEVELOPMENT OF AN ACCEPTING RATIONALE FOR PARANOIA AS A RESPONSE

Exploration of the characteristics of the paranoid mind as an evolved response to survival in the context of a world characterised by interpersonal threat allows the therapist to use normalising information to contextualise paranoia. For example, the therapist might make reference to the evolutionary nature of innately programmed fight/flight responses to explain paranoia and interpersonal distrust. The therapist can give examples of how people might respond in interpersonally threatening situations. The therapist might use hypothetical scenarios to help the person imagine the reactions of others in interpersonally ambiguous situations (for example, meeting a friend in a busy pub in an unknown area of town). The therapist can use simple diagrams to introduce the relationships between thinking, emotion, physiology and behaviour in such scenarios. It can be useful to

Table 7.1 Characteristics of the rational mind, the compassionate mind and the paranoid mind

The rational mind	The compassionate mind	The paranoid mind
The rational mind likes to look at the evidence.	The compassionate mind has empathy and sympathy for those who are in pain and suffering.	The paranoid mind is concerned with detecting threat from other people.
It observes carefully and wants to know as much as possible before coming to a decision.	It is concerned with personal growth and helping people reach their potential.	It is concerned with coming to decisions quickly.
The rational mind likes to have several alternatives to choose from.	It is concerned with healing, supporting and listening to what we and what others need.	It is concerned with survival of the self.
The rational mind likes to test things and run experiments.	It listens and enquires about problems in a kind and friendly way.	It is concerned with safety.
The rational mind does not like being overly influenced by emotional appeal or hasty conclusions.	The compassionate mind is quick to forgive and slow to condemn.	It is not concerned with disconfirming threat or looking for alternative evidence or explanations.
The rational mind knows that knowledge develops slowly.	It does not attack, but seeks to bring healing, reunion and repair.	It needs to act first and think later.
The rational mind knows that we learn most from trial and error – that, in fact, we often learn more from our errors than we do from our successes.	The compassionate mind recognises that life can be painful and that we are all imperfect beings.	It is concerned with keeping people at a distance. Other people are potentially dangerous.
The rational mind will attempt to weigh the pros and cons of a particular view or course of action.	It does not treat ourselves or others simply as objects with a market value.	
The rational mind likes to take a long-term view of things and recognises that we often get to where we are going step by step.		

reflect on the use of a paranoid state of mind as an overdeveloped mental and behavioural strategy or model for dealing with social situations that may have served a positive or adaptive function when developed in the context of particular situations or experiences. This can be crafted against the background of the person's life experience. For example, the therapist and client can work together to develop a timeline showing the relationship between life experiences and the development of beliefs about the self and others. The therapist encourages the person to reflect on the impact of beliefs about self and others on the evolution of interpersonal mistrust and paranoia. The therapist may also consider encouraging the monitoring of elements of the paranoid mind, for example, jumping to conclusions, interpersonal threat appraisals, affective reactions, etc.

BENEFITS AND COSTS OF THE PARANOID MIND

This process allows the therapist to begin to work with the person to reflect upon the way in which interpersonal mistrust and paranoia have been helpful to the person either in the present or historically. This is an important part of the process of validation and the development of therapeutic empathy.

C: There's always been this bit of me that's thought, 'Don't trust anyone, they're just out for themselves.'

Th: Has that bit of you been helpful to you overall?

C: Yeah, it's like, when I was homeless I saw loads of really bad stuff. Like, I remember in this hostel this guy was, like, crying one night. Everyone knew he was weak, he got a kicking. If people see that in you, they can take advantage, use your weakness.

Th: So one benefit is that people don't try to use you. Are there other ways not trusting others is helpful?

C: Well, it's the whole survival of the fittest thing. If you don't trust anyone, they can't hurt you. Like with my uncle, I trusted him and he hurt me really bad.

So, in this example, the client begins to reflect on powerful life experiences including being sexually abused by an uncle and seeing somebody being beaten up after expressing upset and therefore weakness. In this instance the therapist goes on to explore with the client his specific experiences. This process enables the therapist to begin to hypothesise the form and functionality of beliefs underpinning interpersonal mistrust. For example, in the client's case, two key assumptions are identified including, 'If I show weakness, then others will exploit me', and the reciprocal side of that which is, 'If

I am (appear) strong, I will not be harmed.' These are powerful underlying assumptions, which drive cognition, affect and behaviour in social situations and are embedded in the person's life experience. Exploration of associated assumptions and beliefs allows the therapist to work carefully with the client to correctly articulate and verbalise their experiences of interpersonal mistrust. The development of this synchrony in reflecting and understanding affect, experience and meaning is an essential precursor to the process of exploring personal costs of interpersonal mistrust and can become possible in the context of a safe and containing therapeutic relationship where doubts, anxieties and hesitations can be openly reflected and where the experience of these unwanted emotional reactions does not necessarily compel the client to adopt certain safety behaviours:

Th: Your strategy of not trusting others and appearing strong in front of others has had some important benefits in your life. Have there been costs to you also? Of this strategy, I mean?

C: I'm not sure, I guess. You know when I was with my girlfriend there were times that I felt really close. Like when Josh was born. It was nice. But then things went wrong. She couldn't handle me after I started getting angry with her and accusing her of being with the Mafia and the IRA. It was like I couldn't trust her any more. I thought they had hypnotised her, you see, so that they could get at me by controlling her. That led to our break-up. She just freaked out. I thought they were trying to make me a martyr or something, some kind of Jesus.

Th: Thinking about that now, can you tell me what you are feeling?

C: I guess, just feel really stupid. I, I don't know, it's like I miss her and I feel lonely sometimes. I'd really like to be able to see Josh, but she gets really freaked out by me still. She's always watching me to see if I'm getting 'para'. She gets scared that I'll lose the rag and hit someone or something. Her brother gets really protective.

Th: How does that make you feel?

C: Like a loser. I feel really bad. I feel on my own . . . Like, she knows about all that stuff with my uncle and all that, but she doesn't really understand what it's like, you know.

The above narrative provides, albeit in an abridged way, the client's growing awareness of the costs of interpersonal distrust; in this case, the client's experiences of lowered self-esteem, relationship difficulties, loneliness, anxious reactions in others and emotional distress. These costs can be carefully considered within the context of the case formulation and in relation to the client's goals. The therapist might reflect on paranoia and interpersonal mistrust as an evolved, but overly rigid and all-encompassing, strategy. This is a strategy that works well for dealing with threat and this may well have been a very important strategy in the past. However, in an effort to create safety, the strategy itself produces a feeling of lack of safety and personal vulnerability. This undermines the intended functionality of the strategy itself.

DEVELOPMENT OF ALTERNATIVE INTERPERSONAL STRATEGIES

The costs of paranoia and interpersonal mistrust can be translated into intra- and interpersonal behaviours and strategies. Some common costs of paranoia might include the following: over time it may have resulted in an impoverished social network, a lack of close and confiding relationships, the reduced ability to express warmth to others, difficulty trusting people, difficulty reflecting on and communicating feelings, understanding the mental states of others and weighing evidence in decision-making. The process of encouraging self-reflection is important to the development of a metacognitive awareness of the function and personal and interpersonal costs of paranoia. This awareness leads to a consideration of alternative interpersonal strategies. Such strategies can play an important role in re-scripting interpersonal schema, especially if carried out in conjunction with behavioural experiments aimed at testing alternative, more compassionate beliefs about others.

Th: You say that Becky doesn't really understand, that she gets freaked out, she watches for you getting 'para' and that she's scared that you'll lose the rag. Can you describe a recent situation where that happened?

C: Yeah. I came round to see Josh. When I came to the door she said he was sleeping and that she wouldn't disturb him. I heard him upstairs and said, 'Look, he's awake. I just want a wee minute, eh?' She just started freaking out again. Said I was para and to go away. I thought, she's got to have someone in, what's going on?

Th: How did you feel?

C: Ah, just really angry again, like she doesn't care and Josh will grow up without a father. Really upset, but really 'para' again.

Th: OK, that sounds pretty hard. We can spend some time talking about your feelings at that moment, but first I'd like to try something. Can you put yourself in Becky's place, you know, sort of imagine her thoughts and feelings in that situation?

C: Hmmm, OK, well . . . [10-second pause] She wasn't expecting me round, she worries a lot and I don't think she trusts me.

Th: How does that make sense of her reaction to you?

C: I'm not sure, she's always been funny about the wean. She likes everything to be regular, a good routine for Josh, you know.

Th: OK, so she's not expecting you, she likes a regular routine for Josh, she tends to worry. So imagine for a moment the kinds of thoughts she might experience when you arrive that explain why she might freak out.

C: Maybe she thought I wasnae well again, eh? Maybe she thought I was coming round for an argument or something. The day before I had a row with her brother. He was winding me up, saying that his dad doesn't like me.

In this narrative the therapist encourages the client to mentalise Becky's reactions to his arrival. In doing so he encourages a reflective process of mentalising the reactions of others. The therapist is creating opportunities to explore alternative and underdeveloped strategies for managing interpersonal situations. In the client's case the therapist explores the benefits of more open communication with Becky, particularly regarding arrangements to visit Josh. One of the difficulties with this kind of therapeutic narrative is that suspicious or paranoid explanations can be invoked to explain another person's reactions and/or distress. For example, in this instance the client might have thought, 'She had a man in.' It is therefore important to have adequately explored the person's initial responses to interpersonal situations, and established that threat appraisals or jumping to conclusions might act as a barrier to important and value goals in therapy. It is helpful to spend time creating adequate parameters to explore the client's understanding of the reactions of others and to support the development of new positive anchor points and parameters for trust and dependency on others.

The development of alternative behavioural and interpersonal strategies can be achieved through a variety of means, including the use of behavioural experiments, monitoring of the impact of alternative strategies, developing the person's ability to imagine the mental states of others, or the use of interpersonal imagery incorporating new strategies within sessions. Through these therapeutic strategies and within a continuing reflective therapeutic narrative, the therapist works with the person to create new evidence that can then be meshed with alternative beliefs. This process is described in greater detail in Chapter 11 on strategies for working with cognitive interpersonal schemata.

CONCLUSIONS

In this chapter, we have identified that one obstacle to engagement and recovery is the presence of continuing interpersonal distrust and paranoid thinking. We have advocated in this context an approach to conceptualising paranoia that emphasises paranoia and interpersonal distrust as an evolved mental state designed to manage interpersonal threat. This approach implied a therapeutic approach that encourages the development of a mindful and non-judgemental reflectiveness on the origins, development and functionality of paranoia in the person's life context. In doing this, we aim to promote individuals' capacity to represent their paranoid reactions to others as a mental and behavioural response to perceiving interpersonal threat. In addition, we aim to promote a mindful awareness of the alternative explanations for the behaviour of others by encouraging the person to mentalise the thoughts and feelings of others. This process is strongly embedded in the therapeutic relationship, which in itself serves to support the development of self-reflectiveness and mentalisation. As part of this process, the therapist begins to work with the person in identifying alternative and under-developed interpersonal coping behaviours that can be utilised to negotiate difficult interpersonal scenarios and in the development of new and alternative cognitive interpersonal schemata. These strategies will be explored in greater detail in Chapters 9 and 10.

CHAPTER 8

WORKING WITH TRAUMATIC REACTIONS TO PSYCHOTIC EXPERIENCES

INTRODUCTION

In this chapter we build upon the formulation of psychosis as a life event. We particularly focus on the danger-related dimensions of the experience of psychosis. However, as stated in Chapter 6, the reader will note the continuing overlap with appraisals of loss, entrapment and humiliation. We emphasise the importance of careful assessment of individuals' experiences of psychosis and psychiatric treatment, and experiences of other types of trauma that may have occurred prior to, during or after psychosis. In addition, and consistent with the main tenets of cognitive therapy, there continues to be an emphasis on the content of individuals' beliefs, appraisals and attributions. However, we also continue to expand upon the constructs that were introduced in previous chapters, where we have proposed that the structure and form of individual narratives are of clinical importance.

This is particularly relevant to the identification of points within a narrative that is marked by a loss of coherence and collaboration. In the context of trauma, psychosis and recovery, disrupted narratives often signal to the therapist where there may be aspects of the psychotic experience that are avoided and overwhelming, indicating that information processing remains incomplete or unelaborated. The therapist's response is a careful, supportive and collaborative exploration of those aspects of the person's experience. In this scenario, individuals will often experience some level of increased distress in relation to the exploration of a trauma narrative. Therefore, the therapist will carefully prepare the client prior to embarking on such a discourse surrounding the trauma. This preparation involves providing clear information to the client that their emotional distress may increase during this process and that this increase in emotional distress is a normal part of exploring difficult issues that might block recovery, and that increased emotion can be a signal that relevant and important emotional meanings are being focused on. Such a dialogue not only aims to improve collaboration but also provides an opportunity for clients to reflect on their emotional experience. In relation to more complex trauma, this is discussed in Chapter 10. Complex trauma refers to those individuals who are recovering from psychosis, and also have a history of unresolved trauma and/or loss that may include early childhood experiences such as abuse, neglect and loss.

PSYCHOSIS AS A TRAUMATIC EVENT

As we described in Chapter 2, there is growing evidence that psychosis itself is experienced as a traumatic event. To date, seven studies have investigated the prevalence of post-traumatic stress disorder (PTSD) symptomatology following psychosis (McGorry et al., 1991; Shaw et al., 1997; Priebe et al., 1998; Meyer et al., 1999; Frame & Morrison, 2001; Kennedy et al., 2002; Jackson et al., 2004). These studies have reported that somewhere between 11 per cent and 67 per cent individuals meet criteria for PTSD following an acute episode of psychosis, although the prevalence of trauma-related symptom clusters such as recurrent intrusive memories is considerably higher in some studies (e.g. Meyer et al., 1999). Most studies have indicated that the experience of psychotic symptoms themselves was primarily responsible for patients' trauma (Meyer et al., 1999; Frame & Morrison, 2001; Kennedy et al., 2002; Shaw et al., 2002). However, some studies have also suggested that the methods used to treat psychosis may be partially responsible (McGorry et al., 1991; Frame & Morrison, 2001). Although the methodology of these studies has been criticised (Morrison et al., 2003) and despite the fact that acute psychosis is not formally recognised as an event which fulfils DSM-IV (American Psychiatric Association, 1994) criteria for PTSD, the findings still appear to indicate that many patients experience significant PTSD symptomatology which arises following the treatment and experience of acute psychosis. Participants in these studies reported intrusive recollections of stressful hospitalisation events such as police involvement, or symptom-based experiences including uncontrollable auditory hallucinations, persecutory paranoia, thought broadcasting and passivity phenomena. Individuals with a 'sealing-over' recovery style were more likely to report fewer intrusions and greater avoidance using the Impact of Events Scale (Jackson et al., 2004). Those participants with greater levels of peri-traumatic depersonalisation, derealisation and numbing also had greater levels of intrusions and avoidance (Shaw et al., 2002). Consider the following case vignette, which illustrates the emotionally traumatic nature of a first relapse of psychosis:

Amed

Amed is an 18-year-old only child, who was referred to the service following a first episode of psychosis. His first episode occurred in the context of a number of chronic and continuing life problems. There was continuing family disharmony and arguments. His father had left Scotland to work abroad. Amed had started to get into trouble at school due to truanting, fighting and drug taking. When he went to college at 16, Amed continued to have a number of problems in terms of drug use, difficulties in making friends and arguments with his mother. His first episode had a relatively rapid onset of two weeks, followed by a four-week hospital admission. Amed experienced persecutory paranoia, thought broadcasting, thought insertion and was also very conceptually disorganised. However, he made a very quick recovery in terms of his psychotic experiences but was referred for cognitive therapy due to increased depressed mood following remission. He was very preoccupied with the continuing family problems and the break-up of his parents' marriage. He was also distressed regarding his future with respect to the impact of his drug-using lifestyle and psychosis on his future education and employment. Amed was unable to tolerate his antipsychotic medication and gradually discontinued this with the help of his psychiatrist three months following remission.

Over a period of nine months he made an excellent recovery in terms of his social and emotional well-being. He had made new friends, started college, he was no longer depressed and he had successfully reconciled many of his differences with his mother and father. Given the very favourable recovery, Amed's father, who had returned home following the first episode, decided to return to his job abroad. Within two weeks of his departure, Amed was admitted following a second episode of psychosis for a period of five weeks.

Again, Amed's psychotic experiences remitted rapidly. However, at his first appointment following discharge from hospital, there was a marked change in his affect. Amed's psychiatrist was concerned regarding a different presentation on this occasion. He felt that there were strong negative symptoms and asked for further psychological assessment of these. At this assessment, Amed's conversation was slow and stilted. He avoided eye contact. He described being unable to have positive feelings, that his emotions were numb. That it was like he didn't care any more. He felt guilty and ashamed. In relation to this he specifically remembered being admitted to hospital and being asked if he had been drinking alcohol. He realised at that point he had been drinking heavily and thought, 'It's my fault that I'm back here again.' At times Amed's description of events was marked by fragmentation and very general semantic descriptions of his experience, for example, 'You know, it all happened so quickly, one minute I was in (hospital), the next I was out' or 'Yeah, it was fine in hospital, nothing really happened'.

The therapist was struck by the apparent dissymetry between Amed's self-reported affect and the vague descriptions of his experience of his second episode. In further sessions this became a focus for further exploration. Following discussion of this dissymetry, Amed and his therapist agreed to explore this in greater detail. The therapist began to focus on more specific autobiographical details in the weeks prior to and during the second episode. It became apparent that Amed had been experiencing recurring and intrusive recollections of his psychosis. In particular, he reported specific memories of falling out with his friends due to arguments arising from delusional ideas, which included being a famous rock star songwriter. These memories were associated with intense feelings of shame and embarrassment. In relation to this he experienced a vivid visual image of his friends huddled in the classroom, laughing and joking about his misfortune. Associated with these memories, Amed experienced overwhelming feelings of entrapment and loss.

In the above case vignette Amed did not describe a specific threat to his or others' physical integrity or life which can occur in relation to psychotic experiences. For example, severe persecutory paranoia and auditory hallucinations are often associated with a direct threat to the life or physical integrity of the self or others. Rather, Amed's experiences typify many of the traumatic reactions that we see clinically within our services. He described a profound sense of threat to his emotional and social integrity through his own behaviour (i.e. drinking, arguing with friends), his imagined humiliating perception of the behaviour of others (i.e. friends laughing in a huddle) and the possible social vocational consequences of a second episode (e.g. unemployment and being alienated). In relation to these experiences and meanings, Amed describes recurring intrusive memories, nightmares, numbing, cognitive avoidance of thoughts and images, social avoidance of friends and avoidance of mental health facilities.

It is particularly poignant that this is Amed's second episode. While traumatic reactions following a first episode are important and may not be uncommon, we have noted that the second episode can be particularly emotionally and psychologically toxic. The experience of an event repeating itself means that it can no longer be set aside as a 'one-off'. For Amed, psychosis has now acquired the quality of dangerousness via the potential for its recurrence. We think that the extent to which the event is then experienced as threatening and dangerous, via the possibility or probability of relapse, may be important to the understanding of individual traumatic reactions to psychosis. The reader will also note the overlap with other life event dimensions of entrapment, loss and humiliation, which were explored in Chapter 6. The greater the overlap in life event dimensions, the greater the emotional and psychological impact.

TRAUMA THEORY

Ehlers and Clark (2000) have proposed a cognitive model of individuals' reactions to trauma, which specifies multiple sources of appraisal to explain the persistence of traumatic reactions. They propose that PTSD becomes persistent when individuals process a trauma in a way that leads to a sense of serious and current threat and/or danger. This sense of threat arises from disturbances in an individual's personal appraisals and autobiographical memories. First, the appraisals that are responsible for the maintenance of a sense of current threat include excessively negative interpretations of the traumatic event itself and negative interpretations of the consequences of the traumatic event. These appraisals of trauma consequences include the person's interpretations of their specific symptoms (e.g. flashbacks), other people's reactions in the aftermath of the event (e.g. anger, horror) and the consequences of the traumatic event for important areas of life and life goals (e.g. being able to work, finance) and their quality of life (e.g. pain and disability).

Second, disturbances in autobiographical memory characterised by poor elaboration and contextualisation, strong associative memories and strong perceptual priming are also hypothesised to maintain a sense of current threat. Ehlers and Clark also emphasise that behavioural strategies (e.g. avoidance of friends, planning, going outside, carrying a weapon) and cognitive processing styles (e.g. thought suppression, rumination, cognitive avoidance) become maladaptive and problematic because they directly produce PTSD symptoms (e.g. rumination leading to increased intrusions). Consequently, such strategies prevent disconfirmation of negative interpretations of trauma and associated sequelae, and prevent change in the nature of traumatic memories.

Disturbances in Autobiographical Memory

One particularly important factor in the recovery from and vulnerability to relapse in psychosis is the potentially strong stimulus–stimulus or stimulus–response associations between internal events including psychotic experiences (e.g. suspiciousness and ideas of reference), and other internal events such as a sense of dread or external events such as hospitalisation or criticism from others. These strong associations make the triggering of intrusive unwanted memories and intensely distressing emotional re-experiencing more probable.

For example, during treatment one individual described how, during the very early stages of relapse, whispering sounds triggered intrusive memories of hearing voices. She would re-experience the memory of her mother looking at her with horror while she herself was experiencing command hallucinations screaming at her to kill her mother then herself. Shaw and colleagues (1997) found that experiences during psychosis representing a sense of loss of control were rated the most distressing by individuals. These 'loss of control' experiences, which included enforced seclusion, experiencing the self being controlled by external forces, visual hallucinations and thought insertion, were associated with the highest levels of distress. Frame and Morrison (2001) found that, having controlled for the severity of psychotic symptoms, the experience of psychosis accounted for a substantial proportion of PTSD symptoms, whereas experience of hospitalisation only accounted for a small amount of PTSD symptoms. Therefore, it is possible that certain internal processes and events such as particular symptoms or configurations of symptoms cue intrusive vivid visual memories of previous episodes of psychosis and associated events. These memories are likely to form the basis for important experiential meanings and appraisals relevant to recovery and relapse. Indeed, such experiences are likely to maintain a sense of current or impending threat.

However, it is also possible that individuals who 'seal over' their experiences of psychosis and successfully isolate these experiences from other domains of their life may not experience explicit memories of previous episodes. In this case the associations may be more implicit. Therefore, certain internal events reminiscent of relapse or apparently innocuous environmental stimuli may cue feelings of fear and dread. Individuals are likely to struggle to source the origins of these feelings ('affect without recollection') and therefore they will become vigilant for other forms of threat, for example, vigilance for interpersonal danger. Consistent with this, Meyer et al. (1999) found that psychotic symptoms seemed to be minimised by participants. Individuals were often reluctant to discuss them, a response suggestive of avoidance, embarrassment, denial and efforts to avoid being seen as 'crazy'. Psychotic experiences were consistently rated as distressing, particularly persecutory thoughts, visual hallucinations and passivity phenomena, and the patients also reported associated intrusive and recurring thoughts about these experiences. Jackson et al. (2004) reported a significant correlation between individuals' perception of the 'stressfulness' of their initial admission to hospital and their PTSD symptoms, but did not find a relationship between PTSD symptoms and psychotic symptoms. Jackson and colleagues also found a relationship between recovery style and intrusion and avoidance symptoms. Those who had a tendency to 'seal over' their psychotic experiences reported lower levels of intrusions and higher levels of avoidance. Harrison and Fowler (2004) investigated the relationship between negative symptoms, trauma and autobiographical memory among 38 people recovering from psychosis. This group reported a high number of trauma symptoms that were related to both psychosis and hospitalisation experiences. Those who reported greater avoidance of distressing memories of psychotic experiences and hospitalisation also had a higher level of negative symptoms. This was even after controlling for the severity of depressed mood.

According to Ehlers and Clark (2000), poorly elaborated memories are therefore likely to be associated with: (1) problematic intentional recall; (2) a 'here and now' quality (little or no context in time and place) to memories; (3) the absence of subsequent information (e.g. the voices did not make me harm my sister); and (4) the presence of easy triggering by psychologically similar cues. For example, during her admission to hospital, one individual recollected experiencing being rapidly tranquillised by nursing staff. She saw nursing staff as a danger to her physical integrity and well-being, as being predatory and malevolent, and as looking for opportunities to hospitalise and medicate her. Therefore, hospital-related stimuli, including her consultant psychiatrist, became associated with increased suspiciousness and paranoia. This reaction was in turn interpreted by the consultant psychiatrist as evidence of continuing paranoid ideation and the need for further increases in antipsychotic medication. In turn, the client became increasingly exasperated and decided to discontinue her medication.

During cognitive therapy, these experiences were explored in greater detail. Prior to being tranquillised, she had been in a high state of arousal and distress, which compromised a detailed recall of the event. In addition, avoidance of her memories and the overwhelming emotions associated with recollecting the event inhibited elaboration and processing of the trauma. As part of therapy she was encouraged to discuss her experiences with the nursing staff involved. Nursing staff communicated their alarm at her distress and their intention to use rapid tranquillisation to alleviate her distress. Therefore, careful analysis and attention to individual narratives during therapy can reveal disturbances in and fragmentation of autobiographical memories surrounding psychosis. This chain of events was formulated in terms of a process of adaptation that incorporated staff misinterpretations of her apparent suspicious stance and understandable distress. Consider the narrative below:

Th: Can you remember any events prior to developing psychosis?
C: No, not really ... [11-second pause]. It just came out of the blue really, you know? One minute I'm at college doing my work, the next minute

I'm in this night club and this fucking voice is telling me to kill myself ... [4-second pause] no, can't think of anything ... you just can't do anything about it, man, eh?

This person was referred for a persistent and highly disabling fear of relapse. During the process of assessment and engagement he described a number of key beliefs about his recovery. These were that psychosis was an inevitable, sudden and uncontrollable event. Indeed, the structure and content of the narrative above communicate this clearly. In therapy, careful analysis revealed that there were a number of serious life events including a long period of unemployment, leading to feelings of depression (e.g. loss, entrapment), his girlfriend ending their relationship, leading to feelings of loss, and increased self-critical thinking (e.g. humiliation, loss/separation), and in addition his sister developing a episode of severe depression, leading to increased worry and preoccupation regarding the health and well-being of his family (danger/threat). None of the essential contextual factors are apparent in the narrative above and therefore this can easily lead to a sense of psychosis as a sudden, uncontrollable, unpredictable and highly threatening event.

ASSIMILATION AND ACCOMMODATION

Psychotic experiences are processed in the context of individuals' pre-existing beliefs, expectations and attitudes. Janoff-Bulman (1992) proposed that a person's beliefs about self and the world prior to a traumatic event are crucial to understanding their emotional recovery from trauma. According to this theory, a traumatic event shatters an individual's assumptions of the self as invulnerable and worthwhile, and the world as predictable and comprehensible. In this model, negative affect including depression and anxiety are normal and necessary consequences of trauma and the subsequent need to re-evaluate the self and the world. However, as described in previous chapters, people who experience psychosis have often experienced adversity and trauma earlier in life. It would therefore be unreasonable to expect that many individuals who developed psychosis believe that they are invulnerable and the world is a predictable and safe place. Therefore, while Janoff-Bulman's proposal that pre-trauma beliefs may be important determinants of adaptation to psychosis is in line with a developmental understanding of psychosis, it may be that, as Power and Dalgliesh (1997) have suggested, trauma confirms rather than shatters individuals' beliefs and assumptions about themselves and the world. Early adversity may have led to the genesis of beliefs regarding personal vulnerability or defectiveness that are then confirmed by the experience of psychosis.

Adaptation to psychosis and the trauma associated with psychotic experiences or compulsory treatment might best be understood using the Piagetian constructs of assimilation and accommodation. Assimilation refers to the process whereby information is altered and distorted to fit pre-existing beliefs. Accommodation, on the other hand, involves changing existing beliefs to accept new information. The latter process is more difficult and challenging for an individual to achieve.

Hollon and Garber (1988) have proposed that accommodation is necessary for successful integration of a traumatic event. Resick and Schnicke (1993) have also proposed that trauma interacts with individuals' pre-existing beliefs concerning self, world and future, and that in response to a trauma, individuals may reject their pre-existing beliefs (over-accommodation), or distort the trauma to fit with their pre-existing beliefs (assimilation). Over-accommodation involves a radical change in underlying beliefs and assumptions, for example, an individual who viewed themselves as competent and safe prior to psychosis, may view their psychotic experiences as highly dangerous, and as meaning they have no control. Therefore, this appraisal would give rise to high levels of fear concerning relapse. Assimilation, on the other hand, represents an individual's attempt to preserve their pre-existing beliefs, despite their experience of psychosis. For example, the same individual may use cognitive strategies aimed at minimisation (e.g. 'It didn't happen', 'It happened because I wasn't eating properly') or behavioural strategies aimed at avoidance of the trauma. This strategy may lead to reduced depression in the short run; however, the cost may be a corresponding reduced awareness of relapse risk, excessive and unnecessary avoidance, and reduced control of illness in the longer run.

The processes of assimilation and over-accommodation might also help explain the development of shame and humiliation attributions following psychosis and the development of secondary depression. For example, an individual who believes 'good things happen to good people, bad things happen to bad people' may respond to the experience of their psychosis with over-accommodation (e.g. 'It doesn't matter what I do, bad things will happen to me') leading to increased helplessness and hopelessness. Or, alternatively, assimilation (e.g. 'I must have done something wrong to have deserved this') leading to increased self-blame and shame. According to this formulation, what is critical is the interaction between the individual's pre-existing beliefs concerning themselves, the world and future, the occurrence of psychosis as a critical incident, and the individual's attempt to assimilate or accommodate their experience.

The following case example will be used in describing interventions that can be used to support individuals with traumatic reactions in the context of their psychosis:

Susan

Susan first presented to mental health services following an assault at college. She was attacked by a group of fellow college students and developed severe anxiety difficulties that stopped her from further attending college, going into town and eventually leaving the flat at all.

Susan lives with her mother in a small council flat in the centre of a large city. Her father left the family when Susan was two years old and she had no subsequent contact with him. Her mother never remarried or had any intimate relationship since the marital separation. Both Susan and her mother live quite isolated and have few acquaintances or friends. They spend most of their spare time together and enjoy going shopping or to the cinema. As a young child Susan had significant hearing problems for which she had to attend regular hospital treatments for a number of years. As a consequence Susan found it difficult to manage and integrate at primary school and before her transition to secondary school a special education setting was suggested. Throughout her time at school Susan was bullied both by fellow pupils at school but also by peers in her neighbourhood. After her fourth year at secondary school Susan dropped out of school and following a period of non-attendance she went to a local technical college where she managed to attend for about six months. Consequently Susan left her school and college education without having completed any exams. She has been staying at home since and for the past two years Susan's mother has given up work to look after Susan full-time.

At assessment it emerged that she had been hearing multiple voices for a number of years since a significant bullying incident at school. Her voices represented multiple relationships that were reminiscent of peers that she could recognise from school and college. The voices mainly consisted of commentary on her person, her appearance and her actions. She reported that over time she also found the voices to be influencing her decision-making. Susan also suffered from long periods of low mood when she would feel extremely sad, listless and unable to meet people or engage in any activities. At these times of low mood her mother would find Susan sitting on her bed in her room or lying on the floor and 'staring into space'. Over a short period prior to her admission, her mother found Susan cutting up her clothes, shouting at the TV and destroying photographs of herself. When she challenged her about her behaviour, she received no reply. At this point

Susan's mother sought advice from her GP and Susan was referred to a psychiatric emergency team. The psychiatric emergency team diagnosed Susan with schizophrenia and put her on antipsychotic medication; within a short period of time Susan developed severe side effects and her medication treatment was altered several times as a consequence.

EXPLORING TRAUMATIC REACTIONS

From a client's perspective, the emotional distress associated with psychosis appears as a whole. Anxiety, low mood, symptomatic distress related to voices and paranoia are not experienced in a compartmentalised way. Rather, cognitive, emotional and physiological dimensions of psychotic experience are experienced as merged and confusing. Indeed, clients often experience confusion in relation to their traumatic reactions to psychotic experience, and do not necessarily separate these experiences from their psychosis. Therefore, therapists need to take time to help clients separate and differentiate layers of their complex experiences. One of the most distressing aspects of the experience of psychosis can be the pervasive nature of the emotional distress associated with psychosis. It can be difficult for clients to disentangle their experience in order to develop a coherent and self-reflective understanding of their experience. The narrative below gives an example of the confused enmeshment of PTSD and psychosis in the experience of distress:

C: ... and I find it really difficult to get into town to the shops I like.
Th: Explain to me what makes that difficult.
C: I am not sure, I just feel really bad.
Th: When was the last time you planned to go to the shops and that happened?
C: Just last week, when I wanted to get a present for my mum ... I got down to the street and just felt really nervous and I got in my head these thoughts ...
Th: Can you tell me more about these thoughts and that sense of feeling very nervous?
C: I get these thoughts, it's like it's happening again. I feel scared, I don't know what to do, my thoughts are racing and I feel like I can't do this.
Th: Tell me what is happening again.
C: It's like how I felt before. My thoughts are going mental and it's like I can't do anything to stop it. It's like how I was in hospital, I feel like I'm trapped and there is nothing I can do to stop it.

Th: How do you feel just now thinking about this?

C: I feel really bad . . . I can see it happening in my head, I can see myself, it's like I am back there again on the ward, I am pure paranoid.

We see in this brief exchange that the client's description of her emotional distress ('I feel scared', 'I don't know what to do') and reliving experiences ('I can see it happening in my head, I can see myself, it's like I am back there again') involve a state of threat processing. Key to her appraisal of danger is the overlap between PTSD symptoms ('I feel scared') and psychosis symptoms ('I am pure paranoid') in the context of an anxiety reaction. Therefore, an important part of the therapeutic process is a more detailed understanding and formulation of the components of the client's reactions to events symbolising or reminding them of their psychotic experiences. The therapist explores experiences such as intrusive thoughts, images or memories related to psychosis and its associated events. An important part of this is to carefully assess the essential components of possible PTSD reactions, which include clusters of symptoms, associated with intrusions, avoidance and hyperarousal. This needs to go hand in hand with an exploration of the associated cues and triggers to intrusive memories and flashbacks. The narrative below illustrates the process of exploration of cues to experience:

Th: I'd like to explore with you this experience of vividly remembering being back in hospital. In the situation that you just described, what is this like for you?

C: . . . I don't know. I just felt like that, I don't know where that came from.

Th: If you try to take yourself back into the situation, can you remember when that feeling arose?

C: Hmmm, I was at the door, looking out. Everything seemed really busy in the street. I felt frightened. I started to panic. I get this, I don't know, I can't breathe. I was in hospital, that happened. I saw the police bringing somebody in. I thought . . . It's my turn. I'm going to be gassed . . .

Th: What specifically brought that back?

C: The not being able to breathe. The suffocating. I thought, I'm going to die and people are just standing about watching.

We see in this narrative how the client steps out onto the street and how the feelings of anxiety and panic in the context of being in a busy place with other people around cues a reliving experience. What is particularly noteworthy is the sensory quality of this memory where feelings of suffocation activate a vivid visual image of the police bringing a patient onto the ward and the associated meaning 'I'm going to be gassed'. The therapist continues exploration of this experience, although in this example the process has been somewhat shortened to illustrate further exploration of the client's reactions to reliving the experience:

Th: Does this happen at other times?

C: Yeah, it happens all the time, especially when I try to do something on my own, so I hardly ever try now. I couldn't ask Mum to get her to take me to get her birthday present. I couldn't even do that.

Th: How do you normally deal with that reliving?

C: Ah, I just shut it out. I don't think about it. I hate coming here. It, like, reminds me of being in hospital. No offence, like.

Th: None taken. How do you shut it out, not think about it?

C: I try to think of something else. I go to my room to make it stop. Sometimes I pinch myself really hard. But I get nightmares where I'm fighting with people.

Th: What happens when you try to think of something else or pinch yourself?

C: It sometimes stops. Normally I just try to get home.

The narrative begins to highlight the client's attempts to avoid and block out flashbacks, intrusion and reliving experiences. This narrative provides a platform to develop a reflective summary highlighting the links between her experience of her psychosis and the components of her reactions. This provides the basis to develop an individualised formulation of the client's psychological adaptation following psychosis.

EXPLAINING TRAUMATIC REACTIONS

An important step in the evolution of therapeutic work is the sharing of a psychological understanding that incorporates all aspects of the client's trauma reaction. This aids the client's ability to label and differentiate their reactions in different situations and to understand the origins of strong affective, physiological and cognitive experiences that tend to characterise traumatic reactions. The therapist might consider producing a written formulation for the client to support their understanding of their experiences and provide a rationale for important psychotherapeutic tasks. An example of a letter to Susan written by her therapist summarising the previous session is given below:

Dear Susan,

You worked really hard the last time that we met. It was a difficult session for you because you talked about frightening memories of your time in hospital. It was important to talk about these memories because they seem to be related to one of the key areas on your problem list, which is not being able to go outside on your own. It helped me to understand better how these anxieties that you are experiencing now are related to really frightening and traumatic situations when you were in hospital.

Many people have reported experiencing psychosis as frightening and traumatic, and have described very similar reactions to what you described last week. One of the important aspects of a traumatic experience is that because of the state of fear and terror that people experience at the time, memories of those events remain very active. These memories contain lots of very powerful emotions and thoughts that can be so overwhelming that the person feels like they are reliving the event again. It can seem like the only way to deal with these memories is to shut them out.

Similarly, you described a sense of reliving being in hospital when you experienced being frightened and panicky, particularly when there were other people around. This seems to remind you of being in the ward and being terrified that the police were going to kill you. It seemed as if other people just stood back and watched. You've coped with this by trying to blank it out, pinch yourself or by staying at home.

The problem that this leaves you with is that these memories keep intruding back into your mind, as if they haven't been dealt with. This means that you constantly feel under threat and at the same time you don't want to think or talk about it. It feels like how you felt in hospital. But what you are describing is very different to how you were when you were unwell. This is a traumatic reaction to the extreme fear you experienced in hospital. An important therapy task is to help you explore and understand these frightening memories and learn how to deal with them in a way that allows your upsetting feelings to reduce.

A Therapist

There are a number of components to this formulation, which include the following. First, the therapist attempts to validate the client's difficulties in expressing and exploring this experience. Second, the therapist provides a normalising non-pathological description of traumatic reactions that highlights the importance of emotion and meaning. Third, within this context, the therapist then individualises the client's account within this framework and communicates a separation of the traumatic reaction from the psychosis itself. Finally, the therapist defines the task of therapy as addressing the processing of traumatic memories and associated distress. Of course, this sort of dialogue can become threaded through the therapeutic discourse as means for communicating formulation. The therapist might also consider the use of diagrammatical formulations to communicate the specific maintenance mechanisms.

EXPLORING MEANING WITHIN TRAUMATIC MEMORIES AND IMAGERY

By their very nature traumatic memories have a strong sensory quality; they are frequently fragmented, disjointed and show a lack of connectivity. The principal therapeutic task is therefore to support the creation of a consistent, unfragmented and coherent narrative of the traumatic experience(s). In order to do this, the therapist has to attend to ruptures and inconsistencies in the structure, flow and content of discourse. Where patients find initial difficulty in verbally exploring these memories, it can be helpful to invite them to provide a written account of the specific event. The therapist is also aware of gaps in the narrative that may indicate specific aspects of the memory that are unprocessed or avoided. For example, early in therapy Susan agreed to write an account of seeing the police coming onto the ward:

> Susan: I was sitting in the smoking corner and they just appear. It is horrible, they look really angry. They had somebody with them who looked really official. I see them looking at me. . . . They are here to get somebody and to take them away. I heard somebody crying on the ward. Had I hurt them? Are they here to get me? I heard somebody say: 'They are going to gas you! You are evil!' I am all sweaty, I was shaking, I could not breathe properly. One of the nurses came at me and I panicked. He says, 'Stop screaming, you'll upset the other patients.' I pulled the curtains and hid in my bed the rest of the night, I can't remember what happened after that.

Within the above narrative there is a lack of context in terms of the immediate environment, other people, the events beforehand and the events afterwards. Also significant are the switches between past and present tense which give a 'here and now' quality. The narrative is short. There is little elaboration outside her immediate state of alarm and associated appraisals. There is also a sensory quality, particularly regarding her feelings of fear and panic. This characterises the fragmented and unelaborated memories that are characteristic of traumatic reactions. Therefore, it is helpful to support the client in exploring the different qualities of the traumatic experiences. It is helpful to spend time in developing a narrative that fully encompasses the range of the individual's feelings, sensations and thoughts. In this process the therapist uses open questions to allow the client to freely explore. The therapist helps to enrich the narrative by asking the client to describe specific examples and contextual information. This can be facilitated by drawing the client's attention to specific but seemingly arbitrary details of the experience. The discourse below illustrates this process:

Th: I would like you to paint a picture of that scene. In that I want you to fill in as much of the detail as you can remember. Do you remember what you were doing before the police arrived?

C: We had just had lunch and I was sitting in the smoking corner having a fag.

Th: OK, who else was there?

C: Well, there was one guy there, he always smokes, he has these yellow fingers, and he is a nice guy and asks you how you are. The TV was on in the other corner, I think with the news, some train crash . . . It was really busy, there was loads of noise and everybody was rushing about, the nurses, I mean.

Th: Hmmm, OK, what happened next?

C: Well, I am not sure how long it was, but there was all this rushing about . . . I think somebody had hurt themselves, actually, I think somebody had cut themselves.

Th: And then?

C: I think that was what all the rushing was about, I remember people being really upset, Julie started crying, I felt really scared and worried.

Th: What did you do?

C: I was trying to talk to Julie and offered her a fag, I was saying to her it would be OK. I think that was when the police came in . . . I automatically thought they are after me. I got really panicky, I couldn't breathe . . .

Th: Can you describe what that was like?

C: It was terrible. I thought that I was going to suffocate. It was like I was going to die. I was so frightened, and it was then I heard someone say: 'They are going to gas you! You are evil!' It sounds mad now, but I don't know what being gassed feels like but it felt like that was what was happening. It was like at that time I thought everything was my fault and that I was evil, so hearing that was like the worst thing ever!

Th: How do you feel right now talking about this?

C: I feel scared, I feel like I want to panic. I feel stupid, a bit daft. But that feeling of suffocating, it just brings everything back. I never found out if that person was OK or not. I don't know if they died. I never had an experience like that before. How could people put you in a situation like that when you are unwell?

The careful exploration of the traumatic events allows the client to reflect on her experience and begin to explore new meanings. In doing so her narrative becomes more contextualised; she is able to reflect on related events, other people and her emotional reaction at the time. She feels reminded of the emotional intensity of the experience but is able to put her emotional reaction in the here and now and separate that reaction from the original feelings of fear and panic. In addition, she is able to reflect on the significance of suffocation and the coincidence between that feeling, her fear response and the statement of her voice. In so doing she reflects upon one aspect of her unresolved feelings in relation to the event, which was the unresolved outcome of the self-harming incident. The construction of a coherent narrative provides the basis to explore important meanings for the client attached to the traumatic event and how these might resonate with their wider view of themselves, others, the world and the future.

The unfolding of a client's narrative gives rise to an enriched network of important personal meanings that provide important insights into aspects of the trauma that remain unresolved. Themes concerning personal safety, interpersonal trust, power, control and self-esteem may be important in the context of traumatic experiences associated with psychosis. An important consideration in the evolution of traumatic meanings is their historical context. For example, a person with difficult experiences of bullying during their school years who is involuntarily admitted to hospital may experience that admission as confirmatory of their personal vulnerability and the untrustworthiness of others. Development of an understanding of the salient personal meanings therefore gives insight into the individual's process of adaptation to psychosis and how psychotic experiences are assimilated or accommodated into the pre-existing and evolving meaning framework. In addition, personal meanings give shape to individuals' affective responses such as fear, shame, embarrassment or helplessness. These responses are highly idiosyncratic, and therapists cannot assume that there are specific normative responses to specific events. For example, the experience of an involuntary admission to hospital may well generate considerable fear for a person; however, this may not be the essentially traumatic element of the event. It may be the person's sense of humiliation and loss of control that are the central traumatic meaning that drives their distress and avoidance.

In exploring the incident and the associated feelings as described, the client is becoming able to put her emotional reactions and other sequelae in relation to the particular aspects of the event and how these made sense for her at the time. She is now also able to re-evaluate these perceptions within a more coherent narrative that is no longer driven by fear and confusion.

Th: Thinking about what happened, when you were in hospital, what is the most upsetting thing about that?

C: Well, it's really hard, you go through something like that and it's like you can't get over it.

Th: What is the hardest thing to get over?

C: Well, it's like having absolutely no control, being terrified, and thinking that you are going to die and there is nothing you can do.

Th: What does that mean to you now?

C: It could happen any time, there's nothing I can do.

Through the process of identifying salient personal meanings, the therapist explores the roots of those appraisals in terms of resonances with other situations associated with psychosis, or their relationship with other thematically similar experiences. In this sense, the therapist may explore earlier experiences that are relevant to the meaning-making process. This is achieved by tracing recollections of similar emotional experiences:

Th: The sense of there being nothing you can do, is that a feeling that you recognise?

C: Hmmm, maybe. There was a really bad time at college. I was in this group of girls and I thought they were my friends. I didn't know it at the time but I think it had to do with one of their boyfriends fancying me or something. One day after class we went to the park and Gemma started pushing me around, I don't mean physically, like, but she had a right go, you know, saying, 'Who do you think you are?' and stuff like that.

Th: How did you feel?

C: I felt really confused, I remember thinking she's only joking, but then the others joined in and it got really nasty. I didn't go back to college after that.

Th: What happened?

C: They ripped my clothes and told me I was ugly. They made me walk back, my skirt was ripped. I felt so embarrassed. I felt so lost, these were the people I thought were my friends and they just turned on me. I still don't know why. I was really frightened.

Th: Thinking about that, how do you make sense of this now?

C: I don't know, I was scared for ages. I felt I must have done something. Since then I always look behind my shoulder, if you know what I mean, or over my shoulder.

Th: What did you think you had done?

C: I don't know, just something wrong, something bad, I never really found out.

Th: How does that resonate with what happened on the ward?

C: 'Cos it was the first time I felt so scared and panicky, when I was running home, with my skirt, I thought I couldn't breathe, and I remember in the hospital, feeling I must have done something, feeling that they were coming for me.

In this way the process of meaning making enables individuals to develop an active and coherent formulation of their emotional experience via the identification of key meanings. In this instance, the ward experience is assimilated into a developing meaning framework, which encompasses beliefs about undetermined threat, wrongdoing and punishment. Consistent with the approaches developed in Chapter 6, the therapist will work with the client to develop a self-accepting reflective understanding of these experiences.

CONTRASTING EXPERIENCES OF PSYCHOSIS AND PTSD

Specific problems do occur in relation to traumatic reactions to psychosis. For example, it can be difficult to discriminate between experiences of psychosis and traumatic reactions. Both experiences overlap in terms of the presence of intrusive events, anxiety and hyperarousal, accompanying and related affect, and overvalued fear and paranoia. For example, psychosis is characterised by intrusive events such as hearing voices, thought insertion and transmission, passivity and loss of control, whereas PTSD is characterised by intrusive thoughts, images, memories and reliving. Both symptom clusters are phenomenologically similar in that they are intrusive, unwanted and outside the immediate control of the person. This means that for individuals this can be experientially confusing and disorientating. Therefore, it is helpful to work with the client to develop their ability to become aware of the different qualities of their experience. This is important in order to address secondary appraisals of traumatic symptoms that produce a state of heightened fear and alarm. For example, clients may interpret trauma symptoms as signs of relapse, thus producing a state of fear of recurrence. In addition, this is particularly confusing when the content of psychotic symptoms is similar to the material expressed in post-traumatic reactions. For example, clients might misidentify trauma symptoms as being psychotic symptoms. Furthermore, the persistence of a state of threat and danger may also maintain a state of fear in relation to interpersonal threat.

Therefore, the therapist might provide written information on the experiences associated with psychosis and the experiences associated with trauma and invite the person to consider the similarities and differences. On the other hand, the therapist might encourage the person to reflect on the similarities and differences in their own experiences. As a note of caution, if the person has had continuing distressing psychotic experiences, this strategy is likely to be misapplied and might cause undue distress. In allowing the client to explore the different qualities of these experiences, it is helpful to spend time in developing a narrative that fully encompasses the range of the individual's feelings, sensations and thoughts. In this process the therapist uses open questions to allow the client to reconstruct their experience in a safe and containing context. The therapist helps to enrich and contextualise the narrative by asking the client to describe specific examples. The therapeutic task is to create a consistent, unfragmented and coherent narrative of the traumatic. The therapist explores with the client the similarities and differences between traumatic reactions and psychosis itself:

Th: You talked about how what you felt reminded you of the time when you were last in hospital; can you tell me more about that?

C: Yeah, it felt it was frightening in a similar way, I mean, the feeling inside was similar . . . I am not explaining that very well.

Th: You are doing really well; this is a difficult thing to think about.

C: It was like not knowing what would happen next. And then when I get this tightness in my chest, I cannot think straight any more, my thoughts were running away with me.

Th: Is there anything else that is similar?

C: Feeling really confused, and it's like I'm not getting what's happening to me any more.

Th: What does that mean to you?

C: It's like it's happening again. I get frightened.

Th: So, let's do something different for a moment. Let's think about what's different. Can you think of anything that is different about how you feel now compared to before?

C: I don't hear things. It's not that I think I've done something bad, it's more like I think something bad might happen, like I'm going to relapse.

This process is helpful in identifying secondary appraisals responsible for the maintenance of a sense of fear and current danger, to support the person's ability to discriminate between the psychotic experiences and their psychological reactions, and to encourage the development of a reflective self-awareness. The therapist is attentive to the clients' interpretations of their emotional, cognitive and physiological experiences as evidence of further danger, for example, fear of relapse. This process can be supported by creating a safe environment to facilitate further exploration of specific experiences, by developing and testing alternative appraisals, supporting clients in developing coping strategies that alleviate and soothe fearful reactions, and by creating opportunities to explore alternative coping in challenging situations. For example, in Susan's case, the therapist might explore strategies to alleviate her anxiety, reattribute her interpretations of symptoms as evidence of relapse, and apply this learning in situations where these triggers are evoked. For the client, feelings of fear and anxiety evoke appraisals of fear recurrence. Her avoidance of situations which evoke fear prevents disconfirmation of her negative appraisal and reaffirms avoidance as a successful emotion regulation strategy. Therefore, the therapist might work collaboratively to encourage Susan to develop alternative and accepting explanations for her fearful reactions.

CONCLUSIONS

In this chapter we have attempted to build upon some of the core concepts and ideas developed in Chapter 6, but with special reference to traumatic reactions to psychosis. We have emphasised the importance of the therapeutic relationship of narrative in this process and the therapist's attention to fragmentation and disconnections in discourse. This signals the presence of traumatic and unresolved or unprocessed aspects of the experience. The process of exploration is tied closely to the development of meaning making. In this, the therapist's responsibility is to facilitate this process in a way that encourages a sensitive and understanding self-reflection. In addition, the exploration of and development of narrative in the context of traumatic reactions facilitate elaboration and contextualising of the experience. We have emphasised the importance of pursuing emotional resonance in order to allow connectivity with past trauma or life events, or with current appraisals of experience, for example, where the overlap between psychosis and trauma creates a sense of current and persisting threat. Therapists should also be cautious not to overlook other types of appraisal indicating loss, entrapment and shameful humiliation.

CHAPTER 9

INTERPERSONAL STRATEGIES

INTRODUCTION

In consideration of the developmental, social and interpersonal factors outlined in Chapter 3 we would like to discuss aspects of the intervention that focus on the factors of interpersonal vulnerability and interpersonal strategies in the psychotherapeutic treatment of psychosis and staying well. Wide-ranging evidence from research and clinical contexts suggests that the current social environmental context has an important impact on the onset, course and expression of psychosis (e.g. Johnson & Kizer, 2002; Barrowclough & Hooley, 2003).

The role of two kinds of environmental factors has predominantly been highlighted in psychosis: (1) recent negative life events in their interaction with the social environment; and (2) the quality of close social relationships, namely social support in terms of positive and salutogenic social networks and expressed emotion (EE), describing negative interactions with close family members or significant others. As described above, EE is conceptualised through emotionally over-involved and intrusive interactions and critical comments or hostility expressed by close others. The life events literature has been fairly consistent in suggesting that individuals with psychosis experience increased stressful events prior to onset or subsequent episodes. In addition, there is reasonable evidence that social support from significant others leads to a more positive course of psychosis, especially in the face of stressful circumstances. Negative interpersonal relationships, however, EE from family and close others predict higher frequency of relapse. Moreover, there is evidence that psychological interventions developed from the social support and EE literatures, respectively, are effective in the treatment for psychosis and aid recovery and staying well.

THE SOCIAL ENVIRONMENT

Interpersonal Vulnerabilities

A significant characteristic of an individual's current environment that affects the course of psychosis is the quality of supportive or nonsupportive interpersonal relationships and interactions. Support from family and friends can buffer against the adverse effects of stress or directly enhance social functioning and overall quality of life, whereas high degrees of critical interactions and emotional over-involvement (high EE) from caregivers and close others can provide additional stress and significantly worsen the course and prognosis of psychosis.

A number of studies found that individuals with a psychosis experience less social support than various control groups and that low social support is associated with more frequent relapses. Romans and McPherson (1992) found that psychotic participants reported less social support than community controls, but they were not significantly different from the controls with past psychopathology. Individuals with psychosis had less adequate attachments and less available social support as a result of poorer social integration. This was associated with higher levels of residual symptoms and lower quality of life (Schwannauer, 1997). Kulhara et al. (1999) found that lower social support was associated with a higher frequency of lifetime relapses in psychotic inpatients. Stefos and colleagues (1996) found that relapses over the past three years estimated from medical charts in 21 remitted psychotic patients were significantly associated with lower social support, maladjustment in social activities, and poor relationships with extended family.

Prospective studies further established that poor perceived social support predicted greater relapses and longer time to recovery. In a mixed sample of remitted psychotic, depressed and control participants followed for one year with self-report measures of social adjustment and self-esteem, Staner et al. (1997) found that among the psychosis patients, social maladjustment and low self-esteem were predictive of relapse. In two prospective studies of psychotic patients using social support questionnaires, Johnson and colleagues (Johnson et al., 1999, 2000) further found that poorer social support predicted a significantly longer time to recovery and was predictive of residual depression. The association of low social support with depressive symptoms was mediated by low self-esteem.

Some of the findings regarding the quality of the social support networks of psychotic populations, however, appear somewhat contradictory. Cohen and Kochanowicz (1989) found in a sample of Afro-Caribbean persons with schizophrenia in New York that smaller social networks were associated with higher levels of support satisfaction and the frequency of family contacts with family members was highly predictive of hospital readmission. In contrast, Müller et al. (1986) found in a larger sample of people diagnosed with schizophrenia with an illness history of at least 10 years that one-third lived in relative social isolation and a majority reported extremely small social networks. Social isolation and small social networks were associated with poorer social adjustment and overall functioning. Julian Leff and colleagues (1990) investigated the social environments of a large group of chronic psychiatric patients. They found that relatively superficial and infrequent contacts were valued by individuals with schizophrenia, confiding relationships were valued less. Relationships with professionals were valued most for their consistency and instrumental support and that they were emotionally less demanding. The direction or implied causality of these findings, however, appears unclear. Many of the client groups studied in this context had considerable illness histories and had spent a long time in the care of psychiatric services, which in itself is associated with poorer social integration and diminished vocational opportunities. Lipton and colleagues (1981) found in a study looking at the development of the social environment in patients with schizophrenia that network size reduced dramatically following a first episode of psychosis.

Given the somewhat mixed findings, it is therefore difficult to ascertain whether the relative deficits in social support networks are somehow associated with poor social functioning and high levels of social anxiety as part of the nosology of psychosis or whether they portray consequences of an illness model and the individual's relative personal adaptation to the marginalisation and social and socio-economic disadvantages. In the international pilot study of schizophrenia by the World Health Organisation (WHO, 1979), social adaptation remained among the strongest predictors of overall outcome, independent of course and phenomenology. Further, in the WHO 10-country comparison of the course of schizophrenia (Jablensky et al., 1992), comprising a sample of 1,371 patients over a two-year period, low levels of relapse were associated with networks that consisted of a small number of emotionally close and confiding relationships.

Quality of Interpersonal Interactions

The findings outlined above regarding the effects of the social environment on individuals with psychosis over time particularly highlight the importance of the quality of relationships and the characteristics and patterns of interaction on the level of social integration or social adaptation which has long been understood as a stable marker of the deficits associated with psychosis *per se*. Studies of EE and psychosis have focused on the characteristics of individuals' family interactions. EE as an operationalised concept gives an indication of how family members or individuals in other close social contexts (including contexts of institutional care) talk about an individual during a brief interview. In a meta-analysis, Butzlaff and Hooley (1998) established the predictive validity of EE in 26 studies in that living in high EE environments was predictive of increased relapse rates by at least 100 per cent. In looking closely at the associated interactional pattern, Rosenfarb et al. (2001) examined relatives' affective style during a family interaction in 27 psychotic patients followed for nine months. Relatives of patients who relapsed had more critical and supportive statements during the interactions than did relatives of non-relapsers, and among the relapsing group, relatives' criticism was positively correlated with patients' unusual thoughts during the interaction.

In terms of the quality of relationships examined within the EE paradigm, Bromet et al. (1984) found that in a combined sample of psychotic and depressed patients, those with higher level of overall symptomatology symptoms perceived their families more negatively on cohesion, expressiveness, conflict, moral-religious emphasis, and organisation subscales of a family environment scale. Miklowitz et al. (1995) found that during family interactions those patients with higher hostility/suspicion had relatives who made more intrusive statements. Simoneau and colleagues (1998) found that high EE families were more likely than low EE families to show complex negative interaction sequences. Finally, Wendel et al. (2000) assessed both EE levels and attributions of relatives during family interactions with bipolar patients. High EE relatives' causal attributions for the patient's role in negative events were more personal and controllable than those of low EE relatives.

Developmental Factors

There is some evidence regarding some early factors associated with problematic social environments and interactions in individuals with psychosis, namely the influence of parenting and attachment histories. Most of the relevant studies in this area have examined whether the parenting style of parents of psychotic individuals was characterized by low care and high overprotection or psychological control, a pattern of parenting that was predominantly developed in studies examining developmental factors in depression, e.g. Parker (1983) (see Alloy et al., 2001, for a review). In an early qualitative study, Davenport et al. (1979) interviewed six families, including both a parent and an adult child with bipolar disorder. They noted that these families were characterised by avoidance of affect, the absence of intimate relationships apart from the family, domineering mothers, and emotionally or physically absent fathers. Both Joyce (1984) and Cooke and colleagues (1999) did not obtain differences on parenting and family environment between psychosis and normal control groups. Both studies found that within the psychosis group, familial environment was associated with the severity and course of the disorder. In Joyce (1984), individuals who reported low parental care and high overprotection had more hospitalisations than those who did not. In Cooke et al. (1999), within a psychosis group, lower ratings of family expressiveness were associated with a history of co-morbid dysthymia and lower ratings of family cohesiveness were associated with a history of past suicide attempts.

Other studies found that the parenting and attachments of individuals with psychosis differed from those of normal controls. In a comparative study of individuals suffering bipolar and unipolar depression, Rosenfarb et al. (1994) reported that both bipolar and unipolar patients reported less maternal affection than normal controls, but bipolar individuals did not differ from controls on paternal affection or over-control from either parent. On an explicit measure of attachment, both the bipolar and unipolar groups reported less attachment to their mothers than controls, but did not differ from controls on either paternal or peer attachment. In contrast, on an implicit attachment measure, the bipolar group perceived less attachment to their fathers throughout all developmental stages than did the controls.

To summarise the evidence relating parenting practices, there is some suggestion of parenting characterised by low care and high overprotection, poor attachment relations, and childhood abuse in the histories of individuals with psychosis. There is also some evidence that less than optimum parenting and histories of childhood sexual or physical abuse may be associated with a worse course of psychosis.

INTERPERSONAL ENVIRONMENTS AS A BASIS FOR PSYCHOLOGICAL INTERVENTION

In terms of an integration of these concepts and empirical findings into a framework of psychological intervention, it is noteworthy that originally both the social support aspect of social networks and EE in relatives are understood as stable characteristics of an individual's social environments that help explain current level of distress, vulnerability to relapse and chronicity of symptoms. We feel, however, that both interpersonal environments and family interactions need to be conceptualised in a much more dynamic framework that clearly formulates the individual's active part in shaping their relationships and being a forming and prominent part of their social interactions. In that sense the concept of social supports encompasses both positive supportive aspects such as emotional and practical support and social companionship, as well as stressful and negative aspects of personal relationships, in particular, characteristics of communicative styles and interactions which have been conceptualised within the context of EE to be influential in families and close social environments. Schuster et al. (1990) stated that it is often the same individuals who are a source of greatest support and greatest stress. Therefore the concepts of support and interpersonal stress overlap in the client's interpersonal network and processes associated with both therapeutically need to be considered in combination when targeting interpersonal processes therapeutically. In that respect the mechanisms of negative and positive interactions are likely to be equally complex.

In the formulation and treatment of clients with psychosis, it is therefore essential to consider all aspects of their existing social interactions, the quality of attachment, and interpersonal styles and vulnerabilities that influence the quality of their social environment and their ability to utilise existing and possible new sources of social support.

Brown and colleagues (1972) noted early on that there is a significant interaction between the quality of the overall social support network and EE, in that 90 per cent of families with high EE were small in size and socially isolated. The social support and EE literature is also reasonably consistent in indicating that both positive and negative interactions and the resulting interactions with family and friends have an important impact on the overall course of psychosis. There is a strong indication that psychotic individuals with poor social support or relatives with high EE or negative affective style take a longer time to recovery, have a greater likelihood of relapse, and more impairment than those with high social support or relatives with low EE and a positive affective style. Moreover, there is consistent evidence that focused family therapy, designed to reduce relatives' specific high EE interactions, and enhance family communication skills and support, decreases risk for mood episode relapse, and beginning evidence that family interventions may indeed work via its intended mechanisms. However, it is important to remember that much of the literature on the role of the current environment in psychosis is characterised by important methodological limitations including failure to control for current mood state and failure to attend to predictors of specific episodes.

Family Interventions

In relating current family environments and potentially negative interactions between family members and clients to current stressors, it is important to note that one of the main stressors is likely to be the experience of psychosis itself. Multiple consequences of this event for clients and their families include increased socio-economic pressure, societal stigma, associated specific negative life events such as unemployment, institutional care and lack of community resources, etc. The emotional impact of these events on clients and families alike can comprise grief, anger, confusion, guilt and self-blame, all requiring adaptation and assimilation. Individual appraisals and available resources in light of these stressors determine the family's and the individual client's ability to recover from the impact.

Family members report high levels of stress and burden associated with an individual's development of psychosis. These include, besides immediate interferences with daily routines and practical stressors associated with the care and immediate support required by a family member with psychosis, emotional burdens that include confusion, learned helplessness and difficulties in communicating stress and emotional strain with the client. The interaction of these factors as experienced by the family members and the client result in toxic communication styles and patterns of interaction which in turn increase family isolation, and interpersonal negativity which can influence the client's relapse and social and vocational dysfunction (McFarlane, 2002). This interaction is further complicated by the symbolic loss and subsequent grief experienced by family members regarding the perceived expectations of what opportunities the individual might have lost. This experienced family burden is associated with the availability of a wider social support network (Clark, 1994; Solomon & Draine, 1995).

The two main focused family therapy approaches to target these systemic vulnerability factors and to address specific communication and interaction patterns in families following psychosis are Multi-Family Groups (e.g. Marsh, 1994; McFarlane et al., 1995, 2000) and psychoeducational family work focused specifically on the reduction of EE in families (e.g. Barrowclough & Tarrier, 1992; Kuipers et al., 1992; Leff et al., 1995; see Penn & Mueser, 1996, for a review). Overall, all forms of family interventions can be successful in reducing risk of relapse and result in fewer hospital admission (for a review, see Pitschel-Walz et al., 2001; Pilling et al., 2002). These positive effects, however, cannot be generalised to individual patients' outcomes in terms of their personal, interpersonal and social functioning. According to a recent review by Barrowclough and Hooley (2003), this can be attributed to the largely psychoeducational, problem-solving and behavioural orientation of most family-focused treatments, rather than successfully targeting individual clients' and family members' attributions. It further seems inadmissible to include in a formulation of toxic family interactions and this specific vulnerability to staying well the developmental origins of poor communication styles, lack of felt security and the difficulties of a particular family system to contain the emotional strain and stress associated with psychosis, that includes an understanding of the particular parenting and attachment patters that interact with current family functioning.

It is beyond the scope of this treatment manual to provide an outline of a systemic family intervention that would be based on a developmental integration of its techniques and interventions but it appears valuable to include the developmental and cognitive interpersonal aspects of staying well in any individualised formulation that may be the basis for a planned adjunctive family intervention.

THE ROLE OF INTERPERSONAL ANXIETIES AND SOCIAL WITHDRAWAL

As we have outlined above, social anxiety and interpersonal sensitivity play an essential role in the development of psychosis and can be a significant factor affecting recovery and staying well. Social withdrawal and social isolation are common features in the prodromal phase to a psychotic episode but can also characterise the recovery process. Anxiety is a common feature of a psychosis presentation. It may occur historically before any sign of pro-drome (Klosterkoetter et al., 2001), or it could be understood as a main feature of the prodrome manifested in social withdrawal, social phobia and paranoia; these aspects can further be evident during an acute episode and may be a residual symptom post-episode, resulting in difficulties in re-engaging with normal difficulties, distressing symptoms and increased like-lihood of relapse (Preda et al., 2002). This suggests that anxiety about others was a key ingredient in the development of psychotic symptoms such as paranoia, preoccupation and distorted perceptions.

The importance of interpersonal anxiety as a mediator of depression in psy-chosis has also been seen in two studies of group cognitive-behavioural interventions for social anxiety in schizophrenia, in which significant improvements in levels of depression outshone change in anxiety levels (Halperin et al., 2000) and overall perception of quality of life improved (Kingsep et al., 2003). In an early conceptualisation, Sullivan (1962) under-stood social anxiety as a precursor of psychosis and different quantitatively rather than qualitatively from psychosis. According to that view, anxiety would predispose the individual to psychosis. If an individual has devel-oped a view of the world, self and others strongly influenced by anxiety, the person will non-consciously process all information through an anxious filter. Hence the experience of psychosis and its stigmatising (through public perception) and isolating (through symptom content and nature) effects will be easily accommodated within a perception of the self that is inadequate and the world and others as rejecting and threatening.

Social anxiety in psychosis can further be related to the evidence on atten-tional deficits in psychosis with social anxiety, suggesting that early expressed attentional deficit might result in impaired processing of interpersonal infor-mation. This in turn would lead to difficulties in social interaction and com-pensatory social withdrawal (Cornblatt & Keilp, 1994). Green and Phillips (2004) present a more considered approach in their review paper of the evi-dence for cognitive bias in anxiety in the context of psychosis. They refer to the burgeoning literature that taps into evolutionary concepts about survival, from which we can be fairly confident that anxiety develops, providing strong evidence that social anxiety and delusional ideation are associated with greater attention to threat-related facial expressions, albeit not directly. They suggest a vigilance and avoidance mechanism with an affective component.

The Interpersonal Inventory

By including the range of significant relationships in the work with clients, a key aspect of the assessment and formulation of the interpersonal world of the client is the interpersonal inventory. A key tool in interpersonal psychotherapy for depression (Weissman et al., 2000), the interpersonal inventory maps out all significant relationships in the client's world, including their key characteristics for the client and significant qualities that relate to the main problem areas. Essentially the interpersonal inventory provides the therapist with a structure for a systematic assessment and recording of structural and qualitative components of the client's social network. The inventory does include the main contemporary and significant past relationships and considers the interpersonal history of the client's current problems. In the technique of putting clients' difficulties in an interpersonal context, important information is assessed that is relevant for the origin and resolution of interpersonal difficulties, such as particular communication styles and patterns of relating. While the interpersonal inventory can be compiled in a more or less formal manner, it does seem important to keep a record of the client's current description of their interpersonal network that will become a reference point for interpersonal change, and it further provides a tool for the ongoing contextualisation of the client's difficulties.

A particular characteristic of drawing up an interpersonal inventory is to explore in detail what particular significant relationships mean for the client and which aspects they feel are most related to their current difficulties. The essential characteristics of the relationships comprise accessibility (emotional and practical), the predominant nature of individual relationships (confiding, companionship, etc.), reciprocity and level of trust, and elements of conflict or tension. With a particular emphasis on recovery from psychosis and staying well, the interpersonal inventory highlights early on in the treatment where the crucial areas of strength and support are and which are the areas of tension and vulnerability within the client's social network. This is in line with the mixed effects of social support and high EE and other social/interpersonal stressors, as discussed above.

The interpersonal inventory further provides a useful tool for the exploration of the client's attachment behaviour and communication style over time; the way in which clients describe their key relationships and the extent and manner in which they are able to explore and reflect on positive and negative interpersonal experiences help the therapist and client to establish an understanding of their interpersonal functioning, their expectations and perceptions, both regarding their interpersonal history and development and in relation to their current relationships. This technique can be instrumental in identifying patterns of relating and processes that are common to several key relationships in the context of the client's emotional difficulties. The interpersonal inventory therefore provides not only an illustration of the client's current interpersonal world, their key problem areas and goals, but also processes of communication and interaction that form a pattern across several relationships and/or developmental stages.

In the exploration of significant relationships and attachments during the preparation of the interpersonal inventory, the client and therapist explore the history of problematic relationships and attachments, including significant losses and separation, as well as the history of particular problem areas. The investigation of current problematic relationship and social supports includes current problems in communication and interactions with significant others and the client's associated affective responses. This technique not only allows the client and therapist to reach a comprehensive understanding of the current interpersonal context of the client but it also highlights central areas for change in key interpersonal areas. It is important to bear in mind that this initial exploration is guided by the client's current understanding and perception regarding their current relationships and attachments. In focusing on particular interpersonal problem areas throughout treatment, it is likely that these perceptions will change and the interpersonal inventory is hence used as a dynamic and flexible representation that can be revisited in order to illustrate significant changes or to review particular interpersonal difficulties. In fact, areas of apparent contradiction, omissions and tensions can provide constructive insights into the client's current level of interpersonal reflectiveness and areas of interpersonal tension and distress that may be difficult to share and explore at the time of the assessment.

A useful format for the drawing up of the interpersonal inventory is the closeness circles. Figure 9.1 illustrates the interpersonal inventory of Susan whose case vignette we introduced in Chapter 7.

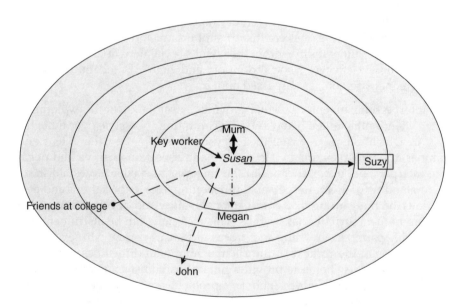

Figure 9.1   Closeness circle of Susan's interpersonal relationships

Interpersonal Formulation

The interpersonal formulation posits the client's current difficulties and expectations for change within the framework of their interpersonal experiences, key attachments and interpersonal context. In this manual, the interpersonal formulation is integrated within the wider formulation of a client's problem areas and recovery framework as outlined above and, dependent on the individual and their key problem areas, the interpersonal aspect of their formulation may be more or less prominent. Apart from formulating aspects of the client's difficulties and goals in relation to their key interpersonal relationships and attachments, the interpersonal formulation also highlights areas for change in the client's current relationships in the context of recovery and staying well.

From the perspective of staying well after psychosis, the interpersonal formulation highlights the potential and desired changes in the client's key relationships following psychosis and identifies sources of interpersonal stress and support. The orientation and emphasis of the interpersonal formulation are that of attachment and interpersonal interactions. The formulation therefore provides a collaborative and shared understanding of the client's difficulties from the perspective of an identification of sources of difficulty and interpersonal change. In the exploration of current and past significant relationships, recent changes in communication and interaction with significant others, and in the formulation of key problem areas and a focus for change, the therapist pays careful attention to the exploration of the affect base for these areas. As we have discussed throughout this manual, developmental and interpersonal aspects and their associated meaning-making and emotional processing play a major part in the vulnerability to relapse and staying well.

Here is an example of an outline of the interpersonal formulation of Susan. The formulation aims to highlight the interpersonal problem areas as described by Susan and an interpersonal perspective of her emotional difficulties:

An Interpersonal Formulation of Susan's Initial Presentation

Susan's interpersonal history is characterised by a number of significant losses and separations from an early age, starting with the loss of her father following her parents' separation at the age of two. She further experienced a lack of positive friendships with peers and found it hard to integrate in social groups; this was compounded by significant hearing difficulties that she suffered as a young child up until the end of primary school. When reflecting on her childhood and her relationships with key figures, Susan displayed a state of mind in relation to her attachment experiences that is characteristic of someone with an insecure dismissing and 'cut off' attachment style. She described a 'generally OK' childhood and upbringing and would abstractly talk about a series of close relationships with friends or relatives throughout her school career. Yet she found it extremely difficult to provide concrete examples of interactions or events and her account of these relationships remained vague and unsubstantiated. A series of adverse interpersonal events such as repeated bullying at school, direct rejection from peers and a more recent unprovoked assault by peers left her feeling extremely wary and fearful of approaching people her own age. It also stopped her leaving the house and following any leisure pursuits.

Throughout her childhood Susan was dependent on her own interpretation of many communications and interactions as she had difficulty following what people were saying. It further appeared that she also relied strongly on her mother's perception and interpretation of events. All her significant relationships appear to be characterised by either relative dependency and are generally labelled as highly positive by Susan, in particular, the relationship with her mother and her key worker; or they can be described as highly conflicted or contradictory in the example of relationships with peers who in the past emotionally and verbally abused her, or peers whom she would describe as close friends but with whom she is unable to report any direct contact.

Susan presented to psychiatric services following a serious assault with a mixture of emotional difficulties in line with symptoms characteristic of post-traumatic stress, social anxiety and psychosis. It appears that Susan developed psychotic experiences in the context of a very impoverished social network with no confiding relationships outside the relationship with her mother and little interpersonal exchange or feedback from others. She experienced psychosis for a period of over one year in the form of multiple voices that would provide her with a social commentary to her experiences, intentions and actions; these were expressed both in positive and extremely negative and derogating terms.

This brief outline of Susan's interpersonal formulation highlights the significant overlap between her attachment style, her interpersonal experiences and her current social context, her self-appraisal as well as her appraisal of her psychotic experiences. It appears as if the voices represent a form of social network for her that carries many of the functions that could be expected of an age-appropriate peer group and of close and confiding relationships. Not always being able to fully rely on her emotional reactions and her understanding of interpersonal interactions, Susan relied on others to structure and validate her experiences. This is apparent in the largely non-reciprocal relationships represented in her current interpersonal inventory. In identifying areas for potential change, the therapist must remain mindful of the important self-regulatory functions that the voices carry for Susan; further, in connection with Susan's dismissive state of mind in relation to her attachment experiences and her high degree of apparent dependency on few relationships, the therapist must further consider the impact of the therapeutic relationship on Susan's internal world and the role that relationship might play in facilitating changes in these few key relationships. The overall goal for Susan to establish greater independence from her mother and to venture out and build up new attachments and peer relationships then seems highly ambitious and is likely to follow a period of appropriate grief and positive adaptation to past events.

AREAS OF INTERPERSONAL DIFFICULTIES

In this treatment manual we do not suggest that psychosis or even its affect base difficulties can be fully explained or alleviated by reformulating them in interpersonal terms or by finding and concentrating on an area of interpersonal change and adaptation alone. We do believe, however, that interpersonal functioning and interpersonal difficulties are an essential factor in the course of psychosis and play a major part in staying well.

Both the interpersonal inventory and an interpersonal formulation are tools for the therapist to illustrate patterns and recurrences in the interpersonal history and the current interpersonal world of clients. These might become apparent in terms of repeated relationship failures, problems to engage with naturalistic peer groups at school, at work or in their neighbourhoods, and a general inability to relate to others might become apparent in a way that is also reflected in the therapeutic relationship.

In its original format, interpersonal psychotherapy for depression is described with four main interpersonal problem areas relative to the resolution of depressive episodes (Klerman et al., 1984). These are described as: (1) interpersonal disputes or unresolved interpersonal conflicts; (2) role transitions, often in the context of significant changes in the individual's life and relationships; (3) grief and loss following a bereavement or interpersonal separations; and (4) interpersonal deficits or interpersonal sensitivity describing an individual's enduring difficulties in establishing and maintaining close relationships. Common to all these problem areas is that significant interpersonal events or changes in key relationships can be clearly formulated in the context of the onset and maintenance of a depressive episode. It is suggested in the original model that the concentration of the psychotherapeutic intervention on the resolution of these interpersonal problem areas leads to an alleviation of depressive symptoms and facilitates lasting adaptation and changes in the individual's interpersonal context that make them less likely to become distressed and unwell in the future. Individuals further develop a better understanding of their patterns of interpersonal functioning that will help them to maintain the positive changes that they have achieved with the support of a psychotherapeutic intervention.

In psychosis, similar to depression, we can identify clear areas of developmental interpersonal vulnerabilities and obvious aspects of interpersonal functioning that interact with the processes of adaptation and recovery. Interpersonal therapeutic techniques help to identify particular focus areas where the main difficulties are located and where a potential or necessity for change can be identified. These may include the adaptation to a loss or separation of a significant other, but also the interpersonal adaptation to a symbolic loss of a particular role within a group or a loss of status as often associated with psychosis. Similarly, this may include difficulties related to the adaptation to a significant change in the interpersonal circumstances or significant life events that necessitate a reorientation of expectations and relationships to others. This may include changes associated with the circumstances of a psychotic episode.

It is often the psychosocial context and the nature of relationships that change following a significant life event such as an episode of psychosis, hospital admission or loss of an educational placement that require considerable adaptation. Markowitz (1998) described a positive context for significant role transitions in his work with individuals suffering from dysthymia, where he describes their current circumstances or roles as defined by 'illness' and their new or aspired role as 'wellness'. This interpersonal treatment concentrates on the implications of these role understandings as carried by others or the individual for their social world and their significant relationships. Therapist and client identify the effects that the old role understanding had on the client's life and work towards an interpersonal context that is not defined by 'illness'. This includes the clear identification of areas where relationships and the psychosocial world of the client have been influenced by their or others' understanding of them as being 'unwell' and focuses on particular aspects of these interpersonal interactions that would be different within a new role understanding.

Similar to any constructive adaptation to significant changes, a transition of role or role understanding includes an acknowledgement of positive and negative aspects of the old role and an anticipation of benefits and potential difficulties associated with the new role. For clients with psychosis, this includes an opportunity to value and validate many experiences associated with their psychosis not simply as illness related but in acceptance of their personal value and meaning. This may, for example, include an exploration of the relationship that a client established with their voice(s), or the way paranoid thinking might have shaped their immediate interpersonal surroundings.

For many individuals the experience of psychosis and its associated circumstances, such as the consequences of long absences from school or work, long periods of poor or problematic communication with family and friends or the stigma attached to hospital admissions, can be conceptualised as being similar in effect to a bereavement. An important part of the therapeutic work is the identification of the interpersonal consequences of this 'loss event' as well as the affective components of this loss. Therapeutically the therapist will want to elicit interpersonal incidents and process affect with the client. This often supports the discussion of the client's changing understanding of the bereavement and its link to the main problem areas. This process can be very difficult for clients as they verbalise and explore negative affect in relation to what they feel they have lost through the event, especially when their previous reactions included a relative 'shutting off' of the affect associated with significant interpersonal changes following psychosis, or when they isolated their emotional reactions. In order to help the client to explore their affective experience, the therapist must establish a containing and safe therapeutic relationship; it is the sense of emotional security within a collaborative and compassionate therapeutic relationship that enables the client to take emotional risks:

Th: We talked about your friends and the way in which your friendships became very difficult to manage for you before you came to hospital. How would you describe these friendships now?

C: I see most of them, well . . . some; especially Tom and Julie did come and see me once in hospital . . . It was horrible.

Th: What felt horrible for you?

C: I actually looked forward to seeing them. It was just them coming in, there was a lot of noise, and I couldn't really talk to them – and then . . . they actually had to see what a basketcase I am.

Th: Have you spoken to them since?

C: No, I feel really awkward speaking to them now . . . they did leave a few messages though.

Th: If they were here in the room, what would you like to tell them?

C: What do you mean?

Th: I understand from what you were saying that you had a good relationship with Tom and Julie before you came to hospital, that there
were some difficult situations when you met them a few times when
you were feeling very anxious and suspicious, and then there was the
time when they came to visit you. It seems that you feel things are different now between you.

C: I don't know how they see me now. I used to be fun; always up for a
party, and I don't think it could ever be the same since they saw me
there . . . I know that I won't be fun any more.

This short exchange highlights the difficulties the client experiences in
accommodating to the possible changes and implications for her relationships following a short stay in hospital. Feelings of shame and fear of rejection seem to be the dominant emotions and an exploration of potential
difficulties seems problematic. The aim for the following interpersonal intervention may be to explore the situation of their visit more closely in an
attempt to explore possible differences between the client's preconceptions
and the emotions linked to her recall of the actual exchange at the time. The
therapist may then offer a short role-play in the session to allow the client
to articulate what she might want to share with her friends in relation to her
experience in hospital and the shame she associates with an encounter before
her inpatient stay and directly in connection to them seeing her there.

Any of these processes of adaptation and interpersonal change require the
client to become aware of their interactions and communication style in their
relationships as well as requiring them to form new social attachments and
to negotiate tense or conflictual interpersonal relationships. Often, however,
clients present with a mode of interpersonal functioning and a pattern of
difficult interpersonal experiences that make it more difficult for them to
develop new social connections and to engage in potentially difficult interactions. This interpersonal sensitivity is often closely linked to the client's
attachment style, in particular, dismissing or preoccupied states of mind in
relation to attachment experiences. This can have a significant effect on the
therapeutic relationship and therapists should feel prepared to use direct
feedback and interactions in therapy sessions to highlight styles of communication or affective reactions. Clients in this group by implication may also
bring less basic social skills that enable them to modify their interpersonal
context, such as inhibited communication styles, lack of empathic or close
engagement with significant others and a hypersensitivity to feedback from
others. They may also prove to be less insightful and self-reflective in their
interpersonal interactions, the very qualities that within a therapeutic
context can facilitate change.

WORKING WITH INTERPERSONAL SENSITIVITY

Persistent social anxiety and withdrawal, or interpersonal sensitivity, relate to an individual's specific difficulty in establishing and maintaining close interpersonal relationships. For many individuals this can develop into a persistent style of attachment and social interaction, especially following an episode of psychosis and/or hospitalisation, even though for many clients this might be a feature that pre-dates their onset of psychosis. This interpersonal sensitivity can often present as a complicating or limiting factor in recovery and staying well after psychosis and is likely to interact with other problematic areas of interpersonal adaptation, in terms of their dealing with loss, role transition and interpersonal conflicts.

As we discussed above, attachment experiences and mental states in relation to attachment styles are inherently related to interpersonal sensitivities and may describe one of the long-standing interpersonal vulnerabilities of some clients with psychosis. Insecure and unresolved attachment styles then become apparent in the way key relationships are described and within the client's description of current interpersonal difficulties. Not least, the therapeutic relationship can initially be compromised by a client's inhibition to communicate emotions, to convey empathy and a hypersensitivity to the reactions of the therapist.

We want to use the following case example to illustrate key problem areas relating to interpersonal relationships and functioning in the context of psychosis:

Deborah

Deborah is 17, living with her parents in a small rural town. She came in contact with services after a long period of social withdrawal over a period of two years. Throughout that time she became increasingly more withdrawn, she stopped achieving at her school work and she stopped following her hobbies. This process was slow and gradual and initially her parents welcomed the slight changes that meant that she stayed home more and she was spending less time drinking with her friends in public places. They consulted their GP who subsequently sought a referral to psychiatric services following Deborah's refusal to attend school.

Deborah grew up with her sister and both her parents; she attended primary school without difficulties and was very successful at horse riding which earned her several prizes and trophies in recent years.

Prior to her social and emotional withdrawal she had a good relationship with her father, mainly through their shared interest in horse riding and his support in getting Deborah to competition events and accompanying her at training sessions. Her relationship with her mother was warm, and at times of emotional upset she would turn to her for support. Her parents' relationship seemed very strained and, apart from their shared concerns regarding Deborah, it was difficult to establish a shared understanding. Deborah's father believed that she was lazy and should 'get her act together'; her mother also admitted that she suffered from periods of depression herself. Deborah's uncle was diagnosed with paranoid schizophrenia and Deborah's father pointed out that she might end up like her uncle unless she got things together, that is, alone, without work and living on disability benefits in a grotty council flat. The family had no contact with the uncle.

At first presentation Deborah had to be seen at home as she refused to go to the clinic. For the first few appointments Deborah was unable to share her inner world and remained largely silent. The assessment and formulation period took, therefore, a few months and involved numerous professionals. The psychological therapist involved in the case initiated walks and other low-key activities to establish a rapport with Deborah and gradually she felt able to talk more about her thoughts and feelings. It emerged that she was hearing voices that told her she was useless and that there was no point in trying to do anything, as she wouldn't achieve anything worthwhile. She further was able to explore her debilitating anxieties and offered that these were fuelled by beliefs that other people were watching her and that they could hear what she was thinking. She further believed that people would be so outraged by the content of her thoughts that the only way they could stop her was by harming her.

In terms of an interpersonal inventory, it is apparent that Deborah had very few positive relationships with her peers and after leaving school she was able to only maintain one friendly relationship with a neighbour and even that relationship was described in very limited terms. In addition, her relationship with her father seemed strained and awkward following her disengagement from horse riding. She further found it very difficult to approach her mother with her difficulties as she felt that her mother was intensely stressed herself and that she would add to her troubles by sharing.

Th: I am interested to hear more about the time after you stopped attending school. What were things like at home around that time?

C: I don't know ... I was just glad to be left alone and not at school ... things got really difficult there.

Th: Tell me a bit more about who was around and how you got on with them.

C: Just my parents.

Th: Could you speak to your mum and dad at the time about what was going on?

C: Nup!

Th: What was it that made that difficult at the time?

C: Don't think they wanted to know! ... Dad was pure grumpy ... and Mum was so stressed all the time anyway.

Th: In what way was that different from before?

C: We would spend all weekend together, going to the shows.

Th: When you felt troubled about things back then, who would you turn to?

C: I'd speak to Mum sometimes.

Th: What makes it difficult for you to speak to her now?

C: Don't know, she's different since I left school ... everyone is different.

Th: In what way would you say your mum is different since then?

C: She is so stressed all the time.

Th: And you think that makes you hesitant to talk to her?

C: Yes, I am not sure she understands any more.

Th: Can you explain to me more what you mean by everyone being different?

C: I don't know what to say to people any more ... and I know they are talking about me.

The therapist is trying to carefully explore current close relationships and to establish an understanding of what might have changed in the key relationship for the client. With clients who have established long-standing interpersonal difficulties, this exploration can be quite limited and may rely on a wide-ranging exploration of possible exceptions and past relationship patterns. In Deborah's example, the therapist is trying to establish a sense of change in her close significant relationships by linking her current difficulties and associated emotions to the current interactions with her parents. This exploration will enable the therapist to link the recent changes linked to the onset of her psychosis with the difficulties in her current close relationships and potential sources for support.

In contrast to the other problem areas, interpersonal sensitivity describes long-standing difficulties of engaging and relating to others. As an underlying style of interaction, interpersonal sensitivities can often complicate the resolution of an acute stressor. In Deborah's example, the initial difficulty came in dealing with the difficulties she experienced with her schoolwork and subsequently with her peers at school, and then the adaptation to leaving school. In contrast to clients who have good skills of social adaptation and a secure interpersonal base, the work with clients presenting with interpersonal sensitivities can be much more challenging, not least as they often present with very few, if any, good enough interpersonal relationships and a relative paucity of social skills which makes the establishment of a more salutogenic social environment much more difficult. In contrast to other areas of interpersonal difficulties, the therapeutic work with interpersonal sensitivities relies much more on a detailed exploration of relevant past relationships. Nonetheless with long-standing interpersonal sensitivities that describe pervasive styles of interacting, it can often be most effective to help clients to overcome more immediate problems and to consider the client's attachment and communication style as a basis for an understanding of current difficulties and to facilitate potential changes. An overall goal is to help the client to become aware of their interpersonal strengths and weaknesses to understand and resolve more acute interpersonal crises.

Clear goals for this problem area are the optimisation of the client's current interpersonal functioning, supporting the client in establishing, where possible, new supportive relationships, and to resolve acute problems and stressors which compound the long-standing difficulties.

The therapist can provide the client with a collaborative, supportive and compassionate therapeutic relationship; the therapeutic relationship often plays an essential role in facilitating the resolution of current problems with interpersonal sensitivity. One immediate aspect is the modelling of an effective, empathic and open interpersonal communication in therapy. This can be facilitated indirectly through the therapeutic stance of the therapist or directly by role-playing difficult interpersonal situations. Following this, the client can directly practise new ways of communication with the therapist and use these to reflect on possible changes within their existing relationships. In many instances, however, the therapeutic relationship is likely to reflect some of the difficulties and interpersonal patterns that the client forms otherwise. It may therefore be characterised by distance, lack of engagement and trust or hostility. These cannot be directly targeted early on in the treatment but an exploration of and reflection on these difficulties become possible as the positive therapeutic alliance develops. In order to facilitate this, the therapist should encourage and reinforce any sign of disclosure or emotional exploration and keep the client focused on the agreed problem areas. When changes become stuck or seem impossible, the therapist may explore the possible anxieties or ambivalences about the proposed changes in behaviour and interactions and link these difficulties in communication and interactions to other relationship problems including the possible difficulties of open exploration within the session.

CONCLUSIONS

In this chapter we have described essential aspects of the interpersonal context of psychosis and key areas of interpersonal vulnerabilities in the context of staying well after psychosis. We identified particular aspects of the interpersonal world of individuals with psychosis that may contribute to their vulnerability to relapse but that may also aid recovery, in particular the influence of social support and positive confiding relationships in the context of stressful or traumatic life events and the effects of negative and toxic interactions and communication styles with family members. There is an obvious overlap with the developmental aspects of self-reflection and reflective functioning, as described in Chapter 3, and their implications for the interpersonal functioning in the context of interpersonal vulnerabilities. We further attempted to describe some of the key therapeutic techniques to effect interpersonal problem areas and particular interpersonal functioning by supporting clients to modify styles of relating, by directly influencing existing relationships that may prove destructive and by utilising clients' interpersonal skills to initiate new attachments and role understandings in social contexts. We further explore the role of the therapeutic alliance and relationship in working directly with interpersonal styles of interactions and communications. Other therapeutic aspects of interpersonal functioning and intervention will be outlined in Chapter 10, working with underlying schema and schema maintenance processes.

CHAPTER 10

WORKING WITH UNDERLYING SCHEMATA AND CORE BELIEFS

INTRODUCTION

Early loss of a significant attachment figure and/or the experience of traumatic events such as sexual abuse, physical abuse and/or neglect all have the potential to profoundly affect and undermine an individual's cognitive, emotional and interpersonal development. Experiences of parental non-availability, neglect and childhood victimisation can produce a long-standing and pervasive impact on a person's schematic representations of the self and others, their interpersonal coping strategies, their ability to form trusting and/or intimate relationships with others, and their ability to seek nurturance, acceptance and love. A substantial body of research has elaborated the links between early loss, abuse, neglect and later psychopathology (e.g. Cichetti & Carlson, 1989; Myers et al., 2002). In attachment terms, these events would be conceptualised as affecting the development of a person's internal working models of the self and others (Bowlby, 1980). Therefore, an understanding of the effects of early adverse experiences upon cognitive interpersonal schemata, interpersonal functioning and affect regulation has important implications for psychotherapy.

EARLY PARENTAL LOSS AND PSYCHOPATHOLOGY

Early parental loss, particularly maternal loss, has repeatedly been associated with later psychopathology. In particular, loss of an individual's mother before the age of 11 has been associated with the development of depression in response to a severe life event (Brown & Harris, 1978). It has been speculated that the link between loss in childhood and later psychopathology is mediated through the provision (or lack of provision) of a caring and stable home environment subsequent to the loss (Harris et al., 1986; Briere, 1988). This may also interact with an individual's interpersonal schemata (Brown & Harris, 1978; Harris et al., 1987; Bowlby, 1988). Early childhood loss of a parent via death or separation has also been implicated in the subsequent development of bipolar affective disorder (Lewinsohn et al. 1995; Mortensen, 2000). Similarly, in a case control study of dissociative disorder (Pasquini et al., 2002), an increased odds ratio for experiencing traumatic experiences (including parental loss) was found in dissociative cases. In psychosis, loss of one's mother in childhood has been linked to the development of co-morbid depression and increased suicide risk (Roy et al., 1983). Historical studies have also reported higher rates of parental loss in general (Pollock et al., 1939; Lidz & Lidz, 1949; Granville-Grossman, 1966), and maternal loss in particular (Barry, 1939), among individuals suffering from psychosis. A recent study into the influence of early traumatic life events on panic disorder reported that 55 per cent of a control group of psychotic patients had an early maternal loss (Friedman et al., 2002). Of course these associations cannot demonstrate clear causality; they do, however, highlight particular vulnerabilities and closely associated areas of difficulties.

CHILDHOOD ABUSE AND NEGLECT

Childhood maltreatment is usually characterised by the division into acts of *omission* and *commission*. Acts of *omission* refer to psychological neglect, e.g. by reducing the contact between parent and child, with resulting effects on the child's access to the parent as a 'secure base'. As has been discussed previously, lack of parental security and appropriate mirroring of the child's needs (Bowlby, 1973, 1988; Fonagy et al., 2002) often leaves the child with an impoverished understanding of the thoughts and feelings of others ('mentalisation') and a reduced ability to regulate their own emotions. Psychological neglect is a clear risk factor for insecure attachment states of mind in later life. Conversely, acts of *commission* are 'actual abusive behaviours directed toward the child' (Briere, 2002). Such acts can be physical, sexual or psychological in nature.

PSYCHOLOGICAL SEQUELAE OF CHILDHOOD ABUSE AND NEGLECT

Suppression of Thoughts and Memories

The psychological ramifications of early abuse and neglect encompass cognitive, affective and interpersonal domains. There is considerable interaction between these domains. One form of cognitive consequence is the suppression of traumatic memories. Briere (2002) proposed that suppression excludes traumatic thoughts and memories from conscious awareness, which on activation can trigger catastrophic emotional responses (Wenzlaff et al., 1991; Wenzlaff & Wegner, 2002). However, suppression requires considerable resources to maintain distressing material beneath awareness, often through distraction or strategies that 'turn off' conscious awareness, such as substance use. Stimuli that are reminiscent of the suppressed material trigger 'rebound' phenomena (Wegner, 1994; Briere, 2002). For example, individuals with avoidant or dismissing states of mind towards attachment relationships often employ 'idealisation' as a strategy to suppress potentially negative material through overtly presenting attachment experiences as positive, without supporting evidence.

Implicit Sensory Memories

It has been hypothesised that the lack of explicit narrative memories involved in sensory flashbacks is a consequence of the emotional 'flooding' present during trauma or abuse, thus disabling higher level, integrative functions such as abstract reasoning that is facilitated through the orbital frontal region of the brain. Instead, phylogenetically older areas of the brain that process the meaning of sensory information, such as limbic circuitry, are given precedence. This is an evolutionary adaptation in that the brain has evolved to process and respond to fearful stimuli rapidly, without attending to fine details (Le Doux, 1996; Siegel, 1999). Unfortunately, fear responses become rapidly engrained, and thus challenging to alter. Alternatively, abuse may have occurred at a very early age, prior to the acquisition of language (Briere, 2002). Furthermore, the hippocampus, the area of the brain which integrates different qualities of a memory, e.g. context (Bremner & Narayan, 1998), develops slowly, over the first few years of life.

Affect Regulation and Interpersonal Functioning

Affect regulation refers to the strategies with which an individual copes with predominantly negative emotional states, both internally through self-regulation and through access to others, such as an attachment figure (Briere, 1992; Sloman et al., 1994). Affect regulation in infancy is acquired through the interactions represented in attentive and sensitive caregiving (Sroufe, 1996). This core interpersonal experience of emotional containment and sensitivity becomes internalised as an expectation about the competence of the self and the responsiveness of others in emotional salient situations (Bowlby, 1988). In general terms, the experience of childhood abuse and neglect has been linked to insecure attachment in adulthood (Alexander, 1992; Styron & Janoff-Bulman, 1997). So-called Avoidant/Dismissing and Anxious/Preoccupied attachment styles, as classified by the Adult Attachment Interview, assessing mental representation of attachment figures and experiences, are predicated by interactions with the attachment figure that lead to an internal model of relationships where the attachment figure is to be avoided, described as a dismissing state of mind, or inconsistently both caring and rejecting in parental responses, characteristic of a preoccupied state of mind. Thus, the individual does not experience sensitive caregiving and the appropriate mirroring of emotional responses by the caregiver which is needed to develop an affectively attuned and socially adept sense of self (Siegel, 1999).

Consistent with the above findings on interpersonal models, in individuals who have experienced significant abuse or neglect, affect regulation is often underdeveloped (Pearlman, 1998). Here, the lack of a reliable and autonomously internalised 'secure base' leads to the child being unable to access their principal source of emotional containment and security in the face of emotional or physical distress when needed, and thus is unable to internalise the sense of security needed for successful and autonomous self-regulation. Instead, the child is left exposed to substantial negative affect; in the case of abuse, the source of this negative affect may often be the caregiver, leaving the child in a 'double bind' as to how to access a 'secure base'. As an adult, the individual who has been unable to achieve adequate affect regulation will often resort to maladaptive methods of coping with affective instability such as substance abuse, inappropriate sexual behaviour, dissociation, avoidance or self-injury (Briere, 1992, 2002). One of the key challenges of therapy with individuals who have experienced abuse or neglect is therefore to provide a framework for developing improved affect regulation, while also providing a safe and containing therapeutic 'secure base' to help the individuals discuss distressing experiences without being overwhelmed by negative emotions (Lineham, 1993; Fonagy et al., 2002).

Abuse and neglect have also been linked with psychopathology, mainly mediated through internal attachment representations. In particular, individuals with a diagnosis of borderline personality disorder have been reported as having notable rates of experiencing, or witnessing, physical or sexual abuse as children (Brown & Anderson, 1991; Herman et al., 1999). Furthermore, emotional neglect is also reported when caregivers were present (Zanarini et al., 1989; Patrick et al., 1994). With regard to attachment classifications, high levels of preoccupied status have been reported, in particular a rare sub-classification of fearfully preoccupied by loss or trauma (Patrick et al., 1994; Fonagy et al., 1996).

UNRESOLVED ATTACHMENT STATUS

The adult attachment classification of 'unresolved with regard to loss/trauma' is the adult analogue of the 'disorganised attachment' classification in infants (Main & Solomon, 1986). Disorganised attachment refers to behaviour in the Strange Situation Test (Ainsworth et al., 1978) that is 'fearful, odd, disorganised, or overtly conflicted' (Lyons-Ruth & Jacobvitz, 1999), including trance-like or disoriented reactions to separation. Behaviour such as this is thought to be indicative of caregiving that is experienced by the infant as frightening (Hesse & Main, 2000). Several studies have suggested that early maltreatment is a substantial risk factor for disorganised attachment in infancy (George & Main, 1979; Carlson et al., 1989; Lyons-Ruth et al., 1990).

As discussed in Chapter 4, Siegel (1999) suggested that there are five basic elements of secure caregiving that in time facilitate secure interpersonal schemas: collaboration, reflective dialogue, repair, coherent narrative and emotional communication. In individuals with unresolved states, the experience of loss or trauma has served to undermine these central elements of discourse, thus presenting a significant challenge during psychotherapy. An association has been made between disorientation/disorganisation in infancy, and elevated scores on the dissociative experiences scale (Carlson & Putnam, 1993; Carlson, 1998). It has also been hypothesised that disorganisation in infancy occurs as a result of multiple incompatible models of self and other, whereby the caregiver cannot be approached in distressing situations, but neither can the infant successfully regulate their own distress. This leads to increased risk of dissociation as a response to threatening situations (Main & Hesse, 1990; Liotti, 1996).

It has been suggested that dissociation is a primitive short-term defensive response for the management of intense distress (van der Kolk et al., 1996). Several studies have found links between dissociation and trauma, usually specified as childhood sexual abuse (Chu & Dill, 1990; Vanderlinden et al., 1993; Hodgins et al., 1996; Draijer & Langeland, 1999). Holowka and colleagues (2003) found significant correlations between dissociation and both emotional and physical abuse in a sample of adult psychotic individuals. Siegel (1999) suggests that emotionally distressing situations, such as childhood trauma, undermine the process of integrating higher and lower neural functioning. In adults, unresolved states are indicative of this lack of *intra*personal integration, and this impaired integration is expressed in dialogue through the breakdown of Siegel's (1999) five basic elements of secure discourse. In psychotherapy the breakdown of secure discourse is linked to an impoverished narrative characterised by a lack of coherence in the expression of self in the context of past events, current task demands and future expectations.

EARLY CHILDHOOD TRAUMA AND PSYCHOSIS

It is becoming increasingly apparent that there are high rates of early childhood trauma and neglect among those individuals who go on to be diagnosed as having schizophrenia (Read et al., 2004). At the age of three, experiencing problematic mother–child interactions characterised by harshness and lack of assistance is associated with a greater likelihood of having a diagnosis of a schizophreniform disorder in adulthood (Cannon et al., 2002). Similarly, in the 1946 British Birth Cohort Survey (Jones et al., 1994), those who experienced poor parenting at the age of four were significantly more likely to be diagnosed with schizophrenia in adulthood. In a group of 8,580 persons living in the UK (Bebbington et al., 2004), experiences including running away from home, being in a children's home and expulsion were significant predictors of having psychosis. These data all suggest that experiences indicating instability of attachments and potentially unsupportive home environments are raised among people with psychosis.

In terms of acts of commission (i.e. early childhood physical and sexual abuse), there is strong evidence for an emerging relationship between trauma and psychotic symptoms (summarised in Table 10.1). These studies show that the relationship between early childhood trauma and hallucinations is particularly strong. Indeed, there appears to be a dose–response relationship between abuse and hallucinatory severity (Read et al., 2004) and psychotic symptom severity (Janssen et al., 2004). Indeed, Janssen and colleagues found that abuse was associated with need for care among those with normally occurring psychotic experiences in the general population. The relationship between abusive experiences and delusions is less clear-cut. Where there does seem to be a relationship between abuse and delusions, this tends to be for persecutory paranoid beliefs (Ross et al., 1994; Read et al., 2003).

TRAUMA, DISSOCIATION AND SCHIZOTYPY

It may be that individuals with a temperamental vulnerability (i.e. schizotypy) to experiencing unusual experiences and culturally peripheral beliefs may be more vulnerable to the long-term effects of traumatic experiences because of a difficulty integrating traumatic intrusions such as memories and flashbacks. Schizotypy refers to a normal personality construct characterised by an enduring tendency to experience attenuated forms of hallucinatory (e.g. hearing one's own thoughts) and delusional experiences (e.g. beliefs in telepathy). Craig Steel and colleagues (Steel et al., 2002, 2005; Holmes & Steel, 2004) have investigated the role of schizotypy in the processing of traumatic material in a non-clinical population. They suggest that a common information processing bias may underlie both post-traumatic stress disorder (PTSD) symptoms and psychotic symptoms. For example, the DSM-IV delineates three types of symptoms characteristic of PTSD (American Psychiatric Association, 1994). These are: (1) re-experiencing of the original trauma via intrusive thoughts and images; (2) increased arousal levels; and (3) avoidance of trauma-related stimuli and/or 'numbing' of emotional responses. PTSD symptomatology has also been proposed as a mediator between severe

Table 10.1   Relationships between child abuse and hallucinations and delusions

	Hallucinations	Delusions
Child abuse (sexual or physical)		
Bryer et al. (1987)	N/A	0
Goff et al. (1991a)	0	N/A
Famularo et al. (1992)	+	0
Ross et al. (1994)	++	++
Read & Argyle (1999)	(+)	(+)
Read et al. (2003)	++	(+)
Resnick et al. (2003)[e]	+	+
Janssen et al. (2004)[f]	++	++
Physical abuse		
Goff et al. (1991b)	N/A	(+)[c]
Read & Argyle (1999)	(+)	0
Read et al. (2003)	++	(+)
Hammersley et al. (2003)	0	0
Sexual abuse		
Bryer et al. (1987)	N/A	0
Sansonnet-Hayden et al. (1987)	++	0
Goff et al. (1991b)	N/A	+[c]
Ensink (1992)	(+)	N/A
Read & Argyle (1999)	(+)	0
Read et al. (2003)	++	(+)
Hammersley et al. (2003)	++	0
Incest		
Beck & van der Kolk (1987)	N/A	(+)[d]
Bryer et al. (1987)[a]	N/A	0
Ellenson (1985)	(+)	N/A
Heins et al. (1990)	(+)	N/A
Read & Argyle (1999)[a]	++	0
Read et al. (2003)[a]	(+)	(+)
Child sexual and physical abuse		
Bryer et al. (1987)[b]	N/A	0
Read & Argyle (1999)[b]	(+)	0
Read et al. (2003)[b]	(+)	0

Notes: $+ = p < 0.05$; $++ = p < 0.01$; (+) = trend or high rates with no controls; 0 = no effect; [a]comparison of incest and non-familial sexual abuse; [b]comparison of those subjected to both child sexual and physical abuse versus those subjected to one form of abuse only; [c]delusions of possession; [d]sexual delusions; [e]measure of positive symptoms in general; [f]combined measure including other forms of trauma and abuse. N/A = not applicable.

negative life events/trauma and psychotic experiences (Mueser et al., 2002). There is also evidence that individuals with psychosis report higher levels of intrusive thoughts and images than general population controls, which are also reported as being significantly more distressing (Morrison & Baker, 2000; Morrison et al., 2002).

Working from the understanding that intrusions are, by their very nature, involuntary, occur outwith conscious awareness, and are triggered by stimuli that correspond to stimuli linked to the original trauma (Ehlers & Clark, 2000; Brewin, 2001), Steel and colleagues (2005) propose a key role for 'contextual integration'. This is the mechanism by which information is processed and stored as memory traces with a relevant spatial and temporal context, where memories refer to the 'right place' and the 'right time'. However, in potentially traumatic situations, there is an immediate associative route to information processing, which routes the memory trace through the amygdala, the neural facilitator of fear processing (Le Doux, 1996). As the amygdala is not organised for conceptual integration, this short cut leads to a 'situationally accessible memory' (Brewin, 2001) that may be involuntarily triggered by stimuli correspondent with traumatic stimuli. This mechanism mirrors the processes involved in traumatic 'flooding' and is akin to models of multi-level emotional processing that require immediate responses.

Crucially, a similar difficulty in integrating information within its spatial and temporal context has been hypothesised to operate in psychosis (Hemsley, 1994). Steel and colleagues (2002) utilise the concept of schizotypy (Claridge, 1997), a continuum model of psychotic personality traits such as susceptibility to unusual experiences. Individuals in the general population scoring highly on schizotypal traits also tend to process information within a framework of relatively weak contextual integration. In addition, after viewing a stressful film specifically designed to induce subsequent intrusions within a controlled framework, those scoring highly on a positive schizotypy measure also reported higher intrusive experiences (Holmes & Steel, 2004). The study also replicated a previously reported association between trait dissociation and positive schizotypy (Startup, 1999; Merckelbach et al., 2000). Therefore, it would appear that schizotypal characteristics (similar to those of psychosis) are linked to both traumatic intrusions and dissociative symptoms.

SCHEMATA AND INTERNAL WORKING MODELS

Schemata develop in response to early childhood experiences, particularly early relationships with close attachment figures. Segal (1988) defines schema as 'organised elements of past reactions and experience that form a relatively cohesive and persistent body of knowledge capable of guiding subsequent perception and appraisals'. They have also been described as evolutionary and become fixed when they are reinforced and/or modelled by parents (Freeman & Leaf, 1989). Later, Young (1994) defined schemata as 'broad pervasive themes regarding oneself and one's relationship with others developed during childhood and elaborated throughout one's life-time'. Young states that early maladaptive schemata arise out of an interaction between in-built temperamental tendencies and negative interpersonal developmental experiences including abuse, criticism, abandonment and/or enmeshment. The emphasis in Young's conceptualisation of schemata is an entrenched pattern of distorted thinking, negative affect and problematic behaviours. One can also consider patterns of thinking and behaviour within a more dynamic and reciprocal framework that shows clear developmental trajectories over time and in conjunction with particular events and corrective experiences. Young has hypothesised that the processes of schema maintenance, schema avoidance and schema compensation maintain schemata.

Bowlby (1973) proposed that, over the period of normal childhood development, the experience of interactions with attachment figures becomes internalised and thus carried forward into adulthood as mental models – also known as internal working models (IWMs) or core relational schemata (Bretheron, 1985; Alexander, 1992; Pearce & Pezzot-Pearce, 1994). These implicit structures produce expectations about the self and others, and regulate responses in subsequent interpersonal interactions. Early attachment relationships therefore come to form the prototype for interpersonal relationships throughout life, through the internal representation of models of the self and others (e.g. Styron & Janoff-Bulman, 1997).

IWMs apply to all self and other representations although this has been articulated mostly in the context of important attachment relationships. They reflect the synthesis of experienced patterns of interaction accumulated throughout development into adulthood. In this sense the cognitive contents of IWMs are products of reciprocal patterns of relating with others over time. In relation to this, IWMs by their very definition are working models, which are updated throughout the lifespan: a process which is supported by the person's self-reflectiveness and subsequent attachment-related experiences. Non-reflective, impoverished IWMs (Fonagy et al., 2002, p. 62) compromise mentalisation and affect regulation. Rigidity of self-reflectiveness and interpersonal coping therefore prevent the IWMs being updated and elaborated. In this context, psychological therapy provides the opportunity for a corrective attachment-related experience that has the potential to reorientate attachment-related behaviours, enhance emotional containment and consequentially update IWMs. In this sense there is no direct access to an IWM. Rather the routes to therapeutic change are via the empathic exploration of the therapeutic narrative, the recognition of affect that is expressed directly or indirectly in the narrative and the therapist's ability to reflect on the process of meaning-making and interpretation of affect that is contained in the client's report. Within this caregiving framework provided by the therapist, there is an explicit attempt to help the person to develop an internal compassionate and self-soothing stance towards their prior experiences and themselves. The therapist works collaboratively with the client to develop and strengthen these underdeveloped self-nurturing strategies. As part of this process, the development of these skills in relating to the self and others is meshed with changes in the clients' beliefs about themselves and others.

Jane

Jane was 22 years old. She experienced two episodes of acute psychosis over an 18-month period. These episodes had been characterised by auditory hallucinations, persecutory paranoia, tactile hallucinations and passivity phenomena. During her acute psychosis Jane was highly distressed by four derogating, male voices that insulted her and commanded her to harm and kill herself. Jane was partially compliant and used self-cutting and starvation as a form of subjugation to them. Jane felt that her thoughts and body were under the external control of another person. She would often sense the presence of another unidentified person. She was often confused whether this presence was a force for good or a force for evil. Tactile experiences were crawling sensations up her legs and in her abdomen. These acute episodes were in the context of multiple substance use including cocaine and cannabis.

Jane described her early experience as 'fine'. She said that she had always been close to her mum and described her as warm, loving, supportive and fun. However, she was unable to recall any specific childhood instances illustrating these facets of her relationship with her mum. During Jane's early development (ages 7 to 12), she and her mum moved frequently in order to escape her abusive father. Jane's mum was highly distressed during this period and was frequently incapacitated by episodes of severe depression leading to psychiatric admission. Jane recalled very little of these events. Jane's father had been an alcoholic who was physically and sexually abusive towards her mother. Again, Jane had few specific memories of her father, except for one memory of him breaking down her mother's bedroom door

and witnessing him assaulting her. In this context, Jane's early school-
ing was highly disrupted. She was also unable to establish lasting
friendships during this time.

During her adolescence, Jane's home circumstances improved. Her
father stopped showing up at the house and her mum's emotional
well-being improved. During this period Jane was able to develop a
strong relationship with both her maternal aunt and uncle. She recalled
specific positive memories of being comforted physically and emotionally by her aunt when upset. She also shared her uncle's love of
music. The loss of her aunt at the age of 16 signalled the beginning
of a difficult period for Jane. She felt extremely distressed by the loss
of her aunt, but unable to articulate the feelings that she was experiencing. Jane became increasingly involved in intense short-term and
unstable romantic relationships and drug taking.

Jane's initial response to treatment was very poor. She didn't respond
to appropriate typical or atypical antipsychotic medication. Jane was
started on Clozapine during her second episode, which reduced many
of her psychotic experiences. However, she still continued to experience distressing derogatory voices. Cognitive therapy focused on
Jane's beliefs about her voices and her compliance and subjugation to
them and led to reduced emotional distress and improved her coping
with the voices. Her frequency of cutting and self-mutilation had also
reduced. However, Jane continued to have marked problems in her
self-esteem, self-harm and interpersonal relationships. Her goals for
recovery were being able to trust some other people, feeling better
about herself and being able to socialise more.

IDENTIFYING SCHEMATA

In cognitive therapy, schemata are understood through the identification of
core beliefs. Core beliefs are regarded as unconditional statements about the
self and others. They are seen as strict rules that are over-learned and which
have their origins in early childhood. In schema theory, these core beliefs act
to guide our attention to and interpretation of events (Davidson, 2000). Core
beliefs can be identified in a number of meanings. Core beliefs can be
accessed through ascertaining the meaning of affect-laden events, through
events within the therapeutic relationship, within imagery, through the
exploration of memories, or via thematic analysis of a client's automatic
thoughts records. The common thread linking these methods is following
and focusing on the presence affect within the therapy sessions. This is illustrated in the extract below taken from a session with Jane and her therapist:

J: I really hated school. I was never really able to settle in. There was a time when it just felt like we were moving all the time.

Th: What was the worst thing about that?

J: Just having to move around. Always having to make new friends.

Th: Is there a particular memory that comes to mind?

J: Hmmm, I remember this group of girls would keep calling me names. One day on my way home from school, they grabbed my schoolbag and threw it in the river, ha ha (*client laughing*).

Th: Do you remember how you felt then?

J: Really bad, really stupid.

Th: What did it mean to you to have your schoolbag thrown in the river by those girls?

J: I felt on the outside, that I didn't belong, that there was nobody around for me. I was really alone.

Th: Thinking about this now, how do you feel?

J: It's like I don't fit in, I'm weird. People don't like me. You can't trust anyone really.

Th: What does that mean to you, that you are weird and people don't like you?

J: Hmmm, just, it's that I'm a misfit. I hate myself sometimes. I'm ugly, I'm horrible, nobody likes me really, at all. I'm horrible.

Th: How do you feel just now, as you are talking?

J: I feel really sad, I feel really angry, really frustrated with myself.

In this scenario, the therapist encourages the client to focus on the affect and meaning contained within a specific childhood memory of being bullied at school. It is often helpful to gently encourage a client to fully explore an image or memory in order to heighten the client's awareness of their associated affect and personal meanings. Importantly, the therapist also encourages a 'here and now' perspective by then encouraging the client to reflect on the meaning of this event in the present.

SCHEMATA AND BEHAVIOUR RELATIONSHIPS

As stated earlier, core beliefs have their origins in very early childhood, have evolved in a specific context and tend to be associated with a series of over-learned habitual intrapersonal and interpersonal strategies. Overdeveloped strategies are important in terms of understanding the processes of schema or core belief maintenance. For example, the core belief 'I am bad' might be expected to be associated with overdeveloped strategies such as self-harm, self-punitiveness, submission and subjugation to others, non-assertiveness, self-neglect and fearful avoidance of attachment. In this way self-punitiveness and isolation serve to maintain the belief that the self is bad either directly through self-punitive and self-critical behaviours, or indirectly through impoverishing life experience and the opportunity for contradictory life experiences via isolation. On the other hand, the belief that 'others are untrustworthy' might be expected to be associated with overdeveloped suspiciousness, hostility, avoidance of intimacy, avoidance of attachment and attachment-related memories. Similarly, suspiciousness and hostility may directly contribute to the maintenance of the belief that 'others are untrustworthy' by, for example, eliciting negative interpersonal responses from others. In addition, avoidance of others might contribute indirectly to schema maintenance via reducing possible alternative positive interpersonal experiences.

Therapeutically, these overdeveloped strategies can be explored by encouraging the client to consider the impact of their experiences, not just on what they believe, but also on the development of ways of behaving towards themselves (intrapersonal strategies) and ways of behaving towards others (interpersonal strategies). This is important to understanding the person, how they relate to themselves and their own thoughts and beliefs, and the roles that they play in their social context. This is illustrated in the continuing narrative of Jane:

Th: You say that you see yourself as horrible, a misfit, so to speak. This seems to make you feel really angry and sad. Can you tell me how you cope with that?

J: I don't know, I get really angry with myself. I just want to scream.

Th: Can you tell me about a recent occasion that you felt that way?

J: Hmmm, well, when Jim found out that I'd been in a psychiatric ward he seemed OK, but then last week he said he wanted to be friends, that the whole psychiatric thing was too complicated for him.

Th: How did you feel?

J: Pretty bad . . .

Th: OK, how did you react when he wanted to be friends?

J: I said that was fine. He was nice about it. It was friendly enough.

Th: Do you remember how you felt inside at that time?

J: Well, kind of OK, I kind of thought at the time that 'Well, here we go again' but later I got really upset. I felt really angry.

Th: Can you describe that reaction in more detail?

J: I just kept thinking that I was stupid, that I was no good. I was a fuckup. That no one could ever love me. I felt really desperate and confused. I wish I had never told him I'd been in hospital.

Th: How did you cope with those feelings?

J: I just locked myself in my room. I cut myself on the legs.

Th: What was that like?

J: It was calming; it's like cutting off from things. I felt a sense of relief, but I felt a sense of being cut off.

We see in this scenario three probable overdeveloped intrapersonal and interpersonal reactions to emotional distress. Interpersonally, Jane appeared to initially react in an emotionally 'cut-off' and possibly submissive manner. Intrapersonally, Jane initially becomes angry and self-critical, and then later she cuts herself as an affect regulation strategy. As part of the initial process of exploration, the therapist forms the hypothesis that Jane's experiences have led her to see herself as a misfit and as horrible, and others as untrustworthy. Associated with these beliefs Jane has developed three important survival strategies, which include cutting off emotionally from people, self-criticism and self-punishment. The therapist would then explore the use of these strategies in other stressful situations either in the here and now or historically. It is important also to explore other problematic or, indeed, helpful coping strategies in this process. It is important to maintain a non-judgemental awareness that the coping strategies utilised by individuals often make sense in their earlier developmental and interpersonal context. Indeed, as part of the therapeutic process, this is communicated directly to the person.

CORE BELIEF CHANGE STRATEGIES IN COGNITIVE THERAPY

Christine Padesky (1994) has outlined a number of cognitive behavioural strategies for modifying clients' core beliefs during cognitive therapy. These strategies involve the use of continua, notebooks to strengthen new beliefs and the involvement of significant others.

Continuum Techniques

In order to introduce some flexibility into core beliefs, therapists can work with clients to produce continua presenting clients' core beliefs on a scale of 0–100 per cent. The therapist can work with the client to establish criterion or evidence that the client cites for their belief. These criteria can then be presented as continua. An example from Jane is given below. In order to understand further what Jane meant by her belief that she was horrible, the therapist was able to explore her specific evidence. From this evidence, specific criteria could be developed to help Jane reflect on and reassess or re-evaluate her belief.

I am horrible.

0 per cent	50 per cent	100 per cent
I always cut myself		I never cut myself
I always avoid people		I never avoid people
I hear voices		I don't hear voices

In addition, the therapist can work with the client to construct alternative valued core beliefs that mesh with the client's goals. For example, two of Jane's goals were to be able to trust some people and to be able to feel good about herself. These goals could be translated into alternative beliefs alongside specific evaluative criteria. An example of this is illustrated below. The evidence for and against clients' core beliefs and their alternatives can then be explored through a number of means. In addition, continua can be used to monitor changes in belief conviction over time.

Some people are trustworthy.

0 per cent	50 per cent	100 per cent
Some people stick around		Nobody sticks around
Some people listen to what I say		Nobody listens
Some people don't hurt me		Everyone hurts me

Use of Notebooks

Directly challenging negative core beliefs can be unhelpful to the client and therapy itself. It can promote an ethos of intellectual change in therapy or, indeed, can be experienced as highly invalidating, thus rupturing the therapeutic alliance. Instead, notebooks can be used as a positive data log, which essentially involves the client keeping a record of all experiences and thoughts that would support the new alternative belief. In this way direct challenge of the core beliefs is avoided. Rather, the aim is to strengthen and elaborate the client's experiential evidence for alternative beliefs. This can be achieved by encouraging the client to self-monitor on a daily basis or by constructing behavioural experiments aimed at testing alternative beliefs.

One of the challenges, however, to the use of schema change strategies is the emphasis on verbal aspects of the client's experience. Meaning is not merely verbally constructed but also reflects individuals' felt sense of their experience. Indeed, the distinction between intellectual meaning and emotional meaning has long been recognised (Teasdale & Barnard, 1993) and this has been explored in relation to psychosis (e.g. Gumley et al., 1999). It is therefore important to promote experiential change, either through the development of new or alternative interpersonal strategies or through clients' intrapersonal strategies and how they relate to themselves.

WORKING WITH UNDERDEVELOPED STRATEGIES

The opposite of overdeveloped intra- and interpersonal strategies is the relative underdevelopment of alternative strategies. In Jane's case her overdeveloped strategies of cutting off from others, self-criticism and self-punishment have as their reciprocal state feeling close to others, compassionate self-nurturance and self-care. These are important strategies that link to both intrapersonal and interpersonal experiences. The therapist therefore works with the client to rehearse both within and between sessions the development of alternative strategies. We shall, for the purposes of this text, divide these into interpersonal and intrapersonal strategies.

Underdeveloped Interpersonal Strategies

Underdeveloped interpersonal strategies are those interpersonal behaviours that the client has not had the opportunity to develop. These interpersonal behaviours can be conceptualised as the opposite of their overdeveloped behaviours. In Jane's case scenario she experiences a number of significant interpersonal problems including expressing positive and negative emotions and saying no to others. As Jane was developing she learned to avoid thinking about her own feelings and to avoid upsetting her mum, who was frequently in a distressed and/or incapacitated state. These experiences probably contributed to Jane adopting an avoidant/dismissing state of mind with respect to attachment experiences. However, Jane was still able to preserve a positive view of her mother despite her own lack of a secure base and specific autobiographical evidence. One cost of this strategy was her difficulty, therefore, in becoming aware of and communicating positive or negative emotions. This is explored in the narrative below:

Th: How has your relationship with your mum changed over the years?
J: I trust her more now than I once did.
Th: How has this happened?
J: I think in the last couple of years and what I've been going through she has stuck by me, she could have chucked me out of the house.
Th: How does that feel that she's stuck by you?
J: Hmmm, I'm not sure; it's a little strange to think about. It feels kind of good, you know. I feel like we have become friends now.
Th: Does she know you feel that way?
J: I don't know.
Th: What do you think it would feel like to tell her?
J: Hmmm, that would be kind of weird saying that.
Th: What would be helpful about telling her?
J: Hmmm, it's kind of weird to think about. She might appreciate it, I guess. I think she has had to cope with a lot over the years, it might feel good to her.

In this transcript the therapist encourages Jane to consider communicating positive expressions of emotion as an opportunity to create new meaning-making experiences. Equally the therapist also focused on expression of negative emotions:

J: I arrived at Jennifer's house. We were planning to go out. She was out of her face on something. I'd been really looking forward to going out. I just went home.

Th: How did you feel?

J: I felt really upset. I got that whole 'I'm a horrible defect' thing all over again. I went home and scratched myself. Even the voices joined in telling me that I was this and that. I felt really stupid. Like I stupidly trusted her and she let me down. I should have known better.

Th: That sounds really hard, you were really upset. Have you managed to speak to her since?

J: No, she won't have a clue. I just feel like I can't speak to her, I feel really upset.

Th: I'd like to try something just now. I know you find it really hard to talk about negative feelings and you get all chewed up inside. This makes you want to cut to get rid of some of the horrible feelings you have. I want to see if we can work together to help you learn to communicate negative feelings. Imagine Jennifer is sitting on that chair, what would you like to say to her?

J: God, I don't know, hmmm, well. She's really upset me and let me down and I don't really want to talk to her again.

Th: OK, so could you try that and see how that feels, like she's here now?

J: Like she's in that chair? (*yip*) OK, 'Jennifer, you let me down "big style", I feel really bad, I don't want to talk to you any more.'

Th: How does that feel for you?

J: I don't know, it feels really bad. I feel like I'm being really hard on her.

Th: Can you tell me why that is?

J: Well, she's been going through a lot recently. Her boyfriend gives her a really hard time, she can't cope with him sometimes, I think that's why she gets out of her face.

Th: How do you imagine she feels?

J: I think she gets upset. I think she doesn't know what to do.

Th: Could you let her know that you know she's having a hard time, but also let her know your feelings?

J: How do you mean?

In this second scenario, the therapist collaborates with Jane to create new circumstances for meaning-making and the development of alternative interpersonal strategies. The reference to the use of a 'two-chair' technique (e.g. Greenberg et al., 1996) opens up the opportunity to encourage the client to begin to reflect on how they feel when they are communicating negative emotions to others or indeed responding to powerful malevolent in difficult interpersonal situations. It also provides an opportunity for the client to reflect upon the feelings and experiences of the other person, thus enabling fine-tuning of emotional communication. This transcript also presents the therapist and client with the opportunity to rehearse and construct more reflective and helpful integrating narratives. These can also be developed through the use of role-play and/or imagery techniques.

Social mentality theory (as outlined by Gilbert, 2005) highlights how contemporary schema theory (Young et al., 2003) has tended to underestimate the role of self-critical, shaming schemata that generate hostile signals (i.e. self-critical thoughts and images) in generating reciprocal defensive responses. This reciprocal self-narrative forms a series of negative intrapersonal reactions. For example, Jane chastises herself for any signal of personal failure. Even when her friend lets her down, Jane responds by automatically generating self-critical statements such as 'I am stupid, I should have known better'. This activates the voices commentating on her stupidity, ugliness and social unloveability. In response, Jane becomes distressed and upset which drives further self-criticism (e.g. 'I am weak, I have no control of my feelings, I should be punished'), which is followed by an increase in voices and submissiveness via self-harm.

We see in this interaction what Gilbert (2005) formulates as an inner social relationship characterised by reciprocal aggressive displays followed by fear and submission. This process encapsulates the complex nature of the client's internal working models, where the absence of an internal model of a compassionate, loving and soothing caregiver generates an aggressive response to perceived failures in self-regulation, interpersonal regulation or affect regulation. This aggressive display has previously been termed the 'pathological critic' by McKay and Fanning (1992). This conceptualisation of aggressive self-critical displays is helpful in terms of encouraging the client to develop a mindful awareness of the characteristics of self-critical displays. The client can be encouraged to mentalise the features of the pathological critic by attending to their emotional tone, manner and content of criticism. Indeed, the client can be encouraged to visualise the appearance of the critic through the use of imagery. In characterising the critic, the client can become aware of a number of important dimensions of this experience including awareness and understanding of personal affective reactions, and an understanding of the function of self-critical narrative. In Jane's case, recurring feelings of stupidity, embarrassment and shame were understood as arising from recurring self-critical narratives. Through the process of reflective dialogue and careful attention to accompanying affect, these self-critical aggressive responses were understood as early attempts to switch off painful feelings:

Th: Can you remember when you first experienced these painful feelings of stupidity?

J: Hmmm, it's hard to remember. It's so difficult. I recall after my Auntie Mags died how I felt really bad, I really hated myself. I didn't even want to eat or nothing.

Th: Can you tell me more about how you felt after your Auntie Mags died? What were your initial feelings?

J: I don't know, totally unexpected, I felt really shocked. I felt really selfish.

Th: What was it about that time that made you feel really selfish?

J: Hmmm, like I had no right to feel bad. My mum was in pieces again. My uncle was really quiet. Who was I? I didn't feel I had a right to have bad feelings about her.

Th: What did it mean to you to be upset?

J: That I was weak, that I was selfish and self-centred.

Th: What did you do?

J: I stopped eating. I didn't talk to anyone. I got on with things, I just got on with things. That's when things got bad with the drugs scene.

Th: Thinking about this now. You are 16 years old, you have recently lost your aunt who you were enormously close to. Can you imagine that there might be anything helpful about telling yourself that you are weak and selfish?

J: . . . [12-second pause] It's like something that drives me, doesn't allow me to think about stuff, or get upset.

Th: What is helpful about that?

J: Well, it's like it drives me, makes me get on with things.

Th: Has that been useful in your life?

J: I've had to at times, I've had to keep going. I was on my own sometimes having to go into foster care when my mum was in hospital and stuff. It's like you grow up.

We see in this narrative the growing awareness of self-criticism and in this growing awareness a developing self-nurturing and compassionate self-view. This growing awareness of intrapersonal dialogue provides an important opportunity for the client to gain clarity into the process of self-attack and the development of a fearful submissive reaction to self-attack.

The use of compassionate mind training as described by Gilbert and Irons (2005) offers a powerful methodology for the development, rehearsal and training in compassionate abilities to self-soothe in response to self-attack. These compassionate abilities encompass important characteristics of the communicative style of optimal attachment figures who show sympathy, distress tolerance, empathy, a non-judgemental attitude, caring for others and for one's own well-being, and sensitivity to distress. Compassionate characteristics can be imagined from experiences with significant others during the life experience. For example, Jane could imagine her Auntie Mags as a compassionate being. For others this may be more challenging. For example, one client imagined Bono from U2 as a compassionate being. The process of exploring compassionate responses to self-critical attack and emotional distress is an important part of helping the client develop self-soothing capabilities.

CONCLUSIONS

Long-standing vulnerabilities to problematic emotional recovery, affective dysregulation and relapse can be understood from the point of view of early cognitive interpersonal schema or internal working models. These internal working models produce an interpersonal and intrapersonal style that maintains negative core beliefs, affective dysregulation and therefore vulnerability to relapse. Careful exploration and formulation of powerful life experiences in shaping rigid and inflexible core beliefs and long-standing behavioural strategies are an important part of developing individuals' awareness of their reactions to negative life events and stresses. The process of therapy is a process of meaning-making. The therapist does not seek to challenge negative core beliefs. Rather, the therapist creates opportunities for the client to explore new ways of relating or new narratives that recreate a revised meaning structure. This is through the development of new interpersonal strategies that aim to support the person in negotiating difficult conflictual interpersonal situations or in developing greater warmth and intimacy. Underpinning this process is the development of compassionate intrapersonal strategies that address internal self-attacking shame and fearful submissive internal dialogues. This is a therapeutic process that is strongly affect-laden and the therapist should maintain a watchful eye on the pacing and emotional temperature of therapy sessions.

CHAPTER 11

AWARENESS, INTRUSIVENESS AND FEAR OF RELAPSE

INTRODUCTION

Relapse has been commonly defined as a recurrence or a deterioration of positive psychotic symptoms, which are associated with increased impairment in day-to-day functioning. There is little doubt that the recurrence of psychosis is a distressing and traumatic experience for individuals, families and loved ones. This is hardly surprising given that relapse is often associated with hospital readmission, slower and less complete recovery, greater loss of social and vocational opportunities and networks, and increased personal disability. Birchwood and colleagues (2000) have shown that relapse is linked to the development of depressed mood and suicidal thinking and that the mechanism for the development of post-psychotic depressed mood is likely to be via personal appraisals of loss ('I'll never be able to work again') arising from the experience of psychosis and entrapment in psychosis ('Relapse just comes out of the blue, there's nothing I can do about it'). In Chapter 6 we focused on the dimensions of humiliation, entrapment and loss in relation to psychosis. In Chapter 8, when working with traumatic experiences arising from psychosis, we focused on the dimension of danger. In this chapter we will focus on two dimensions of beliefs and appraisal: intrusiveness and danger. Here perceptions of danger refer to fear of relapse, and intrusiveness refers to the awareness and experience of involuntary, intrusive and apparently uncontrollable changes in thinking.

PHENOMENOLOGY OF RELAPSE

There is now considerable evidence from retrospective (e.g. Herz & Melville, 1980) and prospective (e.g. Birchwood et al., 1989; Jorgensen, 1998) studies of relapse that the recurrence or exacerbation of psychotic symptoms is preceded by increases in non-psychotic symptoms such as anxiety, sleeplessness, preoccupation, irritability and depressed mood. Prospective studies show that, while there is now strong evidence that these 'non-psychotic' symptoms are sensitive to relapse, they are not specific to relapse: that is, on most occasions when a relapse occurs, it is preceded by increases in non-psychotic symptoms, but increases in symptoms such as anxiety and depression are not necessarily followed by a relapse. In addition, prospective studies show that the specificity of non-psychotic symptoms to relapse is improved when low-level psychotic symptoms such as suspiciousness, paranoia, hearing voices and ideas of reference are incorporated into the formulation of early signs of relapse.

This research evidence has two important implications. First, it suggests that the non-psychotic symptoms, which have been observed during the early stages of relapse, are likely to represent an individual's emotional response to the emergence of subtle and covert changes in low-level psychotic experiences. Second, the lack of specificity of non-psychotic symptoms to relapse suggests that early signs do not signal an inevitable trajectory towards relapse, rather, transition to relapse may depend on other factors including the magnitude or intensity of individuals' emotional and psycho-physiological responses to low-level psychotic experiences. In addition, unhelpful behavioural and interpersonal coping reactions to these experi-ences may promote increased emotional distress and physiological arousal, thus accelerating the speed at which relapse proceeds. We have already pro-posed that individuals' emotional, physiological, behavioural and inter-personal responses to changes in existing or recurring low-level psychotic experiences are: (1) mediated by their cognitive appraisal of these experi-ences; and (2) that these appraisals are based on distressing or traumatic experiences of psychosis or hospitalisation.

SUBJECTIVE EXPERIENCES AND PSYCHOSIS

McGhie and Chapman (1961) first argued that the symptomatology of psy-chosis could be understood as the individual's psychological response to a 'basic disorder'. They interviewed 26 individuals with schizophrenia early in their psychosis and obtained a vivid account of changes in attention, perception, awareness of movement, thinking and emotion. From these accounts they suggested that there was a loss of attentional focality. Atten-tion was not directed in a determined manner by the individual's own voli-tion, but by the diffuse pattern of stimuli existing in the total environment. The perceptual changes reported by these individuals included a heighten-ing of sensory vividness in auditory and visual modalities, and a disturbance in the perception of speech patterns. McGhie and Chapman argued that dis-turbances in attention lead to a widening of the perceptual field, leading to the subjective experience of a changed sense of reality. In terms of the dis-turbance in the perception of speech patterns, McGhie and Chapman proposed that the disturbance in attention meant that information such as the syntax and form of speech, normally processed automatically, overloaded normal information processing. Therefore individuals were unable to appreciate the meaning of speech. Changes in bodily awareness were attributed to heightened awareness of bodily sensation and volitional responses causing overload in the ability of the individuals to process information. The consequences of this overload were a loss of spontaneity of action, and 'self-consciousness' of the minutiae of behaviour.

Freedman (1974) reported on 60 autobiographical accounts of the early experience of psychosis. She described clear perceptual experiences including enhanced sensory awareness, muted sensory awareness, less acute vision, visual illusions, changes in depth perception, and changes in perception of one's own voice. She also found changes in more complex functions including thinking being replaced by emotion, thinking in images, mistaking the identities of other people, experiences of loss of meaning of objects, and physical sensations in the brain. Freedman and Chapman (1973) found that eight subjective experiences distinguished patients with and without schizophrenia. These experiences included thought block, mental fatigue, inability to focus attention, visual illusions, hyperacute auditory perception, and misidentification of people and inability to comprehend others' language. Cutting (1985) interviewed 30 individuals with psychosis (15 remitted, 15 acute) and 15 individuals with depression about their early subjective experience. The features, which characterised psychosis rather than depression, were visual and auditory perceptual distortions, impaired understanding of language, and distortions in memory. Similar findings were also replicated by Docherty et al. (1978), Neuchterlein and Dawson (1984) and Heinrichs et al. (1985).

Chapman and McGhie (1963) suggested that individuals with psychosis become aware of unusual experiences and that their reactions to these experiences can play an important role in the development and maintenance of psychosis. They recommended that a psychotherapeutic understanding of the individuals' perceptual and experiential difficulties would aid improved communication. In addition, they suggested that psychotherapy should aim to discover individuals' subjective experiences and cognitive difficulties, and reduce unhelpful or ineffective reactions to these experiences.

Bowers (1968) argued that self-experienced changes in perception and awareness were critical to the transformation of normal experience to psychosis. In a composite experiential account drawn from interviews with 15 patients, Bowers described changes in heightened awareness of internal and external stimuli. Associated with these perceptual changes, he described individuals as having an increasing sense of urgency, reduced need for sleep, exaggerated affect, and a heightened sense of self. Alongside this heightened experience, internal and external events and stimuli normally outside awareness became meaningful and self-relevant. Individuals described becoming engaged, fascinated, perplexed or indeed scared by their own experience. This state of heightened awareness of self gave way to what Bowers referred to as 'a dissolution of self' or 'loss of mental self-representation'. This loss of meaning combined with a heightened awareness of internal and external stimuli gave way to the development and evolution of delusional beliefs constructed to make sense of 'heightened and altered sensory influx and self-experience, widened categories of relevance and a push for closure or meaning' (1968, p. 352). Indeed, Boker et al. (1984) investigated naturally occurring coping strategies associated with basic experiences among 40 inpatient individuals during the acute phase of psychosis. Most of the coping strategies reported by participants were active problem-solving ones, as opposed to more passive strategies such as avoidance or withdrawal. Such experiences were interpreted by many participants as 'danger signals'. In this sense the subjective experience of cognitive and perceptual dysregulation is by no means a passive experience. Individuals actively attempted to make sense of their experience, and pursue coping strategies to ameliorate these experiences.

APPRAISALS AND RELAPSE

A number of investigators (Thurm & Haefner, 1987; Birchwood, 1995; Gumley et al., 1999) have proposed that relapse is the outcome of a psychological process involving individuals' appraisal of their own experiences. Thurm and Haefner (1987) proposed a model of relapse which placed the individual as an active agent, using coping strategies to decelerate or forestall the process of relapse. Their model emphasised how individuals face numerous adaptational demands as a consequence of their illness, and that individuals' perception of vulnerability to relapse would be associated with anticipatory coping strategies aimed at reducing relapse risk and regulating cognitive and emotional experience. Birchwood (1995) proposed a two-process model of relapse where attributions made by individuals to account for and explain the emergence of disturbing symptoms could serve to either accelerate or retard the process of relapse. In this model, anxiety and depression are seen as a response to the fear of impending relapse (perhaps for those with previous experience of relapse) or expressions of failure to explain symptoms and experiences (perhaps for those with less experience of relapse). In addition, external attributions of negative events drive the development of suspiciousness and paranoia leading to the crystallisation of persecutory beliefs.

Gumley et al. (1999) proposed a conceptualisation of relapse, which emphasised the personal significance of the experience of psychosis. According to this framework, the occurrence of a pattern or configuration of internal and/or external events which have a strong similarity to previous relapses will access negative beliefs concerning self (e.g. 'I am vulnerable') and self in relation to psychosis ('I can never control my symptoms') more rapidly than if the configuration has less similarity. The activation of negative appraisals of psychosis derived from previous experiences of psychosis will initiate the process of relapse. In this model appraisals arise from a variety of sources, including internal information on body state and arousal (Tarrier & Turpin, 1992), and cognitive-perceptual changes (Neuchterlein & Dawson, 1984; Frith, 1992). Indeed, feelings of lack of control over cognitive and perceptual processes during relapse have been reported in a number of phenomenological studies of psychosis (e.g. Bowers, 1968; Freedman & Chapman, 1973; Donlan & Blacker, 1975). Therefore, when trying to conceptualise relapse from a cognitive perspective, one must account for a psychological process that involves different sources of threat appraisal.

AWARENESS, INTRUSIVENESS AND FEAR

Following the Gumley et al. (2003) trial of cognitive therapy for the prevention of relapse, we investigated the cognitive contents of idiosyncratic early signs, which were identified by participants who were allocated to the cognitive therapy treatment condition. This yielded 29 statements that were initially judged to be (1) cognitions specifically relating to relapse or (2) cognitions reflecting idiosyncratic experiences of relapse. Items relating to symptoms such as low mood, suspiciousness, hearing voices or anxiety were excluded. These statements were then formed into a questionnaire, which was then administered to 169 individuals who had been diagnosed with schizophrenia or similar. Of these questions, six were later removed since the content seemed to closely resemble symptomatic experiences. These items were 'I have had difficulty concentrating on things', 'I have felt threatened by other people', 'My thoughts have not felt like my own', 'Other people have seemed different to me', 'I have felt a sense of dread that something bad is going to happen', and 'I have been distractible'. We factor analysed the remaining 23 items using Maximum likelihood with varimax rotation and found three underlying factors which we called Intrusiveness (n=7), Awareness (n=8) and Fear of Relapse (n=8). This is illustrated in Table 11.1.

Table 11.2 illustrates some of the psychometric properties, which show that the Fear of Recurrence Scale has good internal consistency, test–retest relia-

Table 11.1   Fear of Recurrence Scale: maximum likelihood factor loadings

	Intrusiveness	Awareness	Fear of relapse
I have been worrying about relapse			0.59
I have been remembering previous episodes of being unwell			0.54
I have been more aware of my thoughts		0.49	
I have experienced thoughts intruding into my mind	0.70		
I have been worrying about my thoughts	0.73		
I have felt unable to control my illness			0.53
I have been worrying about being in hospital			0.47
I have lacked confidence in my ability to cope			0.50
My thoughts have been uncontrollable	0.75		
My thoughts have been going too fast	0.63		
I have been worrying about losing control			0.56
My thoughts have been distressing	0.73		
I have felt more in touch with my thoughts		0.54	
I have been constantly aware of my thoughts		0.47	0.47
I have been unable to switch of my thinking	0.58		
I have paid close attention to how my mind is working		0.65	
The world has seemed more vivid and colourful		0.63	
My thoughts have been more interesting		0.77	
I have had new insights and ideas		0.72	
Unpleasant thoughts have entered my head against my will	0.71		
My thinking has been clearer than usual		0.67	
I have been checking my thoughts		0.55	
The thought of becoming unwell has frightened me			0.66

bility and strong positive correlations with the Early Signs Scale (Birchwood et al., 1989). A copy of the Fear of Recurrence Scale is available in the Appendix. These appraisals are important in the psychological formulation of vulnerability to future relapse and indeed to understand a person's cognitive, emotional and interpersonal response to the emergence of experiences suggestive of relapse.

Table 11.2 Psychometric properties of the Fear of Recurrence in Psychosis Scale

Subscale	Alpha (95% CI)	Test–retest (two weeks)	Subscale intercorrelations		Correlations with Early Signs Scale (Birchwood et al., 1989)			
			2	3	Anxiety	Depression	Disinhibition	Incipient psychosis
1. Intrusiveness	0.91 (0.88, 0.93)	0.69	0.44	0.75	0.63	0.53	0.40	0.73
2. Awareness	0.85 (0.81, 0.88)	0.71	–	0.43	0.34	0.30	0.45	0.46
3. Fear of Relapse	0.85 (0.81, 0.88)	0.67	–	–	0.65	0.64	0.48	0.69
Total score	0.92 (0.90, 0.94)	0.70	–	–	0.62	0.57	0.50	0.72

COGNITIVE BEHAVIOURAL THERAPY (CBT) AND RELAPSE PREVENTION

Existing treatment manuals of CBT for psychosis have emphasised the psychological treatment of positive symptoms, negative symptoms and co-existing anxiety and depression (for example, Kingdon & Turkington, 1994; Fowler et al., 1995). These manuals detail specific relapse prevention strategies delivered towards the end of treatment. Kingdon and Turkington emphasise the identification of stressors, which may trigger relapse, the development of a relapse profile, which include signs and symptoms indicative of relapse, and the development of a range of response options, for example, medication adherence, seeking help, and coping skills developed during treatment. Fowler et al. provide specific strategies, introduced at the end of therapy, aimed at addressing social disability and risk of relapse. These strategies are embedded in the development of a normalising rationale and a personal formulation of the individual's illness experience. The aim of this phase is to establish hope, develop medium-term and long-term goals, and address any continuing misconceptions regarding diagnosis. Reattribution strategies are specified to reduce self-blame associated with social disabilities. For example, individuals may blame themselves, or feel blamed for negative symptoms. Provision of education regarding negative symptoms is utilised to correct any misconceptions. In addition, individuals are encouraged to actively participate in the management of their illness. The importance of using medication and the use of strategic avoidance during times of increased stress or symptoms are highlighted. However, Tarrier (2005) has recently demonstrated that the evidence that CBT impact on relapse prevention is poor, unless investigators use dedicated relapse prevention programmes:

> Although there is evidence for symptom reduction with CBT in both chronic and acute phases of schizophrenia the evidence that CBT significantly reduces relapse is less impressive. The findings for patients treated during an acute episode are disappointing. In the SoCRATES study of acute patients similar rates for clinical relapse for CBT (33%), SC (29%) and TAU (36%) and rehospitalisation CBT (55%), SC (52%) and TAU (51%) were reported. In patients treated during the chronic phase the results are more equivocal. In their chronic sample, Tarrier et al. reported 14% relapses in TAU compared to none in the CBT or SC groups over the three months treatment period. This changed to relapse rates of 28% for CBT, 19% for SC and 27% for TAU after 15 months. At 27 months there were 27% relapses in the combined CBT and SC group and 39% in the TAU group, However, none of the follow-up results are significant for across group comparisons. Bach & Hayes using Acceptance and Commitment Therapy (ACT) with inpatients found a subsequent reduction in rehospitalisation from 40% in the TAU to 20% in the ACT group over a four-month follow-up period. Gumley et al. used a targeted CBT, which was implemented on the appearance of early signs of relapse. The CBT group showed significantly reduced relapses (14%) compared to the control group (36%) over

a 12-month period. The duration of relapse, but not the severity or time to relapse, was also reduced. These results suggest that a dedicated and intensive relapse prevention programme is necessary to impact upon relapse rates. (2005, p. 141)

EXPLORING EXPERIENCES OF RELAPSE

Developing a relapse formulation is of central importance within treatment. It provides the individual and the therapist with a guide to the key cognitive behavioural factors involved in relapse, and attempts to make sense of the pattern of early signs experienced during the early stages of relapse. The experience of acute psychosis as a critical life event lies at the centre of the case formulation approach for staying well after psychosis. It is proposed that the beliefs and assumptions, which arise from this experience, represent the individual's attempts to accommodate and assimilate their experience, and that these beliefs may represent an enduring cognitive vulnerability to relapse.

The Cognitive Interview for Early Signs (Figure 11.1) provides a prototypic guide and summary to the processes involved in the development of the formulation. During this process the therapist's skills in pacing and being alert to subtle changes in mood, eye contact and behaviour are most important. This is because the individual is being asked to recollect previous episodes of acute psychosis and hospitalisation. This interview utilises cognitive techniques to facilitate the development of an early signs hypothesis. The interview aims to help therapists elicit important beliefs and assumptions, which may be relevant to relapse by identifying specific memories associated with previous episodes. The individual and therapist may choose to focus on the last episode of psychosis or another, which may have more personal significance to the individual, for example, the first or second episode.

The therapist and the individual construct a time line between the onset of early signs and the initiation of acute psychosis on which relevant and personally significant events are 'pegged' to the process of relapse. Birchwood et al. (2000) have described a similar methodology. However, extending this methodology, the therapist collaboratively elicits and prioritises, in terms of personal significance, events that the individual considers critical in the development and evolution of relapse, that is, those events which define the meanings that they attach to becoming unwell. Guided discovery is used to uncover the significance that the individual attaches to these memories, for example, 'I have lost control' or 'I've let others down'. These beliefs are then linked to their associated cognitive, emotional, behavioural and physiological sequelae, for example, fearfulness, shame, avoidance, increased tension and sleeplessness. The configuration of symptoms elicited associated with

Cognitive Interview for Early Signs

ESTABLISH DATE OF LAST RELAPSE

ESTABLISH ONSET OF EARLY SIGNS

CHOOSE EVENT DURING PERIOD BETWEEN ONSET OF EARLY SIGNS
AND RELAPSE

Prototypic questions:
When talking about your last relapse, is there a particular memory that comes to mind?
At what point did this occur?
Are there other events which come to mind?

ESTABLISH TIME LINE FOR EVENTS IN RELATION TO ONSET OF EARLY SIGNS
AND RELAPSE

ESTABLISH EVENT ASSOCIATED WITH 'HOT' COGNITIONS

Prototypic questions:
Which of these events distresses you most?
If only one of these events occurred, which would have been the most upsetting
Why is that?

ELICIT MEMORIES AND IMAGES ASSOCIATED WITH THE EVENT?

Prototypic questions:
What was so upsetting about that?
Are there thoughts and images which come to mind?
Can you describe these?

GUIDED DISCOVERY TO ESTABLISH MEANING

What does that event mean to you?
What was the worst thing about that?

ELICIT COGNITIONS RELATED TO SELF, AND SELF IN RELATION TO ILLNESS

What does it say about your illness?
Do you still think that?
How does it make you feel about your illness?

LINK EVENT AND MEANING THROUGH COGNITIVE, PERCEPTUAL AND
PHYSIOLOGICAL EXPERIENCE

When you think about that now, how do you feel, (probe cognitive, perceptual and
physical experience)?
What do/did you notice about your thoughts?
What do/did you notice about your body?

FORMULATE AND SUMMARISE BY LINKING EVENT, INTERNAL EXPERIENCES,
BELIEFS AND EMOTIONAL/BEHAVIOURAL SEQUELAE

TEST CONFIGURATION OF SYMPTOMS AGAINST PREVIOUS EPISODES
AND ADJUST AS NECESSARY

Figure 11.1   Interview procedure for eliciting early signs
Source: From Tait et al. (2003). Predicting engagement with services for psychosis: insight, symptoms and recovery style. *British Journal of Psychiatry*, **182**, 123–128.

personal meanings is then used as a basis for the early signs hypothesis. This hypothesis can then be tested and evaluated by comparing the configuration and timing of symptoms in relation to previous episodes of relapse. The information gathered by the therapist and the individual is then used to develop an idiosyncratic early signs questionnaire. Relevant beliefs and assumptions are included in this scale in order to help 'bind' the apparent variance in symptoms.

EXPLAINING BELIEFS

Beliefs are regarded as arising from the individual's attempts to either assimilate or accommodate their experience of psychosis with their pre-existing beliefs and assumptions. These beliefs act like rules, which contain predictions about the significance and consequences of internal or external events. Accordingly, the occurrence of experiences reminiscent of previous episodes of psychosis will have implicational meaning for the personal relevance of these beliefs. For example, during the early stages of relapse, physiological changes including increased tension in the head, neck and shoulders might be experienced as if their head is growing out of proportion to their body. Their beliefs about this experience, for example, 'I'm losing control', 'People will start staring at me', 'I'm vulnerable', 'People attack folk who look vulnerable', are elicited. The impact of these beliefs on relapse can be explained with reference to systematically identifying their disadvantages or consequences:

Th: You told me when you feel your body changing, you begin to think that you are losing control, that you are vulnerable, and that people will harm you. When you think that, how does that make you feel?

C: I get frightened. I can't think properly and I can't go out.

Th: What frightens you most?

C: It's the thought of not having control. I need to have control or I'll become unwell and end up in hospital.

Th: Is there anything else that frightens you?

C: It's the thought of looking like a freak. People will see and will attack me. I won't go out, unless it's really late at night.

Th: Is there anything else you do when you feel like that?

C: I can't sleep at night. I clean all the time to keep my mind off things but I keep thinking about it. I have to check myself in the mirror. It's got really bad before. I remember feeling this pain in my stomach. I thought there was an animal inside me, and it was going to eat itself out.

The trauma associated with the experience of psychosis, in this example, is self-evident. This individual describes the implicational meaning of changes in her body. These changes are associated with strong beliefs concerning control and vulnerability to harm by others. Indeed, these core themes are continued and contained in the evolution of delusional beliefs associated with her acute psychosis. The formulation of this example is contained in Figure 11.2 below. The formulation is the key means of communicating the relevance of beliefs in relation to personal experience and the acceleration of relapse. This formulation also contains the key early physiological, emotional, behavioural and cognitive signs of relapse, described diagrammatically to assist the individual in making sense of the process of relapse.

EARLY SIGNS MONITORING

The formulation of an early signs hypothesis informs the development of an individualised early signs questionnaire, which integrates the cognitive, emotional, behavioural and physiological factors that characterise the evo-

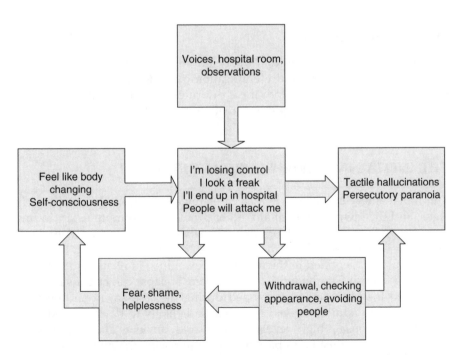

Figure 11.2   A cognitive behavioural formulation of early signs and relapse

lution of relapse. In saying that we find that the use of the case formulation provides a more meaningful way of monitoring. Rather than diagrammatical monitoring early signs, the person is encouraged to monitor at-risk mental states for recurrence. This reduces the emphasis on symptom focus, increases the emphasis on meaning and creates opportunities for the rehearsal of scenarios to optimally respond to increased perception of risk of relapse.

Targeted CBT

Targeted CBT can be provided during the early phase of relapse. In saying this, we have also used the relapse belief transformation strategies described in this chapter during conventional therapy. Given the nature of relapse, the opportunity for intervention is limited. Therefore the strategies employed during treatment are designed: (1) to minimise risk; (2) to reduce the speed of the relapse process, thereby (3) increasing the window of opportunity to prevent the occurrence of a relapse. Targeted CBT is initiated when there has been an increase in early signs of relapse or if there is evidence of stressors which are likely to confer increased relapse risk, for example, the loss of a loved one or being assaulted.

Order of Treatment Tasks

Treatment tasks are prioritised at the beginning of targeted CBT according to the careful assessment and identification of evidence of risk of harm to self and/or harm to others. Once these priorities have been addressed, treatment can move to addressing other treatment priorities.

THE INITIAL INTERVIEW FOR TARGETED CBT

The initial interview begins with a brief review of the individual's early signs, and the identification of any other problems or symptoms, including checks for risk of harm to self or others. The therapist and the individual prioritise problems identified in the review for the session's agenda. Problems and symptoms identified in the review are examined in relation to concerns regarding relapse. The evidence for and against relapse can be considered in relation to the formulation developed during the assessment and engagement phase. In addition, given that relapse is likely to be associated with heightened arousal, high levels of fear and anxiety, and catastrophic thoughts, the therapist takes particular care in pacing the initial and subsequent sessions. The pace of the session is deliberately slowed in order to identify salient beliefs, and, indeed, to provide a model of a non-catastrophic reaction to the threat of an emerging relapse.

TESTING THE FORMULATION

A critically important therapist task at the beginning of targeting is the identification of evidence for and against relapse. This procedure has three functions: (1) the careful assessment of relapse risk; (2) assisting the individual in taking a perspective on their experience; and (3) clarification of the relapse hypothesis. This procedure also provides an opportunity for the therapist and the individual to critically evaluate the accuracy of their formulation. This test can be undertaken using a number of strategies. First, the accuracy of the formulation can be evaluated by comparing the nature and pattern of current early signs, with those predicted by the formulation itself. Second, variations between expected and current experience are examined in terms of the individual's appraisal of their early signs in terms of their current beliefs about relapse, and their recollections of previous relapses. Third, similarities between current and prior experience can also be evaluated.

DECATASTROPHISING RELAPSE

During the initial session the therapist prioritises any catastrophic beliefs concerning relapse. This is an important clinical priority, as catastrophic beliefs will increase physiological arousal and fear, thereby accelerating the speed at which a potential relapse progresses. A number of techniques can be useful in decatastrophising relapse. First, relapse can be reframed as an opportunity for new learning. In particular, historical evidence concerning delayed intervention for relapse can be employed to underline the current opportunities, which may arise from early intervention. On the other hand, previous experiences of failed early intervention can be examined in terms of identifying additional procedures, which may have been helpful. Second, the therapist can further work with the individual to highlight the advantages and disadvantages of early intervention. The results of this can be compared to previous experience. Third, the therapist can elicit experiences where individuals have sought help and/or employed coping skills, which have prevented or reduced the severity of relapse. Evidence of this can be discovered, by asking the individual to recall previous experiences where early signs have been experienced without a subsequent relapse. While this procedure allows the therapist to evaluate the probability of the current episode being a false positive, it also enables the identification of particular coping skills employed by the individual, which have been helpful. Fourth, the therapist remains vigilant throughout for evidence of increased affect. Evidence of increased affect within session is explored by the therapist in order to elicit other negative beliefs concerning self, illness, others and future which may be relevant to relapse, or acting as barriers to reframing relapse itself.

CONTRACTING INTERVENTION

At the end of the initial session, targeted CBT is contracted on the basis of the evidence collected concerning relapse probability. The rationale for CBT is made on the basis of the accuracy of the original or adapted formulation, which provides a focus for targeting key beliefs and behaviours, which seem to be relevant to the relapse process. For example, in explaining the rationale, it can be useful to feed back the relationship between the catastrophic thoughts, which have arisen from negative experiences, and the acceleration of increased fear, arousal and sleeplessness. The use of metaphor can be helpful, where the relapse process is compared to an engine that becomes engaged by frightening thoughts, memories and beliefs, which increase the speed of unpleasant emotions and feelings. By learning new or strengthening existing coping strategies, this engine can be slowed down, or disengaged. The purpose of the metaphor also enables the introduction of realistic hope of increased control over relapse.

SUBSEQUENT SESSIONS

Identifying the Most Emotionally Salient Beliefs

As described, the therapist remains vigilant for any changes in affect, and follows changes in emotion as signals that a particular belief is active. Changes in emotion provide an opportunity to gently enquire about any thoughts and/or images that the individual is experiencing. Ascertaining the meaning of events is a crucial procedure. While increased emotion and distress is an obvious consequence of early relapse, the meaning of the event needs to be established. An example of this process is illustrated below:

Th: You look distressed just now. What is the worst thing about what you are experiencing?

C: I don't know. I'm so confused, I can't think properly; it's all too much for me.

Th: You feel confused, you can't think properly, and it feels too much. (*Summarise to slow pace*) Which one of those things upset you most?

C: It's not being able to think. It's like there's nothing I can do. Everything feels out of control. I'm scared that I'll get unwell.

Th: I can see why you feel so distressed. (*Therapist provides validation*) When you feel confused and unable to think properly, this means that you feel you can't do anything, that you have no control, and that you will become unwell. Have I got that right? (*Check for accuracy*)

C: Yes, (*tearful*) I have no control over what's happening. That's what it's like (*relapse*). It's like something just takes over me, everything speeds up, and I can't do anything about it.

Making specific enquiries about the nature and presence of imagery can be helpful in ascertaining the meaning and psychological significance of early relapse. Given that relapse experience can be traumatic, the therapist needs to be aware of evidence of intrusive imagery in relation to previous events, and that individuals may describe images in an over-general manner (cognitive avoidance). An example of this process is given below:

Th: You say that you've been thinking about the last time you were unwell. Is there a particular aspect of that memory that sticks in your mind?

C: I remember my mum shouting at me. She was screaming; it didn't make any sense. I could hear the voices. They were mad too. The noise wouldn't stop.

Th: Can you see that in your mind as you are speaking?

C: (*Looks away*) I could hear the voices. They were telling me how bad I am. My mum's face was red. I can see her eyes. She looked really angry. She was shouting, but I don't know what she was saying.

Th: What does that image mean to you?

C: I've let her down again. I'm a disappointment to her. I'm no good.

Th: In this image you can see your mum shouting, you remember the voices, but you don't know what your mum was saying. This image means something to you which is distressing, that is that you've let her down, that you're no good, and that you're a disappointment. Is this how you think about yourself when you're worried about relapse?

C: Yes, it's like if I get unwell, then I've let her down again.

The therapist is careful and supportive in eliciting key thoughts, beliefs and images, which occur during relapse. It is important for the therapist to ensure that they have a reasonable sample of cognitions in order not to miss any salient concerns. However, the vast number of thoughts and images, which occur during early relapse, can, understandably, be overwhelming to both individual and therapist. This difficulty can be addressed by identifying the most salient cognition. Most simply this can be achieved by asking which thought or image is most upsetting. On the other hand, careful documentation of thoughts, beliefs and images can then enable the therapist to invite the individual to systematically rate the distress associated with each. By this means the most salient cognition or cognitions can be identified. Furthermore, the therapist can undertake reliability checks by verifying the relationship between specific thoughts and the principal emotions, physiological reactions, and behaviours associated with the relapse process.

INTRODUCING FLEXIBILITY INTO BELIEFS

Beliefs during early relapse can be absolute, acting like unconditional core beliefs, for example, 'I have no control', and 'I am bad'. Critical to the process of decelerating the speed of relapse is the introduction of flexibility into such beliefs through identifying situations where that belief is true or untrue. However, if the individual states that it is true in all situations, then the eliciting evidence for the belief can be used as a means of introducing flexibility. This evidence is then utilised to create conditions where the belief is true for the individual, thereby creating a conditional belief. An example of this process is given below:

Th: You say that you have no control. Can you tell me what makes that true for you?

C: My thoughts are going too fast, I can't think. I can't talk to people properly. There's nothing I can do.

Th: Are there other things that make you feel that you've no control?

C: Yes. Thoughts keep coming into my head (*looks away*), they're awful. It's like I've harmed someone. I can see my sister lying dead.

Th: How does that make you feel?

C: I'm doing something wrong, something bad is going to happen if I don't stop it.

Th: Let me see if I've got this right. Because your thoughts are going too fast, you can't think right, and awful thoughts keep coming into your mind. This makes you feel that you have no control. Is that right?

C: Yes, I can't stop what is happening in my head.

Th: So, if you can't stop what is happening in your head, then you have no control. Does that feel right to you?

C: Yes, that's it; it's what's going on inside my head that is so bad.

Here the therapist balances validation of the belief with an enquiry into the conditions that activate the belief and make it 'feel' true. Creating conditions attached to the belief facilitates the implementation of strategies to transform the belief. Some examples of conditional beliefs that are associated with

> If I relapse, then others will be disappointed in me.
>
> If I lose control of my thoughts, then I'll relapse.
>
> If I don't cope, then I will relapse.
>
> If I relapse, then I'll end up in hospital.
>
> If I tell someone I'm not well, then they'll be angry with me.
>
> If I get unwell, then I'll be punished.
>
> If I relapse, then I am a failure.

Figure 11.3 Conditional beliefs during relapse

relapse acceleration are given in Figure 11.3. These beliefs bind the personal experiences of relapse (e.g. changes in thought, emotion, physiology, cognition and behaviour) to consequences for self (e.g. loss of control, failure), world/others (e.g. anger, punishment) and future (e.g. hospital admission).

TRANSFORMING BELIEFS

Given that a key assumption of targeted CBT is that the beliefs developed concerning relapse emerge as a result of negative experiences, these beliefs are seen as contextually adaptive. During this process the therapist may identify a number of conditional beliefs. This is dealt with by identifying which belief is associated with the strongest emotion, for example, by rating each belief for the amount of distress associated with it. In addition, the therapist does not necessarily take a challenging approach to these beliefs. Rather, the therapist examines the evidence supporting these beliefs in order to establish their function for the individual. For example, the belief 'If I do not control my thoughts, then I will become unwell' will result in a number of safety behaviours such as avoidance of situations that trigger intrusive thoughts, vigilance for changes in thinking, cognitive avoidance, or other thought control strategies. The function of these safety behaviours is the control of thinking. Transforming beliefs involves establishing alternative assumptions that achieve the function (in this case control), without the costs associated with the former conditional belief. The therapist establishes the meaning of 'control' and the parameters which determine control, for example, whether perceived control governed by the individual's cognitive experience alone, whether there are other factors which influence perceived control, and importantly, whether there are alternative behaviours that can enhance the individual's sense of control. By identifying an alternative or existing behaviour that enhances sense of control, this behaviour can be used to bind a new belief. The importance of using behaviour to transform and develop alternative beliefs is related to the subsequent use of behavioural experiments to test transformed beliefs. In this way the therapist does not challenge the logic or truth of the former belief, but works with the individual to develop alternative beliefs. An example of this process is given below:

Th: You say, 'If I do not control my thoughts, then I will become unwell.' Could you tell me how that belief is helpful to you?

C: It means I won't get unwell.

Th: Are there other ways this belief is helpful to you?

C: Well . . . I suppose it means that I feel better, I feel more in control of my head.

Th: OK, so this way of looking at your thoughts means that you're less likely to get unwell, you feel better and feel more in control. Is there anything else that is helpful about this belief?

C: I don't think so, but I never seem to feel better, and I get unwell anyway.

Th: OK, while this belief can be helpful for you, it doesn't work all the time. Are there disadvantages to having to control your thoughts?

C: It's really hard, the harder I try, the harder it gets. I worry about what I'm thinking, and I can't go outside because I might start getting upsetting thoughts, other people might notice. I get really depressed about it.

Th: So this is really hard for you, it leads you to worry about what you're thinking, worry if other people will notice, so you don't go outside, and you get really depressed. So rather than avoiding upsetting thoughts altogether, what if you felt as if you could cope better with upsetting thoughts? How would that be?

C: I'm not sure. I don't like getting these thoughts.

Th: (Therapist checks parameters of control) All right, so when you say that you would like to control these thoughts, what do you mean by that?

C: Well, I mean not get them at all, I should be able to control my thoughts all of the time.

In this example, the therapist decides to address the belief that all thoughts should be controlled and provides some explanation of the difference between voluntary (e.g. planning a shopping list) and involuntary thoughts (e.g. negative automatic thoughts or intrusive thoughts in reaction to stress). Information is provided and discussed on the frequency of intrusive thoughts in the general population, and the role of thought suppression in producing rebound (Wells, 1997). A behavioural experiment investigating the effects of thought suppression is conducted in the session by asking the individual to construct an image of a banana in their imagination and then to avoid thinking about bananas. Once the belief that all thoughts should be controllable is addressed, the belief that 'If I do not control my thoughts, then I will become unwell' can be addressed.

Th: So, what kind of things help you feel more in control?
C: Talking to my friend helps, when I'm not upset, I feel more in control, having a drink helps me as well.
Th: OK, so what is it about these situations that make you feel more in control?
C: I feel more relaxed. I still get upsetting thoughts but they don't bother me so much.
Th: So, what do you do in these situations when you get an upsetting thought?
C: I think about something else or I distract myself by doing something.
Th: So, as a first step, rather than trying to abolish these thoughts altogether, if you were able to ignore these thoughts, what would that mean?
C: I suppose I wouldn't get so upset.
Th: And if you were less upset by them, what would that mean to you.
C: I'd feel better.
Th: So, 'If I can ignore unwanted thoughts, I will feel better.' Does that sound right?

At this point the therapist produces an alternative transformed belief, and as with the former belief ('If I do not control my thoughts, I will become unwell'), the therapist works with the individual to identify the advantages and disadvantages of this belief with respect to self and relapse.

TESTING TRANSFORMED BELIEFS

During the process of relapse individuals adopt a range of behavioural strategies aimed at increasing safety, preventing relapse or increasing control. For example, common signs associated with early relapse include suspiciousness and vigilance, withdrawal and avoidance, use of alcohol and drugs. However, these 'safety behaviours' may result in the acceleration of relapse, thus confirming individuals' beliefs concerning their helplessness, or the inevitability of relapse.

Behavioural experiments provide an ideal methodology of intervention during this process. Behavioural experiments enable the individual to achieve a behavioural change (e.g. implementing a coping skill), which results in a cognitive change (beliefs concerning self or illness). Behavioural experiments can be conducted in sessions and between sessions. Furthermore, behavioural experiments can be also graded according to difficulty. During CBT for relapse, behavioural experiments are targeted on the development of alternative behaviours practised across a number of situations beginning with coaching in a session to applying between session and in vivo. The example given below continues from the example described above. In this example the therapist had begun with the belief that 'If I do not control my thoughts, then I will become unwell' and with the individual had transformed this to 'If I can ignore unwanted thoughts, I will feel better'.

Th: Is there a way to test this belief out?
C: I'm not sure, what do you mean?
Th: Well, how could you find out if this belief is helpful to you or not?
C: I suppose that I could try it out and see what happens.
Th: OK, that seems like a good idea. How could you do that?
C: Well, the next time I get an unwanted thought, I could try to ignore it and do something else.
Th: What kind of problems might happen if you did that?
C: Well, other people might see that there's something going on, and they might get upset or angry.
Th: OK, could anything else go wrong?
C: I could get upset anyway, and then it wouldn't work.
Th: All right, then. There are two problems, first, other people might notice and get upset or angry and you might get upset anyway. Why don't we try and address each of these in turn. Why don't you try this experiment without any other people around first, before trying it out in other situations? Maybe we could try it out just now?

As behavioural interventions are implemented and practised, these changes are consolidated through the review and examination of individuals' beliefs concerning the control, stigma, shame and/or fear associated with illness. The therapist aims to assist the individual in accommodating new information gained during intervention into pre-existing assumptions concerning illness, in comparison with the beliefs tested during treatment.

CONCLUSIONS

In this chapter we have attempted to describe a psychological approach to understanding, conceptualising and responding to relapse. At the centre of this approach is the delineation and targeting of fearful appraisals and beliefs that can accelerate relapse. These appraisals also give shape and form to the characteristic early signs of relapse. It is helpful to use case formulation here as part of the process of meaning-making, where formulation can be used to support maintenance of self-reflective understanding of relapse even in the context of a crisis which might provoke an at-risk mental state for relapse. The formulation also provides the basis for explorative discussion around expectations and individual and service responses in the context of relapse.

CHAPTER 12

CONCLUSION

INTRODUCTION

As stated at the beginning of this book, our overall aim in producing this treatment manual was to outline and operationalise a cognitive interpersonal approach to working with individuals who are at high risk of relapse, to support their emotional recovery and adjustment after psychosis, to reduce psychological vulnerability to relapse, and to provide prompt and immediate support at the early signs of possible relapse. This manual was divided into three main parts. Part I gave a theoretical account of staying well and relapse prevention. Part II gave an overview of the style, structure and organisation of therapy. Part III detailed the specific cognitive, behavioural and interpersonal strategies involved in promoting recovery and staying well.

OVERVIEW OF THE TREATMENT MANUAL

In Part I of this book we aimed to describe and establish the context of the current literature on relapse in psychosis and provide a theoretical and empirical background for our thinking about the structure and content of the treatment manual. In our psychological approach to relapse and staying well after psychosis we outlined a developmental and cognitive interpersonal account of the individual's perspective on their experience of psychosis, their psychosocial situation and the wider service context in which relapse is situated. In providing an integrated cognitive behavioural account of early signs and relapse we aimed to conceptualise the key affective experiences that characterise the early stages of relapse. In fact, we argued that the early signs of relapse are perhaps best conceptualised as an 'at-risk mental state' for relapse. We illustrated that idiosyncratic appraisals and cognitive emotional processes have their origins in the person's wider developmental and psychosocial framework. Indeed, this often includes traumatic memories and processing of previous episodes of psychosis within a vulnerable social and systemic context.

We further outlined a regulatory theory of the interpersonal and developmental context of affect dysregulation in relation to recovery and relapse after psychosis. We argued that the understanding and formulation of individuals' emotional status after psychosis and their interpersonal response to their emotional distress are essential in the understanding of their adaptation to psychosis, their emotional and interpersonal recovery and vulnerability to future possible relapse.

The main body of work that we referred to was that of attachment theory and attachment organisation in terms of a developmental psychopathology of psychosis. The key components that were highlighted related to the internalisation of early attachment experiences and individuals' current states of mind in relation to attachment. In particular, we highlighted the importance of constructs including mindmindedness and reflective function in understanding individual affect regulation and help-seeking. The main implication of adult attachment styles in individuals with psychosis for this manual is related to service engagement and utilisation of available or potential social supports. The establishment of collaborative attachments and a stable and containing therapeutic relationship are essential in the perspective of staying well after psychosis.

We also outlined how early adverse experiences can influence the attachment system. We identified that individuals who develop psychosis are at heightened risk of experiencing events that are likely to reflect problematic early developmental experiences including abuse, neglect and loss separation. These experiences are likely to impair the development of cognitive interpersonal skills necessary for the development of mind mindedness, affect regulation and help-seeking.

Finally, Part I concluded with a closer examination of the role of current social and interpersonal circumstances for the risk of relapse. These included outlining how expressed emotion in close social systems, significant life events, broader socio-economic influences and the individual's social support networks are important contributors in explaining variations in relapse rates and individual vulnerabilities to relapse.

Part II provided the reader with an overview of the style and structure of the individual cognitive interpersonal treatment. Engagement, formulation and therapeutic style are key concepts on which we develop a therapeutic framework for recovery and staying well. We illustrated how assessment and formulation are driven by an integration of the key cognitive behavioural and interpersonal factors contributing to the person's current difficulties. The formulation approach is oriented towards the client's problem list and takes into account essential components of their individual vulnerability and support in terms of staying well. The intervention is designed over about 20 individual sessions that can vary in length and frequency. The principal aim of therapy is the transformation of personal beliefs and the achievement of sustainable changes in problematic interpersonal strategies. The establishment of a containing therapeutic relationship aids the exploration and understanding of complex emotional reactions and is based on an acceptance of negative and positive affective experiences in relation to psychosis. In conjunction with this focused individual treatment approach, staying well requires a coordinated and well-integrated multi-disciplinary response to clients' needs in relation to their recovery and relapse prevention.

We placed particular emphasis on the process of engagement and formulation. The key aspiration of engagement and formulation is the development of a shared and collaborative discourse that is carefully attuned to the client's emotional experiences. Within the elaboration of a shared understanding the therapist pays careful attention to the process of engagement and remains sensitive to the interplay between recovery style, attachment organisation and the therapeutic relationship. The developing therapeutic narrative is a validating and self-accepting one. The experience of negative affect is framed as an important opportunity, allowing the therapist and client to collaborate on the development of experiential meanings. This process aims to support the development of the client's sense of agency, control and hopefulness. The compassionate, productively self-reflective formulation embedded in the client's experiences provides a platform for the client to choose and strengthen alternative perspectives and interpersonal coping.

In Part III, the main body of this text, specific cognitive and interpersonal therapeutic strategies are developed and described that support recovery and staying well after psychosis. The recent discourse on the essential emotional characteristics of psychosis has established the importance of life event dimensions in emotional adaptation to psychosis, in particular, the role and importance of post-psychotic depression and its origin which is essentially linked to negative personal appraisals of humiliation, entrapment and loss arising from the experience of psychosis. These aspects are augmented by the role of social anxiety in the context of psychosis, which is also related to greater feelings of self-blame, entrapment and shame. In the context of the psychotherapeutic treatment, the therapist and the client aim to construct a narrative that allows the client to explore new meanings and resonances integrating the full spectrum of their emotional experiences.

A particular vulnerability in terms of individual recovery and recurrence of psychosis is potential feelings of paranoia, vigilance, suspiciousness and interpersonal threat appraisal. In this manual we suggest understanding paranoid states of mind as strategies of adaptation that developed in the context of particular life events and stressors. We termed this the 'paranoid mind'. In relation to the therapeutic alliance, the paranoid mind could be a block to engagement and recovery via the presence of continuing interpersonal distrust. We have advocated in this context an approach to a conceptualisation of paranoia that emphasises paranoia and interpersonal distrust as an evolved mental state designed to manage interpersonal threat. This framework implied a therapeutic approach that encourages the development of a mindful and non-judgemental reflectiveness on the origins, development and functionality of paranoia in the person's life context. This process is strongly embedded in an evolving therapeutic relationship, which in itself serves to support the development of self-reflectiveness and mentalisation.

We emphasised the importance of careful assessment of individuals' experiences of psychosis and psychiatric treatment as a potentially traumatic life event and the possible interactions with previous traumatic experiences and aspects of trauma processing in the psychological responses of individual clients. Consistent with the main tenets of cognitive therapy, there is an emphasis on the content of individuals' beliefs, appraisals and attributions. In the context of trauma, psychosis and recovery, disrupted client narratives often signal to the therapist where there may be aspects of the psychotic experience that remain avoided and overwhelming, thus indicating that information processing remains incomplete or unelaborated. The therapeutic exploration and development of a coherent narrative in the context of traumatic reactions facilitate the salutogenic elaboration and contextualising of the experience. We have emphasised the importance of pursuing significant emotional resonances in order to allow connectivity with past trauma or life events, or with current appraisals of experience.

In this section we also focused on aspects of the intervention that directly address interpersonal vulnerability factors. We identified particular aspects of the interpersonal world of individuals with psychosis that may contribute to their vulnerability to relapse but also aspects of their interpersonal world that may also aid recovery. In particular we highlighted the influence of social support and positive confiding relationships and the effects of negative interactions and communication styles with family members. In this part of the treatment manual we concentrated on the identification of interpersonal problem areas, which contribute to the vulnerability of relapse. The use of therapeutic techniques such as communication analysis, role-play and exploration of affect in interpersonal scenarios to support the individual to make significant changes in their interpersonal world that help them to address key areas of difficulty.

Particular emphasis was placed on the therapeutic relationship as a model for interpersonal exchange and communication. This focus on the interpersonal world and individual interpersonal strategies within recovery lead us to outline and describe psychological strategies for working with core cognitive interpersonal schemata. This perspective entails an understanding of the effects of early adverse experiences upon the evolution of cognitive interpersonal schemata, and the development of both interpersonal and intrapersonal strategies in affect regulation. Over time these internal working models correspond with personal styles and ways of interacting that maintain negative core beliefs, affective dysregulation and vulnerability to relapse. In therapy the careful exploration of the powerful life experiences that contribute to the shaping of rigid and inflexible core beliefs and long-standing behavioural strategies is an important part of developing an individual's awareness of their reactions to negative life events and stresses. Within this therapeutic frame, the therapist does not seek to challenge negative core beliefs; rather, the therapist creates opportunities for the client to explore new ways of relating or to develop new narratives that recreate a revised meaning structure in relation to significant events and aspects of their self-understanding. Here the emphasis of therapy is on the process of meaning-making. Through development of new interpersonal strategies we aim to support the person in negotiating difficult conflictual interpersonal situations. Underpinning this process is the development of compassionate intrapersonal strategies that address internal self-attacking shame and fearful submissive internal dialogues.

Finally, we revisited the understanding of relapse in terms of strategies that can help to prevent the recurrence or exacerbation of psychotic symptoms. Relapse in terms of recurrence or exacerbation of psychotic symptoms is often preceded by increases in non-psychotic symptoms such as anxiety, sleeplessness, preoccupation, irritability and depressed mood. At the centre of a psychological approach to the understanding and response to relapse is the targeting of fearful appraisals and beliefs that can accelerate relapse. These appraisals also give shape and form to the characteristic early signs of relapse. It is helpful to use case formulation here as part of the process, where formulation can be used to support maintenance of self-reflective understanding of relapse. We detailed a number of psychological early intervention strategies that can be used in the context of individual with 'at-risk mental states' for relapse.

The specific components of the treatment as outlined in the chapters above are meant to be utilised in a fluid and dynamic manner that takes account of the individual's formulation, their particular problem list, their therapy goals, and the processes of therapeutic change throughout the course of treatment. It is vital to remain mindful that the therapeutic work on recovery and staying well takes place in a wider societal and systemic context. It can, in particular, often be the culture of psychiatric services and local communities that drive particular appraisals and reactions that contribute to an individual's vulnerability.

THERAPIST TRAINING

We strongly suggest that therapists using this treatment manual have training and experience in either cognitive behavioural or interpersonal approaches to psychological therapy. Anyone planning to use this treatment manual should also have experience in using these approaches with people with psychosis and with people with anxiety and affective disorders. In addition, therapists should have access to regular clinical supervision that allows them to explore client-based formulation, application of therapeutic strategies and therapy processes. In particular, clinical supervision should also encourage therapists also to reflect on their own emotional reactions within therapy and, indeed, where relevant, on their own developmental and attachment experiences.

THERAPEUTIC CONTEXT

Frequently therapists will need to provide therapy in a multi-disciplinary service context and it is important that therapists are aware of the systemic context of service delivery. Indeed, client-based formulation should be integrated into the organisational arrangements for multi-disciplinary care. Formulation should be integrated into the regular multi-disciplinary review process and the client is encouraged to be actively involved in shaping and determining multi-disciplinary treatment tasks and goals.

Our experience has been that key to the process of encouraging clients to develop an explorative and self-reflective integrative recovery style is the development of the multi-disciplinary team as a 'secure base'. This is not easy. Teams often work in challenging conditions. For example, they are often short-staffed and staff are frequently asked to carry large caseloads. Indeed, different professions in the multi-disciplinary team bring different training experiences and their own unique pressures and responsibilities. It is therefore understandable that mental health staff can sometimes express unhelpful attributions and beliefs in the context of recovery and relapse. For example, staff might attribute relapse to lack of insight where a client refuses to accept an illness model of their experience due to socially degrading and stigmatising dimensions associated with diagnoses such as schizophrenia. On the other hand, staff might insist on medication compliance and/or avoidance of drugs or alcohol in the context of a client wishing to assert their own autonomy and individuation but refusing to submit to psychiatric services. These desynchronous interactions between clients and staff have the potential to create damaging reciprocal interpersonal patterns. These have the capacity to undermine the development of a secure therapeutic base, the provision of appropriate therapeutic interventions, and the development of a robust therapeutic alliance.

The therapist has an important systemic role in fostering the development of a psychological model of care that emphasises early attachment, developmental, cognitive, interpersonal and life event dimensions of clients' experiences. This can be achieved though the provision of regular team-based training, adequate time for a structured multi-disciplinary review that incorporates the presentation and discussion of formulation from multiple view points, the incorporation of clients' narrative and support for user involvement in reviewing and evaluating service provision.

FEAR OF RECURRENCE SCALE (FORSE) QUESTIONNAIRE

Name: _____   Date: _____

This questionnaire is concerned with problems and complaints people some-times have. Please read each item carefully and circle the appropriate number that best describes how you have been over the **last two weeks including today**.

		Do not agree	Agree slightly	Agree moderately	Agree very much
1.	I have been worrying about relapse.	1	2	3	4
2.	I have been remembering previous episodes of being unwell.	1	2	3	4
3.	I have been more aware of my thoughts.	1	2	3	4
4.	I have experienced thoughts intruding into my mind.	1	2	3	4
5.	I have been worrying about my thoughts.	1	2	3	4
6.	I have felt unable to control my illness.	1	2	3	4
7.	I have been worrying about being in hospital.	1	2	3	4
8.	I have lacked confidence in my ability to cope.	1	2	3	4

9.	My thoughts have been uncontrollable.	1	2	3	4
10.	My thoughts have been going too fast.	1	2	3	4
11.	I have been worrying about losing control.	1	2	3	4
12.	My thoughts have been distressing.	1	2	3	4
13.	I have felt more in touch with my thoughts.	1	2	3	4
14.	I have been constantly aware of my thoughts.	1	2	3	4
15.	I have been unable to switch off my thinking.	1	2	3	4
16.	I have paid close attention to how my mind is working.	1	2	3	4
17.	The world has seemed more vivid and colourful.	1	2	3	4
18.	My thoughts have been more interesting.	1	2	3	4
19.	I have had new insights and ideas.	1	2	3	4
20.	Unpleasant thoughts have entered my head against my will.	1	2	3	4
21.	My thinking has been clearer than usual.	1	2	3	4
22.	I have been checking my thoughts.	1	2	3	4
23.	The thought of becoming unwell has frightened me.	1	2	3	4

Fear of Relapse: 1, 2, 6, 7, 8, 11, 23
Awareness: 3, 13, 14, 16, 17, 18, 19, 21, 22
Intrusiveness: 4, 5, 9, 10, 12, 15, 20

DIAGRAMMATICAL FORMULATION OF EARLY SIGNS

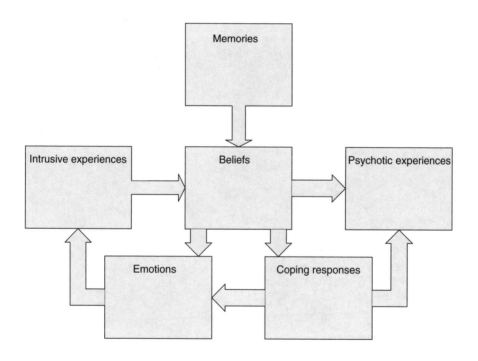

BIBLIOGRAPHY

Abramson LY, Seligman MEP & Teasdale JD (1979). Learned helplessness in humans: critique and reformulation. *Journal of Abnormal Psychology*, **87**, 49–74.

Addington D, Addington J & Maticka-Tyndale E (1993). Assessing depression in schizophrenia: the Calgary Depression Scale. *British Journal of Psychiatry*, **163** (suppl. 22), 39–44.

Addington D, Addington J & Robinson G (1999). Attributional style and depression in schizophrenia. *Canadian Journal of Psychiatry*, **44**, 697–700.

Addington J, van Mastrigt S & Addington D (2004). Duration of untreated psychosis: impact on 2-year outcome. *Psychological Medicine*, **34**, 277–284.

Ainsworth MDS, Blehar MC, Waters E & Wall S (1978). *Patterns of attachment: a psychological study of the strange situation*. Hillsdale, NJ, Erlbaum.

Akiskal HS & Pinto O (1999). The evolving bipolar spectrum: prototypes I, II, III and IV. *Psychiatric Clinics of North America*, **22**(3), 517–534.

Alexander LB & Luborsky L (1986). The Penn Helping alliance scales. In WM Pinsof & LS Greeberg (eds), *The psychotherapeutic process: a research handbook*. New York, Guilford Press, pp. 325–366.

Alexander PC (1992a). Effect of incest on self and social functioning: a developmental psychopathology perspective. *Journal of Consulting and Clinical Psychology*, **60**, 185–195.

Alexander PC (1992b). Application of attachment theory to the study of sexual abuse. *Journal of Consulting and Clinical Psychology*, **60**, 185–195.

Alloway R & Bebbington P (1987). The buffer theory of social support: a review of the literature. *Psychological Medicine*, **17**(1), 91–108.

Alloy LB, Abramson LY, Tashman NA, Berrebbi DS, Hogan ME, Whitehouse WG et al. (2001). Developmental origins of cognitive vulnerability to depression: parenting, cognitive, and inferential feedback styles of the parents of individuals at high and low cognitive risk for depression. *Cognitive Therapy and Research*, **25**(4), 397–423.

American Psychiatric Association (1994). *Diagnostic and statistical manual of mental disorders (DSM-IV)*, 4th edn. Washington, DC, American Psychiatric Association.

Amminger GP, Edwards J, Brewer WJ, Harrigan S & McGorry PD (2002). Duration of untreated psychosis and cognitive deterioration in first-episode schizophrenia. *Schizophrenia Research*, **54**, 223–230.

Andreasen NC (1984). *Scale for the assessment of positive symptoms (SAPS)*. The University of Iowa, Iowa City, Iowa.

Bach P & Hayes S (2002). The use of acceptance and commitment therapy to prevent the rehospitalization of psychotic patients: a randomized controlled trial. *Journal of Consulting and Clinical Psychology*, **70**(5), 1129–1139.

Barbui C, Saraceno B, Liberati A & Garattini S (1996). Low-dose neuroleptic therapy and relapse in schizophrenia: meta-analysis of randomized controlled trials. *European Psychiatry*, **11**(6), 306–313.

Barrowclough C, Haddock G, Tarrier N, Lewis SW, Moring J, O'Brien R et al. (2001). Randomized controlled trial of motivational interviewing, cognitive behavior therapy, and family intervention for patients with comorbid schizophrenia and substance use disorders. *American Journal of Psychiatry*, **158**(10), 1706–1713.

Barrowclough C & Hooley J (2003). Attributions and expressed emotion: a review. *Clinical Psychology Review*, **23**, 849–880.

Barrowclough C, Johnston M & Tarrier N (1994). Attributions, expressed emotion and patient relapse: an attributional model of relatives' response to schizophrenic illness. *Behaviour Therapy*, **25**, 67–88.

Barrowclough C, Lobban Hatton C & Quinn J (1991). An investigation of models of illness in carers of schizophrenia patients using the Illness Perception Questionnaire. *British Journal of Clinical Psychology*, **40**(4), 371–385.

Barrowclough C, Tarrier N & Johnston M (1996). Distress, expressed emotion, and attributions in relatives of schizophrenia patients. *Schizophrenia Bulletin*, **22**, 691–702.

Barry H Jr (1939). A study of bereavement: an approach to problems in mental disease. *American Journal of Orthopsychiatry*, **9**, 355–360.

Bartholomew K (1990). Avoidance of intimacy: an attachment perspective. *Journal of Social and Personal Relationships*, **7**(2), 147–178.

Bebbington P & Kuipers L (1998). Social influences on schizophrenia. In P McGuffin & P Bebbington (eds), *Schizophrenia: the major issues*. Oxford, Heinemann Medical Books/Heinemann Professional Publishing, pp. 201–225.

Bebbington P, Walsh C & Murray R (1993). The causes of functional psychosis. In GG Costello (ed.), *Basic issues in psychopathology*. London, Guilford Press.

Bebbington P, Wilkins S, Jones P, Foerster A, Murray R, Toone B et al. (1993). Life events and psychosis: initial results from the Camberwell Collaborative Psychosis Study. *British Journal of Psychiatry*, **162**, 72–79.

Bebbington PE, Bhugra D, Brugha T, Singleton N, Farrell M, Jenkins G et al. (2004). Psychosis, victimisation and childhood disadvantage: evidence from the second British National Survey of psychiatric morbidity. *British Journal of Psychiatry*, **185**, 220–226.

Bechdolf A, Knost B, Kuntermann C, Schiller S, Klosterkotter J, Hambrecht M et al. (2004). A randomized comparison of group cognitive-behavioural therapy and group psychoeducation in patients with schizophrenia. *Acta Psychiatrica Scandinavica*, **110**(1), 21–28.

Beck AT (1967). *Depression: causes and treatment*. Philadelphia, PA, University of Pennsylvania Press.

Beck AT (1976). *Cognitive therapy and the emotional disorders*. Oxford, International Universities Press.

Beck AT (1978). *The Beck Depression Inventory (BDI)*. New York, Psychological Corporation.

Beck AT, Baruch E, Balter JM, Steer RA & Warman DM (2004). A new instrument for measuring insight: the Beck Cognitive Insight Scale. *Schizophrenia Research*, **68**(2–3), 319–329.

Benn L, Harvey JE, Gilbert P & Irons C. (2005). Social rank, interpersonal trust and recall of parental rearing in relation to homesickness. *Personality and Individual Differences*, **38**, 1813–1822.

Bentall RP, Corcoran R, Howard R, Blackwood N & Kinderman P (2001). Persecutory delusions: a review and theroretical integration. *Clinical Psychology Review*, **21**(8), 1211–1226.

Bentall RP & Kaney S (1989). Content specific information processing and persecutory delusions: an investigation using the emotional Stroop test. *British Journal of Medical Psychology*, **62**, 355–364.

Bentall RP, Kaney S & Bowen-Jones K (1995). Persecutory delusions and recall of threat-related, depression-related and neutral words. *Cognitive Therapy and Research*, **19**, 331–343.

Beuke CJ, Fischer R & McDowall R (2003). Anxiety and depression: why and how to measure their separate effects. *Clinical Psychology Review*, **23**, 831–848.

Beyer JL, Kuchibhatla M, Looney C, Engstrom E, Cassidy F & Krishnan KRR (2003). Social support in elderly patients with bipolar disorder. *Bipolar Disorders*, **5**, 22–27.

Birchwood M (1995). Early intervention in psychotic relapse: cognitive approaches to detection and management. *Behaviour Change*, **12**(1), 2–19.

Birchwood M (1999). Early intervention in psychosis: the critical period. In HJ Jackson & PD McGorry (eds), *The recognition and management of early psychosis: a preventive approach*. New York, Cambridge University Press, pp. 226–264.

Birchwood M (2003). Pathways to emotional dysfunction in first-episode psychosis. *British Journal of Psychiatry*, **182**(5), 373–375.

Birchwood M & Cochrane R (1990). Families coping with schizophrenia: coping styles, their origins and correlates. *Psychological Medicine*, **20**, 857–865.

Birchwood M, Gilbert P, Gilbert J, Trower P, Meaden A, Hay J et al. (2004). Interpersonal and role-related schema influence the relationship with the dominant 'voice' in schizophrenia: a comparison of three models. *Psychological Medicine*, **34**, 1571–1580.

Birchwood M, Iqbal Z, Chadwick P & Trower P (2000a). Cognitive approach to depression and suicidal thinking in psychosis, 1: ontogeny of post-psychotic depression. *British Journal of Psychiatry*, **177**, 516–521.

Birchwood M, MacMillan F & Smith J (1992). Early intervention. In M Birchwood & N Tarrier (eds), *Innovations in the psychological management of schizophrenia*. Chichester, John Wiley & Sons.

Birchwood M, Mason R, MacMillan F & Healy J (1993). Depression, demoralisation and control over illness: a comparison of depressed and non-depressed patients with a chronic psychosis. *Psychological Medicine*, **23**, 387–395.

Birchwood M, Meaden A, Trower P, Gilbert P & Plaistow J (2000b). The power and omnipotence of voices: subordination and entrapment by voices and significant others. *Psychological Medicine*, **30**, 337–344.

Birchwood M & Pelosi A (2003). Is early intervention for psychosis a waste of valuable resources? *British Journal of Psychiatry*, **182**, 196–198.

Birchwood M, Smith J, Macmillan F, Hogg B, Prasad R, Harvey C et al. (1989). Predicting relapse in schizophrenia: the development of implication of an early signs monitoring system using patient and families as observers: a preliminary investigation. *Psychological Medicine*, **19**, 649–656.

Birchwood M, Spencer E & McGovern D (2000c). Schizophrenia: early warning signs. *Advances in Psychiatric Treatment*, **6**, 93–101.

Birchwood M, Todd P & Jackson C (1998). Early intervention in psychosis: the critical period hypothesis. *British Journal of Psychiatry*, **172** (suppl. 33), 53–59.

Birchwood M et al. (1994). A self-report insight scale for psychosis, reliability, validity and sensitivity to change. *Acta Psychiatrica Scandinavica*, **89**, 62–67.

Blain MD, Thompson JM & Whiffen VE (1993). Attachment and perceived social support in late adolescence. *Journal of Adolescent Research*, **8**, 226–241.

Boker H, Hell D, Budischewski K, Eppel A, Hartling F, Rinnert H et al. (2000). Personality and object relations in patients with affective disorders: idiographic research by means of the repertory grid technique. *Journal of Affective Disorders*, **60**, 53–59.

Boker W, Brenner HD, Gerstner G, Keller F, Muller J & Spichtig L (1984). Self-healing strategies among schizophrenics: attempts at compensation for basic disorders. *Acta Psychiatrica Scandinavica*, **69**, 373–378.

Bordin ES (1979). The generalizability of the psychoanalytic concept of the working alliance. *Psychotherapy: Theory, Research and Practice*, **16**(3), 252–260.

Bottlender R, Jager M, Strauss A & Moller H-J (2000). Suicidality in bipolar compared to unipolar depressed inpatients. *European Archives of Psychiatry and Clinical Neuroscience*, **250**, 257–261.

Bottlender R, Tetsuya S, Jager M, Groll C, Strauss A & Moller HJ (2002). The impact of duration of untreated psychosis and pre-morbid functioning on outcome of first inpatient treatment in schizophrenic and schizoaffective patients. *European Archives of Psychiatry and Clinical Neuroscience*, **252**, 226–231.

Bourgeois M, Swendsen J, Young F, Amador X, Pini S, Cassano GB et al. (2004). Awareness of disorder and suicide risk in the treatment of schizophrenia: results of the international suicide prevention trial. *American Journal of Psychiatry*, **161**, 1494–1496.

Bowers MB (1968). Pathogenesis of acute schizophrenic psychosis: an experiential approach. *Archives of General Psychiatry*, **19**, 348–355.

Bowlby J (1969). *Attachment and loss*, vol. 1: *Attachment*. London, Hogarth Press.

Bowlby J (1973). *Attachment and loss*, vol. 2: *Separation, anger and anxiety*. London, Hogarth Press.

Bowlby J (1980). *Attachment and loss*, vol. 3: *Loss, sadness and depression*. London, Hogarth Press.

Bowlby J (1982). *Attachment*, 2nd edn of vol. 1 of *Attachment and loss*. London, Hogarth Press, New York, Basic Books.

Bowlby J (1988). *A secure base: clinical applications of attachment theory*. London, Routledge.

Bramojn E, Croft RJ, McDonald C, Virdi GK, Gruzelier JG, Baldeweg T et al. (2004). Mismatch negativity in schizophrenia: a family study. *Schizophrenia Research*, **67**, 1–10.

Bremner JD & Narayan M (1998). The effects of stress on memory and the hippocampus throughout the life cycle: implications for childhood development and aging. *Developmental Psychopathology*, **10**, 871–886.

Breslau N, Lucia VC & Davis GC (2004). Partial PTSD versus full PTSD: an empirical examination of associated impairment. *Psychological Medicine*, **34**, 1205–1214.

Bretheron I (1985). Attachment theory: retrospect and prospect. In I Bretherton & E Waters (eds), *Growing points of attachment theory and research*. Monographs of the Society for Research in Child Development, **50**(1–2, Serial 129), 3–38.

Bretherton I & Mulholland KA (1999). Internal working models in attachment rela-tionships. In J Cassidy & P Shaver (eds), *Handbook of attachment: theory, research and applications*. New York, Guilford Press, pp. 89–111.

Brewin CR (1989). Cognitive change processes in psychotherapy. *Psychological Review*, **3**, 379–394.

Brewin CR (2001). Memory processes in post-traumatic stress disorder. *International Review of Psychiatry*, **13**(3), 159–163.

Brewin CR, McCarthy B, Duda K, Vaughn CE et al. (1991). Attributions and expressed emotion in the relatives of patients with schizophrenia. *Journal of Abnormal Psychology*, **100**, 546–554.

Brewin CR & Power MJ (1999). Integrating psychological therapies: processes of meaning transformation. *British Journal of Medical Psychology*, **72**, 143–157.

Brieger P, Bloink R, Sommer S & Merneros A (2001). Affective symptoms at index hospitalization in childhood and depressive symptoms in adult-hood: a 'catch-up' study. *Journal of Affective Disorders*, **66**, 263–266.

Brier A & Strauss J (1983). Self-control in psychotic disorders. *Archives of General Psychiatry*, **40**, 1141–1145.

Briere J (1988). Controlling for family variables in abuse effects research: a critique of the 'partialling' approach. *Journal of Interpersonal Violence*, **3**(1), 80–89.

Briere J (1992). *Child abuse trauma: theory and treatment of the lasting effects*. Newbury Park, CA, Sage Publications.

Briere J (2002). Treating adult survivors of severe childhood abuse and neglect: further development of an integrative model. In JEB Myers, L Berliner, J Briere, CT Hendrix, T Reid & C Jenny (eds), *The APSAC handbook on child maltreatment*. 2nd edn, Newbury Park, CA, Sage Publications.

Bromet EJ, Ed V & May S (1984). Family environments of depressed outpatients. *Acta Psychiatrica Scandinavica*, **69**(3), 197–200.

Brown GW (1989). Depression: a radical social perspective. In KR Herbst & ES Paykel (eds), *Depression: An integrative approach*. Oxford, Heinemann Medical Books, pp. 21–44.

Brown GW (2002). Social roles, context and evolution in the origins of depression. *Journal of Health and Social Behavior*, **43**, 255–276.

Brown GW & Anderson B (1991). Psychiatric morbidity in adult inpatients with child-hood histories of sexual and physical abuse. *American Journal of Psychiatry*, **148**, 55–61.

Brown GW, Andrews B, Harris TO, Adler Z & Bridge L (1986). Social support, self-esteem and depression. *Psychological Medicine*, **16**, 813–831.

Brown GW & Birley JL (1968). Crises and life changes and the onset of schizophre-nia. *Journal of Health and Social Behavior*, **9**, 203–214.

Brown GW, Birley JLT & Wing JK (1972). Influence of family life on the course of psychiatric illness. *British Journal of Psychiatry*, **121**, 241–258.

Brown GW & Harris TO (1978). *Social origins of depression: a study of psychiatric disor-der in women*. London, Tavistock.

Brown GW, & Harris TO (1996). Guidelines, examples and LEDS-2 notes on rating for a new classification scheme for humiliation, loss and danger. Unpublished manual.

Brown GW, Harris TO & Hepworth C (1994). Life events and endogenous depres-sion: a puzzle reexamined. *Archives of General Psychiatry*, **51**(7), 525–534.

Brown GW, Harris TO & Hepworth C (1995). Loss, humiliation and entrapment among women developing depression: a patient and non-patient comparison. *Psychological Medicine*, **25**(1), 7–21.

Brown GW & Rutter M (1966). The measurement of family activities and relationships: methodological study. *Human Relations*, **19**, 241–263.

Buchanan A, Reed A, Wessely S, Garety P, Taylor P, Grubin D et al. (1993). Acting on delusions, II: the phenomenological correlates of acting on delusions. *British Journal of Psychiatry*, **163**, 77–81.

Buchkremer G, Klingberg S, Holle R, Schulze Monking H & Hornung WP (1997). Psychoeducational psychotherapy for schizophrenic patients and their key relatives or care-givers: results of a 2-year follow-up. *Acta Psychiatrica Scandinavica*, **96**(6), 483–491.

Burt T, Prudic J, Peyser S, Clark J & Sackeim HA (2000). Learning and memory in bipolar and unipolar major depression: effects of aging. *Neuropsychiatry, Neuropsychology and Behavioural Neurology*, **13**(4), 246–253.

Burton R (1621). *The anatomy of melancholy*. New York, Vintage (reprinted 1977).

Butzlaff RL & Hooley JM (1998). Expressed emotion and psychiatric relapse. *Archives of General Psychiatry*, **55**, 547–552.

Byrne S, Trower P, Birchwood M, Meaden A & Nelson A (2003). Command hallucinations: cognitive theory, therapy and research. *Journal of Cognitive Psychotherapy: An International Quarterly*, **17**(1), 67–84.

Cannon M, Jones P, Gilvarry C, Rifkin L, McKenzie K, Foerster A et al. (1997). Premorbid social functioning in schizophrenia and bipolar disorder: similarities and differences. *American Journal of Psychiatry*, **154**, 1544–1550.

Cannon TD, van Erp TGM, Rosso IM, Huttunen M, Lonnqvist J, Pirkola T et al. (2002). Fetal hypoxia and structural brain abnormalities in schizophrenic patients, their siblings and controls. *Archives of General Psychiatry*, **59**, 35–41.

Carlson EA (1998). A prospective longitudinal study of disorganised/disoriented attachment. *Child Development*, **69**, 1107–1128.

Carlson EB & Putnam FW (1993). An update on the dissociative experiences scale. *Dissociation*, **6**, 16–27.

Carlson, GA (2000). The challenge of diagnosing depression in childhood and adolescence. *Journal of Affective Disorders*, **61**, S3–S8.

Carlson GA, Evelyn MD, Bromet EJ & Sievers S (2000). Phenomenology and outcome of subjects with early- and adult-onset psychotic mania. *American Journal of Psychiatry*, **157**, 213–219.

Carlson V, Cicchetti D, Barnett D & Braunwald K (1989). Disorganized/disoriented attachment relationships in maltreated infants. *Developmental Psychology*, **25**, 525–531.

Carpenter WT & Tamminga CA (1995). Why neuroleptic withdrawal in schizophrenia? *Archives of General Psychiatry*, **52**, 192–193.

Castanzo P, Miller-Johnsen S & Wench H (1995). Social development. In JS Mach (ed.) *Anxiety disorders in children and adolescents*. New York, Guilford Press.

Castine MR, Meador-Woodruff JH & Dalack GW (1998). The role of life events in onset and recurrent episodes of schizophrenia and schizoaffective disorder. *Journal of Psychiatric Research*, **32**(5), 283–288.

Chadwick P, Williams C & Mackenzie J (2003). Impact of case formulation in cognitive behaviour therapy for psychosis. *Behaviour Research and Therapy*, **41**(6), 671–680.

Champion L (1995). A developmental perspective on social support networks. In T Brugha (ed.) *Social support and psychiatric disorder*. Cambridge, Cambridge University Press.

Champion LA, Goodall G & Rutter M (1995). Behaviour problems in childhood and stressors in early adult life, I: a 20-year follow-up of London school children. *Psychological Medicine*, **25**(2), 231–246.

Chang KD, Blasey CM, Ketter TA & Steiner H (2002). Temperament characteristics of child and adolescent bipolar offspring. *Journal of Affective Disorders*, **77**(1), 11–19.

Chapman J (1966). The early symptoms of schizophrenia. *British Journal of Psychiatry*, **112**, 225–251.

Chapman J (1967). Visual imagery and motor phenomena in acute schizophrenia. *British Journal of Psychiatry*, **113**, 771–778.

Chapman J & McGhie A (1963). An approach to the psychotherapy of cognitive dysfunction in schizophrenia. *British Journal of Medical Psychology*, **36**, 253–255.

Christensen EM, Gjerris A, Larsen JK, Larsen BH, Rolff H, Ring G et al. (2003). Life events and onset of a new phase in bipolar affective disorder. *Bipolar Disorders*, **5**, 356–361.

Chu JA & Dill DL (1990). Dissociative symptoms in relation to childhood physical and sexual abuse. *American Journal of Psychiatry*, **147**, 887–892.

Churchill R, Hunot V, Corney R, Knapp M, McGuire H, Tylee A et al. (2001). A systematic review of controlled trials of the effectiveness of brief psychological treatments for depression. *Health Technology Assessment*, **5**, 35.

Cicchetti D & Carlson V (1989). *Child maltreatment: theory and research on the causes and consequences of child abuse and neglect*. Cambridge, Cambridge University Press.

Clare L & Singh K (1994). Preventing relapse in psychotic illness: a psychological approach to early intervention. *Journal of Mental Health*, **3**, 541–50.

Claridge G (ed.) (1997). *Schizotypy: implications for illness and health*. Oxford, Oxford University Press.

Clark R (1994). Family costs associated with severe mental illness and substance use. *Hospital and Community Psychiatry*, **45**, 808–813.

Clarkin JF, Carpenter D, Hull J, Wilner P & Glick I (1998). Effects of psychoeducational intervention for married patients with bipolar disorder and their spouses. *Psychiatric Services*, **49**(4), 531–533.

Clayton PJ (1986). Commentary: psychosocial factors in manic-depressive disease. *Integrative Psychiatry*, **4**, 265.

Clement S, Singh SP & Burns T (2003). Status of bipolar disorder research. *British Journal of Psychiatry*, **182**, 148–152.

Close H & Garety P (1998). Cognitive assessment of voices: further developments in understanding the emotional impact of voices. *British Journal of Clinical Psychology*, **37**, 173–188.

Cochran SD (1984). Preventing medical noncompliance in the outpatient treatment of bipolar affective disorders. *Journal of Consulting and Clinical Psychology*, **52**, 873–878.

Cohen AS & Docherty NM (2003). Affective reactivity of speech and emotional experience in patients with schizophrenia. *Schizophrenia Research*, **69**(1), 7–14.

Cohen CI & Kochanowicz N (1989). Schizophrenia and social network patterns: a survey of black inner-city outpatients. *Community Mental Health Journal*, **25**(3), 197–207.

Cohen S & Willis T (1985). Stress and social support and the buffering hypothesis. *Psychological Bulletin*, **98**, 310–357.

Cole DA & Rehm LP (1986). Family interaction patterns and childhood depression. *Journal of Abnormal Child Psychology*, **14**(2), 297–314.

Cole PM & Putnam FW (1992). Effect of incest on self and social functioning: a developmental psychopathology perspective. *Journal of Consulting and Clinical Psychology*, **60**, 174–184.

Colom F, Vieta E, Martinez-Aran A, Reinares M, Goikolea JM, Benabarre A et al. (2003). A randomized trial on the efficacy of group psychoeducation in the prophylaxis of recurrences in bipolar patients whose disease is in remission. *Archives of General Psychiatry*, **60**, 402–407.

Cook RG, Robb JC, Young LT & Joffe RT (1996). Well-being and functioning in patients with bipolar disorder assessed using the MOS 20-ITEM short form (SF-20). *Journal of Affective Disorders*, **39**, 93–97.

Cook WL, Strachan AM, Goldstein MJ & Miklowitz DJ (1989). Expressed emotion and reciprocal affective relationships in families of disturbed adolescents. *Family Process*, **28**(3), 337–348.

Cooke RG, Young LT, Mohri L, Blake P & Joffe RT (1999). Family-of-origin characteristics in bipolar disorder: a controlled study. *Canadian Journal of Psychiatry*, **44**, 379–381.

Copolov D, Trauer T & Mackinnon A (2003). On the non-significance of internal versus external auditory hallucinations. *Schizophrenia Research*, **69**(1), 1–6.

Corcoran R, Cahill C & Frith CD (1997). The appreciation of visual jokes in people with schizophrenia: a study of 'mentalising' ability. *Schizophrenia Research*, **24**, 319–327.

Corcoran R, Mercer G & Frith CD (1995). Schizophrenia, symptomatology and social inference: investigating 'theory of mind' in people with schizophrenia. *Schizophrenia Research*, **77**, 5–13.

Cornblatt BA & Keilp JG (1994). Impaired attention, genetics and the pathophysiology of schizophrenia. *Schizophrenia Bulletin*, **20**(1), 31–46.

Costa PT & McCrae RR (1992). *NEO-PI-R professional manual*. PAR Inc.

Craig T, Hwang MY & Bromet EJ (2003). Obsessive-compulsive and panic symptoms in patients with first-admission psychosis. *American Journal of Psychiatry*, **159**, 592–598.

Cranach MV (1981). Psychiatrische Versorgung durch niedergelassene Ärzte und ambulante Dienste. In M Bauer & HK Rose (eds), *Ambulante Dienste für psychische Kranke*. Cologne, Rheinland-Verlag, pp. 31–41.

Craney JL & Geller B (2003). A prepubertal and early adolescent bipolar disorder-I phenotype: review of phenomenology and longitudinal course. *Bipolar Disorders*, **5**, 243–256.

Creer C & Wing JK (1974). *Schizophrenia at home*. London, National Schizophrenia Fellowship.

Crow TJ et al. (1986). The Northwick Park study of first episode schizophrenia, II: a randomized controlled trial of prophylactic neuroleptic treatment. *British Journal of Psychiatry*, **148**, 120–127.

Curran C, Byrappa N & McBride A (2004). Stimulant psychosis: systematic review. *British Journal of Psychiatry*, **185**, 196–204.

Cutting J (1985). *The psychology of schizophrenia*. Edinburgh, Churchill Livingstone.

Cutting LP & Docherty NM (2000). Schizophrenia outpatients' perceptions of their parents: is expressed emotion a factor? *Journal of Abnormal Psychology*, **109**(2), 266–272.

Daniels BA, Kirkby KC, Mitchell P, Hay D & Bowling A (2003). Heterogeneity of admission history among patients with bipolar disorder. *Journal of Affective Disorders*, **75**, 163–170.

Daniels L (1998). A group cognitive-behavioral and process-oriented approach to treating the social impairment and negative symptoms associated with chronic mental illness. *Journal of Psychotherapy Practice and Research*, **7**(2), 167–176.

Davenport YB, Adland ML, Gold PW & Goodwin FK (1979). Manic-depressive illness: psychodynamic features of multigenerational families. *American Journal of Orthopsychiatry*, **49**(1), 24–35.

Davidson K (2000). *Cognitive therapy for personality disorders*. Oxford, Butterworth-Heinemann.

de Jong PJ, Haenen M-A, Schmidt A & Mayer B (1998). Hypochondriasis: the role of fear-confirming reasoning. *Behaviour Research and Therapy*, **36**, 65–74.

de Jong PJ, Weertman A, Horselenberg R, van den Hout MA (1997). Deductive reasoning and pathological anxiety: evidence for a relatively strong 'belief bias' in phobic subjects. *Cognitive Therapy and Research*, **21**, 647–662.

de Novaes Soares C & Almeida OP (2001). *Depression during the perimenopause.* (reprinted) *Archives of General Psychiatry*, **58**, 306, Mar.

Dixon T, Kravariti E, Frith C, Murray RM & McGuire PK (2004). Effect of symptoms on executive function in bipolar illness. *Psychological Medicine*, **34**, 811–821.

Docherty JP, Van Kammen DP, Siris SG & Marder SR (1978). Stages of onset of schizophrenic psychosis. *American Journal of Psychiatry*, **135**, 420–426.

Donaldson C & Lam D (2004). Rumination, mood and social problem-solving in major depression. *Psychological Medicine*, **34**, 1309–1318.

Donlan PT & Blacker KH (1975). Clinical recognition of early schizophrenic decompensation. *Disorders of the Nervous System*, **36**(6), 323–327.

Dooley L (1921). A psychoanalytic study of manic depressive psychoses. *Psychoanalytic Review*, **8**, 38–72.

Doughty CJ, Wells JE, Joyce PR, Olds RJ & Walsh AES (2004). Bipolar-panic disorder comorbidity within bipolar disorder families: a study of siblings. *Bipolar Disorders*, **6**, 245–252.

Douglas JD, Cooper J, Amos T, Webb R, Guthrie E & Appleby L (2004). 'Near-fatal' deliberate self-harm: characteristics, prevention and implications for the prevention of suicide. *Journal of Affective Disorders*, **79**, 263–268.

Dozier M (1990). Attachment organization and the treatment use for adults with serious psychopathological disorders. *Development and Psychopathology*, **2**(1), 47–60.

Dozier M, Cue K & Barnett L (1994). Clinicians as caregivers: role of attachment organization in treatment. *Journal of Consulting and Clinical Psychology*, **62**(4), 793–800.

Dozier M, Cue K & Barnett L (2002). Impact of case formulation in cognitive behaviour therapy for psychosis. *Behaviour Research and Therapy*, **41**, 671–680.

Dozier M & Kobak RR (1992). Psychophysiology in attachment interviews: converging evidence for deactivating strategies. *Child Development*, **63**(6), 1473–1480.

Dozier M & Lee SW (1995). Discrepancies between self and other report of psychiatric symptomatology: effects of dismissing attachment strategies. *Development and Psychopathology*, **7**(1), 217–226.

Dozier M & Lomax L (1994). Clinicians as caregivers: role of attachment organization in treatment. *Journal of Consulting and Clinical Psychology*, **62**, 793–800.

Dozier M, Lomax L, Lee CL & Spring W (2001). The challenge of treatment for clients with dismissing states of mind. *Attachment and Human Development*, **3**(1), 62–76.

Dozier M, Stovall KC & Albus KE (1999). Attachment and psychopathology in adulthood. In PR Shaver & J Cassidy (eds), *Handbook of attachment: theory, research, and clinical applications*. New York, Guilford Press, pp. 497–519.

Dozier M & Tyrrell C (1997). Attachment and communication among persons with serious psychopathological disorders. In JA Simpson & WS Rholes (eds), *Attachment theory and close relationships*. New York, Guilford Press.

Draijer N & Langeland MA (1999). Childhood trauma and percieve parental dysfunction in the etiology of dissociative symptoms in psychiatric inpatients. *American Journal of Psychiatry*, **156**, 379–385.

Drake R, Haley C & Akhtar S (2000). Causes and consequences of duration of untreated psychosis in schizophrenia. *British Journal of Psychiatry*, **177**, 511–515.

Drayton M, Birchwood M & Trower P (1998). Early attachment experience and recovery from psychosis. *British Journal of Clinical Psychology*, **37**, 269–284.

Drury V, Birchwood M & Cochrane R (2000). Cognitive therapy and recovery from acute psychosis: a controlled trial, 3: five-year follow-up. *British Journal of Psychiatry*, **177**, 8–14.

Drury V, Birchwood M, Cochrane R & Macmillan F (1996). Cognitive therapy and recovery from acute psychosis, a controlled trial, II: impact on recovery time. *British Journal of Psychiatry*, **169**(5), 602–607.

Dudley REJ & John CH (1997). The effect of self-referent material on the reasoning of people with delusions. *British Journal of Clinical Psychology*, **36**, 575–584.

Dudley REJ & Over DE (2003). People with delusions jump to conclusions: a theoretical account of research findings on the reasoning of people with delusions. *Clinical Psychology and Psychotherapy*, **10**(5), 263–274.

Dunner DL & Hall KS (1980). Social adjustment and psychological precipitants in mania. In RH Belmaker & HM van Praag (eds), *Mania: an evolving concept*. New York, Spectrum Publications.

Dunner DL, Patrick V & Fieve RR (1979). Life events at the onset of bipolar affective illness. *American Journal of Psychiatry*, **136**(4B), 508–511.

Dupuy J-B, Beaudoin S, Rheaume J, Ladouceur R & Dugas MJ (2001). Worry: daily self-report in clinical and non-clinical populations. *Behaviour Research and Therapy*, **39**, 1249–1255.

Durham RC, Guthrie M, Morton RV, Reid DA, Treliving LR, Fowler D et al. (2003). Tayside-Fife clinical trial of cognitive-behavioural therapy for medication-resistant psychotic symptoms. *British Journal of Psychiatry*, **182**, 303–311.

Edwards J, Maude D, McGorry PD, Harrigan SM & Cocks JT (1998). Prolonged recovery in first-episode psychosis. *British Journal of Psychiatry*, **172**(33), 107–116.

Ehlers A & Clark DM (2000). A cognitive model of posttraumatic stress disorder. *Behaviour Research and Therapy*, **38**, 319–345.

Eich E, Macaulay D & Lam RW (1997). Mania, depression and mood dependent memory. *Cognition and Emotion*, **11**, 607–618.

Eichenbaum H (1997). Declarative memory: insights from cognitive neurobiology. *Annual Review of Psychology*, **48**, 547–572.

Fagiolini A, Frank E, Cherry CR, Houck PR, Novick DM, Buysse DJ et al. (2002). Clinical indicators for the use of antidepressants in the treatment of bipolar 1 depression. *Bipolar Disorders*, **4**, 277–282.

Falloon IR, Boyd JL, McGill CW, Razani J, Moss HB & Gilderman AM (1982). Family management in the prevention of exacerbations of schizophrenia: a controlled study. *New England Journal of Medicine*, **306**(24), 1437–1440.

Falloon IR, Boyd JL, McGill CW, Williamson M, Razani J, Moss HB et al. (1985). Family management in the prevention of morbidity of schizophrenia: clinical outcome of a two-year longitudinal study. *Archives of General Psychiatry*, **42**(9), 887–896.

Farmer AE & McGuffin P (2003). Humiliation, loss and other types of life events and difficulties: a comparison of depressed subjects, healthy controls and their siblings. *Psychological Medicine*, **33**, 1169–1175.

Favazza AR & Rosenthal RJ (1993). Diagnostic issues in self-mutilation. *Hospital and Community Psychiatry*, **44**(2), 134–140.

Fear C, Sharp H & Healy D (1996). Cognitive processes in delusional disorders. *British Journal of Psychiatry*, **168**, 61–67.

Feeney JA, Noller P & Hanrahan M (1994). Assessing adult attachment. In MB Sperling & WH Berman (eds), *Attachment in adults: clinical and developmental perspectives*. New York, Guilford Press, pp. 122–158.

Fenigstein A & Vanable PA (1984). Self-consciousness and over-perception of self as target. *Journal of Personality and Social Psychology*, **47**, 860–870.

Fenigstein A & Vanable PA (1992). Paranoia and self-consciousness. *Journal of Personality and Social Psychology*, **62**, 129–134.

First MB, Spitzer RL, Gibbon M & Williams JBW (1997). *Structured clinical interview for DSM-IV Axis I disorders (SCID I) – Clinical Version*. Washington, DC, American Psychiatric Press.

Fombonne E, Wostear G, Cooper V, Harrington R & Rutter M (2001a). The Maudsley long-term follow-up of child and adolescent depression, 1: psychiatric outcomes in adulthood. *British Journal of Psychiatry*, **179**, 210–217.

Fombonne E, Wostear G, Cooper V, Harrington R & Rutter M (2001b). The Maudsley long-term follow-up of child and adolescent depression, 2: Suicidality, criminality, and social dysfunction in adulthood. *British Journal of Psychiatry*, **179**, 218–223.

Fonagy P (1998). Moments of change in psychoanalytic theory: discussion of a new theory of psychic change. *Infant Mental Health Journal*, **19**, 163–171.

Fonagy P, Gergely G, Jurist E & Target M (2002). *Affect regulation, mentalization, and the development of the self*. London, Karnac.

Fonagy P, Leigh T, Steele M, Steele H, Kennedy R, Mattoon G et al. (1996). The relation of attachment status, psychiatric classification, and response to psychotherapy. *Journal of Consulting and Clinical Psychology*, **64**, 22–31.

Fonagy P, Steele M, Steele H, Leigh T, Kennedy R, Mattoon G et al. (1995). Attachment, the reflective self, and borderline states. In S Goldberg, R Muir & J Kerr (eds), *Attachment theory: social, developmental and clinical perspectives*. Hillsdale, NJ, Analytic Press, pp. 233–278.

Fonagy P & Target M (1997). Attachment and reflective function: their role in self-organization. *Development and Psychopathology*, **9**, 679–690.

Fonagy P, Target M, Cottrell D, Phillips J & Kurtz Z (2002). *What works for whom? A critical review of treatments for children and adolescents*. New York, Guilford Press.

Fonagy P, Target M, Gergely G, Allen JG & Bateman A (2004). The developmental roots of borderline personality disorder: reflective functioning and attachment. *PTT: Personlichkeitsstörungen Theorie und Therapie*, 8(4), 217–229.

Forrester A, Owens DGC & Johnstone EC (2001). Diagnostic stability in subjects with multiple admissions for psychotic illness. *Psychological Medicine*, **31**, 151–158.

Fowler D, Garety P & Kuipers E (1995). *Cognitive behaviour therapy for psychosis*. Chichester, John Wiley & Sons.

Fraley RC & Shaver PR (1999). Loss and bereavement: attachment theory and recent controversies concerning 'grief work' and the nature of detachment. In J Cassidy & P Shaver (eds), *Handbook of attachment, theory, research and applications*. New York, Guilford Press, pp. 735–759.

Frame L & Morrison AP (2001). Causes of posttraumatic stress disorder in psychotic patients. *Archives of General Psychiatry*, **58**, 305–306.

Frankle WG, Perlis RH, Deckersbach T, Grandin LD, Gray SM, Sachs GS et al. (2002). Bipolar depression: relationship between episode length and antidepressant treatment. *Psychological Medicine*, **32**, 1417–1423.

Franko DL, Streigel-Moore RH, Brown KM, Barton BA, McMahon RP, Screiber GB et al. (2004). Expanding our understanding of the relationship between negative life events and depressive symptoms in black and white adolescent girls. *Psychological Medicine*, **34**, 1319–1330.

Free ML, Tian PS & Sanders MR (1991). Treatment outcome of a group cognitive therapy program for depression. *International Journal of Group Psychotherapy*, **41**(4), 533–547.

Freedman BJ (1974). The subjective experience of perceptual and cognitive disturbances in schizophrenia. *Archives of General Psychiatry*, **30**, 333–340.

Freedman BJ & Chapman LJ (1973). Early subjective experience in schizophrenic episode. *Journal of Abnormal Psychology*, **82**, 46–54.

Freeman A & Leaf RC (1989). Cognitive therapy applied to personality disorders. In A Freeman, KM Simon, LE Bleutler & H Arkowitz (eds), *Comprehensive handbook of cognitive therapy*. New York, Plenum, pp. 403–433.

Freeman D, Garety PA & Kuipers E (2001). Persecutory delusions: developing the understanding of belief maintenance and emotional distress. *Psychological Medicine*, **31**, 1293–1306.

Freeman D, Garety PA & Phillips ML (2000). The examination of hypervigilance for external threat in individuals with generalized anxiety disorder and individuals with persecutory delusions using visual scan paths. *Quarterly Journal of Experimental Psychology: Human Experimental Psychology*, **53A**(2), 549–567.

Freud S (1917). *Lectures: introduction to psychoanalysis*. Frankfurt, Fischer.

Friedlander RI & Donnelly T (2004). Early-onset psychosis in youth with intellectual disability. *Journal of Intellectual Disability Research*, **48**, 540–547.

Friedman S, Smith L, Fogel D, Paradis C, Viswanathan R, Ackerman R et al. (2002). The incidence and influence of early traumatic life events in patients with panic disorder: a comparison with other psychiatric outpatients. *Anxiety Disorders*, **16**, 259–272.

Frith CD (1992). *The cognitive neuropsychology of schizophrenia*. Hove, Erlbaum.

Frith CD & Corcoran R (1996). Exploring 'theory of mind' in people with schizophrenia. *Psychological Medicine*, **26**, 521–530.

Fujiwara Y, Honda T, Tanaka Y, Aoki S & Kuroda S (1998). Comparison of early- and late-onset rapid cycling affective disorders: clinical course and response to pharmacotherapy. *Journal of Clinical Psychopharmacology*, **18**, 282–288.

Gabbard GO, Lazar SG, Hornberger J & Spiegel D (1997). The economic impact of psychotherapy: a review. *American Journal of Psychiatry*, **154**(2), 147–155.

Gaebel W, Frick U, Kopcke W, Linden M et al. (1993). Early neuroleptic intervention in schizophrenia: are prodromal symptoms valid predictors of relapse? *British Journal of Psychiatry*, **163**(suppl. 21), 8–12.

Gaebel W & Frommann N (2000). Long-term course in schizophrenia: concept methods and research strategies. *Acta Psychiatrica Scandinavica*, **102**(suppl. 407), 49–53.

Gaebel W, Janner M, Frommann N, Pietzcker A, Kopcke W, Linden M et al. (2002). First vs multiple episode schizophrenia: two-year outcome of intermittent and maintenance medication strategies. *Schizophrenia Research*, **53**, 145–159.

Garber J, Weiss B & Shaney N (1993). Cognitions, depressive symptoms and development in adolescents. *Journal of Abnormal Psychology*, **102**(1), 47–57.

Garety PA, Dunn G, Fowler D & Kuipers E (1998). The evaluation of cognitive behavioural therapy for psychosis. In N Tarrier, T Wykes et al. (eds), *Outcome and innovation in psychological treatment of schizophrenia*. New York, John Wiley & Sons, pp. 101–118.

Garety PA & Freeman D (1999). Cognitive approaches to delusions: a critical review of theories and evidence. *British Journal of Clinical Psychology*, **38**, 113–154.

Garety PA, Kuipers E, Fowler D, Chisholm D, Freeman D, Dunn G et al. (1998). London-East Anglia randomised controlled trial of cognitive-behavioural therapy for psychosis, III: follow-up and economic evaluation at 18 months. *British Journal of Psychiatry*, **173**, 61–68.

Geller B, Bolhofner K, Craney JL, Williams M & DelBello MP (2000). Psychosocial functioning in a prepubertal and early adolescent bipolar disorder phenotype. *Journal of American Academy of Child and Adolescent Psychiatry*, **39**(12), 1543–1548.

Georgaca E (2000). Reality and discourse: a critical analysis of the category of 'delusions'. *British Journal of Medical Psychology*, **73**, 227–242.

George C, Kaplan N & Main M (1985). The adult attachment interview. Unpublished manuscript, University of California at Berkeley.

George C & Main M (1979). Social interactions of young abused children: approach, avoidance, and aggression. *Child Development*, **50**, 306–318.

George EL, Miklowitz DJ, Richards JA, Simoneau TL & Taylor DO (2003). The comorbidity of bipolar disorder and axis II personality disorders: prevalence and clinical correlates. *Bipolar Disorders*, **5**, 115–122.

Ghaemi SN, Hebben N, Stoll AL & Pope HG (1996). Neuropsychological aspects of lack of insight in bipolar disorder: a preliminary report. *Psychiatry Research*, **65**, 113–120.

Gibson RW (1963). Psychotherapy of manic-depressive states. *Psychiatric Research Reports*, **17**, 91–102.

Gibson RW, Cohen MB & Cohen RA (1959). On the dynamics of the manic-depressive personality. *American Journal of Psychiatry*, **115**, 1101–1107.

Gilbert P (1989). *Human nature and suffering*. Hove, Erlbaum.

Gilbert P (1992). *Depression: the evolution of powerlessness.* Hove, Erlbaum.

Gilbert P (2000). Social mentalities: internal 'social' conflicts and the role of inner warmth and compassion in cognitive therapy. In P Gilbert & KG Bailey (eds), *Genes on the couch: explorations in evolutionary psychotherapy.* Hove, Psychology Press, pp. 118–150.

Gilbert P (2001). Evolutionary approaches to psychopathology: the role of natural defences. *Australia and New Zealand Journal of Psychiatry,* **35,** 17–27.

Gilbert P (ed.) (2005). *Compassion: conceptualizations, research, and use in psychotherapy.* London, Brunner-Routledge.

Gilbert P, Birchwood M, Gilbert J, Trower P, Hay J, Murray B et al. (2001). An exploration of evolved mental mechanisms for dominant and subordinate behaviour in relation to auditory hallucinations in schizophrenia and critical thoughts in depression. *Psychological Medicine,* **31,** 1117–1127.

Gilbert P, Boxall M, Cheung M & Irons C (2005). The relation of paranoid ideation and social anxiety in a mixed clinical population. *Clinical Psychology and Psychotherapy,* **12,** 124–133.

Gilbert PL, Harris MJ, McAdams LA & Jeste DV (1995). Neuroleptic withdrawal in schizophrenic patients: a review of the literature. *Archives of General Psychiatry,* **52,** 173–188.

Gilbert P & Irons C (2005). Focused therapies and compassionate mind training for shame and self-attacking. In P Gilbert (ed.), *Compassion, conceptualiations, research and use in psychotherapy.* London and New York, Routledge, pp. 263–325.

Gitlin MJ, Neuchterlein K, Subotnik KL, Ventura J, Mintz J, Fogelson DL et al. (2001). Clinical outcome following neuroleptic discontinuation in patients with remitted recent-onset schizophrenia. *American Journal of Psychiatry,* **158,** 1835–1842.

Gitlin MJ, Swendsen J, Heller TL & Hammen C (1995). Relapse and impairment in bipolar disorder. *American Journal of Psychiatry,* **152,** 1635–1640.

Gleeson JF, Rawlings D, Jackson HJ & McGorry PD (2005). Agreeableness and neuroticism as predictors of relapse after first-episode psychosis: a prospective follow-up study. *Journal of Nervous and Mental Disease,* **193**(3), 160–169.

Goldberg DP & Williams P (1988). *A user's guide to the general health questionnaire.* Windsor, NFER Nelson.

Goldberg TE (1999). Some fairly obvious distinctions between schizophrenia and bipolar disorder. *Schizophrenia Research,* **39,** 127–132.

Goldberg TE, Dodge M, Aloia M, Egan MF & Weinberger DR (2000). Effects of neuroleptic medications on speech disorganization in schizophrenia: biasing associative networks towards meaning. *Psychological Medicine,* **30,** 1123–1130.

Goldstein MJ, Rodnick EH, Evans JR, May PR & Steinberg MR (1978). Drug and family therapy in the aftercare of acute schizophrenics. *Archives of General Psychiatry,* **35**(10), 1169–1177.

Goodwin I, Holmes G, Cochrane R & Mason O (2003). The ability of adult mental health services to meet clients' attachment needs: the development and implementation of the service attachment questionnaire. *Psychology and Psychotherapy: Theory, Research and Practice,* **76,** 145–161.

Gotlib IH & Avison WR (1993). Children at risk for psychopathology. In GG Costello (ed.), *Basic issues in psychopathology.* London, Guilford Press.

Gould RA, Mueser KT, Bolton E, Mays V & Goff D (2002). Cognitive therapy for psychosis in schizophrenia: an effect size analysis. *Schizophrenia Research,* **48,** 335–342.

Gourovitch ML, Torrey EF, Gold JM, Randolph C, Weinberger DR & Goldberg TE (1999). Neuropsychological performance of monzygotic twins discordant for bipolar disorder. *Biological Psychiatry*, **45**, 639–646.

Granville-Grossman KL (1966). Early bereavement and schizophrenia. *British Journal of Psychiatry*, **112**, 1027–1034.

Graves JS (1993). Living with mania: a study of outpatient group psychotherapy for bipolar patients. *American Journal of Psychotherapy*, **47**, 113–126.

Green MJ & Phillips ML (2004). Social threat perception and the evolution of paranoia. *Neuroscience and Biobehavioural Reviews*, **28**(3), 333–342.

Greenberg LS & Pascual-Leone J (1997). Emotion in the creation of personal meaning. In M Power & CR Brewin (eds), *The transformation of meaning in psychological therapies*. Chichester, John Wiley & Sons.

Greenberg LS, Rice LN & Elliott R (1996). *Facilitating emotional change*. New York, Guilford Press.

Greenhouse WJ, Meyer B & Johnson SL (2000). Coping and medication adherence in bipolar disorder. *Journal of Affective Disorders*, **59**, 237–241.

Grof P, Robbins W, Alda M, Berghoefer A, Vojtechovsky M, Nilsson A et al. (2000). Protective effect of pregnancy in women with lithium-responsive bipolar disorder. *Journal of Affective Disorders*, **61**, 31–39.

Grubb D (1995). Three bipolar women: the boundary between bipolar disorders and disorders of the self. In JF Masterton & R Klein (eds), *Disorders of the self*. New York, Brunner/Mazel.

Grunebaum MF, Galfalvy HC, Oquendo MA, Burke AK & Mann JJ (2004). Melancholia and the probability and lethality of suicide attempts. *British Journal of Psychiatry*, **184**, 534–535.

Gumley A, O'Grady M, McNay L, Reilly J, Power K & Norrie J (2003). Early intervention for relapse in schizophrenia: results of a 12-month randomized controlled trial of cognitive behavioural therapy. *Psychological Medicine*, **33**, 419–431.

Gumley A, O'Grady M, Power K & Schwannauer M (2004). Negative beliefs about self and illness: a comparison of individuals with or without comorbid social anxiety disorder. *Australian and New Zealand Journal of Psychiatry*, **38**, 960–964.

Gumley A, White CA & Power K (1999). An interacting cognitive subsystems model of relapse and the course of psychosis. *Clinical Psychology and Psychotherapy*, **6**, 261–279.

Gupta RD & Guest JF (2002). Annual cost of bipolar disorder to UK society. *British Journal of Psychiatry*, **180**, 227–233.

Haarasilta L, Marttunen M, Kaprio J & Aro H (2001). The 12-month prevalence and characteristics of major depressive disorder in a representative nationwide sample of adolescents and young adults. *Psychological Medicine*, **31**, 1169–1179.

Haas GL, Glick ID, Clarkin JF, Spencer JH, Lewis AB, Peyser J et al. (1988). Inpatient family intervention: a randomized clinical trial. *Archives of General Psychiatry*, **45**, 217–224.

Hackmann A (1998). Working with images in clinical psychology. In A Bellack & M Hersen (eds), *Comprehensive clinical psychology*. London, Pergamon, pp. 301–317.

Haddock G, Barrowclough C, Tarrier N, Moring J, O'Brien R, Schofield N et al. (2003). Cognitive-behavioural therapy and motivational intervention for schizophrenia and subtance misuse. *British Journal of Psychiatry*, **183**, 418–426.

Haddock G, McCarron J, Tarrier N & Faragher EB (1999). Scales to measure dimensions of hallucinations and delusions: the psychotic symptom rating scales (PSYRATS). *Psychological Medicine*, **29**, 879–889.

Haddock G, Slade PD, Bentall RP, Reid D & Faragher EB (1998). A comparison of the long-term effectiveness of distraction and focusing in the treatment of auditory hallucinations. *British Journal of Medical Psychology*, **71**, 339–349.

Haddock G, Tarrier N, Morrison AP, Hopkins R, Drake R & Lewis S (1999). A pilot study evaluating the effectiveness of individual inpatient cognitive-behavioural therapy in early psychosis. *Social Psychiatry and Psychiatric Epidemiology*, **34**(5), 254–258.

Hallensleben A (1994). Group psychotherapy with manic-depressive patients on lithium: 10 years' experience. *Group Analysis*, **27**, 475–482.

Halperin S, Nathan P, Drummond P & Castle D (2000). A cognitive-behavioural, group-based intervention for social anxiety in schizophrenia. *Australian and New Zealand Journal of Psychiatry*, **34**, 809–813.

Hamera EK, Peterson KA, Young LM & Schaumloffel MM (1992). Symptom monitoring in schizophrenia: potential for enhancing self-care. *Archives of Psychiatric Nursing*, **6**(6), 324–330, Dec.

Hammen C (1988). Self-cognitions, stressful events and the prediction of depression in children of depressed mothers. *Journal of Abnormal Psychology*, **16**(3), 347–360.

Hammen C (1992). Cognitive, life stress, and interpersonal approaches to a developmental psychopathology model of depression. *Development and Psychopathology*, **4**, 189–206.

Hammen C, Gordon D, Burge D, Adrian C, Jaenicke C & Hiroto D (1987). Maternal affective disorders, illness and stress: risk for children's psychopathology. *American Journal of Psychiatry*, **144**, 736–741.

Hammersley P, Dias A, Todd G, Bowen-Jones K, Reilly B & Bentall RP (2003). Childhood trauma and hallucinations in bipolar affective disorder: preliminary investigation. *British Journal of Psychiatry*, **182**, 543–547.

Han-Joo L, Jesse R, Cougle M & Telch J (2005). Thought-action fusion and its relationship to schizotypy and OCD symptoms. *Behaviour Research and Therapy*, **43**, 29–41.

Harrington R, Campbell F, Shoebridge P & Whittaker J (1998). Meta-analysis of CBT for depression in adolescents. *Journal of the American Academy of Child and Adolescent Psychiatry*, **37**(10), 1005–1100.

Harrington R, Whittaker J, Shoebridge P & Campbell F (1998). Systemic review of efficacy of cognitive behaviour therapies in childhood and adolescent depressive disorder. *British Journal of Medicine*, **316**(7144), 1559–1563.

Harris TO (2003). Depression in women and its sequelae. *Journal of Psychosomatic Research*, **54**, 103–112.

Harris TO (2004). Chef or chemist? Practicing psychotherapy within the attachment paradigm. *Attachment and Human Development*, **6**(2), 191–207.

Harris TO, Brown GW & Bifulco A (1987). Loss of parent in childhood and adult psychiatric disorder: the role of social class position and premarital pregnancy. *Psychological Medicine*, **17**, 163–183.

Harris TO, Brown GW & Robinson P (1999). Befriending as an intervention for chronic depression among women in an inner city, 2: role of a fresh-start experiences and baseline psychosocial factors in remission from depression. *British Journal of Psychiatry*, **174**(3), 225–232.

Harrison CL & Fowler D (2004). Negative symptoms, trauma and autobiographical memory: an investigation of individuals recovering from psychosis. *Journal of Nervous and Mental Disease*, **192**(11), 745–753.

Harrop C & Trower P (2001). Why does schizophrenia develop at late adolescence? *Clinical Psychology Review*, **21**(2), 241–266.

Hartman LM (1983). A meta-cognitive model of social anxiety: implications for treatment. *Clinical Psychology Review*, **3**, 435–456.

Hawton K, Arensman E, Townsend E, Bremner S, Feldman E, Goldney R et al. (1998). Deliberate self harm: systemic review of efficacy of psychosocial and pharmacological treatments in preventing repetition. *British Journal of Medicine*, **317**, 441–447.

Hayes AM & Harris MS (2000). The development of an integrative therapy for depression. In SL Johnson, AM Hayes, TM Field, N Schneiderman & PM McCabe (eds), *Stress, coping and depression*. New Jersey, Erlbaum.

Hayes SC, Strosahal KD & Wilson KG (2002). Acceptance and commitment therapy: an experimental approach to behavior change. *Child and Family Behavior Therapy*, **24**(4), 51–57.

Hazan C & Shaver PR (1987). Romantic love conceptualized as an attachment process. *Journal of Personality and Social Psychology*, **52**, 511–524.

Healey A, Knapp M, Astin J, Beecham J, Kemp R, Kirov G et al. (1998). Cost-effectiveness evaluation of compliance therapy for people with psychosis. *British Journal of Psychiatry*, **172**(5), 420–424.

Healy D & Williams JMG (1989). Follow up of 53 bipolar manic-depressive patients. *Psychiatric Developments*, **1**, 49–70.

Heinrichs DW & Carpenter WT Jr (1985). Prospective study of prodromal symptoms in schizophrenic relapse. *American Journal of Psychiatry*, **142**, 371–373.

Heinrichs DW, Cohen BP & Carpenter WT (1985). Early insight and the management of schizophrenic decompensation. *Journal of Nervous and Mental Disease*, **173**, 133–138.

Heller K (1990). Social and community intervention. *Annual Review of Psychology*, **41**, 141–168.

Hemsley DR (1994). Perceptual and cognitive abnormalities as the bases for schizophrenic symptoms. In AS David & JC Cutting (eds), *The neuropsychology of schizophrenia*. Hove, Erlbaum, pp. 97–116.

Henry C, Bullivier F, Sorbara F, Tangwongchai S, Lacoste J, Faure-Chaigneu M et al. (2001). Bipolar sensation seeking is associated with a propensity to abuse rather than to temperamental characteristics. *European Psychiatry*, **16**, 289–292.

Henry C & Nassir Ghaemi S (2004). Insight in psychosis: a systematic review of treatment interventions. *Psychopathology*, **37**, 194–199.

Herman D, Opler L, Felix A, Valencia E, Wyatt RJ & Susser E (1999). A critical time intervention with mentally ill homeless men: impact on psychiatric symptoms. *Journal of Nervous and Mental Disease*, **188**, 135–140.

Herold R, Tenyi T, Lenard K & Trixler M (2002). Theory of mind deficit in people with schizophrenia during remission. *Psychological Medicine*, **32**, 1125–1129.

Herz MI, Lamberti JS, Mintz J, Scott R, O'Dell SP, McCartan L et al. (2000). A program for relapse prevention in schizophrenia. *Archives of General Psychiatry*, **57**, 277–283.

Herz MI & Melville C (1980). Relapse in schizophrenia. *American Journal of Psychiatry*, **137**(7), 801–805.

Hesse E (1996). Discourse, memory and the adult attachment interview: a note with emphasis on the emerging cannot classify category. *Infant Mental Health Journal*, **17**, 4–11.

Hesse E (1999). The adult attachment interview: historical and current perspectives. In J Cassidy & P Shaver (eds), *Handbook of attachment: theory, research and applications*. New York, Guilford Press, pp. 395–433.

Hesse E & Main M (2000). Disorganized infant, child, and adult attachment: collapse in behavioral and attentional strategies. *Journal of American Psychoanalytical Association*, **48**(4), 1097–1127.

Hillegers MH, Burger H, Wals M, Reichart CG, Verhulst FC, Nolen WA et al. (2004). Impact of stressful life events, familial loading and their interaction on the onset of mood disorders: study in a high-risk cohort of adolescent offspring of parents with bipolar disorder. *British Journal of Psychiatry*, **185**, 97–101.

Hills P & Argyle M (2001). Emotional stability as a major dimension of happiness. *Personality and Individual Differences*, **31**, 1357–1364.

Hirsch S, Bowen J, Emami J, Cramer P, Jolley A, Haw C et al. (1996). A one-year prospective study of the effect of life events and medication in the aetiology of schizophrenic relapse. *British Journal of Psychiatry*, **168**(1), 49–56.

Hirsch SR & Jolley AG (1989). The dysphoric syndrome in schizophrenia and its implications for relapse. *British Journal of Psychiatry*, **155**(suppl. 5), 46–50.

Hlastala SA, Frank E, Mallinger AG, Thase ME, Ritenour AM & Kupfer DJ (1997). Bipolar depression: an underestimated treatment challenge. *Depression and Anxiety*, **5**, 73–83.

Hodgins S, Mednick SA, Brennan PA, Schulsinger F & Engberg M (1996). Mental disorder and crime: evidence from a Danish cohort. *Archives of General Psychiatry*, **53**, 489–496.

Hoencamp E, Haffmans PMJ, Griens AMGF, Huijbrechts IPAM & Heycop ten Ham BF (2001). A 3.5-year naturalistic follow-up study of depressed out-patients. *Journal of Affective Disorders*, **66**, 267–271.

Hofstra MB, van der Ende J & Verhulst FC (2001). Adolescents' self-reported preoblems as predictors of psychopathology in adulthood: 10-year follow-up study. *British Journal of Psychiatry*, **179**, 203–209.

Hofstra MB, van der Ende J & Verhulst FC (2002). Child and adolescent problems predict DSM-IV disorders in adulthood: a 14-year follow-up of a Dutch epidemiological sample. *Journal of the American Academy of Child and Adolescent Psychiatry*, **41**, 182–189.

Hogarty GE, Anderson CM, Reiss DJ, et al. (1991). Family psychoeducation, social skills training and maintenance chemotherapy in the aftercare treatment of schizophrenia, II: two-year effects of a controlled study on relapse and adjustment. *Archives of General Psychiatry*, **48**, 340–341.

Hogarty GE, Greenwald D, Ulrich RF, Kornblith SJ, DiBarry AL, Cooley S et al. (1997b). Three-year trials of personal therapy among schizophrenic patients living with or independent of family, II: effects of adjustment of patients. *American Journal of Psychiatry*, **154**(11), 1514–1524.

Hogarty GE, Kornblith SJ, Greenwald D, DiBarry A-L, Cooley S, Ulrich R-F et al. (1997a). Three-year trials of personal therapy among schizophrenic patients living with or independent of family, I: description of study and effects of relapse rates. *American Journal of Psychiatry*, **154**(11), 1504–1513.

Hogarty GE, McEvoy JP, Munetz M, DiBarry AL, Bartone P, Cather R et al. (1988). Dose of fluphenazine, familial expressed emotion, and outcome in schizophrenia: results of a two-year controlled study. *Archives of General Psychiatry*, **45**, 797–805.

Hollis C (2000). Adult outcome of child and adolescent-onset schizophrenia: diagnostic stability and predictive validity. *American Journal of Psychiatry*, **157**(10), 1652–1659.

Hollis C (2003). Developmental precursors of child and adolescent-onset schizophrenia and affective psychoses: diagnostic specificity and continuity with symptom dimensions. *British Journal of Psychiatry*, **182**, 37–44.

Hollon SD & Garber J (1988). Cognitive therapy. In LY Abrahamson (ed.), *Social cognition and clinical psychology: a synthesis*. New York, Guilford Press, pp. 204–253.

Holmes EA & Steel C (2004). Schizotypy: a vulnerability factor for traumatic intrusions. *Journal of Nervous and Mental Disease*, **192**(1), 28–34.

Holmes J (1993). *John Bowlby and attachment theory*. London, Routledge.

Holmes J (2003). Borderline personality disorder and the search for meaning: an attachment perspective. *Australian and New Zealand Journal of Psychiatry*, **37**(5), 524–531.

Holowka DW, King S, Saheb D, Pukall M & Brunet A (2003). Childhood abuse and dissociative symptoms in adult schizophrenia. *Schizophrenia Research*, **60**, 87–90.

Honer WG, Kopala LC, Locke JJ & Lapointe JS (1996). Left cerebral hemiatrophy and schizophrenia-like psychosis in an adolescent. *Schizophrenia Research*, **20**, 231–234.

Honig A, Hofman A, Rozendaal N & Dingemans P (1997). Psycho-education in bipolar disorder: effect on expressed emotion. *Psychiatry Research*, **72**, 17–22.

Hooley J (1985). Expressed emotion: a review of the critical literature. *Clinical Psychology Review*, **5**, 119–139.

Hooley J (1998). Expressed emotion and locus of control. *Journal of Nervous and Mental Disease*, **186**(6), 374–378.

Hope DA, Rapee RM, Heimberg RG & Dombeck MJ (1990). Representations of the self in social phobia: vulnerability to social threat. *Cognitive Therapy and Research*, **14**, 177–189.

Horowitz LM, Alden LE, Wiggins JS & Pincus AL (2000). IIP: inventory of interpersonal problems. San Antonio, TX, The Psychological Corporation.

Horowitz LM, Rosenberg SE, Baer BA, Ureno G & Villasenor VS (1988). The inventory of interpersonal problems: psychometric properties and clinical applications. *Journal of Consulting and Clinical Psychology*, **56**, 885–895.

Houston K, Hawton K & Sheppard R (2001). Suicide in young people aged 15–24: a psychological autopsy study. *Journal of Affective Disorders*, **63**, 159–170.

Hoyer EH, Olesen AV & Mortensen PB (2004). Suicide risk in patients hospitalised because of an affective disorder: a follow-up study, 1973–1993. *Journal of Affective Disorders*, **78**, 209–217.

Hultman CM, Wieselgren IM & Ohman A (1997). Relationships between social support, social coping and life events in the relapse of schizophrenic patients. *Scandinavian Journal of Psychology*, **38**(1), 3–13.

Huxley NA, Parikh SV & Baldessarini RJ (2000). Effectiveness of psychosocial treatments in bipolar disorder: state of the evidence. *Harvard Review of Psychiatry*, **8**(3), 126–140.

Hyman SE (2000). Goals for research on bipolar disorder: the view from NIMH. *Biological Psychiatry*, **48**, 436–441.

Inderbitzin LB, Lewine RRJ, Scheller-Gilkey G, Swofford CD, Egan GJ, Gloersen BA et al. (1994). A double-blind dose-reduction trial of fluphenazine decanoate for chronic, unstable schizophrenic patients. *American Journal of Psychiatry*, **151**, 1753–1759.

Infrasca R (2002). Childhood adversities and adult depression: an experimental study on childhood depressogenic markers. *Journal of Affective Disorders*, **76**(1–3), 103–111.

Ingram RE & Wisnicki KS (1988). Assessment of positive automatic cognition. *Journal of Consulting and Clinical Psychology*, **56**, 898–902.

Inskip HM, Harris EC & Barraclough B (1998). Lifetime risk of suicide for affective disorder, alcoholism and schizophrenia. *British Journal of Psychiatry*, **172**(1), 35–37.

Iqbal Z, Birchwood M, Chadwick P & Trower P (2000). Cognitive approach to depression and suicidal thinking in psychosis, 2: testing the validity of a social ranking model. *British Journal of Psychiatry*, **177**, 522–528.

Iqbal Z, Birchwood M, Hemsley D, Jackson C & Morris E (2004). Autobiographical memory and post-psychotic depression in first episode psychosis. *British Journal of Clinical Psychology*, **43**, 97–104.

Irons C & Gilbert P (2005). Evolved mechanisms in adolescent anxiety and depression symptoms: the role of the attachment and social rank systems. *Journal of Adolescence*, **28**, 325–341.

Isometsa E, Heikkinen M, Henriksson M, Aro H & Lonnqvist J (1995). Recent life events and completed suicide in bipolar affective disorder: a comparison with major depressive suicides. *Journal of Affective Disorders*, **33**, 99–106.

Jablensky A, Sartorius N, Ernberg G & Anker M (1992). Schizophrenia: manifestations, incidence and course in different cultures: a world health organisation ten country study. *Psychological Medicine*, (suppl. 20), 97.

Jackson C, Knott C, Skeate A & Birchwood M (2004). The trauma of first episode psychosis: the role of cognitive mediation. *Australian and New Zealand Journal of Psychiatry*, **38**, 327–333.

Jamison KR & Goodwin FK (1983). Psychotherapeutic issues in bipolar illness. In FK Goodwin & KR Jamison (eds), *Manic-depressive illness*. New York, Oxford University Press.

Janoff-Bulman R (1992). *Shattered assumptions*. New York, Lexington Books.

Janowsky DS, El-Yousef MK & Davis JM (1974). Interpersonal maneuvers of manic patients. *American Journal of Psychiatry*, **131**, 250–255.

Janowsky DS, Leff M & Epstein RS (1970). Playing the manic game: interpersonal maneuvers of the acutely manic patient. *Archives of General Psychiatry*, **22**, 252–261.

Janowsky DS, Morter S, Hong L & Howe L (1999). Myers Briggs type indicator and tridimensional personality questionnaire differences between bipolar patients and unipolar depressed patients. *Bipolar Disorders*, **2**, 98–108.

Janssen I, Hanssen M, Bak M, Bijl RV, De Graaf R, Vollebergh W et al. (2003). Discrimination and delusional ideation. *British Journal of Psychiatry*, **182**, 71–76.

Janssen I, Krabbendam L, Bak M, Hanssen M, Vollebergh W, de Graaf R et al. (2004). Childhood abuse as a risk factor for psychotic experiences. *Acta Psychiatrica Scandinavica*, **109**(1), 38–45.

Janssen I, Krabbendam L, Jolles J & van Os J (2003). Alterations in theory of mind in patients with schizophrenia and non-psychotic relatives. *Acta Psychiatrica Scandinavica*, **108**, 110–117.

Joel D, Sathyaseelan M, Jayakaran R, Vijayakumar C, Muthurathnam S & Jacob KS (2003). Explanatory models of psychosis among community health workers in South India. *Acta Psychiatrica Scandinavica*, **108**, 66–69.

Johannessen JO, McGlashan TH & Larsen TK (2001). Early detection strategies for untreated first-episode psychosis. *Schizophrenia Research*, **51**, 39–46.

Johannessen JO, McGlashan TH, Larsen TK, Horneland M, Joa I, Mardal S et al. (2001). Early detection strategies for untreated first-episode psychosis. *Schizophrenia Research*, **51**(1), 39–46.

Johns LC, Cannon M, Singleton N, Murray RM, Farrell M, Brugha T et al. (2004). Prevalance and correlates of self-reported psychotic symptoms in the British population. *British Journal of Psychiatry*, **185**, 298–305.

Johns LC & van Os J (2001). The continuity of psychotic experiences in the general population. *Clinical Psychological Review*, **21**(8), 1125–1141.

Johnson DAW, Ludlow JM, Street K & Taylor RDW (1987). Double-blind comparison of half-dose and standard-dose flupenthixol decanoate in the maintenance treatment of stabilized outpatients with schizophrenia. *British Journal of Psychiatry*, **151**, 634–638.

Johnson JG, Cohen P, Skodol AE, Oldham JO, Kasen S & Brook JS (1999). Personality disorders in adolescence and risk of major mental disorders and suicidality during adulthood. *Archives of General Psychiatry*, **56**, 805–811.

Johnson SL & Kizer A (2002). Bipolar and unipolar depression: a comparison of clinical phenomenology and psychosocial predictors. In CL Hammen & IH Gotlib (eds), *Handbook of depression*. New York, Guilford Press, pp. 141–165.

Johnson SL, Meyer B, Winett C & Small J (2000). Social support and self-esteem predict changes in bipolar depression but not mania. *Journal of Affective Disorders*, **58**, 79–86.

Johnson SL, Meyer B, Winters RW, Sandrow D & Goodnick P (2003). The behavioural activation system and the course of mania. In T Scrimali & L Grimaldi (eds), *Cognitive psychotherapy toward a new millenium*. New York, Kluwer Academic/Plenum.

Johnson SL & Nowak A (2002). Dynamical patterns in bipolar depression. *Personality and Social Psychology Review*, **6**(4), 380–387.

Johnson SL, Turner RJ & Iwata N (2003). BIS/BAS levels and psychiatric disorder: an epidemiological study. *Journal of Psychopathology and Behavioural Assessment*, **25**(1), 25–36.

Johnson SL, Winett C, Meyer B, Greenhouse W & Miller I (1999). Social support and the course of bipolar disorder. *Journal of Abnormal Psychology*, **108**, 558–566.

Johnstone EC, Crow TJ, Johnson AL & MacMillan JF (1986). The Northwick Park Study of first episode schizophrenia, I: presentation of the illness and problems relating to admission. *British Journal of Psychiatry*, **148**, 115–120.

Jolley AG, Hirsch SR, Morrison E et al. (1990). Trial of brief intermittent neuroleptic prophylaxis for selected schizophrenic outpatients: clinical and social outcome at two years. *British Medical Journal*, **301**, 837–842.

Jones C, Cormac I, Silveira da Mota Neto JI & Campbell C (2004). Cognitive behaviour therapy for schizophrenia. *Cochrane Database of Systematic Reviews*, Update for 2nd quarter, 2005.

Jones M (2002). Cognitive-behavioural therapy for psychosis: implications for the way that psychosis is managed within community mental health teams. *Journal of Mental Health*, **11**(6), 595–603.

Jones P, Rodgers B, Murray R & Marmot M (1994). Child development risk factors for adult schizophrenia in the British 1946 birth cohort. *Lancet*, **344**, 1398–1402.

Jorgensen P (1998). Early signs of psychotic relapse in schizophrenia. *British Journal of Psychiatry*, **172**, 327–330.

Joyce PR (1984). Parental bonding in bipolar affective disorder. *Journal of Affective Disorders*, **7**, 319–324.

Kahn D (1990). The psychotherapy of mania. *Psychiatric Clinics of North America*, **13**, 229–240.

Kaltiala-Heino R, Rimpela M, Rantanen P & Laippala P (2001). Adolescent depression: the role of discontinuities in life course and social support. *Journal of Affective Disorders*, **64**, 155–166.

Kanai T, Takeuchi H, Furukawa TA, Yoshimura R, Imaizumi T, Kitamura T et al. (2003). Time to recurrence after recovery from major depressive episodes and its predictors. *Psychological Medicine*, **33**, 839–845.

Kanas N (1993). Group psychotherapy with bipolar patients: a review and synthesis. *International Journal of Group Psychotherapy*, **43**, 321–333.

Kanas N (1999). Group therapy with schizophrenic and bipolar patients: integrative approaches. In M Pines & V Schermer (eds), *Group Psychotherapy of the Psychoses*. London, Jessica Kingsley.

Kanas N & Cox P (1998). Process and content in a therapy group for bipolar outpatients. *Group*, **22**, 39–44.

Kane JM, Rifkin A, Woerner M, Reardon G, Sarantakos S, Schiebel D et al. (1983). Low-dose neuroleptic treatment of outpatient schizophrenics, I: preliminary results for relapse rates. *Archives of General Psychiatry*, **40**, 893–896.

Kaney S, Bowen-Jones K & Bentall RP (1999). Persecutory delusions and autobiographical memory. *British Journal of Clinical Psychology*, **38**, 97–102.

Kaney S, Bowen-Jones K, Dewey ME & Bentall RP (1997). Two predictions about paranoid ideation: deluded, depressed and normal participants' subjective frequency and consensus judgements for positive, neutral and negative events. *British Journal of Clinical Psychology*, **36**, 349–364.

Kaney S, Wolfendon M, Dewey M & Bentall R (1992). Persecutory delusions and the recall of threatening and non-threatening propositions. *British Journal of Clinical Psychology*, **31**, 85–87.

Karatzias T, Gumley AI, Power KG & O'Gady M (in submission). Axis I comorbidity in a group of outpatients with Schizophrenia Spectrum Disorders: demographic and clinical correlates.

Kaufman J, Birmaher B, Clayton S, Retano A & Wongchaowart B (1997). Case study: trauma-related hallucinations. *Journal of the American Academy of Child and Adolescent Psychiatry*, **36**(11), 1602–1606.

Kavanagh DJ (1992). Recent developments in expressed emotion and schizophrenia. *British Journal of Psychiatry*, **160**, 601–620.

Kay SR, Fiszbein A & Opler LA (1987). The positive and negative syndrome scale (PANSS) for schizophrenia. *Schizophrenia Bulletin*, **13**, 261–276.

Keck PE, McElroy SL, Strakowski SM, West SA, Hawkins JM, Huber TJ et al. (1995). Outcome and comorbidity in first- compared with multiple-episode mania. *Journal of Nervous and Mental Disease*, **183**, 320–324.

Keitner GI, Solomon DA, Ryan CE, Miller IW, Mallinger A, Kupfer DJ et al. (1996). Prodromal and residual symptoms in bipolar I disorder. *Comprehensive Psychiatry*, **37**(5), 362–367.

Keller MB, Lavori PW, Coryell W, Endicott J & Mueller TI (1993). Bipolar I: a five-year prospective follow-up. *Journal of Nervous and Mental Disease*, **181**, 238–245.

Kelly GR & Scott JE (1990). Medication compliance and health education among outpatients with mental disorders. *Medical Care*, **28**(12), 1181–1197.

Kemp R & David A (1996a). Compliance therapy: an intervention targeting insight and treatment adherence in psychotic patients. *Behavioural and Cognitive Psychotherapy*, **24**, 331–350.

Kemp R & David A (1996b). Psychological predictors of insight and compliance in psychotic patients. *British Journal of Psychiatry*, **169**(4), 444–450.

Kendler KS, Hettema JM, Butera F, Gardner CO & Prescott CA (2003). Life event dimensions of loss, humiliation, entrapment, and danger in the prediction of onsets of major depression and generalized anxiety. *Archives of General Psychiatry*, **60**(8), 789–796.

Kendler KS, McGuire M, Gruenberg AM & Walsh D (1995). Examining the validity of DSM-III-R schizoaffective disorder and its putative subtypes in the Roscommon family study. *American Journal of Psychiatry*, **152**, 755–764.

Kennedy BL, Dhaliwal N, Pedley L, Sahner C, Greenberg R & Manshadi MS (2002). Post-traumatic stress disorder in subjects with schizophrenia and bipolar disorder. *Journal of Kentucky Medical Association*, **100**, 395–399.

Kent L & Craddock N (2002). Is there a relationship between hyperactivity disorder and bipoar disorder? *Journal of Affective Disorders*, **73**(3), 211–221.

Keshavan MS, Rabinowitz J, DeSmedt G, Harvey PD & Schooler N (2004). Correlates of insight in first episode psychosis. *Schizophrenia Research*, **70**(2–3), 187–194.

Kessing LV (2004). Gender differences in the phenomenology of bipolar disorder. *Bipolar Disorders*, **6**, 421–425.

Kessing LV, Agerbo E & Mortensen PB (2004). Major stressful life events and other risk factors for first admission with mania. *Bipolar Disorders*, **6**, 122–129.

Kinderman P (1994). Attentional bias, persecutory delusions and the self concept. *British Journal of Medical Psychology*, **67**, 53–66.

Kinderman P & Humphris G (1995). Clinical communication skills teaching: the role of cognitive schemata. *Medical Education*, **29**, 436–442.

King S & Dixon MJ (1996). The influence of expressed emotion, family dynamics and symptom type on the social adjustment of schizophrenic young adults. *Archives of General Psychiatry*, **53**, 1098–1104.

King M, Sibbald B, Ward E, Bower P, Lloyd M, Gabbay M et al. (2000). Randomised controlled trial of non-directive counselling, cognitive-behaviour therapy and usual general practitioner care in the management of depression as well as mixed anxiety and depression in primary care. *Health Technology Assessment 2000*, **4**, 19.

Kingdon D & Turkington D (1991). The use of cognitive behavior therapy with a normalizing rationale in schizophrenia. *Journal of Nervous and Mental Disease*, **179**(4), 207–211.

Kingdon D & Turkington D (1994). *Cognitive behaviour therapy of schizophrenia*. Hillsdale, NJ, Erlbaum.

Kingsep P, Nathan P & Castle D (2003). Cognitive behavioural group treatment for social anxiety in schizophrenia. *Schizophrenia*, **63**(1–2), 121–129.

Klerman GL, Weismann NM, Rounsaville BJ & Chevron ES (1984). *Interpersonal therapy of depression*. New York, Basic Books.

Klimes-Dougan B, Free K, Ronsaville D, Stilwell J, Welsh CJ & Radke-Yarrow M (1999). Suicidal ideation and attempts: a longitudinal investigation of children of depressed and well mothers. *Journal of the American Academy of Child and Adolescent Psychiatry*, **38**(6), 651–665.

Klosterkoetter J, Hellmich M, Steinmeyer EM & Schultze-Lutter F (2001). Diagnosing schizophrenia in the initial prodromal phase. *Archives of General Psychiatry*, **58**(2), 158–164.

Knapp M, et al. (2002). Comparing patterns and costs of schizophrenia care in five European countries: the EPSILON study. *Acta Psychiatrica Scandinavica*, **105**, 42–54.

Kobak R, Cole H, Ferenz-Gillies R, Fleming WS et al. (1993). Attachment and emotion regulation during mother teen problem solving: a control theory analysis. *Child Development*, **64**(1), 231–245.

Kobak RR & Sceery A (1988). Attachment in late adolescence: working models, affect regulation, and representations of self and others. *Child Development*, **59**, 135–146.

Kochanska G, Murray KT & Harlan E (2000). Effortful control in early childhood: continuity and change, antecedents, and implications for social development. *Developmental Psychology*, **36**, 220–232.

Krabbendam L, Myin-Germeys I, De Graff R, Vollebergh W, Nolen EW, Iedma J et al. (2004). Dimensions of depression, mania and psychosis in the general population. *Psychological Medicine*, **34**, 1177–1186.

Kravariti E, Morris RG, Rabe-Hesketh SR, Murray RM & Frangou S (2003). The Maudsley early onset shcizophrenia study: cognitive function in adolescents with recent onset schizophrenia. *Schizophrenia Research*, **61**, 137–148.

Krawiecka M, Goldberg D & Vaughan M (1977). A standardized psychiatric assessment scale for rating chronic psychotic patients. *Acta Psychiatrica Scandinavica*, **55**, 299–308.

Kroll L, Harrington R, Jayson D, Fraser J & Gowers S (1996). Pilot study of continuation cognitive-behavioural therapy for major depression in adolescents psychiatric patients. *Journal of the American Academy of Child and Adolescent Psychiatry*, **35**(9), 1156–1161.

Krstev H, Jackson H & Maude D (1999). An investigation of attributional style in first-episode psychosis. *British Journal of Clinical Psychology*, **38**, 181–194.

Kruse A & Schmidt E (1997). Emotionalität, Alter und Altern- Forschungsperspektiven, methodische Zugänge und empirische Ergbnisse. *Therapeutische Umschau*, **54**(6), 326–335.

Kuipers L & Bebbington P (1988). Expressed emotion research in schizophrenia: theoretical and clinical implications. *Psychological Medicine*, **18**(4), 893–909.

Kuipers L, Birchwood M & McCreadie RG (1992). Psychosocial family intervention in schizophrenia: a review of empirical studies. *British Journal of Psychiatry*, **160**, 272–275.

Kulhara P, Basu D, Mattoo SK, Sharan P & Chopra R (1999). Lithium prophlaxis of recurrent bipolar affective disorder: long-term outcome and its psychosocial correlates. *Journal of Affective Disorders*, **54**, 87–96.

Kumar S, Thara R & Rajkumar S (1989). Coping with symptoms of relapse in schizophrenia. *European Archives of Psychiatry and Neurological Sciences*, **239**, 213–215.

Kusznir A, Cooke RG & Young LT (2000). The correlates of community functioning in patients with bipolar disorder. *Journal of Affective Disorders*, **61**, 81–85.

Lacro J, Dunn LB, Dolder CR et al. (2002). Prevalence of risk factors for medication nonadherence in patients with schizophrenia: a comprehensive review of recent literature. *Journal of Clinical Psychiatry*, **63**, 892–909.

Laible DJ & Thompson RA (1998). Attachment and emotional understanding in preschool children. *Developmental Psychology*, **34**, 1038–1045.

Lam DH, Bright J, Jones S, Hayward P, Schuck N, Chisholm D et al. (2000). Cognitive therapy for bipolar illness – a pilot study of relapse prevention. *Cognitive Therapy and Research*, **24**(5), 503–520.

Lam DH, Green B, Power MJ & Checkley S (1996). Dependency, matching adversities, length of survival and relapse in major depression. *Journal of Affective Disorders*, **37**, 81–90.

Lam DH, Schuck N, Smith N, Farmer A & Checkley S (2002). Response style, interpersonal difficulties and social functioning in major depressive disorder. *Journal of Affective Disorders*, **75**(3), 279–283.

Lam DH & Wong G (1997). Prodromes, coping strategies, insight and social functioning in bipolar affective disorders. *Psychological Medicine*, **27**, 1091–1100.

Lam DH, Wong G & Sham P (2001). Prodromes, coping strategies and course of illness in bipolar affective disorders: a naturalistic study. *Psychological Medicine*, **31**, 1397–1402.

Landerman R, George LK, Campbell RT & Blazer DG (1989). Alternative models of the stress buffering hypothesis. *American Journal of Community Psychology*, **17**(5), 625–642.

Langdon R, Davies M & Coltheart M (2002). Understanding minds and understanding communicated meanings in schizophrenia. *Mind and Language*, **17**, 68–104.

Laufer M (1986). Adolescence and psychosis. *International Journal of Psycho-Analysis*, **67**, 367–371.

Lay B, Blanz B, Hartmann M & Schmidt MH (2000). The psychosocial outcome of adolescent-onset shizophrenia: a 12-year follow-up. *Schizophrenia Bulletin*, **26**(4), 801–816.

Lazarus RS & Folkman S (1984). *Stress, appraisal and coping*. New York, Springer.

Leahy R (2002). A model of emotional schemas. *Cognitive and Behavioural Practice*, **9**(3), 177–190.

Leahy R (2005). A social-cognitive model of validation. In P Gilbert (ed.), *Compassion, conceptualisations, research and use in psychotherapy*. London and New York, Routledge, pp. 195–217.

Lecompte D (1996). The management of drug-resistant, persistent and unpleasant auditory hallucinations. *Acta Psychiatrica Belgica*, **96**(1), 21–29.

Le Doux J (1996). *The emotional brain*. New York, Simon & Schuster.

Lee CS, Chang JC & Cheng TA (2002). Acculturation and suicide: a case-control psychological autopsy study. *Psychological Medicine*, **32**, 133–141.

Lee K-H, Farrow SA, Spence SA & Woodruff PWR (2004). Social cognition, brain networks and schizophrenia. *Psychological Medicine*, **34**, 391–400.

Leff J (1995). Family management of schizophrenia. In HA Nasrallah & CL Shriqui (eds), *Contemporary issues in the treatment of schizophrenia.* Washington, DC, American Psychiatric Association, pp. 683–702.

Leff J, Kuipers L, Berkowitz R & Sturgeon D (1985). A controlled trial of social intervention in the families of schizophrenic patients: two year follow-up. *British Journal of Psychiatry*, **146**, 594–600.

Leff J & Vaughn C (1985). *Expressed emotion in families.* New York, Guilford Press.

Leff J, Wig NN, Bedi H & Menon DK (1990). Relatives' expressed emotion and the course of schizophrenia in Chandigarh: a two-year follow-up of a first contact sample. *British Journal of Psychiatry*, **156**, 351–356.

Leff J, Wig NN, Ghosh A, Bedi H, Menon DK, Kuipers L et al. (1987). Expressed emotion and schizophrenia in north India, III: influence of relatives' expressed emotion on the course of schizophrenia in Chandigarh. *British Journal of Psychiatry*, **151**, 166–173.

Levitan RD, Rector NA & Bagby RM (1998). Negative attributional style in seasonal and nonseasonal depression. *American Journal of Psychiatry*, **155**(3), 428–430.

Lewinsohn PM, Klein DN & Seeley JR (1995). Bipolar disorders in a community sample of older adolescents: prevalence, phenomenology, comorbidity, and course. *Journal of the American Academy of Child and Adolescent Psychiatry*, **34**, 454–463.

Lewinsohn PM, Klein DN & Seeley JR (2000). Bipolar disorder during adolescence and young adulthood in a community sample. *Bipolar Disorders*, **2**, 281–293.

Lewis S, Tarrier N, Haddock G, Bentall RP, Kinderman P, Kingdon D et al. (2002). Randomised controlled trial of cognitive-behavioural therapy in early schizophrenia: acute-phase outcomes. *British Journal of Psychiatry*, **181**(suppl. 43), s91–s97.

Liang B & Bogat A (1994). Culture, control, and coping: new perspectives on social support. *American Journal of Community Psychology*, **22**(1), 123–147.

Lidz RW & Lidz T (1949). The family environment of schizophrenic patients. *American Journal of Psychiatry*, **106**, 332–345.

Lineham MM (1993). *Cognitive-behavioural treatment of borderline personality disorder.* New York, Guilford Press.

Lineham MM, Armstrong HE, Suarez A, Allmon D & Heard HL (1991). Cognitive-behavioral treatment of chronically parasuicidal borderline patients. *Archives of General Psychiatry*, **48**, 1060–1064.

Linszen DH, Dingemans P, Van der Does JW, Nugter A, Scholte P, Lenior R et al. (1996). Treatment, expressed emotion and relapse in recent onset schizophrenic disorders. *Psychological Medicine*, **26**, 333–342.

Liotti G (1996). L'attaccamento. In BG Bara (ed.), *Manuale di psicoterapia cognitiva.* Torino, Bollati Boringhieri.

Lipton FR, Cohen CI, Fischer E & Katz SE (1981). Schizophrenia: a network crisis. *Schizophrenia Bulletin*, **7**, 144–151.

Low G, Jones D, Macleod A, Power M & Duggan C (2000). Childhood trauma, dissociation and self-harming behavior: a pilot study. *British Journal of Medical Psychology*, **73**, 269–278.

Lozano BE & Johnson SL (2001). Can personality traits predict increases in manic and depressive symptoms? *Journal of Affective Disorders*, **63**, 103–111.

Ludwig AM & Ables MF (1974). Mania and marriage: the relationship between biological and behavioral variables. *Comprehensive Psychiatry*, **15**(6), 411–421.

Lukoff D, Snyder K, Ventura J & Nuechterlein KH (1984). Life events, familial stress, and coping in the developmental course of schizophrenia. *Schizophrenia Bulletin*, **10**(2), 258–292.

Lutgendorf S, Antoni MH, Ironson G, Starr K, Costello N, Zuckerman M et al. (1998). Changes in cognitive coping skills and social support during cognitive behavioral stress management intervention and distress outcomes in symptomatic human immunodeficiency virus (HIV)-seropositive gay men. *Psychosomatic Medicine*, **60**(2), 204–214.

Lyons-Ruth K, Connell DB, Grunebaum H & Botein S (1990). Infants at social risk: maternal depression and family support services as mediators of infant development and security of attachment. *Child Development*, **61**, 85–98.

Lyons-Ruth K & Jacobvitz D (1999). Attachment disorganisation: unresolved loss, relational violence and lapses in behavioural and attentional strategies. In J Cassidy & PR Shaver (eds), *Handbook of attachment: theory, research and applications*. New York, Guilford Press, pp. 520–554.

MacDonald EM, Pica S, Mcdonald S, Hayes RL & Baglioni AJ Jr (1998). Stress and coping in early psychosis: role of symptoms, self-efficacy, and social support in coping with stress. *British Journal of Psychiatry*, **33**(suppl. 172), 122–127.

MacQuenn GM, Galway TM, Hay J, Young LT & Joffe RT (2002). Recollection memory deficits in patients with major depressive disorder predicted by past depressions but not by current mood state or treatment status. *Psychological Medicine*, **32**, 251–258.

MacVane JR, Lange JD, Brown WA & Zayat M (1978). Psychological functioning of bipolar manic-depressives in remission. *Archives of General Psychiatry*, **35**, 1351–1354.

Mahler MS (1971). A study of the separation-individuation process: and its possible application to borderline phenomena in the psychoanalytic situation. *Psychoanalytic Study of the Child*, **26**, 403–424.

Mahler MS (1974). Symbiosis and individuation: the psychological birth of the human infant. *Psychoanalytic Study of the Child*, **29**, 89–106.

Maier W, Lichtermann D, Minges J, Delmo C & Heun R (1995). The relationship between bipolar disorder and alcoholism: a controlled family study. *Psychological Medicine*, **25**, 787–796.

Maier W, Lichtermann D, Minges J, Hallmayer J, Heun R, Benkert O et al. (1993). Continuity and discontinuity of affective disorders and schizophrenia: results of a controlled family study. *Archives of General Psychiatry*, **50**, 871–883.

Main M (1990). Cross-cultural studies of attachment organization: recent studies, changing methodologies, and the concept of conditional strategies. *Human Development*, **33**, 48–61.

Main M (1999). Epilogue: attachment theory: eighteen points with suggestions for future studies. In J Cassidy & PR Shaver (eds), *Handbook of attachment: theory, research and applications*. New York, Guilford Press.

Main M & Goldwyn R (1985). The adult attachment classification system. Unpublished manuscript, University of California at Berkeley.

Main M, Goldwyn R & Hesse E (2002). Adult attachment scoring and classification systems. (Version 7.1), Unpublished manuscript, University of California.

Main M & Hesse E (1990). Parents' unresolved traumatic experiences are related to infant disorganized attachment status: is frightened and/or frightening parent behaviour the linking mechanism? In M Greenberg, D Cicchetti & E Cummings (eds), *Attachment in the preschool years*. Chicago, University of Chicago Press, pp. 161–182.

Main M, Kaplan N & Cassidy J (1985). *Security in infancy, childhood and adulthood: a move to the level of representation*. Monographs of the Society for Research in Child Development, **50**(1–2), 66–104.

Main M & Solomon J (1986). Discovery of a new, insecure-disorganised/disoriented attachment pattern. In TB Brazelton & MW Yogman (eds), *Affective development in infancy*. Norwood, NJ, Ablex, pp. 95–124.

Main M & Solomon J (1986). Discovery of an insecure-disorganised/disorientated attachment pattern. In MW Yogman & TB Brazelton (eds), *Affective development in infancy*. Westport, CT, Ablex, pp. 95–124.

Main M & Solomon J (1990). Procedures for identifying infants as disorganized/disoriented during the Ainsworth Strange Situation. In MT Greenberg, D Cicchetti & EM Cummings (eds), *Attachment in the preschool years: theory, research, and intervention*. Chicago, University of Chicago Press, pp. 121–160.

Maj M, Pirozzi R, Formicola AMR & Tortorella A (1999). Reliability and validity of four alternative definitions of rapid-cycling bipolar disorder. *American Journal of Psychiatry*, **156**, 1421–1424.

Maj M, Pirozzi R, Magliano L & Bartoli L (2003). Agitated depression in bipolar I disorder: prevalence, phenomenology, and outcome. *American Journal of Psychiatry*, **160**(12), 2134–2140.

Malin A (1988). A short history of the psychoanalytic approach to the treatment of psychotic disorders. In A Goldberg (ed.), *Frontiers in self psychology: progress in self psychology*, vol. 3. Hillsdale, NJ, Analytic Press.

Malkoff-Schwartz S, Frank E, Anderson B, Sherrill JT, Siegel L, Patterson D et al. (1998). Stressful life events and social rhythm disruption in the onset of manic and depressive bipolar episodes: a preliminary investigation. *Archives of General Psychiatry*, **55**(8), 702–707.

Malla AK & Norman RMG (1994). Prodromal symptoms in schizophrenia. *British Journal of Psychiatry*, **164**, 487–493.

Malla AK, Norman RMG, Manchanda R, Ahmed MR, Scholten D, Harrichan R et al. (2002). One year outcome in first epsiode psychosis: influence of DUP and other predictors. *Schizophrenia Research*, **54**, 231–242.

Malla AK, Norman RMG, McClean TS & McIntosh E (2001). Impact of phase-specific treatment of first episode of psychosis on Wisconsin Quality of Life Index. *Acta Psychiatrica Scandinavica*, **103**, 355–361.

Malmberg A, Lewis G, David A et al. (1998). Premorbid adjustment and personality in people with schizophrenia. *British Journal of Psychiatry*, **172**, 308–313.

Malone RP, Delaney MA, Luebbert JF, Cater J & Campbell M (2000). A double-blind placebo-controlled study of lithium in hopitalized aggressive children and adolescents with conduct disorder. *Archives of General Psychiatry*, **57**, 649–654.

Marcelis M, Myin-Germeys I, Suckling J, Woodruff P, Hofman P, Bullmore E et al. (2003). Cerebral tissue alterations and daily life stress experience in psychosis. *Acta Psychiatrica Scandinavica*, **107**, 54–59.

Marder SR (1999). Antipsychotic drugs and relapse prevention. *Schizophrenia Research*, **35**(suppl.), s87–s92.

Marder SR (2000). Integrating pharmacological and psychosocial treatments for schizophrenia. *Acta Psychiatrica Scandinavica*, **102**(suppl. 407), 87–90.

Marder SR, van Putten T, Mintz J et al. (1984). Costs and benefits of two doses of fluphenazine. *Archives of General Psychiatry*, **41**, 1025–1029.

Marder SR, van Putten T, Mintz J et al. (1987). Low and conventional dose maintenance therapy with fluphenazine decanoate. *Archives of General Psychiatry*, **44**, 518–521.

Marder SR, Wirshing WC, van Putten T et al. (1994). Fluphenazine vs placebo supplementation for prodromal signs of relapse in schizophrenia. *Archives of General Psychiatry*, **51**, 280–288.

Mari JJ & Streiner DL (1994). An overview of family interventions and relapse on schizophrenia: meta-analysis of research findings. *Psychological Medicine*, **24**, 565–578.

Mari JJ & Streiner D (1996). The effects of family intervention on those with schizophrenia. In C Adams et al. (eds), *Schizophrenia module*. Cochrane Database of Systematic Reviews, London, Cochrane Library.

Markowitz J (1998). *Interpersonal psychotherapy for dysthymic disorder.* Washington, DC, American Psychiatric Press.

Marneros A, Pillmann F, Haring A, Balzuweit S & Bloink R (2002). The relation of 'acute and transient psychotic disorder' (ICD-10 F23) to bipolar schizoaffective disorder. *Journal of Psychiatric Research*, **36**, 165–171.

Marsh DT (1994). The psychodynamic model and services for families: issues and strategies. In M Wasow & HP Lefley (eds), *Helping families cope with mental illness*. Langhorne, PA, Harwood Academic Publishers/Gordon, pp. 105–128.

Mason O, Startup M, Halpin S, Schall U, Conrad A & Carr V (2004). Risk factors for transition to first episode psychosis among individuals with 'at-risk mental states'. *Schizophrenia Research*, **71**, 227–237.

McCabe R, Heath C, Burns T, Priebe S & Skelton J (2002). Engagement of patients with psychosis in the consultation: conversation analytic study. *British Medical Journal*, **325**, 1148–1151.

McCandless-Glimcher L, McKnight S, Hamera E, Smith BL, Peterson KA & Plumlee AA (1986). Use of symptoms by schizophrenics to monitor and regulate their illness. *Hospital and Community Psychiatry*, **37**(9), 929–933.

McClennan J & Werry J (1997). AACAP official action: practice parameters for the assessment and treatment of children and adolescents with bipolar disorder. *Journal of the American Academy of Child and Adolescent Psychiatry*, **36**, 138–157.

McDermut W, Mattia J & Zimmerman M (2001). Comorbidity burden and its impact on psychosocial morbidity in depressed outpatients. *Journal of Affective Disorders*, **65**, 289–295.

McElroy SL, Keck PE & Strakowski SM (1996). Mania, psychosis and antipsychotics. *Journal of Clinical Psychiatry*, **57**, 14–26.

McEvoy JP & Wilkinson ML (2000). The role of insight in the treatment and outcome of bipolar disorder. *Psychiatric Annals*, **30**(7), 496–498.

McFarlane WR (2000). Psychoeducational multi-family groups: adaptations and outcomes. In A Bateman & B Martindale (eds), *Psychosis: psychological approaches and their effectiveness*. London, Gaskell/Royal College of Psychiatrists, pp. 68–95.

McFarlane WR (2002). *Multifamily groups in the treatment of severe psychiatric disorders.* New York: Guilford Press.

McGhie A & Chapman J (1961). Disorders of attention and perception in early schizophrenia. *British Journal of Medical Psychology*, **34**, 103–116.

McGlashan TH, Levy ST & Carpenter WD (1975). Integration and sealing over: clinically distinct recovery styles from schizophrenia. *Archives of General Psychiatry*, **32**, 1269–1272.

McGorry P, Yung A, Phillips L, Yuen HP, Francey S, Cosgrave E et al. (2002). Randomised controlled trial of interventions designed to reduce the risk of progression to first-episode psychosis in a clinical sample with subthreshold symptoms. *Archives of General Psychiatry*, **59**, 921–928.

McGorry PD (1995). Psychoeducation in first-episode psychosis: a therapeutic process. *Psychiatry*, **58**, 313–328.

McGorry PD, Chanen A, McCarthy E, Van Riel R, McKenzie D & Singh BS (1991). Posttraumatic stress disorder following recent-onset psychosis: an unrecognised postpsychotic syndrome. *Journal of Nervous and Mental Disease*, **179**(5), 253–258.

McKay M & Fanning P (1992). *Self esteem: a proven program of cognitive techniques for assessing, improving and maintaining your self esteem*, 2nd edn. Oakland, CA, New Harbinger Publishers.

McPherson H, Herbison P & Romans S (1993). Life events and relapse in established bipolar affective disorder. *British Journal of Psychiatry*, **163**, 381–385.

Meins E, Fernyhough C, Russell J & Clark-Carter D (1998). Security of attachment as a predictor of symbolic and mentalising abilities: a longitudinal study. *Social Development*, **7**, 1–24.

Menezes NM & Milovan E (2000). First-episode psychosis: a comparative review of diagnostic evolution and predictive variables in adolescents versus adults. *Canadian Journal of Psychiatry*, **45**, 710–716.

Merckelbach H, Rassin E & Muris P (2000). Dissociation, schizotypy and fantasy proneness in undergraduate students. *Journal of Nervous and Mental Disorder*, **188**, 428–431.

Mercy JA, Kresnow M-J, O'Carroll PW, Lee RK, Powell KE, Potter LB et al. (2001). Is suicide contagious? A study of the relation between exposure to the suicidal behaviour of others and nearly lethal suicide attempts. *American Journal of Epidemiology*, **154**(2), 120–127.

Meyer B, Beevers CG & Johnson SL (2004). Goals appraisals and vulnerability to bipolar disorder: a personal projects analysis. *Cognitive Therapy and Research*, **28**, 173–182.

Meyer H, Taiminen T, Vuori T, Aeijaelae A & Helenius H (1999). Posttraumatic stress disorder symptoms related to psychosis and acute involuntary hospitalisation in schizophrenic and delusional patients. *Journal of Nervous and Mental Disease*, **187**, 343–352.

Middleton W, Raphael B, Martinek N & Misso V (1993). Pathological grief reactions. In MS Stroebe, W Stroebe & RO Hanssen (eds), *Handbook of bereavement: theory, research and intervention*. New York, Cambridge University Press, pp. 44–61.

Miklowitz DJ, George EL, Richards J-A, Simoneau T-L & Suddath R-L (2003). A randomized study of family-focused psychoeducation and pharmacotherapy in the outpatient management of bipolar disorder. *Archives of General Psychiatry*, **60**(9), 904–912.

Miklowitz DJ & Goldstein MJ (1990). Behavioral family treatment for patients with bipolar affective disorder. *Behavior Modification*, **14**, 457–489.

Miklowitz DJ, Goldstein MJ & Falloon IRH (1983). Premorbid and symptomatic characteristics of schizophrenics from families with high and low levels of expressed emotion. *Journal of Abnormal Psychology*, **92**(3), 359–367.

Miklowitz DJ, Goldstein MJ & Neuchterlein KH (1995). Verbal interactions in the families of schizophrenic and bipolar affective patients. *Journal of Abnormal Psychology*, **104**, 268–276.

Miklowitz DJ, Goldstein MJ, Neuchterlein KH, Snyder KS & Mintz J (1988). Family factors and the course of bipolar affective disorder. *Archives of General Psychiatry*, **45**, 225–231.

Miklowitz DJ & Hooley JM (1998). Developing family psychoeducational treatments for patients with bipolar and other severe psychiatric disorders: a pathway from basic research to clinical trials. *Journal of Marital and Family Therapy*, **24**(4), 419–435.

Miklowitz DJ, Simoneau TL, George EL & Richards JA (2000). Family-focused treatment of bipolar disorder: 1-year effects of a psychoeducational program in conjunction with pharmacotherapy. *Biological Psychiatry*, **48**, 582–592.

Mikulincer M & Florian V (1997). Are emotional and instrumental supportive interactions beneficial in times of stress? The impact of attachment style. *Anxiety, Stress and Coping, An International Journal*, **10**, 109–127.

Mikulincer M, Florian V & Weller A (1993). Attachment styles, coping strategies, and posttraumatic psychological distress: the impact of the Gulf War in Israel. *Journal of Personality and Social Psychology*, **64**(5), 817–826.

Mikulincer M, Hirschberger G, Nachmias O & Gillath O (2001). The affective component of the secure base schema: affective priming with representations of attachment security. *Journal of Personal and Social Psychology*, **81**(2), 305–321.

Miller F, Dworkin J, Ward M & Barone D (1990). A preliminary study of unresolved grief in families of seriously mentally ill patients. *Hospital and Community Psychiatry*, **12**, 1321–1325.

Miller FE (1996). Grief therapy for relatives of persons with serious mental illness. *Psychiatric Services*, **47**, 633–637.

Mojtabai R (1999). Duration of illness and structure of symptoms in schizophrenia. *Psychological Medicine*, **29**, 915–924.

Mojtabai R (2000). Heterogeneity of cycloid psychoses: a latent class analysis. *Psychological Medicine*, **30**, 721–726.

Moller H-J, Bottlender R, Wegner U, Wittman J & Stauss A (2000). Long-term course of schizophrenic, affective and schizoaffective psychosis: focus on negative symptoms and their impact on global indicators of outcome. *Acta Psychiatrica Scandinavica*, **102**(suppl. 407), 54–57.

Montagnon F, Said S & Lepine JP (2002). Lithium: poisoning and suicide prevention. *European Psychiatry*, **17**, 92–95.

Montgomery SA, Taylor P & Montgamery D (1978). A comprehensive psychopathological rating scale. *Acta Psychiatrica Scandinavica*, **271**(suppl.), 5–27.

Moore E, Ball RA & Kuipers L (1992). Expressed emotion in staff working with the long-term adult mentally ill. *British Journal of Psychiatry*, **161**, 802–808.

Moore E & Kuipers L (1992). Behavioral correlates of expressed emotion in staff-patient interactions. *Social Psychiatry and Psychiatric Epidemiology*, **27**, 298–303.

Moore E, Kuipers L & Ball R (1992). Staff-patient relationships in the care of the long-term adult mentally ill: a content analysis of expressed emotion interviews. *Social Psychiatry and Psychiatric Epidemiology*, **27**, 28–34.

Moorhead S & Scott J (2000). Clinical characteristics of familial and non-familial bipolar disorder. *Bipolar Disorders*, **2**, 136–139.

Morgan G, Buckley C & Nowers M (1998). Face to face with the suicidal. *Advances in Psychiatric Treatment*, **4**, 188–196.

Morrison AP (1998). A cognitive analysis of the maintenance of auditory hallucinations: are voices to schizophrenia what bodily sensations are to panic? *Behavioural and Cognitive Psychotherapy*, **26**, 289–302.

Morrison AP (2001). The interpretation of intrusions in psychosis: an integrative cognitive approach to hallucinations and delusions. *Behavioural and Cognitive Psychotherapy*, **29**, 257–276.

Morrison AP & Baker CA (2000). Intrusive thoughts and auditory hallucinations: a comparative study of intrusions in psychosis. *Behaviour Research and Therapy*, **38**, 1097–1106.

Morrison AP, Frame L & Larkin W (2003). Relationships between trauma and psychosis: a review and integration. *British Journal of Clinical Psychology*, **42**, 331–353.

Morrison AP, French P, Walford L, Lewis SW, Kilcommons A, Green J et al. (2004). Cognitive therapy for the prevention of psychosis in people at ultra-high risk. *British Journal of Psychiatry*, **185**, 291–297.

Morrison AP, Gumley AI, Schwannauer M, Campbell M, Gleeson A, Griffin E et al. (2005). The beliefs about paranoia scale: preliminary validation of a metacognitive approach to conceptualizing paranoia. *Behavioural and Cognitive Psychotherapy*, **33**(2), 153–164.

Morrison AP, Haddock G & Tarrier N (1995). Intrusive thoughts and auditory hallucinations: a cognitive approach. *Behavioural and Cognitive Psychotherapy*, **23**, 265–280.

Morrison AP, Wells A & Nothard S (2002). Cognitive and emotional predictors of predisposition to hallucinations in non-patients. *British Journal of Clinical Psychology*, **41**, 259–270.

Mortensen PB (2000). Urban–rural differences in the risk for schizophrenia. *International Journal of Mental Health*, **29**, 101–110.

Mueser KT, Rosenburg SD, Goodman LA & Trumbetta SL (2002). Trauma, PTSD, and the course of severe mental illness: an interactive model. *Schizophrenia Research*, **53**, 123–143.

Mulder RT, Joyce PR, Sullivan PF, Bulik CM & Carter FA (1999). The relationship among three models of personality psychotherapy psychopathology: DSM-III-R personality disorder, TCI scores and DSQ defences. *Psychological Medicine*, **29**(4), 943–951.

Muller E, Schapowahl A & Seelander A (1984). Katamnestische Erhebungen zur somato-psychosozialen Entwicklung in Kindheit und Jugend von Patienten mit monopolar depressiven und bipolar manischdepressiven Psychosen. *Psychiatrie, Neurologie und Medische Psychologie*, **36**, August, 8, S, 480–488.

Muller MJ (2002). Letter to the editors: overlap between emotional blunting, depression and extrapyramidal symptoms in schizophrenia. *Schizophrenia Research*, **57**, 307–309.

Müller P, Günther U & Lohmeyer J (1986). Behandlung und Verlauf schizophrener Psychosen über ein Jahrzehnt. *Nervenarzt*, **57**, 332–341.

Muris P (2002). Relationships between self-efficacy and symptoms of anxiety disorder and depression in a normal adolescent sample. *Personality and Individual Differences*, **32**, 337–348.

Murphy FC, Sahakian BJ, Rubinsztein JS, Michael A, Rogers RD, Robbins TW et al. (1999). Emotional bias and inhibitory control processes in mania and depression. *Psychological Medicine*, **29**, 1307–1321.

Myers JEB, Berliner L, Briere J, Hendrix CT, Reid T & Jenny C (2002). *The APSAC handbook on child maltreatment*, 2nd edn. Newbury Park, CA, Sage Publications.

Myin-Germeys I, Krabendam L, Delespaul PAEG & van Os J (2003). Do life events have their effect on psychosis by influencing the emotional reactivity to daily life stress? *Psychological Medicine*, **33**, 327–333.

Myin-Germeys I, Peeters F, Havermans R, Nicolson NA, deVries MW, Delespaul P et al. (2003). Emotional reactivity to daily life stress in psychosis and affective disorder: an experience sampling study. *Acta Psychiatrica Scandinavica*, **107**, 124–131.

Myin-Germeys I, van Os J, Schwartz JE, Stone AA & Delespaul PA (2001). Emotional reactivity to daily life stress in psychosis. *Archives of General Psychiatry*, **58**(12), 1137–1144.

Nayani TH & David AS (1996). The auditory hallucination: a phenomenological survey. *Psychological Medicine*, **26**(1), 179–192.

Neria Y, Bromet EJ, Sievers S, Lavelle J & Fochtmann LJ (2002). Trauma exposure and posttraumatic stress disorder in psychosis: findings from a first-admission cohort. *Journal of Consulting and Clinical Psychology*, **70**(1), 246–251.

Nesse RM (2000). Is depression an adaptation? *Archives of General Psychiatry*, **57**, 14–20.

Neuchterlein KH & Dawson ME (1984a). Information processing and attentional functioning in the developmental course of schizophrenia disorders. *Schizophrenia Bulletin*, **10**, 160–203.

Neuchterlein KH & Dawson ME (1984b). A heuristic vulnerability/stress model of schizophrenic episodes. *Schizophrenia Bulletin*, **10**(2), 300–309.

Neuchterlein KH et al. (2002). The structure of schizotypy: relationships between neurocognitive and personality disorder features in relatives of schizophrenic patients in the UCLA Family Study. *Schizophrenia Research*, **54**, 121–130.

Newcomb MD & Bentler PM (1986). Loneliness and social support: a confirmatory hierarchical analysis. *Personality and Social Psychology Bulletin*, **12**(4), 520–525.

Nordentoft N, Jeppesen P, Abel M, Kassow P, Petersen L, Thorup A et al. (2002). OPUS study: suicidal behaviour, suicidal ideation and hopelessness among patients with first-episode psychosis. *British Journal of Psychiatry*, **181**(suppl. 43), s98–s106.

Norman RMG & Malla AK (1995). Prodromal symptoms of relapse in schizophrenia: a review. *Schizophrenia Bulletin*, **21**(4), 527–539.

Norman RMG, Townsend L & Malla AK (2001). Duration of untreated psychosis and cognitive functioning in first-episode patients. *British Journal of Psychiatry*, **179**, 340–345.

O'Connor LE, Berry JW, Weiss J & Gilbert P (2002). Guilt, fear, submission and empathy in depression. *Journal of Affective Disorders*, **71**, 19–27.

Ognibene TC & Collins NL (1998). Adult attachment styles, perceived social support and coping strategies. *Journal of Social and Personal Relationships*, **15**, 323–345.

Oken RJ & Mcgeer PL (1995). Schizophrenia: a 100-year retrospective. *American Journal of Psychiatry*, **152**(11), 1692–1693.

O'Leary D & Costello F (2001). Personality and outcome in depression: an 18-month prospective follow-up study. *Journal of Affective Disorders*, **63**, 67–78.

Olin SS & Mednick SA (1996). Risk factors of psychosis: identifying vulnerable populations premorbidly. *Schizophrenia Bulletin,* **22,** 223–240.

Oliver N & Kuipers E (1996). Stress and its relationship to expressed emotion in community mental health workers. *International Journal of Social Psychiatry,* **42**(2), 150–159.

Osher Y, Cloninger CR & Belmaker RH (1996). TPQ in euthymic manic-depressive patients. *Journal of Psychiatric Research,* **30,** 353–357.

Osher Y, Mandel B, Shapiro E & Belmaker RH (2000). Rorschach markers in offspring of manic-depressive patients. *Journal of Affective Disorders,* **59,** 231–236.

Overall JE & Gorham DR (1962). The brief psychiatric rating scale. *Psychological Reports,* **10,** 799–812.

Overholser JC & Adams DM (1997). Stressful life events and social support in depressed psychiatric inpatients. In TW Miller (ed.), *Clinical disorders and stressful life events.* Madison, WI, International Universities Press.

Ozerdem A, Tunca Z & Kaya N (2001). The relatively good prognosis of bipolar disorders in a Turkish bipolar clinic. *Journal of Affective Disorders,* **64,** 27–34.

Padesky CA (1994). Schema change processes in cognitive therapy. *Clinical Psychology Psychotherapy,* **1,** 267–278.

Pallanti S, Quercioli L & Pazzagli A (1997). Relapse in young paranoid schizophrenic patients: a prospective study of stressful life events, P300 measures and coping. *American Journal of Psychiatry,* **154**(6), 792–798.

Parker G (1983). Parental 'affectionless control' as an antecedent to adult depression: a risk factor delineated. *Archives of General Psychiatry,* **40,** 956–960.

Parker G, Roy K, Hadzi-Pavlovic D, Wilhelm K & Mitchell P (2001). The differential impact of age on the phenomenology of melancholia. *Psychological Medicine,* **31,** 1231–1236.

Parker G, Roy K, Wilhelm K, Mitchell P & Hadzi-Pavlovic D (2000). The nature of bipolar depression: implications for the definition of melancholia. *Journal of Affective Disorders,* **59,** 217–224.

Parkes CM (1985). Bereavement. *British Journal of Psychiatry,* **146,** 11–17.

Parkes CM & Weiss RS (1983). *Recovery from bereavement.* New York, Basic Books.

Parry G, Shapiro DA & Davies L (1989). Reliability of life-event ratings: an independent replication. In TW Miller (ed.), *Stressful life events.* Madison, WI, International Universities Press, pp. 123–126.

Pasquini P, Liotti G, Mazzotti E, Fassone G & Picardi A (2002). Risk factors in the early family life of patients suffering from dissociative disorders. *Acta Psychiatrica Scandinavica,* **105**(2), 110–116.

Pataki CS & Carlson GA (1992). Bipolar disorders: clinical manifestations, differential diagnosis and treatment. In M Shaffi & SL Shaffi (eds), *Clinical guide to depression in children and adolescents.* Washington, DC, American Psychiatric Publishing.

Patrick M, Hobson RP, Castle D, Howard R & Maughan B (1994). Personality disorder and the mental representation of early social experience. *Development and Psychopathology,* **6,** 375–388.

Patterson C, Birchwood M & Cochrane R (2000). Preventing the entrenchment of high expressed emotion in first episode psychosis: early developmental attachment pathways. *Australian and New Zealand Journal of Psychiatry,* **34,** S191–S197.

Paykel ES, Ramana R, Cooper Z, Hayhurst H, Kerr J & Baroker A (1995). Residual symptoms after partial remission: an important outcome in depression. *Psychological Medicine*, **25**(6), 1171–1180.

Paykel ES, Scott J, Teasdale JD, Johnson AL, Garland A, Moore R et al. (1999). Prevention of relapse in residual depression by cognitive therapy: a controlled trial. *Archives of General Psychiatry*, **56**(9), 829–835.

Pearce JW & Pezzot-Pearce TD (1994). Attachment theory and its implications for psychotherapy with maltreated children. *Childhood Abuse and Neglect*, **18**(5), 425–438.

Pearlin LI (1985). Social structure and processes of social support. In S Cohen & SL Syme (eds), *Social support and health*. Orlando, FL, Academic Press.

Pearlman L (1998). Trauma and the self: a theoretical and clinical perspective. *Journal of Emotional Abuse*, **1**, 7–25.

Pencer A, Addington J & Addington D (2005). Outcome of a first episode of psychosis in adolescence: a 2-year follow-up. *Psychiatry Research*, **133**(1), 35–43.

Penn DL & Mueser KT (1996). Research update on the psychosocial treatment of schizophrenia. *American Journal of Psychiatry*, **153**(5), 607–617.

Peralta V & Cuesta MJ (2003). Cycloid psychosis: a clinical and nosological study. *Psychological Medicine*, **33**, 443–453.

Perlick D, Clarkin JF, Sirey J, Raue P, Greenfield S, Struening E et al. (1999). Burden experienced by care-givers of persons with bipolar affective disorder. *British Journal of Psychiatry*, **175**, 56–62.

Perry A, Tarrier N, Morriss R, McCarthy E & Limb K (1999). Randomised controlled trial of efficacy of teaching patients with bipolar disorder to identify early symptoms of relapse and obtain treatment. *British Medical Journal*, **318**, 149–153.

Persons JB (1989). *Cognitive therapy in practice: a case formulation approach*. New York, Norton.

Pevalin DJ & Goldberg DP (2003). Social precursors to onset and recovery from episodes of common mental illness. *Psychological Medicine*, **33**, 299–306.

Peven DE & Shulman BH (1983). The psychodynamics of bipolar affective disorder: some empirical findings and their implications for cognitive theory. *Journal of Adlerian Theory, Research and Practice*, **39**(1), 2–16.

Pharoah FM, Mari JJ & Streiner DL (1999). Family intervention for schizophrenia. *Cochrane Review*, **4**.

Pickup GJ & Frith CD (2001). Schizotypy, theory of mind and weak central coherance. *Schizophrenia Research*, **49**(1–2 suppl.), 118.

Pilkonis PA, Feldman H, Himmelhoch J & Cornes C (1980). Social anxiety and psychiatric diagnosis. *Journal of Nervous Mental Disorders*, **168**(1), 13–18.

Pilling S, Bebbington P, Kuipers E, Garety P, Geddes J, Orbach G et al. (2002). Psychological treatments in schizophrenia, I: meta-analysis of family intervention and cognitive behavioural therapy. *Psychological Medicine*, **32**(5), 763–782.

Pinto A, La-Pia S, Mennella R, Giorgio D & DeSimone L (1999). Cognitive-behavioral therapy and clozapine for clients with treatment-refractory schizophrenia. *Psychiatric Services*, **50**(7), 901–904.

Pitschel-Walz G, Baeuml J & Kissling W (1998). Psychoedukative Gruppen bei schizophrenen Psychosen – Ergebnisse der Muenchner PIP-Studie. *Schizophrenie*, **8**.

Pitschel-Walz G, Leucht S, Bauml J, Kissling W & Engel RR (2001). The effect of family interventions on relapse and rehospitalization in schizophrenia: a meta-analysis. *Schizophrenia Bulletin*, **27**(1), 73–92.

Pollack LE (1999). Why the cycle in a cyclical psychosis? An analytic contribution to the understanding of recurrent manic-depressive psychosis. *Allied Nursing Research*, **12**, 143–152.

Pollack LE & Cramer RD (1999). Patient satisfaction with two models of group therapy for people hospitalized with bipolar disorder. *Allied Nursing Research*, **12**(3), 143–152.

Pollock HM, Malzberg B & Fuller RG (1939). *Hereditary and environmental factors in the causation of manic-depressive psychoses and dementia praecox.* Utica, NY, State Hospitals Press.

Pollock LR & Williams JMG (2004). Problem-solving in suicide attempters. *Psychological Medicine*, **34**, 163–167.

Posner CM, Wilson KG, Kral MJ, Lander S & McIlwraith RD (1992). Family psychoeducational support groups in schizophrenia. *American Journal of Orthopsychiatry*, **62**(2), 206–218.

Posternak MA & Miller I (2001). Untreated short-term course of major depression: a meta-analysis of outcomes from studies using waiting list control groups. *Journal of Affective Disorders*, **66**, 139–146.

Power M & Dalgliesh T (1997). *Cognition and emotion.* Hove, Psychology Press.

Power PJR, Bell RJ, Mills T, Herrman-Doig M, Davern M, Henry L et al. (2003). Suicide prevention in first episode psychosis: the development of a randomised controlled trial of cognitive therapy for acutely suicidal patients with early psychosis. *Australian and New Zealand Journal of Psychiatry*, **37**, 414–420.

Preda A, Madlener A & Hetherington P (1998). Premature polypsychopharmacology. *Journal of the American Academy of Child and Adolescent Psychiatry*, **37**(4), 348–349.

Preda A, Miller TJ, Rosen JL, Somjee L, McGlashan TH & Woods SW (2002). Treatment histories of patients with a syndrome putatively prodromal to schizophrenia. *Psychiatric Services*, **53**(3), 342–344.

Priebe S, Broker M & Gunkel S (1998). Involuntary admission and posttraumatic stress disorder symptoms in schizophrenia patients. *Comprehensive Psychiatry*, **39**, 220–224.

Provencher HL & Fincham FD (2000). Attributions of causality, responsibility and blame for positive and negative symptom behaviours in caregivers of persons with schizophrenia. *Psychological Medicine*, **30**, 899–910.

Quinlan DM, Glazer W, Schuldberg D & Morgenstern H (1995). Positive and negative symptom course in chronic community-based patients: a two-year prospective study. *The British Journal of Psychiatry*, **166**(5), 634–641.

Quraishi S & Frangou S (2002). Neuropsychology of bipolar disorder: a review. *Journal of Affective Disorders*, **72**(3), 209–226.

Rabiner CJ, Wegner JT & Kane JM (1986). Outcome study of first episode psychosis. *American Journal of Psychiatry*, **143**(9), 1155–1158.

Rae MM, Tompson MC, Miklowitz DJ, Goldstein MJ, Hwang S & Mintz J (2003). Family-focused treatment versus individual treatment for bipolar disorder: results of a randomized clinical trial. *Journal of Consulting and Clinical Psychology*, **71**(3), 482–492.

Raja M & Azzoni A (2004). Clinical management of obsessive-compulsive disorder comorbidity: a case series. *Bipolar Disorder*, **6**, 264–270.

Ramana R & Bebbington P (1995). Social influences on bipolar affective disorders. *Social Psychiatry and Psychiatric Epidemiology*, **30**, 152–160.

Randall F, Corcoran R, Day JC & Bentall RP (2003). Attention, theory of mind and causal attributions in people with persecutory delusions: a preliminary investigation. *Cognitive Neuropsychiatry*, **8**(4), 287–294.

Randolph EA, Eth S, Glynn SM, Paz GG, Leong GB, Shaner AL et al. (1994). Behavioral family management in schizophrenia: outcome of a clinic-based intervention. *British Journal of Psychiatry*, **164**, 501–506.

Rasanen P, Tiihonen J & Hakko H (1998). The incidence and onset-age of hospitalized bipolar affective disorder in Finland. *Journal of Affective Disorders*, **48**, 63–68.

Rathod S, Kingdon D, Smith P & Turkington D (2005). Insight into schizophrenia: the effects of cognitive behavioural therapy on the components of insight and association with sociodemographics data on a previously published randomised controlled trial. *Schizophrenia Research*, **74**, 211–219.

Read J, Agar K, Argyle N & Aderhold V (2003). Sexual and physical abuse during childhood and adulthood as predictors of hallucinations, delusions and thought disorder. *Psychological Psychotherapy*, **76**(Pt 1), 1–22.

Read J, Goodman L, Morrison A et al. (2004). Childhood trauma, loss and stress. In J Read, L Mosher & R Bentall (eds), *Models of madness: psychological, social and biological approaches to schizophrenia*. Hove, Brunner-Routledge, pp. 223–252.

Rector NA, Seeman MV & Segal ZV (2002). Cognitive therapy for schizophrenia: a preliminary randomized controlled trial. *Schizophrenia Research*, **63**, 1–11.

Remschmidt H (2001). Early-onset schizophrenia as a progressive-deteriorating developmental disorder: evidence from child psychiatry. *Journal of Neural Transmission*, **109**, 101–117.

Resick PA & Schnicke MK (1993). *Cognitive processing therapy for rape victims: a treatment manual*. Newbury Park, CA, Sage Publications.

Rijsdijk FV, Scham PC, Sterne A, Purcell S, McGuffin P, Farmer A et al. (2001). Life events and depression in a community sample of siblings. *Psychological Medicine*, **31**, 401–410.

Roberts G (1991). Delusional belief systems and meaning in life: a preferred reality? *British Journal of Psychiatry*, **159**(14), 19–28.

Roberts RE, Chen Y-W & Solovitz BL (1995). Symptoms of DSM-III-R major depression among Anglo, African and Mexican American adolescents. *Journal of Affective Disorders*, **36**, 1–9.

Robinson DG, Woerner MG, Alvir JMJ, Bilder RM, Hinrichsen GA & Lieberman JA (2002). Predictors of medication discontinuation by patients with first-episode schizophrenia and schizoaffective disorder. *Schizophrenia Research*, **57**, 209–219.

Robinson DG, Woerner MG, Alvir JMJ, Geisler S, Koreen A, Sheitman B et al. (1999). Predictors of treatment response from a first episode of schizophrenia or schizoaffective disorder. *American Journal of Psychiatry*, **156**(4), 544–549.

Robinson EAR (1996). Causal attributions about mental illness: relationship to family functioning. *American Journal of Orthopsychiatry*, **66**, 282–295.

Roder V, Brenner HD, Muller D, Lachler M, Zorn P, Reisch T et al. (2002). Development of specific social skills training programmes for schizophrenia patients: results of a multicentre study. *Acta Psychiatrica Scandinavica*, **105**, 363–371.

Romans SE & McPherson HM (1992). The social networks of bipolar affective disorder patients. *Journal of Affective Disorders*, **25**, 221–228.

Romans-Clarkson SE & McPherson HM (1991). The social networks of bipolar affective disorder patients. *Biological Psychiatry*, **29**, 308S.

Romme MAJ & Escher ADMAC (1989). Hearing voices. *Schizophrenia Bulletin*, **15**(2), 209–216.

Rooke O & Birchwood M (1998). Loss, humiliation and entrapment as appraisals of schizophrenic illness: a prospective study of depressed and non-depressed patients. *British Journal of Clinical Psychology*, **37**, 259–268.

Rosenberg M (1965). *Society and the adolescent self-image*. Princeton, NJ, Princeton University Press.

Rosenfarb IS, Becker J & Khan A (1994). Perceptions of parental and peer attachments by women with mood disorders. *Journal of Abnormal Psychology*, **103**(4), 637–644.

Rosenfarb IS, Miklowitz DJ, Goldstein MJ, Harmon L, Neuchterlein KH & Rea MM (2001). Family transactions and relapse in bipolar disorder. *Family Process*, **40**(1), 5–14.

Rosenstein DS & Horowitz HA (1996). Adolescent attachment and psychopathology. *Journal of Consulting and Clinical Psychology*, **64**, 244–253.

Ross CA, Anderson G & Clark P (1994). Childhood abuse and positive symptoms of schizophrenia. *Hospital and Community Psychiatry*, **45**, 489–491.

Rossi A, Daneluzzo E, Arduini L, Domenico M Di, Stratta P & Petruzzi C (2000). Cognitive symptoms of mania in pure and mixed episodes evaluated with the positive and negative syndrome scale. *European Archives of Psychiatry and Clinical Neuroscience*, **250**, 254–256.

Rossler W, Haung H-J & Munk-Jorgensen P (2002). The psychosocial basis of schizophrenia. *Acta Psychiatrica Scandinavica*, **102**(suppl. 407), 5.

Roth DA, Coles ME & Heimberg RG (2002). The relationship between memories for childhood teasing and anxiety and depression in adulthood. *Journal of Anxiety Disorders*, **16**, 149–164.

Rothbart MK, Derryberry D & Hershey K (2000). Stability of temperament in childhood: laboratory infant assessment to parent report at seven years. In VJ Molfese & DL Molfese (eds), *Temperament and personality development across the life span*. Mahwah, NJ, Erlbaum, pp. 85–119.

Rothbart MK, Derryberry D & Posner MI (1994). A psychobiological approach to the development of temperament. In JE Bates & TD Wachs (eds), *Temperament: individual differences at the interface of biology and behavior*. Washington, DC, American Psychological Association, pp. 83–116.

Ro-Trock GK, Wellisch DK & Schoolar JC (1977). A family therapy outcome study in an inpatient setting. *American Journal of Orthopsychiatry*, **47**(3), 514–522.

Roy A, Thompson R & Kennedy S (1983). Depression in chronic schizophrenia. *British Journal of Psychiatry*, **142**, 465–470.

Rund BR, Melle I, Friis S, Larsen TK, Midboe LJ, Opjordsmoen S et al. (2004). Neurocognitive dysfunction in first-episode psychosis: correlates with symptoms, premorbid adjustment, and duration of untreated symptoms. *American Journal of Psychiatry*, **161**, 466–472.

Rutter M (2000). Resilience reconsidered: conceptual considerations, empirical findings, and policy implications. In JP Shonkoff & SJ Meisels (eds), *Handbook of early childhood intervention*, 2nd edn. New York, Cambridge University Press, pp. 651–682.

Salkovskis PM, Atha C & Storer D (1990). Cognitive-behavioural problem solving in the treatment of patients who repeatedly attempt suicide: a controlled trial. *British Journal of Psychiatry*, **157**, 871–876.

Sandberg S, Rutter M, Giles S, Owen A, Champion L, Nicholls J et al. (1993). Assessment of psychosocial experiences in childhood: methodological issues and some illustrative findings. *Journal of Child Psychology and Psychiatry*, **34**(6), 879–897.

Sandler IN & Ramsay IN (1980). Dimensional analysis of children's stressful life events. *American Journal of Community Psychology*, **8**(3), 285–302.

Sanz M, Constable G, Lopez-Ibor I, Kemp R & David AS (1998). A comparative study of insight scales and their relationship to psychopathological and clinical variables. *Psychological Medicine*, **28**(2), 437–446.

Sarason BR, Pierce GR & Sarason IG (1990). Social support: the sense of acceptance and the role of relationships. In BR Sarason, IG Sarason & GR Pierce (eds), *Social support: an interactional view*. New York, John Wiley & Sons.

Sarason BR, Pierce GR, Shearin EN, Sarason IG, Waltz JA & Poppe L (1991). Perceived social support and working models of self and actual others. *Journal of Personality and Social Psychology*, **60**, 273–287.

Sato T, Narita T, Hirano S, Kusunoki K, Sakado K & Uehara T (2001). Is interpersonal sensitivity specific to non-melancholic depressions? *Journal of Affective Disorders*, **64**, 133–144.

Sax KW, Strakowski SM, Keck PE, McElroy SL, West SA, Bourne ML et al. (1997). Comparison of patients with early-, typical-, and late-onset affective psychosis. *American Journal of Psychiatry*, **154**, 1299–1301.

Saxe GN, van der Kolk BA, Berkowitz R, Chinman G, Hall K, Lieberg G et al. (1993). Dissociative disorders in psychiatric inpatients. *American Journal of Psychiatry*, **150**, 1037–1042.

Scazufca M & Kuipers E (1996). Links between expressed emotion and burden of care in relatives of patients with schizophrenia. *British Journal of Psychiatry*, **168**(5), 580–587.

Scheller-Gilkey G, Moynes K, Cooper I, Kant C & Miller AH (2004). Early life stress and PTSD symptoms in patients with comorbid schizophrenia and substance abuse. *Schizophrenia Research*, **69**, 67–74.

Schulze B, Richter-Werling M, Matschinger H & Angermeyer MC (2003). Crazy? So what! Effects of a school project on students' attitudes towards people with schizophrenia. *Acta Psychiatrica Scandinavica*, **107**, 142–150.

Schuster TL, Kessler RC & Aseltine RH (1990). Supportive interactions, negative interactions and depressed mood. *American Journal of Community Psychology*, **18**, 423–438.

Schwannauer M (1997). Social networks, social support and expressed emotion significance of psychosocial factors in the long-term community care of patients with schizophrenia and major depression. Thesis, Philis-University, Marburg, Germany.

Scott J, Cole A & Eccleston D (1991). Dealing with persisting abnormalities of mood. *International Review of Psychiatry*, **3**, 19–33.

Scott J, Stanton B, Garland A & Ferrier IN (2000). Cognitive vulnerability in patients with bipolar disorder. *Psychological Medicine*, **30**, 467–472.

Scott WCM (1963). The psychoanalytic treatment of mania. *Psychiatric Research Reports*, **17**, 84–90.

Segal ZV (1988). Appraisal of the self-schema construct in cognitive models of depression. *Psychological Bulletin*, **103**, 147–162.

Segal ZV, Pearson JL & Thase ME (2003). Challenges in preventing relapse in major depression: report of a National Institute of Mental Health Workshop on state of the science of relapse prevention in major depression. *Journal of Affective Disorders*, **77**, 97–108.

Segrin C (2000). Social skills deficits associated with depression. *Clinical Psychology Review*, **20**(3), 379–403.

Seidlitz L, Conwell Y, Duberstasin P, Cox C & Denning D (2001). Emotion traits in older suicide attempters and non-attempters. *Journal of Affective Disorder*, **66**, 123–131.

Seidman LJ, Kremen WS, Koren D, Faraone SV, Goldstein JM & Tsuang MT (2002). A comparative profile analysis of neuropsychological function in patients with schizophrenia and bipolar psychoses. *Schizophrenia Research*, **53**(1–2), 31–44.

Seligman MEP, Schulman P & DeRuibes RJ (2002). The prevention of depression and anxiety. *Prevention and Treatment*, **2**, article 8 (electronic journal).

Sellwood W, Barrowclough C, Tarrier N, Quinn J, Mainwaring J & Lewis S (2001). Needs-based cognitive-behavioural family intervention for carers of patients suffering from schizophrenia: 12-month follow-up. *Acta Psychiatrica Scandinavica*, **104**, 346–355.

Sellwood W, Tarrier N, Quinn J & Barrowclough C (2003). The family and compliance in schizophrenia: the influence of clinical variables, relatives knowledge and expressed emotion. *Psychological Medicine*, **33**, 91–96.

Selten JP, Gernaat H, Nolen WA, Wiersma D & Van den Bosch RJ (1998). Experience of negative symptoms: comparison of schizophrenic patients to patients with a depressive disorder and to normal subjects. *American Journal of Psychiatry*, **155**, 350–354.

Selten JP, Patino LR, Van Engeland H, Duyx JH, Kahn RS & Burger H (2005). Migration, family dysfunction and psychotic symptoms in children and adolescents. *British Journal of Psychiatry*, **186**, 442–443.

Selten JP, Veen N, Feller W, Blom JD, Schols D, Camoenie W et al. (2001). Incidence of psychotic disorders in immigrant groups to The Netherlands. *British Journal of Psychiatry*, **178**, 367–367.

Sensky T, Turkington D, Kingdon D, Scott JL, Scott J, Siddle R et al. (2000). A randomised controlled trial of cognitive-behavioural therapy for persistent symptoms in schizophrenia resistant to medication. *Archives of General Psychiatry*, **57**, 165–172.

Shahar G, Trower P, Iqbal Z, Birchwood M, Davidson L & Chadwick P (2004). The person in recovery from acute and severe psychosis: the role of dependency, self-criticism, and efficacy. *American Journal of Orthopsychiatry*, **74**, 480–488.

Shapiro DA, Rees A, Barkman M & Hardy G (1995). Effects of treatment duration and severity of depression on the maintenance of gains after cognitive-behavioral and psychodynamic-interpersonal psychotherapy. *Journal of Consulting and Clinical Psychology*, **63**(3), 378–387.

Shapiro J, Sank LI, Sank C, Shaffer CS & Donovan DC (1982). Cost effectiveness of individual vs. group cognitive behavior therapy for problems of depression and anxiety in an HMO population. *Journal of Clinical Psychology*, **38**(3), 674–677.

Sharma V, Khan M & Smith A (2005). A closer look at treatment resistant depression: is it due to a bipolar diathesis? *Journal of Affective Disorders*, **84**, 251–257.

Shaver PR & Brennan KA (1992). Attachment styles and the 'Big Five' personality traits: their connections with each other and with romantic relationship outcomes. *Personality and Social Psychology Bulletin*, **18**(5), 536–545.

Shaw K, McFarlane A & Bookless C (1997). The phenomenology of traumatic reactions to psychotic illness. *Journal* of *Nervous and Mental Diseases*, **185**(7), 434–441.

Shaw K, McFarlane A, Bookless C & Air T (2002). The aetiology of postpsychotic post-traumatic stress disorder following a psychotic episode. *Journal of Traumatic Stress*, **15**, 39–47.

Shaw M & Singh SP (2004). Management of early-onset psychosis. *Current Opinions in Psychiatry*, **17**, 249–254.

Sheri J & Kizer A (2002). Bipolar and unipolar depression: a comparison of clinical phenomenology and psychosocial predictors. In CL Hammen & IH Gotlib (eds), *Handbook of depression*. New York, Guilford Press, pp. 141–165.

Sherrington JM, Hawton K, Fagg J, Andrew B & Smith D (2001). Outcome of women admitted to hospital for depressive illness: factors in the prognosis of severe depression. *Psychological Medicine*, **31**, 115–125.

Siegel DJ (1999). *The developing mind: toward a neurobiology of interpersonal experience.* New York: Guilford Press.

Simoneau TL, Miklowitz DJ & Saleem R (1998). Expressed emotion and interactional patterns in the families of bipolar patients. *Journal of Abnormal Psychology*, **107**, 497–507.

Skeate A, Jackson C, Birchwood M & Jones C (2002). Duration of untreated psychosis and pathways to care in first-episode psychosis. *British Journal of Psychiatry*, **181**(suppl. 43), s73–s77.

Slade A, Belsky J, Aber JL & Phelps JL (1999). Mothers' representations of their relationships with their toddlers: links to adult attachment and observed mothering. *Developmental Psychology*, **35**, 611–619.

Sloman L, Gilbert P & Hasey G (2003). Evolved mechanisms in depression: the role and interaction of attachment and social rank in depression. *Journal of Affective Disorders*, **74**(2), 107–121.

Smith TE, Hull J, Romanelli S, Fertuch E & Weiss KA (1999). Symptoms and neurocognition as rate limiters in skills training for psychotic patients. *American Journal of Psychiatry*, **156**(11), 1817–1818.

Soares CN & Almeida OP (2001). Depression during the perimenopause. *Archives of General Psychiatry*, **58**(3), 306.

Solomon DA, Ristow R, Keller MB, Kane JM, Gelenberg AJ, Rosenbaum JF et al. (1996). Serum lithium levels and psychosocial function in patients with bipolar I disorder. *American Journal of Psychiatry*, **153**, 1301–1307.

Solomon P & Draine J (1995). Subjective burden among family members of mentally ill adults: relation to stress, coping, and adaptation. *American Journal of Orthopsychiatry*, **65**(3), 419–427.

Somnath CP, Reddy YCJ & Jain S (2002). Is there a familial overlap between schizophrenia and biolar disorder? *Journal of Affective Disorders*, **72**, 243–247.

Sourander A, Helstela L, Haavisto A & Bergroth L (2001). Suicidal thoughts and attempts among adolescents: a longitudinal 8-year follow-up study. *Journal of Affective Disorders*, **63**, 59–66.

Spangler DL, Simons AD & Monroe SM (1997). Response to cognitive-behavioral therapy in depression: effects of pretreatment cognitive dysfunction and life stress. *Journal of Consulting and Clinical Psychology*, **65**, 568–575.

Spanier C, Fank E, McEachran AB, Grochocinski VJ & Kupfer DJ (1996). The prophylaxis of depressive episodes in recurrent depression following discontinuation of drug therapy: integrating psychological and biological factors. *Psychological Medicine*, **26**(3), 461–476.

Spauwen J, Krabbendam L, Lieb R, Wittchen HU & van Os J (2004a). Does urbanicity shift the population expression of psychosis? *Journal of Psychiatric Research*, **38**(6), 613–618.

Spauwen J, Krabbendam L, Lieb R, Wittchen HU & van Os J (2004b). Early maternal stress and health behaviours and offspring expression of psychosis in adolescence. *Acta Psychiatrica Scandinavica*, **110**(5), 356–364.

Spencer JH, Glick ID, Haas GL, Clarkin JF, Lewis AB, Peyser J et al. (1988). A randomised clinical trial of inpatient family intervention, III: effects at 6-month and 18-month follow-ups. *American Journal of Psychiatry*, **145**(9), 1115–1121.

Spiegel D & Wissler T (1987). Using family consultation as psychiatric aftercare for schizophrenic patients. *Hospital and Community Psychiatry*, **38**(10), 1096–1099.

Spielberger CD, Gorsuch RL & Lushene RE (1968). *The state-trait anxiety inventory (STAI): test manual for Form X*. Palo Alto, CA, Consulting Psychologists Press.

Squire LR (1992). Memory and the hippocampus: a synthesis from findings with rats, monkeys and humans. *Psychological Review*, **99**(2), 195–231.

Sroufe LA (1996). *Emotional development: the organisation of emotional life in the early years*. New York: Cambridge University Press.

Stafanis NC et al. (2002). Evidence that three dimensions of psychosis have a distribution in the general population. *Psychological Medicine*, **32**, 347–358.

Staner L, Tracy A, Dramaix M, Genevrois C, Vanderelst M, Vilane A et al. (1997). Clinical and psychosocial predictors of recurrence in recovered bipolar and unipolar depressives: a one-year controlled prospective study. *Psychiatry Research*, **69**, 39–51.

Stark KD, Humphrey LL, Laurent J, Livingston R & Christopher J (1993). Cognitive, behavioral and family factors in the differentiation of depressive and anxiety disorders during childhood. *Journal of Consulting and Clinical Psychology*, **61**, 878–886.

Stark KD, Rouse LW & Livingston R (1991). Treatment of depression during childhood and adolescence: cognitive-behavioral procedures for the individual and family. In P Kendall (ed.), *Child and adolescent therapy*. New York, Guilford Press, pp. 165–206.

Startup M (1996). Insight and cognitive deficits in schizophrenia: evidence for a curvilinear relationship. *Psychological Medicine*, **26**(6), 1277–1281.

Startup M (1999). Schizotypy, dissociative experiences and childhood abuse: relationships among self-report measures. *British Journal of Clinical Psychology*, **38**, 333–344.

Startup M, Jackson MC & Bendix S (2004). North Wales randomized controlled trial of cognitive behaviour therapy for acute schizophrenia spectrum disorders: outcomes at 6 and 12 months. *Psychological Medicine*, **34**, 413–422.

Steel C, Fowler D & Holmes EA (2005). Trauma related intrusions in psychosis: an information processing account. *Behavioural and Cognitive Psychotherapy*, **33**(2), 139–152.

Steel C, Hemsley DR & Pickering AD (2002). Distractor cueing effects on choice reaction time and their relationship with schizotypal personality. *British Journal of Clinical Psychology*, **41**(2), 143–156.

Stefos G, Bauwens F, Staner L, Pardoen D & Mendlewicz J (1996). Psychosocial predictors of major affective recurrences in bipolar disorder: a 4-year longitudinal study of patients on prophylactic treatment. *Acta Psychiatrica Scandinavica*, **93**, 420–426.

Stirling J, Tantam D, Thomas P, Newby D, Montague L, Ring N et al. (1993). Expressed emotion and schizophrenia: the ontogeny of EE during an 18-month follow-up. *Psychological Medicine*, **23**, 771–778.

Strauss J (2000). The interactive development model revisited. *Acta Psychiatrica Scandinavica*, **102**(suppl. 407), 19–25.

Strober M, Schmidt-Lackner S, Freeman R, Bower S, Lampert C & DeAntonio M (1995). Recovery and relapse in adolescents with bipolar affective illness: a five-year naturalistic, prospective follow-up. *Journal of the American Academy of Child and Adolescent Psychiatry*, **34**, 724–731.

Strober MA (1996). Outcome studies of mania in children and adolescents. In KI Shulman, M Tohen et al. (eds), *Mood disorders across the life-span*. New York, Wiley-Liss.

Stuart S & Robertson M (2003). *Interpersonal psychotherapy: a clinician's guide*. London, Edward Arnold.

Styron T & Janoff-Bulman R (1997). Childhood attachment and abuse: long-term effects on adult attachment, depression and conflict resolution. *Child Abuse and Neglect*, **21**, 1015–1023.

Subotnik KL & Neuchterlein KH (1988). Prodromal signs and symptoms of schizophrenic relapse. *Journal of Abnormal Psychology*, **97**, 405–412.

Subotnik KL, Neuchterlein KH, Ventura J, Green MF & Hwang SS (1998). Prediction of the deficit syndrome from initial deficit symptoms in the early course of schizophrenia. *Psychiatry Research*, **80**(1), 53–59.

Sullivan HS (1962). *Schizophrenia as a human process*. Oxford, Norton.

Sundquist K, Frank G & Sundquist J (2004). Urbanisation and incidence of psychosis and depression. *British Journal of Psychiatry*, **184**, 293–298.

Sutherland S (1998). Cognitive therapies. In *Breakdown: a personal crisis and a medical dilemma*, 2nd edn. New York, Oxford University Press.

Swann AC, Pazzaglia P, Nicholls A, Dougherty DM & Moeller FG (2003). Impulsivity and phase of illness in bipolar disorder. *Journal of Affective Disorders*, **73**, 105–111.

Swartz HA & Frank E (2001). Psychotherapy for bipolar depression: a phase-specific treatment strategy? *Bipolar Disorders*, **3**, 11–22.

Swendsen J, Hammen C, Heller T & Gitlin M (1995). Correlates of stress reactivity in patients with bipolar disorder. *American Journal of Psychiatry*, **152**, 795–797.

Swendson JD & Merikangas KR (2000). The comorbidity of depression and substance abuse disorders. *Clinical Psychology Review*, **20**(2), 173–189.

Tai S, Haddock G & Bentall R (2004). The effects of emotional salience on thought disorder in patients with bipolar affective disorder. *Psychological Medicine*, **34**, 803–809.

Tait L, Birchwood M & Trower P (2002). A new scale (SES) to measure engagement with community mental health services. *Journal of Mental Health*, **11**, 191–198.

Tait L, Birchwood M & Trower P (2003). Predicting engagement with services for psychosis: insight, symptoms and recovery style. *British Journal of Psychiatry*, **182**, 123–128.

Tait L, Birchwood M & Trower P (2004). Adapting to the challenge of psychosis: personal resilience and the use of sealing-over (avoidant) coping strategies. *British Journal of Psychiatry*, **185**(5), 410–415.

Tam W-CC, Sewell KW & Deng H-C (1998). Information processing in schizophrenia and bipolar disorder: a discriminant analysis. *Journal of Nervous and Mental Disease*, **186**(10), 597–603.

Tanna VL (1974). Paranoid states: a selected review. *Comprehensive Psychiatry*, **15**(6), 453–470.

Tarrier N (2005). Cognitive behaviour therapy for psychotic disorders: current issues and future developments. *Clinical Psychology, Science and Practice*, **12**(1), 51–56.

Tarrier N, Barrowclough C & Bamrah JS (1991). Prodromal signs of relapse in schizophrenia. *Social Psychiatry and Psychiatric Epidemiology*, **26**(4), 157–161.

Tarrier N, Barrowclough C, Haddock G & McGovern J (1999). The dissemination of innovative cognitive-behavioural psychosocial treatments for schizophrenia. *Journal of Mental Health*, **8**, 569–582.

Tarrier N, Barrowclough C, Vaughn C, Bamrah JS, Porceddu K, Watts S et al. (1989). Community management of schizophrenia: a two-year follow-up of a behavioural intervention with families. *British Journal of Psychiatry*, **154**, 625–628.

Tarrier N, Beckett R, Harwood S, Baker A, Yusupoff L & Ugarteburu I (1993). A trial of two cognitive-behavioural methods of treating drug-resistant psychotic symptoms in schizophrenic patients, I: outcome. *British Journal of Psychiatry*, **162**, 524–532.

Tarrier N, Haddock G, Morrison AP, Hopkins R, Drake R & Lewis S (1999). A pilot study evaluating the effectiveness of individual inpatient cognitive-behavioural therapy in early psychosis. *Social Psychiatry and Psychiatric Epidemiology*, **34**(5), 254–258.

Tarrier N, Harwood S, Yusupoff L, Beckett R & Baker A (1990). Coping strategy enhancement (CSE): a method of treating residual schizophrenic symptoms. *Behavioural Psychotherapy*, **18**(4), 283–293.

Tarrier N, Lewis S, Haddock G, Bentall R, Drake R, Kinderman P et al. (2004). Cognitive-behavioural therapy in first-episode and early schizophrenia. *British Journal of Psychiatry*, **184**, 231–239.

Tarrier N & Turpin G (1992). Psychosocial factors, arousal and schizophrenic relapse. *British Journal of Psychiatry*, **161**, 3–11.

Tavares JVT, Drevets WC & Sahakian BJ (2003). Cognition in mania and depression. *Psychological Medicine*, **33**, 959–967.

Teasdale JD & Barnard PJ (1993). *Affect, cognition and change: re-modelling depressive thought*. Hove, Erlbaum.

Teixeira MA (1992). Psychoanalytic theory and therapy in the treatment of manic-depressive disorders. *Psychoanalysis and Psychotherapy*, **11**(2), 162–177.

Telles C, Karno M, Mintz J, Paz G, Arias M, Tucker D et al. (1995). Immigrant families coping with schizophrenia: behavioral family intervention v. case management with a low-income Spanish-speaking population. *British Journal of Psychiatry*, **167**, 473–479.

Thase ME, Friedman ES, Berman SR, Fasiczka AL, Lis JA, Howland RH et al. (2000). Is cognitive behavior therapy just a 'nonspecific' intervention for depression? A retrospective comparison of consecutive cohorts treated with cognitive behavior therapy or supportive counseling and pill placebo. *Journal of Affective Disorders*, **57**, 63–71.

Thase ME, Greenhouse JB, Frank E, Reynolds CF, Pilkonis PA, Hurley K et al. (1997). Treatment of major depression with psychotherapy or psychotherapy-pharmacotherapy combinations. *Archives of General Psychiatry*, **54**, 1009–1015.

Thompson KN, Conus PO, Ward JL, Phillips LJ, Koutsogiannis J, Leicester S et al. (2003). The initial prodrome to bipolar affective disorder: prospective case studies. *Journal of Affective Disorders*, **77**, 79–85.

Thurm I & Haefner H (1987). Perceived vulnerability, relapse risk and coping in schizophrenia: an explorative study. *European Archives of Psychiatry and Neurological Sciences*, **237**, 46–53.

Tohen M, Zarate CA, Hennen J, Khalsa H-MK, Strakowski SM, Gebre-Medhin P et al. (2003). The McLean first-episode mania study: prediction of recovery and first recurrence. *American Journal of Psychiatry*, **160**(12), 2099–2121.

Torgersen S, Edvardsen J, Oien PA, Onstad S, Skre I, Lygren S et al. (2002). Schizotypal personality disorder inside and outside the schizophrenic spectrum. *Schizophrenia Research*, **54**, 33–38.

Torrey EF (1999). Epidemiological comparison of schizophrenia and bipolar disorder. *Schizophrenia Research*, **39**, 101–106.

Tracey TJ & Kokotovic AM (1989). Factor structure of the Working Alliance Inventory. *Psychological Assessment: A Journal of Consulting and Clinical Psychology*, **1**, 207–210.

Trauer T & Sacks T (2000). The relationship between insight and medication adherence in severely mentally ill clients treated in the community. *Acta Psychiatrica Scandinavica*, **102**, 211–216.

Trower P, Birchwood M, Meaden A, Byrne S, Nelson A & Ross K (2004). Cognitive therapy for command hallucinations: RCT. *British Journal of Psychiatry*, **184**, 312–320.

Trower P & Chadwick P (1995). Pathways to defense of the self: a theory of two types of paranoia. *Clinical Psychology: Science and Practice*, **2**, 263–278.

Tsuang MT, Stone WS, Tarbox SI & Faraone SV (2002). An integration of schizophrenia with schizotypy: identification of schizotaxia and implications for research on treatment and prevention. *Schizophrenia Research*, **54**, 169–175.

Tsuchiya KJ, Agerbo E, Byrne M & Mortensen PB (2004). Higher socio-economic status of parents may increase risk for bipolar disorder in the offspring. *Psychological Medicine*, **34**, 787–793.

Turkington D & Kingdon D (2000). Cognitive-behavioural techniques for general psychiatrists in the management of patients with psychoses. *British Journal of Psychiatry*, **177**, 101–106.

Turkington D, Kingdon D, Turner T et al. (2002). Effectiveness of a brief cognitive-behavioural therapy intervention in the treatment of schizophrenia. *British Journal of Psychiatry*, **180**, 523–527.

Valbak K, Koster A, Larsen KA, Nielsen JR & Norrie B (2003). The Danish national multicenter schizophrenia project: assessment of psychotic patients for dynamic psychotherapy (APPP). *Nordic Journal of Psychiatry*, **57**(5), 333–338.

Valevski A, Ratzoni G, Sever J, Apter A, Zalsman G, Shiloh R et al. (2001). Stability of diagnosis: a 20-year retrospective cohort study of Israeli psychiatric adolescent inpatients. *Journal of Adolescence*, **24**, 625–633.

van der Kolk BA, McFarlane AC & Weisaeth L (1996). *Traumatic stress: the effects of overwhelming experience on mind, body and society.* New York, Guilford Press.

Vanderlinden J, Vandereycken W, van Dyck R & Vertommen H (1993). Dissociative experiences and trauma in eating disorders. *International Journal of Eating Disorders*, **13**, 187–193.

van Os J (2004). Does the urban environment cause psychosis? *British Journal of Psychiatry*, **184**, 287–288.

van Os J, Gilvarry C, Bale R, van Horn E, Tattan T, White I et al. (1999). A comparison of the utility of dimensional and categorical representations of psychosis. *Psychological Medicine*, **29**, 595–606.

van Os J & Jones PB (2001). Neuroticism as a risk factor for schizophrenia. *Psychological Medicine*, **31**, 1129–1134.

van Os J, Jones P, Lewis G, Wadsworth M & Murray R (1997). Developmental precursors of affective illness in a general population birth cohort. *Archives of General Psychiatry*, **54**, 625–631.

van Os J, Jones P, Sham P, Bebbington P & Murray RM (1998). Risk factors for onset and persistence of psychosis: social support. *Psychiatry and Psychiatric Epidemiology*, **33**, 596–605.

van Os J, Pedersen CB & Mortensen PB (2004). Confirmation of synergy between urbanicity and familial liability in the causation of psychosis. *American Journal of Psychiatry*, **161**(12), 2312–2314.

van't Wout M, Aleman A, Kessels RPC, Laroi F & Kahn RS (2004). Emotional processing in a non-clinical psychosis-prone sample. *Schizophrenia Research*, **68**(2–3), 271–281.

Vaughan K, Doyle M, McConaghy N, Blaszczynski A, Fox A & Tarrier N (1992). The Sydney intervention trial: a controlled trial of relatives' counselling to reduce schizophrenic relapse. *Social Psychiatry and Psychiatric Epidemiology*, **27**(1), 16–21.

Vazquez-Barquero JL, Cuesta MJ, Castanedo SH, Lastra I & Herran A (1999). Cantabria first-episode schizophrenia study: three-year follow-up. *British Journal of Psychiatry*, **174**, 141–149.

Veen ND, Selten JP, Van der Tweel I, Feller W, Hoek HW & Kahn RS (2004). Cannabis use and age at onset of schizophrenia. *American Journal of Psychiatry*, **161**, 501–506.

Ventura J, Lukoff D, Snyder K & Nuechterlein KH (1984). Life events, familial stress, and coping in the developmental course of schizophrenia. *Schizophrenia Bulletin*, **10**(2), 258–292.

Ventura J, Nuechterlein KH, Subotnik KL, Green MF & Gitlin MJ (2004). Self-efficacy and neurocognition may be related to coping responses in recent-onset schizophrenia. *Schizophrenia Research*, **69**, 343–352.

Wallace JL & Vaux A (1993). Social support network orientation: the role of adult attachment style. *Journal of Social and Clinical Psychology*, **12**, 354–365.

Walsh J & Connelly PR (1996). Supportive behaviors in natural support networks of people with serious mental illness. *Health and Social Work*, **21**(4), 296–303.

Watanabe H, Takahashi T, Tonoike T, Suwa M & Akahori K (2003). Cenesthopathy in adolescence. *Psychiatry and Clinical Neurosciences*, **57**, 23–30.

Waters E, Merrick S, Treboux D, Crowell J & Albersheim L (2000). Attachment security in infancy and early adulthood: a twenty-year longitudinal study. *Child Development*, **71**, 684–689.

Watts FN, Powell GE & Austin SV (1973). The modification of abnormal beliefs. *British Journal of Medical Psychology*, **46**, 359–363.

Wearden A, Tarrier N, Barrowclough C, Zastowny TR & Rahill AA (2000). A review of expressed emotion research in health care. *Clinical Psychology Review*, **20**, 633–666.

Wegner DM (1994). Ironic processes of mental control. *Psychological Review*, **101**, 34–52.

Weiner B (1985). An attributional theory of achievement motivation and emotion. *Psychological Review*, **92**, 548–573.

Weinfeld NS, Sroufe LA & Egeland B (2000). Attachment from infancy to early adulthood in a high risk sample: continuity, discontinuity, and their correlates. *Child Development*, **71**, 695–702.

Weissman M, Markowitz JC & Klerman GL (2000). *Comprehensive guide to interpersonal psychotherapy*. New York, Basic Books.

Weller E & Weller R (2000). Treatment options in the management of adolescent depression. *Journal of Affective Disorders*, **61**, S23–S28.

Weller EB, Weller RA & Fristad MA (1995). Bipolar disorder in children: misdiagnosis, underdiagnosis and future directions. *Journal of the American Academy of Child and Adolescent Psychiatry*, **34**, 709–714.

Wells A (1997). *Cognitive therapy for anxiety disorders*. Chichester, John Wiley & Sons.

Wendel JS, Miklowitz DJ, Richards JA & George EL (2000). Expressed emotion and attributions in the relatives of bipolar patients: an analysis of problem-solving interactions. *Journal of Abnormal Psychology*, **109**(4), 792–796.

Wenzlaff RM & Wegner DM (2000). Thought suppression. *Annual Review of Psychology*, **51**, 59–91.

Wenzlaff RM, Wegner DM & Klein SB (1991). The role of thought suppression in the bonding of thought and mood. *Journal of Personality and Social Psychology*, **60**, 500–508.

Whitehead C, Moss S, Cardno A & Lewis G (2003). Antidepressants for the treatment of depression in people with schizophrenia: a systematic review. *Psychological Medicine*, **33**, 589–599.

Whitehorn D, Lazier L & Kopala L (1998). Psychosocial rehabilitation early after the onset of psychosis. *Psychiatric Services*, **49**(9), 1135–1137.

Wiersma D, Nienhuls FJ, Slooff CJ & Giel R (1998). Natural course of schizophrenic disorders: a 15 year follow-up of a Dutch incidence cohort. *Schizophrenia Bulletin*, **24**, 75–85.

World Health Organisation (1979). *The international pilot study of schizophrenia*. Chichester, John Wiley & Sons.

Wulsin L, Bachop M & Hoffman D (1988). Group therapy in manic-depressive illness. *American Journal of Psychotherapy*, **42**, 263–271.

Xiong W, Phillips MR, Hu X, Wang R, Dai Q, Kleinman J et al. (1994). Family-based intervention for schizophrenic patients in China: a randomised controlled trial. *British Journal of Psychiatry*, **165**(2), 239–247.

Yildiz A & Sachs GS (2003). Age onset of psychotic versus non-psychotic bipolar illness in men and in women. *Journal of Affective Disorders*, **74**(2), 197–201.

Young JE (1994). *Cognitive therapy for personality disorders: a schema focused approach* (rev. edn). Sarasota, FL, Professional Resource Press.

Young JE, Klosko JS & Weishaar ME (2003). *Schema therapy: a practitioner's guide.* New York, Guilford Press.

Zahn-Waxler C, Mayfield A, Radke-Yarrow M, McKnew DH, Cytryn L & Davenport YB (1988). A follow-up investigation of offspring of parents with bipolar disorder. *American Journal of Psychiatry*, **145**, 506–509.

Zanarini MC, Gunderson JG, Marino MF, Schwartz EO & Frankenberg FR (1989). Childhood experiences of borderline patients. *Comprehensive Psychiatry*, **30**, 18–25.

Zarate CA & Tohen M (1996). Outcome of mania in adults. In KI Shulman, M Tohen et al. (eds), *Mood disorders across the life-span*. New York, Wiley-Liss.

Zarate CA, Tohen M, Land M & Cavanagh S (2000). Functional impairment and cognition in bipolar disorder. *Psychiatric Quarterly*, **71**(4), 309–329.

Zaretsky A (2003). Targeted psychosocial interventions for bipolar disorder. *Bipolar Disorder*, **5**(suppl. 2), 80–87.

Zaretsky AE, Zindel VS & Gemar M (1999). Cognitive therapy for bipolar depression: a pilot study. *Canadian Journal of Psychiatry*, **44**, 491–494.

Zhang M, Wang M, Li J & Phillips MR (1994). Randomized-control trial of family intervention for 78 1st episode of male schizophrenic patients: an 18 month study in Suzhou, Jiangsu. *British Journal of Psychiatry*, **165**(suppl. 24), 19–27.

Zisook S, McAdams LA, Kuck J, Harris MJ, Bailey A, Patterson TL et al. (1999). Depressive symptoms in schizophrenia. *American Journal of Psychiatry*, **156**(11), 1736–1743.

Zlotnick C, Kohn R, Keitner G & Della Grotta SA (2000). The relationship between quality of interpersonal relationships and major depressive disorder: findings from the National Comorbidity Survey. *Journal of Affective Disorders*, **59**(3), 205–215.

INDEX